Legal and Economic Perspectives on the Nexus of AI and Copyright

Burcu Gülseren Özcan Büyüktanır
Hacettepe University, Turkey

Pelin Varol İyidoğan
Hacettepe University, Turkey

Péter Krisztián Zachar
Ludovika University of Public Service, Hungary

IGI Global
Scientific Publishing
Publishing Tomorrow's Research Today

Vice President of Editorial | Melissa Wagner
Director of Acquisitions | Mikaela Felty
Director of Book Development | Jocelynn Hessler
Production Manager | Mike Brehm
Cover Design | Phillip Shickler

Published in the United States of America by
IGI Global Scientific Publishing
701 East Chocolate Avenue
Hershey, PA, 17033, USA
Tel: 717-533-8845
Fax: 717-533-7115
Website: https://www.igi-global.com E-mail: cust@igi-global.com

Library of Congress Cataloging-in-Publication Data

Names: Büyüktanır, Burcu G. Özcan, editor. | Varol İyidoğan, Pelin, 1981- editor. | Zachar, Péter Krisztián, 1976- editor.
Title: Legal and economic perspectives on the nexus of AI and copyright / Burcu Özcan Büyüktanır, Pelin Varol İyidoğan, Péter Zachar.
Description: Hershey : IGI Global Scientific Publishing, 2025. | Includes bibliographical references and index. | Summary: "This book aims to analyze effects of AI on law and economy policy and to make policy recommendations that will guide policy makers on the axis of these analyses"-- Provided by publisher.
Identifiers: LCCN 2024055216 (print) | LCCN 2024055217 (ebook) | ISBN 9798369387047 (hardcover) | ISBN 9798369387054 (paperback) | ISBN 9798369387061 (ebook)
Subjects: LCSH: Artificial intelligence--Law and legislation. | Artificial intelligence--Economic aspects. | Copyright--Economic aspects.
Classification: LCC K564.C6 L43 2025 (print) | LCC K564.C6 (ebook) | DDC 343.09/998--dc23/eng/20241119
LC record available at https://lccn.loc.gov/2024055216
LC ebook record available at https://lccn.loc.gov/2024055217

British Cataloguing in Publication Data
A Cataloguing in Publication record for this book is available from the British Library.

Table of Contents

Detailed Table of Contents

The most important question, as defined by the author, is whether in a more advanced and integrated society with artificial intelligence (such as the Japanese Society 5.0) the "artificial human" can appear in its legal forms, economic, and socio-political consequences leading to a new paradigm shift in the future. The key questions is whether the self-learning "artificial human" who produces intellectual products has the rights to those products produced by it. In other words, whether such a humanoid robot, which functions as a user (as a worker) as well as a consumer (as a learner) of intellectual properties, holds any legal status regarding the products it creates. In addition, artificial intelligence, a humanoid robot in question as a registered legal entity, can also be considered a rights holder, and to what extent does this affect the 'traditional' GDP calculation and 'structure' and its definition when the value added of the technology exceeds the (additional) value of human resources in the value creation/production, especially in an IP-driven and depopulating economy?

Intellectual products created by artificial intelligence have caused some difficult problems in various branches of law. One of these problems is whether the income obtained from the transfer or granting of the right to use these products can be taxed or not. While there are some suggestions in the doctrine for the taxation of these incomes within the current system, some states have tried to create new taxes on this issue. In terms of Turkish tax law, there is no need to create a new tax in order to tax the income obtained from the intellectual products created by artificial intelligence. Although the intellectual products created by artificial intelligence are not considered as "works" in Turkish intellectual property rights law, they will be subject to taxation in accordance with the Turkish income tax, Turkish corporate tax law, or Turkish value added tax, if their investors earn income from the transfer or right to use of these products.

The rapid development of artificial intelligence (AI) has introduced novel challenges and opportunities within the domain of copyright law. This chapter explores the intersection of AI and copyright, specifically focusing on the legal problems and regulatory frameworks in the United Kingdom. It examines how AI-generated works are situated within the existing copyright law, the implications for traditional copyright principles, and the evolving regulatory responses. At the heart of the discussion is the question of authorship of AI-generated works. Traditional copyright law presumes a human author, raising significant questions about the legal status of works created autonomously by AI systems. The chapter further delves into the implications of AI on copyright infringement and fair use. AI systems, particularly those employing machine learning algorithms, often require large datasets to train on, which may include copyrighted material.

The formulation and development of cultural policies are important for achieving the social goals set by states. In this context, all kinds of cultural activities should be supported, protected, and developed. Transferring the evidence of the social culture's history to the digital environment through artificial intelligence (AI) may lead to copyright issues for the works. States make and implement legal regulations to solve copyright issues arising from digitalization. Preservation of the copyrights for the artifacts exhibited at the Ephesus Experience Museum, where artifacts of the ancient city of Ephesus are exhibited with a realistic experience, is important. The fact that the Ephesus Experience Museum was designed with the support of the Republic of Türkiye Ministry of Culture and Tourism helps prevent problems that may arise regarding copyrights.

think the fundamental concepts of intellectual property law. Once it is accepted as a work of authorship, the question of who the copyright holder arises. Is there really a need to re-think these conventional concepts or is the answer clear enough? Indeed, the legal debate of whether works created by non-human beings deserve copyright protection is not a problem specific to the digital age. The copyright status of a selfie taken by a monkey has been the subject of another extraordinary lawsuit, Naruto v. Slater. The purpose of this study is to examine the impacts of AI-generated artistic works on copyright law. In order to address the challenges created by non-human authors, with focus on AI-generated artistic works, the conventional concepts of intellectual property law are discussed to determine whether they are sufficient to handle the novel problems AI systems created.

Chapter 8
A Complex Intersection of Deepfakes and Copyright Infringement 155
Pranjal Khare, O.P. Jindal Global University, India
Vishambhar Raghuwanshi, Manipal University, India

The advent of deepfake technology has introduced new challenges to copyright law due to its ability to manipulate media content. This chapter delves into the intricate relationship between deepfakes and copyright law, examining the legal frameworks in key jurisdictions and the ethical implications for creators. Beyond the legal considerations, deepfakes also raise significant ethical concerns which need to be addressed. Deepfakes, generated by artificial intelligence, can reproduce, transform, and adapt existing copyrighted material, raising questions about authorship and originality. It is crucial to address the challenges posed by deepfakes while balancing the interests of creators, copyright holders, and the public.

Chapter 9
Is Turkish Copyright Law Well-Equipped to Handle Artificial Intelligence? .. 181
Cemre Polat, Ankara Medipol University, Turkey

This chapter provides an overview of Turkish law as regards the most-frequently debated copyright problems within the realm of artificial intelligence. The problems which are observed to be the most prominent are probable copyright infringements in the training and testing phase of AI, copyright infringement as a result of the output of AI, and copyright protection of AI outputs. Although these copyright issues can be observed in various AI applications, they are more pronounced in generative AI. The success and wide reach of OpenAI's ChatGPT revealed that the question which needs the most urgent answer was not "Will robot kill us and who will be liable?" This is not to undermine the need for clarity for AI involved accidents, but copyright problems emerged more widely and have already been subject to lawsuits, especially in the US. Global use of Generative AI makes the copyright problems relevant for all jurisdictions. However, Turkish copyright law has not been amended

Preface

In recent decades, there has been a significant transformation in the relationship between the social/human sciences and the natural sciences. Rather than being regarded as distinct disciplines, they are increasingly conceptualized as a complex network of interactions and interrelationships. From this perspective, we propose that the study of the intertwining of artificial intelligence (AI) and copyright from a social science perspective represents a highly productive and dynamically evolving field of research. The accelerated evolution of AI technologies is precipitating profound societal transformations, with concomitant legal and ethical ramifications. It is imperative that copyright law evolve to align with these developments, and it falls upon the social sciences to investigate and examine the novel challenges that arise. Concurrently, at the nexus of AI and copyright, a multifaceted and comprehensive approach can be achieved through the integration of tools and methodologies drawn from a diverse array of disciplines, including but not limited to law, computer science, philosophy, and sociology. Furthermore, the outcomes of social science research can assist the state and legislators in formulating a regulatory structure that harmonizes innovation with copyright protection.

It is a well-known fact that technological developments have a profound impact on legal systems all over the world. This has given rise to a number of significant legal issues about AI and copyright. It is an irrefutable fact that the utilization of AI technologies in the field of copyright is the source of both new threats as well as new opportunities. From generating art, music and literature to producing software and media, artificial intelligence (AI) is becoming increasingly involved in creative process. However, throughout the history, the creation of art and other forms of creative work has been considered unique to human beings, and the law has been shaped accordingly reflecting this reality. Currently, it is necessary to shed light on two distinct yet interrelated matters: on the one hand, AI innovations and on the other, several legal issues pertaining to AI and copyright. These issues bear upon one aspect of the original value of the book.

Moreover, it is extremely important to consider the economic implications of these legal developments, which have been shaped by technological advancements from a holistic perspective. A review of the literature reveals a growing consensus that AI is reshaping the creative industry, with significant economic implications for copyright law and market dynamics. It is essential to emphasize the necessity for policy reforms to address legal ambiguities, fair income distribution, and the protection of economic interests for traditional creators. The debate on whether AI-generated works should be granted copyright protection, and the potential impact this may have on the broader economy, remains a topic of ongoing debate. There is a clear need for adaptable frameworks that can balance the objectives of innovation and economic fairness. At this juncture, it is of utmost importance that public policies are meticulously designed to establish and maintain a balance between economic and legal structure. This balance aims not only to promote sustainable economic growth but also to protect the rights of individuals and society at large. By ensuring the efficient use of resources, advocating for fairness in income distribution, and upholding the rule of law, public policies should support both economic development and social welfare.

CHAPTER OVERVIEW

From this perspective, this edited book is organized into 15 chapters addressing the relationship between AI and copyright from the angle of current critical debates in the literature, theory and practice. Following an introductory part, the remarkable study of László Gábor Lovászy examines the nexus of artificial intelligence (AI) and intellectual property (IP), with a particular emphasis on the prospective legal and economic challenges posed by AI-generated works and the concept of "artificial persons". The text also draws attention to Japan's pioneering Society 5.0 strategy, which integrates robotics and AI to address demographic challenges and promote sustainable development, with the ultimate goal of creating a super-smart society. The paper underscores the importance of re-examining the concepts of personhood, IP rights, and economic paradigms in light of AI's evolving capabilities. It urges policymakers to prepare for a future where robots and AI systems may play autonomous roles in society.

The study of Oytun Canyaş examines the challenges of taxing intellectual products created by AI, with a particular focus on the Turkish tax law. It also considers s whether such products qualify as "works" under intellectual property law. It analyzes legal issues regarding the authorship and ownership of AI-generated works, as well as the taxation implications associated with royalties and licensing income derived from these creations. The study concludes that, despite AI-generated works not being classified as “works” under current Turkish law, income derived from their transfer or licensing can still be subject to taxation within the framework of business or corporate income tax provisions.

Zehra Özkan Üner & Pınar Çağlayan Aksoy examine the intersection of artificial intelligence (AI) and copyright law in the UK, focusing on challenges such as the authorship of AI-generated works and the use of copyrighted data for training AI models. The study discusses existing legal frameworks, including the Copyright, Designs, and Patents Act, and evaluates regulatory efforts to balance innovation with the protection of creators' rights.

İrem Didinmez & Zeynep Coşkun provide an insight about the role of digitalization and artificial intelligence in preserving cultural heritage, focusing on the Ephesus Experience Museum as a case study. The study highlights how alternative immersive technologies enhance cultural sustainability by providing interactive and realistic representations of historical artifacts. They also emphasizes the importance of copyright protections for AI-generated digital content to ensure the ethical and legal safeguarding of cultural heritage.

Nazmiye Tekdemir & Ayşegül Durucan & Eda Yeşil explore the nexus of artificial intelligence (AI) and intellectual property (IP) rights, underscoring the necessity for revised legal frameworks as AI contributes to innovation and invention. The paper addresses challenges such as authorship, ownership, and the economic impact of protecting AI-generated works, proposing that adaptive public policies can foster economic growth and attract international investment. The study highlights that modernizing IP laws will enable effective integration of AI into innovation ecosystems.

Derya Ateş investigates the legal implications of AI in the context of IP and Turkish civil law, with a particular focus on the concept of authorship for AI-created works. It elucidates the difficulties inherent in defining AI's legal personhood, assessing whether AI-generated outputs qualify for copyright, and determining who holds rights over such creations. The chapter emphasizes the need for updated legal frameworks to address the evolving role of AI in creative and economic processes.

Dila Okyar explores the legal challenges posed by AI-generated works and their implications for copyright law. The author draws parallels with the “Monkey Selfie” case, in which a macaque's photograph sparked debates about non-human authorship. It highlights the growing complexity of determining ownership and authorship for creations by autonomous AI systems and the necessity for updated legal frameworks. The chapter emphasizes the necessity of striking a balance between innovation and intellectual property rights while addressing questions of liability and creative ownership in a rapidly evolving technological landscape.

In their contribution Pranjal Khare & Vishambhar Raghuwanshi address the legal challenges posed by deepfake technology in relation to copyright law, highlighting issues of originality, unauthorized reproduction, and liability. The article examines the ways in which deepfakes blur the lines between creativity and violation, emphasizing the need for updated legal frameworks to address AI-generated content. The study highlights the complexities of regulating deepfakes across jurisdictions, advocating for global collaboration to balance technological innovation with intellectual property rights.

In her study, Cemre Polat discusses whether Turkish copyright law is equipped to handle the challenges posed by artificial intelligence (AI), focusing on issues like input and output infringements and the authorship of AI-generated works. The study identifies deficiencies in the current Turkish copyright law, particularly the lack of text and data mining exceptions, and contrasts this with frameworks like the EU's AI Act. The study recommends a balanced legal regime to address systemic copyright infringements while fostering innovation and suggests defining new legal norms to manage the autonomy of AI in creative processes.

Barış Gözübüyük examines the legal challenges posed by deepfake technology, particularly its intersection with copyright law. The author addresses a number of key issues, including the concept of originality, the question of unauthorized use, and the question of liability. The paper demonstrates the inadequacy of existing copyright frameworks in addressing deepfake-related concerns and emphasizes the need for updated legal norms and international cooperation to regulate the ethical and legal use of synthetic media. Moreover, Ankita Roy & Abhisikta Basu explore the legal and ethical challenges surrounding AI-generated content, particularly its impact on intellectual property and copyright law. It emphasizes the need for updated frameworks to address issues like authorship, originality, and data privacy while balancing innovation with legal protections.

David Lopez & Eduardo Carlos Dittmar & Jenny Patricia Vargas analyze the complex intersection of artificial intelligence (AI) and copyright law across Asia, Europe, and the United States, emphasizing the challenges of regulating AI-generated content within traditional legal frameworks. It highlights regional differences in policy approaches, the role of self-regulation, and the need for international harmonization to address authorship, intellectual property rights, and ethical considerations in the AI era.

Erman M. Demir & Nihan Gider Işıkman investigate the impact of generative AI technologies on the film industry, emphasizing their potential to enhance efficiency and creativity while raising concerns about labor displacement, copyright, and ethical implications. It underscores the need for updated legal frameworks and international collaboration to address issues such as authorship, data ownership, and the preservation of cultural diversity in AI-generated content. The study also advocates for educational programs and stakeholder engagement to ensure the responsible and ethical integration of AI into creative industries.

Utku Topcan explores the challenges posed by artificial intelligence (AI) in the realm of copyright law, focusing on issues like authorship, ownership, and liability for AI-generated works. It examines international frameworks, including Turkish, EU, and U.S. laws, and emphasizes the need for clear regulations to address the legal status of AI-created content and prevent misuse. The study advocates for a case-by-case approach to authorship and highlights the potential role of AI as a legal entity to ensure accountability and foster innovation.

The objective of Burcu Özcan Büyüktanır & Barış Gözübüyük is to present an analysis of the legal challenges surrounding the protection of artificial intelligence (AI) under Turkish intellectual property law, with a particular focus on copyright and patents. The study highlights the inadequacy of current laws, which treat AI as akin to computer programs, and advocates for AI-specific patent regulations that consider novelty, inventive step, and industrial applicability. The study emphasizes that short-term patent protection would better balance societal and economic interests, ensuring innovation while mitigating risks such as unemployment and corporate dominance.

As the editors of this book, we are very gratified and honored to host these esteemed scholars and present their research in this collection. Furthermore, we would like to express our gratitude to the Republic of Türkiye, Ministry of Culture and Tourism, Directorate General of Copyrights for the support of our project work titled "Artificial Intelligence and Copyright: Country Comparative Legal and Economic Analysis" which inspired this book. The content of each chapter in this book is solely the responsibility of the respective chapter authors. No other individual or institution holds any liability regarding the content presented in this book. It is our hope that this book will prove a valuable resource for researchers interested in the subject, offering an enjoyable and worthwhile reading experience.

Burcu Gülseren Özcan Büyüktanir
Faculty of Law, Hacettepe University, Turkey

Pelin Varol Iyidogan
Hacettepe University, Turkey

Péter Krisztián Zachar
Ludovika University of Public Service, Hungary

Chapter 1
Some Questions on the Possible Advent of the "Artificial Person"

László Gábor Lovászy
https://orcid.org/0000-0001-9064-0930
University of Public Service, Hungary

ABSTRACT

The most important question, as defined by the author, is whether in a more advanced and integrated society with artificial intelligence (such as the Japanese Society 5.0) the "artificial human" can appear in its legal forms, economic, and socio-political consequences leading to a new paradigm shift in the future. The key questions is whether the self-learning "artificial human" who produces intellectual products has the rights to those products produced by it. In other words, whether such a humanoid robot, which functions as a user (as a worker) as well as a consumer (as a learner) of intellectual properties, holds any legal status regarding the products it creates. In addition, artificial intelligence, a humanoid robot in question as a registered legal entity, can also be considered a rights holder, and to what extent does this affect the 'traditional' GDP calculation and 'structure' and its definition when the value added of the technology exceeds the (additional) value of human resources in the value creation/production, especially in an IP-driven and depopulating economy?

INTRODUCTION

As it is stated in the introduction to a resolution[1] of the European Parliament: „(...) now that humankind stands on the threshold of an era when ever more sophisticated robots, bots, androids and other manifestations of artificial intelligence ('AI') seem to

DOI: 10.4018/979-8-3693-8704-7.ch001

be poised to unleash a new industrial revolution, which is likely to leave no stratum of society untouched, it is vitally important for the legislature to consider its legal and ethical implications and effects, without stifling innovation". Moreover, the EP „notes that there are no legal provisions that specifically apply to robotics, but that existing legal regimes and doctrines can be readily applied to robotics, although some aspects appear to call for specific consideration; calls on the Commission to support a horizontal and technologically neutral approach to intellectual property applicable to the various sectors in which robotics could be employed." (section 18). In addition, the European legislative body „calls on the Commission and the Member States to take into account the rapid technological evolution in the field of robotics, including the advancement of cyber-physical systems, and to ensure that Union law does not stay behind the curve of technological development and deployment." (Point 19)

Although it may have seemed too early back in February 2017, MEP Gilles Lebreton, a right-wing (ID Group) lawmaker in the European Parliament, stated in the debate on the so-called Delvaux report: "Mr President, intelligent robots have become a reality. These are machines programmed to make decisions, such as driverless cars or certain surgical robots. The Delvaux report is right to be concerned about this, because their intelligence will, in the near future, exceed the intellectual capacities of human beings. (…) I object to this perspective for two reasons: first of all, since it will remove all responsibility from their manufacturers and users, which would undoubtedly please the powerful lobbies; secondly, and this is important, because I believe, like Jacques Maritain,[2] that the human is endowed with a spiritual existence, with which no artificial intelligence can be compared". The MEP referred to such robots in question as «des personnes électroniques responsables».[3]

This study tries to look behind the current development of robotics in the sphere of intellectual property (IP), based on the performance of leading countries and sectors. In this paper, Japan is in the focus of attention due to its new vision of Society 5.0, and we also scrutinize the perspective of the possible arrival of artificial persons – *«des personnes électroniques responsables»* – in addition to natural and legal persons in legal systems, within the context of the importance of IP in developed economies, in view of global trends in robotics and AI. Finally, the author also studies the question whether the theory of an artificial person could cast doubt on current theories and the interpretation of modern economies.

The issue of IP within the context of AI seems to be not only critical but also varied. As Myers remarks: "Although some countries follow the current U.S. approach of declining to protect AI-generated content, a number of jurisdictions are finding ways to offer such works copyright protection, including Japan, Ireland, New Zealand and South Africa" (Myers, 2024).

1) Society 5.0 as a New Societal Model?

In Japan, society traditionally rejects immigration, while the population is rapidly aging, in parallel with an almost uniquely high and continuously rising life expectancy. Japan's population is expected not only to age but to shrink by as much as one third in the next 50 years. The Japanese government recognized the seriousness of the problem early on and took initiatives to increase the activity and employment of the elderly, as well as to improve productivity through robotization. Robotics was intended to play a key role not only in industry, but also in terms of active aging and the mitigation of women's household work. The most successful Japanese Prime Minister of all time, Shinzo Abe, who was assassinated two years ago, announced at the end of 2016 that robotics would be the most important socio-political answer to demographic and other problems, based on the "New Robot Strategy" adopted in 2015. For this purpose, a National Special Robotics Zone was created in the Kanagawa district, which is also iconic in terms of the Western influence experienced in the Middle Ages, and the historical Japanese opening in the 19th century. They also set the goal of quadrupling the robotics industry in order to replace expensive workforce through automation instead of mass immigration. The New Robot Strategy has proven comprehensive, involving developments from agriculture to the food industry and even healthcare services (Japan External Trade Organization, 2024).

The robotics industry is developing at an amazing pace: according to forecasts, new-generation robots may increase the productivity of certain industries by up to 30% by 2025, while labour costs may decrease by almost 20%, primarily in the USA, China and Germany. The most economically significant Asian countries - China, Korea and Japan - have already produced five times more robots than the leading EU member states (Germany, Italy, France) and three times more robots than Europe and the USA combined (IFR Press Room, 2023). Japan could be a clear leader in terms of industrial robot manufacturing companies: the five most profitable companies in the world are Japanese in this industry, and it is also believed that Japan will be one of the most important countries and economies in terms of the paradigm shift regarding human-robot collaboration. Based on its history and traditions, the Japanese society has always been very open to 'smart' puppets or machines (, karakuri ningyō) (Law, 2015) or robots as we call them today.

But this proved to be just the beginning. As it turned out, the New Robot Strategy as an initiative was part of a broader plan: the Japanese government came forward with a comprehensive strategy supported by philosophical and "evolutionary" arguments. The Society 5.0 (5.0) concept is a long-term strategy for sustainable development, prepared by the Science, Technology and Innovation Council based on the 5th Basic Science and Technology Plan adopted by the cabinet in a January

2016 decision. An even more interesting development occurred in 2017, when a chatbot programmed to be a seven-year-old boy became the first AI bot to be granted official residence in Tokyo, Japan (Cuthbertson, 2017) which means that the bot was considered eligible for a residence permit. (Recognition of residence is in fact a prerequisite to formal citizenship.)

Another milestone was reached in 2021, when the Japanese government released the comprehensive Moonshot project ( ) (*Moonshot Research and Development Program - Science, Technology and Innovation,* n.d.) which includes targeted and revolutionary research and health developments (, *mibio*) (Kanagawa Prefecture, 2024) from agriculture and the food industry to health and rehabilitation services. In this ambitious project, the Japanese government set almost sci-fi-like, amazing targets. By 2050, the country wants to (1) create a society in which people are free from the limitations of body, brain, space and time through technology, and (2) predict and prevent diseases at an extremely early stage - of course the with the help of artificial intelligence and robotics. To this end, they also want to (3) produce robots for the economy that learn and act by themselves (autonomously) and live in harmony with humans through artificial intelligence and the “co-evolution” of robots. Also, they plan to (4) implement sustainable resource circulation - also by robots and artificial intelligence - in order to restore the global environment, and (5) create sustainable food supply chains that are free from environmental overload and waste. To facilitate that, (6) general-purpose and low-error quantum computers will be created, also fundamentally improving the economy, industry, productivity and security; and finally, (7) a sustainable health and care system based on robots will be implemented by 2040, which prevents and overcomes serious diseases and enables people to live much healthier, more active and independent lives up to the age of 100. China and South Korea, countries that already exhibit much worse demographic trends than Japan, are also planning to follow this path (*Fertility rate: children per woman,* 2024).

The presented concept asserts nothing less than humanity essentially entering a new evolutionary level: after the gathering and hunting society, the farming lifestyle, the industrial revolution, and then the information society, the “super-smart” society follows. On the international stage, the Japanese government presented the Society 5.0 concept as an official national strategic objective in 2019 at the annual meeting of the World Economic Forum (*Speech by Prime Minister Abe at the World Economic Forum Annual Meeting,* n.d). The Japanese Society 5.0 concept not only focuses on technological development, digitalization, and economic competitiveness per se, but also on individuals, and specifically persons as well as their family and quality of life. Japan is the first developed industrial country that, in addition to creating a digital infrastructure, aims to exceed Industry 4.0 as both a social policy goal and a tool. The country now wants to achieve a breakthrough in daily life and quality of life, in order to make life in society pleasant. People are to be freed from their previous, burdensome and tiring obligations, which should allow them time to take care of themselves and even have more children. If we take a step back, we may realize that this strategy may involve a change in the image of man (introducing a kind of "enhanced man"). This goal may also be promoted by seemingly extensive support and a focused financial framework from the Japanese government in the field of biotechnology, in order to improve the quality of human longevity.

Society 5.0 is therefore Japan's comprehensive vision of the future, and at the same time a response to the demographic crisis. This presents a vision of a "smart society" in which the most advanced technologies – primarily big data, the Internet of Things (IoT) and artificial intelligence (AI) – create a system using robots, carefully designed and cooperating in close symbiosis, in every industry and practically every social segment, including culture. (That symbiosis may also bring future robots which can learn and improve like today's human children.) At the heart of the idea is that digitalization can provide solutions to the challenges and problems of both the economy and society, so that they can better utilize and optimize the infrastructure, products and services vacated by a declining population. As Myers concluded: "Society has already reached the point at which the Turing test, which involves the question whether AI works are indistinguishable from human creations – has been satisfied." (Myers, 2024). According to Brian Merchant of Wired magazine, the gaming market, a nearly 200-billion-dollar sector, may be the biggest industry which AI stands poised to conquer. Although Merchant believes that generative AI will be no different from the previous industrial revolutions, it can most capably produce 2D images that managers in cost-squeezed studios may already consider "good enough". In fact, Leo Li, a Hangzhou-based gaming recruiter cited by Merchant, said that the number of illustrator jobs in his country had fallen by 70%. Similar patterns are noted in Japan, too, where the cost of illustrations has plunged by a staggering 95%. As Merchant concludes, "US law insists that any work seeking copyright must have a human author—a fact that gives, say, Hollywood studios pause. But it's still an open question whether using unlicensed intellectual property to train AI systems violates copyright. Even in cases in which an AI program generates work based on human prompts, [U.S.] courts have ruled against copyright protection. For things like concept art, character descriptions, or code that doesn't wind up in the game, it's harder to determine what is out of line." (Merchant, 2024).

Consequently, one of the most important questions for the next period will revolve around the future (legal) status of increasingly autonomous and "intelligent" robots (artificial intelligence), as well as the extent to which this could change our perception of humans as well as economic and intellectual products, and especially those that are closely resemble human output or skills. Within this, a particularly interesting and important issue involves the assessment of intellectual products generated by artificial intelligence (and how the interests of investors in AI will be protected in the long run), when it comes to the scope of copyright covering unique creativity, regardless of art form.

2) A New Symbiosis Between the Labour Market and Artificial Intelligence: The Digital Revolution and the Emergence of IP-Driven Economies

Before discussing the issue of intellectual property, it is important to review the big picture of technological advancement in general. Naturally, technological progress will not only terminate jobs but also create new ones, leaving us with the ultimate dilemma, namely the relative ratio of the jobs lost and created. The National Intelligence Council, a renowned futurologist think-tank advising the presidents of the United States, raises questions about the labour market for human workforce after 2030, when the significance of growth perspectives will be less important, and growth itself will be less relevant (Lovászy, 2022). However, this development could be different from the previous industrial revolutions where natural and physical forces were replaced by machines. When it comes to outsourced skills, fire replaced digestion and promoted food storage. Wheels helped movement and transportation. Books helped the recording of knowledge. Glasses helped shortsighted people work. Spinning jennies replaced weavers, and robots replaced mass workers in factories. Computers replaced most of the mathematicians calculating planetary orbits at NASA, just to name one example. This time is different because the 'outsourced' skill is the most complex one: the increasing complexity of the human mind.

Looking into the near future, the reputable analysis firm McKinsey points out (Manyika et al., 2017) that productivity rose by 0.3% annually between 1850 and 1910, while it is expected to increase by up to 1.5% between 2015 and 2060, including the sector of services where 70-80% of the labour force is employed. This could put the growth rate at 300-400% compared to the first industrial revolution. Thus, the impacts of full or partial automation on the services sector remain unpredictable. Meanwhile, according to US federal labour statistics, demand for less skilled or even unskilled workers (in personal care) will increase the most in the future. At the same time, somewhat shockingly, the productivity of conventional service and production sectors has declined sharply since 2008. According to the OECD, the most productive and innovative services – mostly driven by AI-related solutions – improved by 50% in that regard between 2001 and 2010, while their traditional competitors failed to achieve productivity improvements and could only match the figures (growth rate) seen before 2000 (Lovászy, 2022). Finally, there is a little-known aspect of digitisation which is also of worth mentioning: as our world becomes a digital copy (metaverse), (Lovászy, 2021) the role of culture is being re-assessed, as more and more programmers need to provide culturally based responses to modelling the situations and preferences to be decided in advance, in order to make increasingly complex systems coherent.

All these developments could also lead to the evolution of the digitalization of (human) culture, a new kind revolution of knowledge, a new version or layers of knowledge strengthened by AI. As governor of the Hungarian National Bank Matolcsy put it in 2021: “Underlying the emergence of the human and artificial human, the real and virtual world, or the new dual world system is the dichotomy of the 0-1 digital code. The new society will be twofold in everything, so it will be a more diverse and colourful decade, a decade of contrasts, stronger competition and stronger cooperation.” (Matolcsy, 2021). Matolcsy also points to a new model of sustainability: the knowledge revolution will connect human communities, where the human-human relations defined by culture (civilization) will become crucial, rather than the previous world connections based on the differentiation of living from things. Thus, sustainability will also be about human civilization, and therefore human relationships will be at the heart of sustainable economics in societies powered by artificial intelligence and robotisation. However, this vision may also be overwritten by the surging development of the mental capacities of robots, which could lead to a new, “enhanced” culture based on AI capacities, as pieces of art made by AI will increasingly resemble the products of human creativity. This is already an obvious trend.

This phenomenon brings us to the topic of copyright as one of the most personal activities in economy when it comes to culture and the production of cultural services and goods based on accelerated automation. This issue also involves the possible recognition of ownership of intellectual property (IP) of robots. IP remains a massive economic driver for jobs and investment. According to the U.S. Department of Commerce, in the United States alone, IP supports over $6 trillion in GDP and more than 45 million jobs (U.S. Chamber Staff, 2022). (This amount equals the combined market value of Apple, Microsoft, Google, Amazon, Nvidia, Facebook and Tesla.) (Hilotin, 2023). Consequently, innovation, and intellectual property behind it, are becoming one of the most important driving forces that lead to a more developed economy based on R&D.

Currently, in the field of copyrights, the guiding principle is that an intellectual product (work or piece of art) has one core feature: it must be unique. The second, but less clear condition, which is basically a historical axiom, is that the author must be *human*. But that is not always the case today. As Anikó Grad-Gyenge notes: “In addition, regional and international standards take into account the fact that different national regulators provide different scopes of rights for interested parties that are not natural persons. Just think of the Software Directive which enables the national legislators of the European Union to define, as the original owner of software copyright, the legal entity that stands in the interest of the development of the software [cf. Article 2(1) of Directive 2009/24/EC]. In addition, international copyright standards avoid regulating who can be the original copyright holder, opening the possibility for contracting parties to develop regulations according to their own legal, cultural, and economic aspects." (Grad-Gyenge, 2023). According to Grad-Gyenge, copyright protection was never aimed at personal, creative performance (with the exception of the protection of artists), but rather at the legal recognition of material and human investment and organization. And the copyright can be held by a natural or legal person. Therefore, copyright, patents etc. have been regulated for numerous existing scenarios (e.g. the work and product made by an employee of a legal entity). But in these cases, the individual creator was always to be found. Gyertyanfy adds that the author's 'personality' is also important when it comes to originality, which adds a subjective and fundamental element to IP rights. There must be an evident personal relationship between the author and the work. However, Gyertyánfy also adds that the so-called *'prompting'* process can, in most cases, create an individual author's work. Still, the question could indeed be whether evolving AI can, by collecting and interpreting ever-growing data and coherent pieces of knowledge, turn into a sort of 'original' and 'unique' personality reminiscent of humans (Gyertyánfy, 2023).

Most recently, in the United States as one of the most important markets in terms of AI, a court in Washington D.C. ruled (case Thaler – Shire Perlmutter, 22-1564(BEH)) that a work of art created by artificial intelligence without any human input cannot be copyrighted under U.S. law. This put an end to a five-year-long legal debate. Judge Howell took the side of the Copyright Office, alleging that human authorship is a "bedrock requirement for copyright" based on "centuries of settled understanding" (Brittain, 2023).

However, referring to the previous argument, the question remains what happens if direct human contribution to economic and intellectual output fully disappears in the future, which can lead to a new theory in economics as well. In addition, what if the AI in question can individually produce original works bearing economic value? And how can the owner of the AI (the investment in AI) be protected if the product (work, art) in question is not protected at all?

3) Advent of the Artificial Person: Can a Third Person Appear After the Natural and Legal Person?

As noted above, the labour market, education and personal life in Japan are affected by the proliferation of robots. The Japanese society has traditionally been surprisingly open to robotics and automation, humanlike robots included. (One could also note the manufacturing of lifelike dolls for sexual purposes since the 1950s for people with disabilities, and for the few workers living at the South Pole

– East Ongul Island – employed by the Japanese Ministry of Education) (Galbraith, 2008). In addition, the second half of the 20th century brought another boost when, in 1952, the first comic book series featuring a robot boy (Astro Boy or Tetsuwan Atomu) was published. The popularity of comics also influenced the creation of the first fully anthropomorphic robot, WABOT-1, in 1970-1973, which could grasp objects and speak. Honda is at the forefront of robotics developments: in 1996, the company released the first realistic movement-imitating humanoid robot called P2. In 2000, Asimo appeared, who could already communicate in several languages. In 2013, Japanese robots conquered space: the 34-centimetre Kirobot was created by Honda's rival, Toyota, for the crew of the International Space Station. In 2014, Softbank Robotics' Pepper robot was released, which was capable of analysing human emotions (Sanz, n.d.).

What is the main question regarding Society 5.0 when it comes to the co-evolution of machines and humans? Regarding robotization and sustainable development, a fundamental question which inevitably arises in the long term is whether demand, i.e. consumers, will be needed in the current economic model to maintain sustainability, if technology and robotics develop at the current rate. Of course, a basic question is how to define sustainability in connection with disruptive technologies, when demographic changes are completely cut off compared to the growth and speed of innovation and transformation. In other words, in a society operated by (humanoid) robots, who would qualify not only as tools but also consumers? Also, can the needs (e.g. maintenance, energy) of the robots replacing humans – similarly to clothing for children who do not qualify as workers - also be interpreted as consumer demand? If so, to what extent does this affect the conventional calculation and structure of GDP, as well as its definition, when the added value of technology already exceeds the value of human resources in terms of value creation/production? In relation to this, how does an AI or robot with self-learning and creativity-like capacities, one that can create works which traditionally only humans could make, count in terms of either intellectual property (and property rights) or contribution to GDP?

Furthermore, the more autonomously a robot can learn under the influence of various stimuli (information), the more unique that machine can become, presumably with an increasingly specific neural system. In this paper, we cannot discuss and decide whether, for example, two artificial intelligences, launched at the same time but accessing different databases at different times and to different extents, would ultimately develop similarly or completely uniquely. But this probably also concerns the question of 'uniqueness'.

Looking into the more distant but not unforeseeable future, the development of artificial intelligence may radically reshape both the concept of legal capacity and the ability to act, as well as the concept of productivity. Currently, persons have two manifestations in law and economy: natural persons and legal persons. (In contrast to civil law, only natural persons can principally and basically be held responsible in national criminal law, especially in the EU. But there are few exceptions in the EU and in France, for example, criminal law sanctions legal persons as well, e.g. by deletion from the register (*Criminal responsibility of legal persons in "France - Criminal Code 1994, (2005) EN,* 2024). However, according to Latham & Watkins, even the French Supreme Court had to emphasize that, in its opinion, there is no dogmatic parallel between deregistration and capital punishment, however similar they may be: "The French Supreme Court thus retains an interpretation of the principle of the personal nature of offences and penalties, according to which the dissolution of a legal entity cannot be assimilated to the death of a natural person" (Latham & Watkins, 2020).

The issue of natural persons also has further ramifications as a natural person can only be human, but not all people were (had been) natural persons. The most glaring example is the institution of slavery as regulated in Roman law, where a slave was considered a thing. Still, slaves could also have personal property, and they could buy and sell in their own name and on behalf of their masters (meaning partial legal capacity). Moreover, there are controversial situations such as the special legal status of the foetus (e.g. limited legal capacity in terms of inheritance), while a foetus can be "erased" based on rights granted by lower-level legislation. In addition, various legal statuses (capacities to act) exist with regard to mental capacity, since in most legal systems not even children under the age of 14 or 12 can make decisions freely and independently, as their discernment (intellectual) capacities are not yet adequate for making responsible and independent decisions. Legal systems allow for the restriction of severely mentally disabled adult persons based on a similar principle.

In future, will self-learning artificial intelligence with an artificial nervous system (neural network) reach the status of, for example, ancient slaves, including the ability to do legal business? In essence, this could mean the arrival of the artificial person after the natural and legal person. For example, on stock exchanges, algorithms can already enter into legal transactions, i.e. "free" contracts within a specified framework, and most transactions are already concluded by such programs in the USA. This is not that different from the legal status of slaves.

All of that is not primarily a technical or technological issue, but a civilizational and cultural challenge. Unlike Christianity, which never considers objects as "living things" with consciousness and only deems humans as spiritual beings, in Asia, through animism (shamanism), any object can have a soul, personality and consciousness. This can result in a completely different attitude towards humanoid machines.

Consequently, in Japan, a country standing on the ground of Shintoism, the attitude towards artificial beings and persons may differ significantly from the European approach. In the Shinto religion,[4] everything has a *kami*, i.e. a spirit. From this point of view, perhaps it was not surprising that the Tamagotchi - a keychain-sized virtual pet simulation that had a "soul" and had to be constantly cared for - appeared in Japan in 1996.[5] Japan can therefore be a special example of how the legal status of a robot with both a *kami* and a personality can change if it is capable of mental performance similar to or even greater than that of a human. What reactions will a "Tamagotchi" with feelings and thinking, or even a "superhuman" humanoid body, evoke not only in Japan, but worldwide? (According to news reports, a robot with human brain tissue is already built in China.) How will humanoid robots as "individuals" (similar to ancient slaves who were intellectually full-fledged or could even surpass their masters, and had a special legal status and even freedom, a name and citizenship) fit into the ranks of production means? What will be the legal status of the unique works they produce? Whom will those enrich? In addition, as previously mentioned, the added value of technology already exceeds the value of human resources in terms of value creation/production. According to McKinsey, by 2030, activities that account for up to 30 percent of the hours currently worked across the US economy could be automated—a trend that is accelerated by generative AI.[6]

The challenge at hand is far from minor and not only dogmatic in nature, in view of the reshaping labour market and the demand for human workers in the longer run. More specifically and broadly: can robots, i.e. "artificial humans", statistically influence (more precisely: offset) even the demographic transition - and thus, for example, the variable of the dependency ratio - in relation to GDP and productivity? Specifically, if we consider the decreasing fertile female population, even with a theoretically targeted fertility rate of 2.1 – which in fact still does not ensure even a stagnating population –, we should expect a declining population in the coming decades, so the role and importance of intellectual property in developed economies may continue to increase.

This could well be the most important question of the future, to which we do not yet know the answer. What is more: these developments entail a paradigm shift in the current economic thinking. As for the risks: before assessing the real and substantive risks, we have to face an even greater threat: many people are not even willing to ask this "preliminary question", even though the topic should be dealt with in the same way and with the same weight as, for example, mass migration, artificial insemination, or the issue of abortion with the possible accessibility of artificial wombs, to name just some dogmatic challenges.

CONCLUSION

In conclusion, it can be said that humans and those what could be considered as humans in terms of skills and performance might soon become the most important political issue, since the question to be decided will be whether our fellows, ourselves (and our children) are merely biological factors as well as that what could perform like humans in society and economy and how those(/they?) shall be identified and valued, or whether there is a value and a conception that goes beyond humans, based on which there is an inalienable, unchangeable dignity of human beings stemming from traditional religions, which cannot be touched under any circumstances, either for individual or for state interests and purposes, including the IP realm.

But it is also easy to imagine that these 'complex' issues might not be addressed by EU policy makers, who would think that these issues will 'sort themselves out' in the long run and intentionally keep distance from religions within the framework of antidiscrimination and based on universal (human) civic rights by citing equal opportunities, creating even more problems for both human rights and IP rights as well as social and employment policies.

The explanation is that equal opportunity itself is being undermined at a time when AI and robotization, as well as socioeconomical visions and practices, are also likely to redraw the current patterns and even perspectives in societies especially in terms of different civilizational ideas and understanding, and not to mention the realm of competitiveness, too.

This issue will especially be crucial in Europe in terms of the restricted idea of personhood when it will come to humanoid robots, which may well run counter to the interest of having more competitive EU economies in the 21st century especially when more competing Asian countries in the field of robotics will arise due to their different visions. This issue will also affect the cherished score values of the EU in terms of human rights and their understandings and framework, which stem from basically – however less expressed nowadays – the spiritual foundations of the European culture (Christianity and recently Islam, too).

The most important European value that is the objective set out in Article 3 of the TEU: The Union's aim is to promote the well-being of its peoples. The Treaty also puts that: “It shall work for the sustainable development of Europe based on balanced economic growth and price stability, a highly competitive social market economy, aiming at full employment and social progress, and a high level of protection and improvement of the quality of the environment. It shall promote scientific and technological advance.” Therefore, we, Europeans, shall be ready for the advent of the artificial person if it happens - since that could be the third person after the recognition of natural and legal persons that already happened long ago in the past as well. Given that, it is worth considering looking to as well as examining the current and the future Asiatic and Japanese developments and their understanding of AI-related legislation and practices in the long run, especially when AI and its learning and understanding skills leading to individual and independent abilities to 'think' leading to leaping forward to currently unknown areas.

Finally, based on the beforementioned values that may be at risk in the not-too-distant future if we do not understand of and neither are we ready for the change that is inevitably approaching to us. Perhaps that is why the Japanese Society 5.0 as a new vision could be a new path to the evolution of robotics that shall be considered in the future.

REFERENCES

Brittain, B. (2023, August 21). *AI-generated art cannot receive copyrights, US court says.* Reuters. https://www.reuters.com/legal/ai-generated-art-cannot-receive-copyrights-us-court-says-2023-08-21/

Criminal responsibility of legal persons in "France - Criminal Code 1994 (2005) EN." (2024). Nottingham.ac.uk. https://cjad.nottingham.ac.uk/en/legislation/174/keyword/521/

Cuthbertson, A. (2017, November 6). *Tokyo: Artificial Intelligence "Boy" Shibuya Mirai Becomes World's First AI Bot to Be Granted Residency.* Newsweek. https://newsweek.com/tokyo-residency-artificial-intelligence-boy-shibuya-mirai-702382

Fertility rate: children per woman. (2024). Our World in Data. https://ourworldindata.org/grapher/fertility-rate-with-projections?time=1988.2040&country=JPN~CHN~KOR

Galbraith, P. W. (2008, May 16). *Plastic fantastic: Japan's doll industry booming - Japan Today.* Japantoday.com. https://japantoday.com/category/features/lifestyle/plastic-fantastic-japans-doll-industry-booming?comment-order=popular

Grad-Gyenge, A. (2023) *A mesterséges intelligencia által generált tartalmak értelmezésének lehetőségei a szerzői jog útján.* https://szakcikkadatbazis.hu/doc/2441007

Gyertyánfy, P. (2023). *A mesterséges intelligencia hatályos szerzői jogi törvényünk szerint.* https://www.sztnh.gov.hu/sites/default/files/files/kiadv/szkv/industrial-property-and-copyright-review-2023-6/02-gyertyanfypeter.pdf

Hilotin, J. (2023, July 4). *6 trillion-dollar companies: World's super-exclusive club of mega global businesses.* Gulfnews.com; Gulf News. https://gulfnews.com/business/markets/6-trillion-dollar-companies-worlds-super-exclusive-club-of-mega-global-businesses-1.1688486130909?slide=5

IFR Press Room. (2023, September 26). World Robotics 2023 Report: Asia ahead of Europe and the Americas. IFR International Federation of Robotics. https://ifr.org/ifr-press-releases/news/world-robotics-2023-report-asia-ahead-of-europe-and-the-americas

Japan External Trade Organization. (2024). *Where to invest in Japan's local regions: Kanagawa.* JETRO. https://www.jetro.go.jp/en/invest/region/data/kanagawa.html

Kanagawa Prefecture. (2024). Improving preventive measures (for prefectural residents). Kanagawa Prefecture. https://www.pref.kanagawa.jp/docs/cz6/me-byokaizen/index.html

Latham & Watkins. (2020). *France Reverses Position on Transfer of Criminal Liability in Mergers.* Number 2834. https://www.lw.com/admin/upload/SiteAttachments/Alert%202834.v6.pdf

Law, J. M. (2015). *Puppets of Nostalgia: The Life, Death, and Rebirth of the Japanese "Awaji Ningyo" Tradition.* Princeton University Press. DOI: 10.1515/9781400872954

Lovászy, L. (2021, December 18). *A szemünk láttára kettőződik meg a világunk – Asimovnak lesz igaza?* Portfolio.hu. https://www.portfolio.hu/gazdasag/20211218/a-szemunk-lattara-kettozodik-meg-a-vilagunk-asimovnak-lesz-igaza-515908

Lovászy, L. (2022). Ember és robot – múlt, jelen és jövő: Munkaerőpiaci és foglalkoztatási kihívások. In: PARRAGH, Bianka – BÁGER, Gusztáv (Eds.): Az ösztönző állam válságkezelése II. - A sikeres gazdasági újraindítás. Budapest, pp. 269-302. Ludovika Egyetemi Kiadó.

Manyika, J., Chui, M., Miremadi, M., Bughin, J., George, K., Willmott, P., & Dewhurst, M. (2017, January 12). *Harnessing automation for a future that works.* McKinsey & Company. https://www.mckinsey.com/featured-insights/digital-disruption/harnessing-automation-for-a-future-that-works

Matolcsy, G. (2021, June 7). *Az évtized kihívásai.* Növekedés.hu. https://novekedes.hu/mag/matolcsy-gyorgy-az-evtized-kihivasai

Merchant, B. (2024, July 23). *AI Is Already Taking Jobs in the Video Game Industry.* Wired. https://www.wired.com/story/ai-is-already-taking-jobs-in-the-video-game-industry/

Moonshot Research and Development Program - Science, Technology and Innovation. (n.d.). Cabinet Office Home Page. https://www8.cao.go.jp/cstp/english/moonshot/top.html

Myers, G. (2024). *The Future is Now: Copyright Protection for Works Created by Artificial Intelligence.* Texas Law Review Online. https://texaslawreview.org/wp-content/uploads/2023/10/Myers.10.2.23.FINAL_-2.pdf

Sanz, V. M. Á. (n.d.) *The evolution of japanese robotics: from the beginning to the newest tendencies.* University of Barcelona. https://diposit.ub.edu/dspace/bitstream/2445/126059/1/TFG-GEI-Alvarez-VictorManuel-Jun18.pdf

Speech by Prime Minister Abe at the World Economic Forum Annual Meeting. (n.d.). Ministry of Foreign Affairs of Japan. https://www.mofa.go.jp/ecm/ec/page4e_000973.html

U.S. Chamber Staff. (2022, February 24). *Intellectual Property Drives Economic Prosperity as World Emerges from Pandemic, New Report Shows.* Uschamber.com; U.S. Chamber of Commerce. https://www.uschamber.com/intellectual-property/intellectual-property-drives-economic-prosperity-as-world-emerges-from-pandemic-new-report-shows

ENDNOTES

1 European Parliamentary (2017) European Parliament P8_TA(2017)0051 *Civil Law Rules on Robotics European Parliament Resolution of 16 February 2017 with Recommendations to the Commission on Civil Law Rules on Robotics* (2015/2103(INL)). https://www.europarl.europa.eu/doceo/document/TA-8-2017-0051_EN.pdf

2 *Jacques Maritain (1882–1973) was a French Catholic philosopher. He was raised as a Protestant and was agnostic before converting to Catholicism in 1906. He helped to rediscover Thomas Aquinas for modern times, and took influential part in the development and drafting of the Universal Declaration of Human Rights.*

3 Verbatim report of proceedings of the European Parliament - Civil Law Rules on Robotics (debate) - Wednesday, 15 February 2017. (2017). Europa.eu. https://www.europarl.europa.eu/doceo/document/CRE-8-2017-02-15-ITM-014_EN.html#top

4 *Shinto.* (n.d.). Www.japan-Guide.com. https://www.japan-guide.com/e/e2056.html

5 *History | Official Tamagotchi Site*. (2023). History | Official Tamagotchi Site. https://tamagotchi-official.com/us/history/

6 Ellingrud, K., Sanghvi, S., Singh Dandona, G., Madgavkar, A., Chui, M., White, O., & Hasebe, P. (2023, July 26). *Generative AI and the Future of Work in America.* Www.mckinsey.com; McKinsey Global Institute. https://www.mckinsey.com/mgi/our-research/generative-ai-and-the-future-of-work-in-america

Chapter 2
Taxation Problem of Copyright Income Obtained From Intellectual Products Created by Artificial Intelligence in Turkish Tax Law

Oytun Canyaş
Hacettepe University, Turkey

ABSTRACT

Intellectual products created by artificial intelligence have caused some difficult problems in various branches of law. One of these problems is whether the income obtained from the transfer or granting of the right to use these products can be taxed or not. While there are some suggestions in the doctrine for the taxation of these incomes within the current system, some states have tried to create new taxes on this issue. In terms of Turkish tax law, there is no need to create a new tax in order to tax the income obtained from the intellectual products created by artificial intelligence. Although the intellectual products created by artificial intelligence are not considered as "works" in Turkish intellectual property rights law, they will be subject to taxation in accordance with the Turkish income tax, Turkish corporate tax law, or Turkish value added tax, if their investors earn income from the transfer or right to use of these products.

DOI: 10.4018/979-8-3693-8704-7.ch002

INTRODUCTION

The use of artificial intelligence (AI) has increased rapidly in recent years due to technological developments, such that AI contributes to our daily lives and the development of many sectors, such as healthcare, industry, and services (Bak, 2018). The AI market has doubled from approximately $90 billion in 2020 to $184 billion in 2024. Undoubtedly, the main reason for this rapid growth is that AI can solve complex problems that computers could not do before. Indeed, AI can be trained to compose or paint, write poems and newspaper articles, or shoot short films (Naqvi, 2020).

Like other technological developments, this rapid increase in the use of AI has also led to unexpected and difficult-to-solve social and legal problems. The decisions and applications of AI challenge, contradict, and even violate existing legal rules, and therefore a fundamental change is needed. In this sense, developments in AI technology have made certain legal problems even more apparent. For example, according to research by Oxford University, approximately half of all occupations can be undertaken by computers (Frey & Osbourne, 2013), which has raised social and public problems caused by the loss of human labor. Indeed, the increase in the use of AI and robots instead of human labor, especially in the production sector, has reduced income tax revenue from wage incomes and social security premium incomes due to falling employment. Meanwhile, public spending (e.g., on unemployment benefits) due to unemployment has increased as required by the principle of the social state. One way to resolve such problems is to use taxation, as suggested both in the doctrine (Kovacev, 2020; Kou et al., 2024) and as enacted by some states (*2018 tax amendments in effect*).

New legal problems have also emerged due to AI's ability to create intellectual products like paintings, musical compositions, and poems that computers could not create before. Examples of such problems concerning intellectual property law include whether the intellectual work created by artificial intelligence will be considered a work and therefore whether it will benefit from the legal protection regime provided for copyrights, and if so, who will own the copyright of the intellectual product (Naqvi, 2020; Zeytin & Gençay, 2019). One of the proposed solutions for copyright infringements regarding intellectual products created by AI is the use of taxation authority. Here, it is first necessary to distinguish between ideal law and existing-positive law in the discussion of taxation of intellectual products of AI. The problem of taxation of artificial intelligence in general and taxation of intellectual products created by AI specifically is a problem of ideal law at the level of doctrine.

Examining such a normative taxation problem requires answering a number of fundamental questions, specifically whether artificial intelligence and robots will be taxed. If they are taxable, which of the income, corporate, or value added taxes they will fall under, what the subject of the tax will be, and who the taxpayer will be. Discussing these questions, which are outlined below, means discussing normative proposals for the use of taxation authority as a tool for various purposes of taxation (such as income redistribution, equality promotion, or prevention of copyright violations). However, proposals regarding the financial and social consequences of the use of AI are beyond the scope of the present study.

For now, the issue we are trying to investigate relates to positive law. In other words, the study focuses on the question of whether the copyright income arising from the intellectual products created by AI can be taxed in positive law. Undoubtedly, considering the variety of legal systems across the world, this question needs to be examined separately in terms of the tax laws of each state.

On the other hand, this discussion on positive law should be carried out with great care and sensitivity due to the possibility of infringing on fundamental rights and freedoms. This is because the issues lies at the intersection of the principle of legality of taxes, which is the fundamental taxation principle of modern states, and the financing of public spending and the use of taxation authority for extra-fiscal purposes. Indeed, states are obliged not to violate the principle of legality of taxes when they use taxation as an instrument for purposes like income redistribution, promotion of science or art, with the purpose of financing public spending, which is the fiscal purpose of taxation authority. Otherwise, the state's taxation authority could be used arbitrarily and unpredictably, and thereby infringe on many fundamental individual rights and freedoms, especially property rights. We believe that our discussion of Turkish tax law while taking into account the above principles and reservations can also guide discussions regarding tax laws in other states.

Thus, the main aim of the present study is to examine the taxation of AI-created intellectual products under Turkish tax law within the framework of Turkey's intellectual property law regime, along with tax issues and liability concepts. To answer these questions, we first present a conceptual framework regarding the process of creating intellectual products by AI. We then examine whether AI-created intellectual products can be considered works in terms of Turkish intellectual property law, the problem of authorship, and financial rights. In the third part of the study, we comprehensively discuss whether AI-created intellectual products can be taxed under Turkish tax law.

THE RELATIONSHIP BETWEEN AI CREATION OF INTELLECTUAL PRODUCTS AND COPYRIGHT

Taxation of AI-created intellectual products depends on answering fundamental questions, particuarly whether the product can be considered a “work” under intellectual property law and, if so, who earns the copyright income. To answer these two questions, we must first determine the relationship between the process of creating an intellectual product by artificial intelligence and copyright, limited to our subject of study.

In this context, AI[1] refers, in its most general sense, to a computer program or machine that can imitate what humans do, evaluate phenomena like humans, make decisions, and implement them according to these qualifications, and therefore exhibit problem-solving ability (Bak, 2018; Kılıçarslan, 2019; Zeytin & Gençay, 2019). In other words, AI is designed to imitate certain biological cognitive activities (Naqvi, 2020), particularly through neural network models that are similar to biological neural networks[2]. AI operates in areas that currently require human intelligence, such as learning, problem solving, and decision making. AI can operate autonomously because it is programmed to learn and adapt by itself (*Introduction to AI Applications in Robotics*, n.d.). However, AI is not sentient (Naqvi, 2020).

AI learns through machine learning and deep learning methods. In machine learning, AI algorithms improve themselves to perform a specific task (Naqvi, 2020; Bak, 2018). These algorithms allow the AI to perform the task in the best way possible without being reprogrammed with specific instructions. In machine learning, the programmer can see the input and output, but cannot observe the AI's learning process. Some AIs have been designed to rewrite their own code to improve their performance. (Naqvi, 2020).

Deep learning, on the other hand, is a method developed to solve more complex problems on larger and more complex computers. It is an advanced branch of machine learning associated with big data. (Bak, 2018). In deep learning, big data presented in a complex form as a multi-layered learning model is made understandable by performing calculations between layers. (Gözübüyük, 2021).

Although machine learning and deep learning methods enable AI to collect, process, develop information, and choose among different alternatives, an AI program/machine lacks free will because it is programmed through a set of instructions given to it (Zorluer, 2019; Naqvi, 2020). Hence, while AI's learning activity requires a certain ability, AI cannot make choices that would demonstrate free will or disobey instructions (Naqvi, 2020).

What AI can do is to create intellectual products using machine learning and deep learning methods. As seen from examples of musical compositions and Haiku poems created by an AI named Annie, developed by David Cope, a professor of

Musicology and an artist robot called e-David, AI can act alone to create intellectual products (Yanisky-Ravid, 2017). Another example of AI's creativity are the chatbots developed by Facebook. Although these robots were not programmed to do so, they created a new means of English-language communication as they understand it (Zorluer, 2019).

The creation of intellectual products by AI has given rise to the concept of generative AI, defined as a technology that can produce intellectual products that would be subject to copyright if created by humans, such as texts, images, videos, and audio recordings (including imitating the human voice). Generative AI is trained on a large dataset that often includes works that are or may be copyrighted (*Artificial Intelligence and Copyright,* 2023).

This development has stimulated new discussions regarding private and public law. In particular, the creation of intellectual products by artificial intelligence has led to discussions in intellectual property law, which is a branch of private law, regarding whether the created intellectual product qualifies as a work, and whether training it on a data set containing copyrighted works leads to copyright infringement. Here, the first question to consider regarding intellectual property law is whether AI-created intellectual products can be considered as work. If they can, then this raises the question of who owns the rights to the work in question, such as the AI investor or programmer (Zorluer, 2019). If an AI-created intellectual product can be considered a work then the author can benefit from the legal protection regime granted to copyrights (Gözübüyük, 2021).

To understand the subject of this study more clearly, it is necessary here to distinguish between the AI code and the AI-created intellectual product. the issue here is not the invention of a certain AI technology by a person or its use as a tool to create a work. Rather, the issue is whether the intellectual product created by the AI itself can be considered as a work and, if so, who will own the copyright (Zorluer, 2019). This matters because, when AI creates an intellectual product, the resulting product code is different from the initial algorithm code (Naqvi, 2020).

Discussions have already started in various legal systems to consider whether AI-created intellectual products can be considered as works and, if so, whether they can benefit from the legal regime granted to copyright. Regarding US law, for example, the US Copyright Office has clearly stated in Paragraph 306 of the document stating the basic rules and principles regarding copyright that an intellectual product can be considered as an original work if created by a human[3]. Therefore, according to US law, AI-created intellectual products cannot be considered as works and AI cannot be the author or copyright owner of the intellectual product it creates[4]. In a very recent decision, the US Distict Court for the District of Columbia ruled that intellectual products created by an tAI cannot be protected by US intellectual property law[5]. The lawsuit in question was filed by Stephen Taler, the owner of an AI called the Creativity Machine, after the US Copyright Office rejected his application to register an intellectual product created by the AI. The court found lawful the defendant's action of rejecting the copyright application for a work not created by a human.

English law also has relevant regulations. Article 178 of the English Copyright, Design and Patent Act of 1988 defines a computer-generated work as a work produced by a computer where the author is not a human. The law states that this provision does not cover products created by fully autonomous AI, but covers situations where the intellectual product is created by AI when the inputs are given to the AI by humans (Gözübüyük, 2021).

As noted earlier, another fundamental problem that for intellectual property law regarding AI-created intellectual products is that AI may violate copyright while being trained on other intellectual products using machine learning and deep learning methods. This is because AI can use copyrighted intellectual products without permission and without payment while being trained with machine learning methods or can violate the author's copyright by plagiarizing an article by copying it (Naqvi, 2020). Following recent developments in AI technology, AI companies have faced many copyright infringement disputes (Kou et al., 2024). For example, on June 29, 2023, two authors filed a copyright infringement class action lawsuit against OpenAI in California. The plaintiffs accused OpenAI of using the books for which they own the copyright without permission to train ChatGPT (*Lawsuit says OpenAI violated US authors' copyrights to train AI chatbot,* 2023). Similarly, The New York Times accused OpenAI and Microsoft of using millions of copyrighted articles without permission to train their chatbots (*NY Times sues OpenAI, Microsoft for infringing copyrighted works,* 2023). Finally, The Hollywood Reporter reported that well-known Hollywood actress Scarlett Johansson is considering suing OpenAI for imitating her voice and facial expressions, despite her explicit refusal to give them permission (Cho, 2024). In January 2023, some artists filed a class action lawsuit against Stability AI, Deviant Art, and Midjourney in the US Court of California, claiming that the companies' AI programs used thousands of artists' copyrighted works in the form of images without permission and without payment[6]. Due to the growth of such legal disputes, the US Copyright Office published a Notice of Inquiry in August 2023, providing information on how to select and use data sets for training generative AI in US Law, what permissions should be obtained from copyright owners, and how they should be compensated[7].

As noted before, this study addresses the issue from the perspective of tax law, which is a sub-branch of public law. Within this framework, it is possible to examine both of the private law issues presented above in terms of the use of taxation authority. However, the study focuses on the issue of taxation of royalties obtained from intellectual products created by artificial intelligence in Turkish law. Therefore, the issue is primarily examined below in terms of Turkish intellectual property law. Since taxation authority as a rule is based on private law concepts and principles, the issue cannot be examined in terms of Turkish tax law before determining the nature of AI's intellectual products under Turkish intellectual property law.

Evaluation of AI-Created Intellectual Products in Terms Of Turkish Intellectual Property Law

Copyrights or intellectual property rights refer to all rights and authorities granted by a legal regime over the products created by individuals' intellectual labor (Cangüven, 2019; Zorluer, 2019). In Turkish law, intellectual property rights broadly cover both the rights to works regulated according to FSEK[8] number 5846 and the rights on patents, utility models, and designs regulated by the Industrial Property Law number 6769. More narrowly, only the rights to intellectual and artistic works, such as ideas, designs, computer programs, and music, regulated in FSEK fall within the scope of copyrights (Zorluer, 2019). It should be noted that we address the taxation issue only in terms of AI-created intellectual products within the scope of FSEK. Copyrights are divided into financial and moral rights. Of these, the relevant financial rights according to the provisions of FSEK Article 20 et seq. include the right to process, the right to reproduce, the right to distribute, the right to represent, and the right to transmit. The financial rights to a work can be transferred to third parties partially or completely through copyright transfer agreements, or license transfer agreements that only transfer the right to use the financial right (İncel, 2023). The copyright income is obtained by establishing the contractual relations in question. Copyright income refers to the income obtained as a result of the valuation of intellectual and artistic works. The income obtained by the authors by selling their works and patents or by transferring or renting their existing rights to them falls within the scope of copyright income. Copyright income is obtained by transferring the financial rights on the work (İncel, 2023). Therefore, in terms of various tax laws, financial rights may constitute the subject of tax in tax laws, while their transfer may constitute the event that gives rise to tax (İncel, 2023).

There are already examples of transferring AI-created intellectual products and earning royalties from them. In 2018, for example, an AI-created portrait, titled "Edmond de Belamy, from La Famille de Belamy," was sold at an auction for $432,500[9]. Therefore, there is both an intellectual product and profit obtained from its sale.

As far as we can determine, such a transfer of financial rights has not occurred under Turkish law. Nevertheless, it raises the question of whether the royalty income from selling an AI-created intellectual product in Turkey would be subject to tax. Answering this question requires a detailed analysis regarding tax law-private law relations under Turkish law.

Whether Intellectual Products Created by Artificial Intelligence Can Be Considered Works

Work and Its Conditions Under FSEK

Under Turkish law, the author of a work acquires the material and moral rights set forth in FSEK upon creating an intellectual product that qualifies as a "work" without the need for any process like registration or enrollment (Gözübüyük, 2021; Karahan et al., 2011). That is, the intellectual product must first be accepted as a work in order for the rights to it to be protected under FSEK (Tekinalp, 2004; Karahan, et al., 2011; Cangüven, 2019; Zorluer, 2019). Intellectual products are non-material products that have emerged as a result of human intelligence and have a separate existence and legal regime from the objects they embody (Zorluel, 2019; Cangüven, 2019). Given that not every intellectual product can benefit from the legal protection regime provided by FSEK, the important issue here is which intellectual products qualify as "works" worthy of protection within the scope of FSEK (Gözübüyük, 2021; Zorluer, 2019).

FSEK 1/B-a provision defines works as "all kinds of intellectual and artistic products that bear the identity of their owner and are considered as works of science, literature, music, fine arts or cinema". Thus, for an intellectual product to be considered a work and be protected under FSEK, it must bear the characteristics of its owner, be shaped to reflect the characteristics in question, be one of the types of works envisaged in FSEK, and be the product of intellectual effort (Tekinalp, 2004)[10].

The first of these elements is "specialty" (Karahan et al., 2011; Gözübüyük, 2021; Cangüven, 2019). The condition of bearing the specialty of the author is related to the expression or style of the author that reveals their creativity. However, specialty is broader than content, expression, or style (Karahan et al., 2011) because it also includes the existence of the free shaping area of the creator of the intellectual product. Conversely, specialty does not apply in cases where everyone has to shape an intellectual product in one specific way because there is no free shaping area. Examples of such products include everyday letters and recipes (Karahan et al., 2011).

On the other hand, while specialty refers to individual, subjective expression, reducing this expression to the quality of originality narrows the concept of work considerably. Intellectual products that are specific to the original author undoubtedly have the quality of a work. However, it is also clear that specificity includes a level that is not ordinary. Thus, we can differentiate the result of such mental labor from ordinary, everyday activities (Tekinalp, 2004; Cangüven, 2019).

The condition of specificity means that non-human agents, such as animals, plants, or nature, cannot create works. Therefore, if a person finds and exhibits an object found in nature, that object does not have the characteristics of a work. Conversely, if the author has used computers or other machines while creating their work, and has participated in its creation to a certain extent, then it can be considered a work. However, if the author has only accessed the computer or other machine without making any creative contribution, then the product cannot be considered a work (Karahan et al., 2011; Gözübüyük, 2021). This implies that computer-generated works do not have the characteristics of a work because they are not created by humans, whereas computer-aided products can be considered works provided that they meet the conditions discussed above (Gözübüyük, 2021).

The second element is that the work must be shaped in a way that reflects the author's personality and must be presented in a particular form (Tekinalp, 2004Shaped means that the work must be objectively perceivable. Hence, in order for the work to benefit from FSEK's legal protection regime, it does not necessarily have to be embodied as an object or recorded on a technical device. Rather, as long as it is objectively perceivable, even an oral discourse is legally protected (Karahan et al., 2011). On the other hand, as long as it remains at the stage of mere idea thought, it cannot be considered a work (Tekinalp, 2004; Karahan et al., 2011; Gözübüyük, 2021).

Thirdly, the intellectual product must fall into one of the types of works stipulated in FSEK (Tekinalp, 2004). Also called the objective element of being considered a work, these types include "all kinds of intellectual and artistic products that are considered as works of science and literature, music, fine arts or cinema". They are listed in a restricted manner (numerus clausus) in FSEK art.1/B-a (Karahan et al., 2011; Gözübüyük, 2021; Cangüven, 2019). According to FSEK art. 6, "processes" and compilations that bear the characteristics of the creator are also considered "works". Therefore, provided that they do not harm the rights of the author, they should also be considered within this scope (Karahan et al., 2011).

The final condition is that the work must be an intellectual product and a product of activity, which means that the work is created by humans. Hence, Tekinalp (2004) does not accept a computer translation as a work because it is the product of a machine, not an idea. If the options are determined by the machine or if everyone who uses that machine reaches the same result, a work cannot exist (Tekinalp, 2004). Zorluer explains this condition as the need for an intellectual product to have an owner (Zorluer, 2019).

As stated above, FSEK's definition of work is not limited to those listed in FSEK art.1/B-a. The law also includes works related to the main work, created by making use of that work, putting the work into another genre, re-arranging it, or translating it into another language. These are called "adapted works" because they are connected to the main work but are works of thought and art that are not independent of the main work (Tekinalp, 2004; Karahan et al., 2011). Accordingly, FSEK article 1/B-c defines adapted works as "products of thought and art that are created by making use of another work and are not independent of that work and that carry the idiosyncrasy of the adaptor". A processed work is legally defined as a work provided that it meets the condition of speciality and is the product of a creative effort.

Given that the right to process a work belongs exclusively to its owner, the original work cannot be processed without the owner's permission. Hence, the permission of the independent owner of the work is required to use the processed work commercially. However, the owner of the processed work has the same financial and moral rights as the owner of the work (Karahan et al., 2011). Finally, the condition of specialty in the independent work applies to the processed work (Tekinalp, 2004; Karahan et al., 2011).

Evaluation in Terms of Intellectual Products Created by Artificial Intelligence

In the above discussion about whether AI-created intellectual products can be considered as works, the important conditions were that the work should be the result of the intellectual product and activity, along with specialty (Zorluer, 2019; Gözübüyük, 2021). Because AI-created intellectual products do not exist as mere thoughts, they have taken shape. In addition, these intellectual products can often fall under the types of works specified in FSEK art. 1/B-a. We therefore claim that AI-created intellectual products meet the condition of specificity, as in the example of Annie, the AI that was trained to compose music yet wrote poetry (Zorluer, 2019).

However, there are also views in the doctrine arguing that AI-created intellectual products cannot be considered works. According to Gözübüyük (2021), these do not qualify under FSEK because there is no clear regulation on this issue. According to Gözübüyük, although FSEK does not specifically state that AI-created products cannot be considered works, it is not possible to say that the essence and spirit of FSEK, which is an old law, has changed. In addition, as stated before, others argue that a work can only be created by humans because it results from intellectual production and activity (Tekinalp, 2004; Şahin & Şahin, 2022).

Yet, it can also be argued that, unlike other computer programs, AI does create intellectual products. Some computer programs or software create products within a mechanical process, without making any choices, within the framework drawn for them. Therefore, the product they create does not meet the conditions of creativity and specialty. Because they do not meet the conditions that the work results from an intellectual product and activity restricted to "people", they cannot be considered works as defined by FSEK. (Tekinalp, 2004; Zorluer, 2019). AI, however, can create a new and non-random product without external human intervention by processing the information it collects from different sources through machine learning or deep learning and choosing between alternatives.

Nevertheless, we still believe that despite having the required characteristics and meeting the conditions discussed above, an AI-created intellectual product still cannot be considered a "work". The purpose and systematics of FSEK prevent the acceptance of an AI-created intellectual product. Article 1, which regulates the purpose of FSEK, clearly states that its purpose is to determine and protect the moral and financial rights to their products of the owners of intellectual and artistic works and other related rights holders, to regulate the conditions for benefiting from these works, and to impose sanctions in case of non-compliance. As will be explained below, because AI is not considered a person in the legal order, it cannot be the owner of a work whose "financial rights to its work will be determined and protected". Moreover, neither the AI itself nor its investor can be a related rights holder. In this case, qualifying the AI-created intellectual product as a work yet concluding that there is no author (or related rights holder) according to FSEK means reaching a conclusion that is inconsistent with the law's wording and purpose through systematic interpretation. Thus, as the doctrine rightly states, the legislator has regulated authorship in terms of natural persons and has not foreseen authorship in terms of AI-created intellectual products.

Finally, it is necessary to consider whether AI-created intellectual products can be considered as processed works. Under art. 6/10 of FSEK, AI-created works could arguablly be considered as adaptations and editings in the sense of "adaptation, editing or any change made to a computer program". However, adaptation and editing are used to correct program errors and make the product more functional, whereas in AI-created intellectual products discussed in this study, new code is created by changing the initial source codes. Hence, AI-created intellectual product cannot be considered as a "processed work" according to FSEK (Gözübüyük, 2021). On the other hand, even if it can be said that the work in question meets the condition of specialness in the event that AI creates a processed intellectual product by using other copyrighted works, we believe that this processed intellectual product cannot be considered as a work according to FSEK, in line with our conclusion regarding independent works.

Authorship of AI-Created Intellectual Products

Authority in FSEK

According to FSEK Article 8/1, the owner of a work is the person who creates it, and who gains the status of authorship at the moment the work is created. This principle, that the owner of the work is the person who creates it, is a natural consequence of the work having the characteristics of its owner because creating a work is a material act. Therefore, when the work is created, authorship arises automatically

(Tekinalp, 2004; Zorluer, 2019). Hence, those lacking the capacity to act can also be the owner of the work (Karahan et al., 2011), which is parallel to capacity in tax law. This is because, in terms of tax obligations like liability and responsibility, the capacity to act is not required according to the Tax Procedure Law (VUK) Article 9/1.

Given that this principle aims to encourage intellectual effort, it is impossible for those who do not or cannot make an intellectual creative effort to be an author. This principle exists in continental European legal systems, such as those in Germany and Switzerland. Under Turkish law, the principle prevents the acceptance of a legal entity as an author. That is, legal entities cannot produce intellectual products, although, as can be seen in works created by employees, this principle can be exempted in favor of certain financial rights. This does not prevent employees from being authors, but employers can use their financial rights (Tekinalp, 2004; Karahan et al., 2011; Zorluer, 2019). According to FSEK Article 18/2, workers employed to create works in accordance with the employment relationship are the owners of the works they create. The moral rights to the work belong to the employee. However, since the work is done in accordance with a service contract, the use of the financial rights belongs to the employer (Tekinalp, 2004). The situation is different in Anglo-Saxon legal systems. In the USA, for example, the work-for-hire system implies that employers hire people, create a work, and own it. This allows workers to provide their services while the owners of the works they create are those who employ them (Tekinalp, 2004).

As for the rights of the author, as previously stated, FSEK accords the author both moral[11] and financial[12] rights, of which the latter are relevant here. Financial rights, consisting of "right to process", "right to reproduce", "right to distribute", "right to represent" and "right to communicate to the public" in FSEK art. 20 et seq., are rights that grant the author an exclusive right to benefit economically from the work and the right to prevent third parties from benefiting economically (Karahan et al., 2011).

Although the ownership of a work cannot be transferred, the financial rights to the work can be transferred, mortgaged, or seized (Tekinalp, 2004). Thus, financial rights can be subject to legal transactions, such as transfer and license, or inherited (Karahan et al., 2011; Tekinalp, 2004). Indeed, a financial right can be transferred through obligatory (commitment) or savings transactions and thus leave the property of the right holder. Alternatively, it is also possible to grant the other party the opportunity to use that right, in other words, a license, without leaving the property of the transferor. FSEK names the authority to use financial rights "license" (Tekinalp, 2004; Karahan et al., 2011). The point that should be emphasized here is that since financial rights are independent, they can be subject to separate legal transactions, such as the right to process or reproduce, with each being subject to transfer or license (Karahan, Suluk, Saraç, Nal, 2011).

Here, it is necessary to mention the concept of related rights in FSEK because of its relevance to our topic. In some cases, FSEK protects investments and acquisitions in addition to the work. That is, producers, publishers, and performers who contribute to the adaptation of a work benefit from the copyright protection regime in accordance with FSEK Article 80. Rights related to the rights of the owner of the work, which are different from the work due to the lack of a creative element are rights adjacent to the rights of the owner of the work (FSEK article 80/1) and the rights of film producers (FSEK Article 80/2). The rights adjacent to the rights of the owner of the work in FSEK Article 80/1 are the rights of artists who interpret, introduce, narrate, sing, play, or perform a work in an original way, record producers as regulated in FSEK Article 80, provided that they do not harm the moral and financial rights of the owner of the work.

As can be seen, through related rights, FSEK aims to grant certain rights to some performers, record producers, radio-TV organizations, and film producers, who are not actually able to be owners of works. This enables them to benefit from the legal protection regime regarding their products that cannot be considered "works" according to FSEK (Tekinalp, 2004). Related rights are absolute rights and cannot change, limit, or remove the rights of the owner of the work. Hence, under FSEK art. 1/b-j, art. 1/B-k and art. 80, the existence of related rights is recognized on condition that they do not harm the moral and material rights of the owner of the work (Tekinalp, 2004).

The explanations so far demonstrate that authorship and the issue of who can use the financial rights on the work are distinct. As will be explained below, because AI lacks a personality, it cannot be an owner of a work. However, this does not prevent discussion of whether a natural person or legal entity can own the financial rights to an AI-created intellectual product. What is also important in terms of taxation is to determine which real or legal person is the rightful owner of an AI-created intellectual product.

Ownership of Intellectual Products Created by Artificial Intelligence

As stated above, in order to benefit from the financial and moral rights stipulated in FSEK, an intellectual product must be considered a work; therefore, there must be an author who has these rights. If the author transfers their financial rights or grants a license, taxable income becomes relevant, but this is only meaningful if the intellectual product created by artificial intelligence has the quality of a work.

Although we do not agree with this opinion, presenting the discussions in the doctrine will help convey our opinion on this issue more easily.

In this case, it is necessary to determine who will have financial rights over the intellectual product created by AI. In the doctrine, it has been discussed whether, for an AI-created work, the public, the AI itself, the person who made necessary adjustments while creating the work, or the investor in the AI can be considered as the work's author (Gözübüyük, 2021; Zorluer, 2019). It should be noted that we will address the issue narrowly in terms of its effect on the use of taxation authority. This limitation means that there has been no examination of whether the public can have rights in an AI-created intellectual product[13] because public legal entities cannot be taxpayers themselves. In addition, another view in the doctrine has not been examined, namely the question of whether the person who makes the necessary arrangements for the creation of the work can be the owner of the work. This is because it is a debate arising from the legislation of countries subject to the Anglo-Saxon legal system, such as England, Ireland, and New Zealand, rather than Turkish Law[14].

Here, it can be discussed whether the AI can be the rights holder for a work it created itself. Since only individuals can have rights in the legal system, an AI can gain rights by granting it personality. However, AI lacks rights capacity, meaning being able to have rights and obligations. Therefore, as long as AI is not granted personality, it cannot have gain the rights to the work it creates (Gözübüyük, 2021; Zorluer, 2019; Zeytin & Gençay, 2019)[15].

Turkish law also raises the question of whether an AI can be considered as a worker in terms of the discussion about who can own the copyright of an AI-created product(Zorluer, 2019). As stated earlier, in Turkish law, the right of ownership of the work produced by workers belongs to the employee unless otherwise provided. However, the employer can only have financial rights over the work. This suggests that an AI cannot be considered as a worker or a work's author. Because Turkish law does not consider AI to be a person, it cannot benefit from the status of worker envisaged for natural persons[16]. Therefore, the concept of work and hire in US law mentioned above is not valid in Turkish law. As outlined above, in US law, the concepts of employer and employee are interpreted broadly in accordance with the concept of work made for hire, raising the question of whether AI can be considered as an employee and employers as owners of AI. This suggests that if the programmer or owner of the AI uses the AI to create a new product then they can be considered to be employers (Zorluer, 2019).

Another possibility regarding the discussion of the right of ownership of AI is whether the developer of the AI can be a rightful owner. As stated before, for an intellectual product to have the quality of a "work", it must have the "personality" of its owner. However, the work created by the AI cannot be known by the developer because AI constantly changes its source codes in the process. In other words, the specificity of the programmer is not included in the intellectual product created by the AI. Therefore, the doctrine rightfully states that the software developer cannot have rights to the work created by AI (Gözübüyük, 2021).

In our opinion, the discussion of whether the investor of artificial intelligence has copyright is of key importance in terms of taxation, which is the subject of the study. It is first necessary to make the following determination. In Turkish law, AI, as a computer program, is accepted as a "scientific and literary work" and benefits from FSEK's legal protection regime. FSEK article 1/B-g defines a computer program as "a computer command system organized in a way that will enable a computer system to perform a specific operation or task, and preparatory studies that will ensure the formation and development of this command system". FSEK article 2/1 states, "Works expressed in any form of language and writing and computer programs expressed in any form and their preparatory designs, provided that they result in a program at the next stage" are protected under FSEK as scientific and literary works. In parallel, the Industrial Property Law No. 6769 article 82/2-c[17] states that computer programs are not considered inventions and are excluded from industrial property protection.

Since the creation of AI programs requires a certain amount of capital and organization, they can mostly be created by legal entities like companies, and exceptionally by natural persons. If AI is created by a company's software developers, the authors of this AI computer program are workers (software developers) employed to create a work in accordance with the employment relationship, according to FSEK art. 18/2. However, because the work must be done in accordance with the service contract, the use of financial rights belongs to the company, unless otherwise understood from the special contract between them or the nature of the work. In short, the financial rights to the AI computer program will belong to the legal entity – the artificial intelligence investor – unless otherwise provided. According to FSEK art. 13, the company does not need to register or record the AI computer program.

However, there is a difference between copyrights on AI and AI-created intellectual products. In our opinion, if AI-created intellectual products are considered as works according to FSEK, the owner of the work cannot be the investor/employer. This is because, according to FSEK art. 18/2, the investor/employer can only be the owner of financial rights. Since, as explained above, the AI that created the work is not a person, it cannot be the owner of the work. In this case, an inconsistent result emerges in terms of the legal order.

Another question that needs to be discussed regarding taxation of AI-created works is whether the artificial intelligence investor can be a related right holder. As noted earlier, FSEK art. 80-82 protects under the name of the author's related rights both literary works, such as stories, novels, compositions, paintings, sculptures, and works of art, that emerged through human intellectual creativity and also products that cannot be considered intellectual products (Bülter, 2005). Related right holders other than the author are protected because they convey the work to the public. In many cases, the author cannot perform or present the work publicly on their own (Bülter, 2005). Therefore, in Turkish law, as previously stated, the rights of performing artists, and neighboring right holders like record producers and film producers are protected within the scope of related rights.

Within the conditions set by the law, related right holders also have moral and/or financial rights[18]. For example, according to FSEK Art. 80/A-2, performing artists have the exclusive right to authorise or prohibit the fixation of their performance, the reproduction, sale, distribution, rental, and lending of this fixation, communication to the public by means of signs, sounds, and/or images, and retransmission and representation of their performance. Therefore, relevant articles of FSEK include regulations governing the use or transfer of financial rights by the owners of the related rights (Bülter, 2005).

Analysis of FSEK provisions suggests that an AI investor cannot be a related rights holder. This is because, in FSEK Art.s 80-82, the related right holders are numerically listed as neighboring right holders (performing artists, record and film producers, radio and television organizations). Because the investor in AI is not counted among the holders of related rights, even if the AI-created intellectual product qualifies as a work, the investor cannot be protected under the FSEK to this extent. On the other hand, the doctrine states that since AI-created intellectual products are not considered works, the AI investor cannot benefit from the legal regime granted for the related rights (Gözübüyük, 2021).

Consequently, in the legal regime envisaged by FSEK in Turkish law, AI-created intellectual products cannot be described as works and cannot have an author, whether human or AI. Therefore, such intellectual products are not protected by Turkish intellectual property rights law, and the fundamental question remains unanswered: How should an AI-created intellectual product be characterized in terms of private law? We believe that the correct characterization can be given based on the investor (employer) of the AI program. As noted above, because an AI program is a computer program, it is a work recognized under FSEK. Regardless of the owner of the work in question, the financial rights belong to the investor of the AI. The most important financial rights are the right to process, regulated in FSEK art. 21. Here, the AI investor makes the necessary arrangements for the creation of the intellectual product in the AI program; in other words, the investor processes artificial intelligence in a broad sense[19].

However, an intellectual product is created irrespective of AI. FSEK regulates the processing right within the framework of a work in progress. As explained above, the AI-created intellectual product is not a work in progress. In our view, the correct characterization here is that the intellectual product is created in the context of the investor's right to process artificial intelligence in a broad sense. However, such a broad interpretation does not allow the resulting intellectual product to be recognized as a work of art under FSEK Art. s 6 and 21. Similarly, under this interpretation, FSEK does not make the investor in AI a holder of financial rights. In short, FSEK does not provide an answer to the question.

This result has a limited impact on the assessment to be made in terms of Turkish tax law. As demonstrated below, even if the AI-created intellectual product is not considered a work, the income derived from its transfer or use may be taxable.

Approaches to the Taxation of Intellectual Products Created by Artificial Intelligence

As the topic is related to the taxation of AI in general, it is useful to outline approaches to this issue. Proposals to tax AI are oriented towards the use of taxation for extra-fiscal purposes, such as encouraging technological investment and preventing job losses, rather than the main purpose of taxation, which is to finance public expenditure. The first approach focuses on compensating for tax loss due to the employment-reducing effect of the widespread use of AI in various sectors (Chand et al., 2020; Kovacev, 2020). Accordingly, the owner of AI will also pay the tax arising from it. Hence, in order to ensure neutrality, the taxation of robots or AI should in theory be the same amount as the taxation of the wage income of a worker doing the same job. The wage will be calculated on the basis of arm's length salary. Thus, compensation for the loss of income tax and insurance premium due to the worker's unemployment will follow the neutrality principle (Chand et al., 2020; Kostić, & Reis, 2020).

The second approach focuses on changes to corporate taxation. It suggests that corporate taxpayers who reduce their labor force by automating to a certain level through the use of AI should not benefit from tax incentives, or their ability to benefit should be reduced (Abbott & Bogenschneider, 2018; Chand et al, 2020). Another proposal suggests that the tax rate for corporate taxpayers who automate by using AI should increase in line with their increasing profitability due to the decrease of labor force expenses (Abbott & Bogenschneider, 2018; Chand et al., 2020).

According corporate-focused proposal is to tax employers through unemployment insurance at a level based on the size of their human labor force. The aim is to compensate the state for increased public spending due to the unemployment caused companies replacing human workers with robots or AI (Abbott & Bogenschneider, 2018; Chand et al., 2020). It has also been suggested that the products of companies using AI should be taxed at a higher VAT rate, given that their use of

AI increases their profitability (Chand et al., 2020). Some of these proposals have already been enacted[20].

To the best of our knowledge, no country currently specifically taxes AI-created intellectual products, although some legislative proposals and doctrinal opinions exist that specifically address this taxation issue. For example, in France, within the framework of the French National Artificial Intelligence Strategy, a legislative proposal (No. 1630) to amend the French Intellectual Property Code was presented on 12.9.2023 by the party of President E. Macron. The purpose of the proposed legislation is to ensure that AI respects copyright and creativity. Under the proposal, companies that own AI systems would be required to obtain permission from the copyright holder or owner before the AI uses the copyrighted work. Furthermore, the AI-created intellectual product would have to be labeled "work created by AI" while the AI should also identify the author it was inspired by in creating the work. Finally, the author of the AI-created intellectual product would be the author whose work was used by the AI to create the intellectual product[21].

Regarding the tax-related part of the proposal, the companies that own AI systems will pay tax to the copyright collective management organization. More specifically, if their AI creates an intellectual product based on works of uncertain origin, a tax will be levied (at a rate to be established by a regulatory act) to increase the value of the intellectual product in favor of the copyright collective management organization. This ensures that the company owning the AI that creates the intellectual product becomes the payer of the tax[22].

In the doctrine, taxation is proposed to prevent the reduction of the incentive to create original works due to copyright infringement due to AI-created works, the loss of labor in the original work sector, and the reduction in social welfare. According to this approach, the taxation of AI and the by-product art or art sector will financially support the original work or art sector, thereby maintaining employment within the sector and ultimately increasing overall social welfare (Kou et al., 2024).

However, as will be shown below, there is no need for such normative discussions regarding Turkish law. This is because, although not directly aimed at protecting copyright, the provisions of Turkish law allow for the taxation of AI-created intellectual products.

The Problem of Taxation of AI-Created Intellectual Products Under Turkish Law

In this section, we evaluate our conclusions in the context of FSEK with respect to Turkish tax law. Instead of explaining how copyrights are taxed under Turkish tax law, we highlight problematic areas and suggest solutions. Before discussing the issue in terms of income tax, corporate tax, and value added tax, we first analyze the impact of FSEK on the application of tax laws in the context of the relationship between tax law and private law. This is because our conclusions are based on the components of this relationship.

The Effect of FSEK on Tax Laws in the Context of Tax Law–Private Law Relationships

Because the subject of the tax is the economic element on which the tax is collected and the taxable event occurs as a result of legal transactions and events, the legislator mostly applies private law concepts, such as residence, marriage, and contract, when regulating the subject of tax and the taxable event. The fact that tax laws determine the subject of tax and the taxable event with private law transactions and events makes it necessary to look closely at the relationship between private law and tax law. Here, the first question regarding the taxation of AI-regarding intellectual products is whether FSEK provisions will affect the application of tax laws. The second question is whether the FSEK (private-law) terms "work" and "author" will have the same meaning when applying tax laws.

It should be noted that FSEK has a different purpose to tax laws. The purpose of tax laws is to achieve some extra-fiscal goals by financing tax duty relationships and public spending. The purpose of FSEK, as stated in Art. 1, is to determine and protect the moral and financial rights of the authors who create intellectual and artistic works and related rights holders to their products, to regulate the conditions for benefiting from these products, and to determine sanctions in case of exploitation contrary to the stipulated principles and procedures. Thus, for example, if income is generated from the transfer of an intellectual product that is not within the scope of the FSEK, this intellectual product may be taxable for income tax purposes, even if it cannot qualify as a work under FSEK. According to Art. 73/3 of the Constitution, the principle of legality of taxes obliges the tax administration to establish subjective taxation procedures in accordance with tax laws. Therefore, if the transfer of an intellectual product is regulated as a taxable event in a tax law – for example, in the Income Tax Act – the tax administration must establish taxation procedures. In this sense, tax law is neutral with respect to the private law situation. In other words, it is not interested in the private law situation. To return to our example, even if this intellectual product cannot benefit from the legal protection regime granted to a work in FSEK, the tax administration must establish a taxable transaction when it defines the taxable person and the taxable event in the tax laws.

However, as noted above, tax legislation often draws on private law concepts. Thus, the concepts of work[23], computer program[24] and copyright[25] in the FSEK are also used in tax legislation. For example, the terms "work" is used in art. 18 of the Income Tax Act, art. 11/1 of the Value Added Tax Act; "computer program" is used in art. 18 of the Income Tax Act, art. 70/6, 80/3, 94/4 of the Income Tax Act; and "copyright" is used in art. 26, art. 30/2 of the Corporation Tax Act.

There are three approaches in Turkish tax law doctrine in this regard (Öncel et al, 2019; Karakoç, 2017). The first is that tax law is bound by the concepts and forms of private law in all cases. The second is that tax law is not bound by the concepts and principles of private law, and can apply these concepts and forms in accordance with its own principles and objectives. The third approach is that, unless otherwise specified, the private law approach will be valid regarding the concepts and principles of private law. Furthermore, if the relevant concept and form is specifically regulated in tax law, these regulations will be taken as a basis (Öncel et al., 2019; Karakoç, 2017). The doctrine states that in tax law the concepts and forms of private law will, as a rule, be applied with their meaning in private law (e.g., marriage, domicile, and contract); on the other hand, if the relevant concept or form has a different meaning in tax law, this meaning will be valid in the application of tax law (Öncel, et.al, 2019; Karakoç, 2017). We agree with the third approach.

In light of this argument, we will next examine the taxation of an AI-created intellectual product in terms of basic tax laws, such as income tax, corporation tax, and value added tax.

Evaluation in Terms of Income Tax Law and Corporate Tax Law

In Turkish tax law, two separate taxes are levied on income: income tax and corporate tax. While the Turkish Income Tax Law[26] (TGVK) taxes the income of real persons, the Turkish Corporate Tax Law (TKVK)[27] taxes the income of corporations. Therefore, there is a difference between the two in terms of the legal taxpayer. In addition, the Turkish Tax Procedure Law (TPL) refers to TGVK in basic taxation elements, such as determining corporate income or the taxable event[28].

According to TGVK art. 1, the Income Tax Law taxes income, defined as the net amount of income and revenue obtained by real persons within a calendar year. Here, it is necessary to recall TPL art. 8/1[29], which states that[30] the legal taxpayer of the tax can be a real person or a legal entity, unless otherwise stipulated in the tax laws[31]. The provision in art. 1 of the Income Tax Law, which states that the legal taxpayer of income tax is a real person, is parallel to the main provision in TPL art. 8.

Thus, in Turkish tax law, AI cannot be the legal taxpayer of any tax, income tax, according to TGVK art. 1. This provision is aligns with the FSEK provision that AI cannot be the author of an AI-created intellectual product. Although AI cannot be the legal taxpayer of income tax, if the human investor in AI receives royalty income from the transfer or licence right of the AI-created intellectual product, such income will be subject to TGVK. Similarly, since AI does not fall within the scope of TPL art. 2, it cannot be a legal taxpayer of corporate income tax. TPL art. 2 lists the following kinds of corporate taxpayers: capital companies, cooperatives, public economic institutions, economic enterprises of associations and foundations, and business partnerships.

In our opinion, according to the TGVK, a human investor can obtain commercial income through the transfer of an AI-created intellectual product or through the transfer of the licence right[32]. In the Turkish income tax system, income can only be taxed if it fall into one of seven types of income and profits (commercial income, agricultural income, self-employment income, wages, income from real estate capital, income from movable capital, other income and profits) regulated in TGVK art. 2. In order for the income from the transfer of an AI-created intellectual product or from the use of the licence right to be taxed according to the provisions of business income, the income must be obtained within the framework of a commercial or industrial activity according to the provisions of TGVK art.s 37 et seq.

Thus, if the author has created the work within the framework of a commercial organization and the work is subject to private law transactions such as transfer, rent, and use of the license right, and income has been obtained, then the income of the real person is taxed according to the provisions of business income (Cangüven, 2019). Therefore, if the investor in AI has implemented an AI computer program within the framework of a commercial organization and has generated income by subjecting the AI-created intellectual products to private law transactions, such as transfer, rent, or use of licensing rights, then the income obtained will be taxed as business income. On the other hand, the investor in AI may have created an AI computer program, which is a work of art, through the software developers they employ instead of creating it themselves. In this case, if the AI created by the software developers creates an intellectual product, the income obtained from the transfer of the intellectual product in question should also be considered the business income of the investor.

Here, it is useful to recall our findings regarding FSEK. That is, because an AI-created intellectual product is not considered a work under FSEK, it is not possible to have a financial right to it under FSEK. As mentioned above, the rules and principles of private law apply to the application of tax laws, unless otherwise stated. Hence, it does not seem possible to include an intellectual product, which is not considered a work under FSEK, in the commercial enterprise as a financial right under FSEK. However, because FSEK considers an AI computer program a work, the financial rights to it can be registered as an intangible right of a commercial enterprise. However, the same legal characterization cannot be applied to AI-created intellectual products because the term "copyright" is used in art. 70/6, art. 80/3, art. 94/4 of the TKVK and art. 26, art. 30/2 of the Corporate Tax Law (KVK). For example, art. 70/1 of the Income Tax Act defines real estate capital income as income from the rental of goods and rights specified in the article by their owners, possessors, holders of easements and usufruct rights or lessees ; art. 70 /6 defines real estate capital income as income from the rental of copyrights (although the income from the rental of copyrights by authors or their legal heirs is self-employment income); TGVK art. 70/9 states that if these rights are included in a commercial enterprise, the income from their rental is subject to the provisions on business income. In other words, TGVK art. 70 clearly defines the concept of copyright, which is a private law concept. Therefore, the problem here is whether the concept of copyright in TGVK is to be interpreted in accordance with its meaning in private law or for the purposes of tax law.

It should be noted that FSEK does not mention the term copyright, although FSEK Provisional art. 1/3 states that "copyright, authorship, literary property, artistic property and similar expressions used in legislation and contracts shall be understood as the rights and authorisations granted by this Law in similar cases". According to FSEK art. 90, the effective date of the provision is 1 January 1952. The Income Tax Act[33] entered into force on 1.1.1961 and the Corporation Tax Act[34] on 1.1.12006, i.e. after FSEK. Nevertheless, we believe that the reference to copyright in the legislation in FSEK Provisional art. 1/3 remains valid. Therefore, in accordance with this reference, it can be concluded by the method of systematic interpretation that the provisions of the Turkish Income Tax Act and TKVK, which mentions the concept of copyright, refer to financial rights as in FSEK. This suggests that by using the term copyright, both the Income Tax Act and TKVK mean a right that can be qualified as a financial right under FSEK in order for an intellectual right to be included in a commercial enterprise. Therefore, an investor in AI cannot include an AI-created intellectual product as an intangible right[35] in their commercial enterprise because it is not considered a work under FSEK, the investor is not the work's owner, and cannot be the owner of a financial right under FSEK.

How then can an intellectual product, which cannot be valued as an intangible right and cannot be included in a commercial enterprise, be included in a commercial enterprise? In our opinion, an AI-created intellectual product can be included in a commercial enterprise as a good or service. Hence, the income obtained from transfering it or providing services can be taxed according to the commercial income provisions of TGVK. This is because an AI-created intellectual product may become a physical asset like a painting. In this case, it must be registered as a commodity in the commercial enterprise. However, it is also possible that an AI-created intellectual product is given to another person as a service. In either case, the income from the transfer or use under licence of an intellectual product that is not considered a work under FSEK is subject to income tax as business income.

On the other hand, an AI-created intellectual product cannot be characterized as self-employment income because it is a continuous activity carried out within a specific commercial organization with the aim of making a profit in a capital-intensive way. In contrast, self-employment income is derived from an independent activity that requires knowledge and expertise rather than capital, is non-commercial in nature, and is independent in continuity. The creation of AI by a human software developer is undoubtedly a self-employment activity. Thus, if a human software developer independently creates a work by designing another person's AI, they will, as the author, become the owner of the financial rights to that AI. Therefore, the software developer's transfer or lease of artificial intelligence may, if it is not continuous, qualify as self-employment income under articles 65, 70/6, and 82/4 of the Income Tax Act. This is because it involves "computer program work", which may be subject to financial rights. However, once the AI has been developed, the creation of intellectual products by operating the AI and the transfer of these intellectual products are commercial activities. That is, they are commercial activities carried out continuously within a specific capital-intensive and profit-oriented commercial organization. Therefore, such activities are taxed according to the rules for business income rather than the rules for self-employment income under TGVK.

All of the above also apply to the Turkish corporate tax code. This is because, as explained above, net corporate income is calculated according to the business income provisions of TGVK, as referred to in TKVK art. 6. Thus, a capital company, joint venture, etc., in which AI is included as a work, the corporate taxpayer will receive corporate income in return for the transfer or use of the intellectual product created by artificial intelligence and will be taxed according to TKDVK.

Evaluation in Terms of VAT

AI-created intellectual products will also be subject to VAT. This is because, according to art. 1/1 of the Turkish Value Added Tax Law (TKDVK), supplies and services provided within the framework of commercial, industrial, agricultural, and self-employed activities are subject to VAT; according to art. 8/1 of TKDVK, in cases of supply of goods and services, those who perform this work are the legal taxpayers of TKDVK. Therefore, if the natural or legal taxpayer who is the author of the work in which AI is included in the business enterprise supplies an AI-created intellectual product or provides an AI-created service, such supply or service provision is subject to the provisions of TKDVK.

CONCLUSION

Efforts to tax AI-created intellectual products have intensified in recent years. There are various doctrinal opinions regarding this issue and even efforts to legislate, as in France. Under Turkish tax law, however, there is no need to introduce a new tax on AI-created intellectual products. According to FSEK, AI-created intellectual products are not works and there is no author; hence, no financial right can be established to the product. Nevertheless, the business income provisions of TGVK allow for taxation of such AI-created intellectual products. The same conclusion applies to TKVK and TKDVK.

Thus, the differences between Turkey's tax laws and FSEK in their purpose and scope allows for the taxation of AI-created intellectual products, even if they do not benefit from FSEK's legal protection regime under private law. This is because the income obtained from the transfer of an AI-created intellectual product or the granting of the right of use arises as a result of a commercial activity that is carried out continuously within a certain commercial organization on a for-profit, capital-intensive basis. It therefore falls within the scope of the tax law and the taxable event for income and corporation tax purposes.

Regarding VAT, the supply or provision of services is subject to VAT because TGVK's commercial activity provisions apply. Because AI itself lacks legal personality, it cannot be a legal taxpayer pursuant to TPL, TGVK, TKVK, and TKDVK. On the other hand, the real person or corporate taxpayer who owns the financial rights to an AI will be the income or corporate taxpayer of the business income obtained from transferring the AI-created intellectual product or from offering right of use. The same persons will also be the taxpayers of VAT in the case of supplying or providing services. In short, the transfer of an AI-created intellectual product or the presentation of the right of use is already taxable under Turkish tax law.

REFERENCES

Abbott, R., & Bogenschneider, B. (2017). *Should Robots Pay Taxes? Tax Policy in the Age of Automation* (SSRN Scholarly Paper 2932483). DOI: 10.2139/ssrn.2932483

AI Art at Christie's Sells for $432,500. Retrieved July 26, 2024, from https:// www .nytimes.com/2018/10/25/arts/design/ai-art-sold-christies.html

Ansel Adams Estate Calls Out Adobe for Selling AI-Generated Art Using Photographer's Name. (n.d.). Retrieved July 25, 2024, from https://www.artnews.com/art-news/ news/ansel-adams-estate-ai-generated-images-adobe-controversy-1234708739/

Artificial intelligence (AI) market size worldwide from 2020 to 2030. (n.d.). Retrieved July 20 2024, https://www.statista.com/forecasts/1474143/global-ai-market -size#:~:text=The%20market%20for%20artificial%20intelligence,billion%20U.S. %20dollars%20in%202030

Artificial Intelligence and Copyright, 24.07.204, 88 Fed. Reg. 59,942, https://www .federalregister.gov/documents/2023/08/30/2023-18624/artificial-intelligence-and -copyright

Bak, B. (2018). Medeni Hukuk Açısından Yapay Zekanın Hukuki Statüsü ve Yapay Zeka Kullanımından Doğan Hukuki Sorumluluk. *Türkiye Adalet Akademisi Dergisi*, 9(35), 211–232.

Bowler-Smith, M. (2021). A new-knowledge approach to AI and tax policy. *Australian Tax Forum*. https://search.informit.org/doi/abs/10.3316/informit.250136285387518

Bülter, A. (2005). Eser Sahibinin Haklari İle Bağlantili Haklar. *TBB Dergisi*, 2005(59), 90–107.

Cangüven, M. B. (2019). *Telif Haklarinin Vergilendirilmesi*. Marmara Üniversitesi Sosyal Bilimler Enstitüsü.

Chand, V., Kostić, S., & Reis, A. (2020). Taxing Artificial Intelligence and Robots: Critical Assessment of Potential Policy Solutions and Recommendation for Alternative Approaches – Sovereign Measure: Education Taxes/Global Measure: Global Education Tax or Planetary Tax. *World Tax Journal*, 12(4), 711–761. DOI: 10.59403/2sjxe4d

Cho, W. (2024, May 21). *Scarlett Johansson's AI Legal Threat Sets Stage for Actors' Battle With Tech Giants*. Retrieved July 25, 2024, from https://www.hollywoodreporter .com/business/business-news/scarlett-johanssonai-legal-threat-1235905899

European Parliament resolution of 16 February 2017 with recommendations to the Commission on Civil Law Rules on Robotics (2015/2103(INL)). (n.d.). Retrieved July 22. 2024, https://eur-lex.europa.eu/legal-content/EN/TXT/PDF/?uri=CELEX: 52017IP005

France mulls taxing AI works based on copyrighted material. (n.d.). Retrieved August 25, 2024, from https://www.medianama.com/2023/09/223-france-law-tax-ai-works-copyrighted-material/

French National Assembly Proposes New Law to Secure Copyright in AI. (n.d.). Retrieved August 12, 2024, from https://www.fieldfisher.com/en/locations/belgium/insights/french-national-assembly-proposes-new-law-to-secur

Frey & Osborne. (2013). *The Future of Employment: How Susceptible Are Jobs to Computerisation?* Retrieved July 20 2024, https://www.oxfordmartin.ox.ac.uk/downloads/academic/The_Future_of_Employment.pdf

Gözübüyük, B. (2021). Yapay Zekanin Meydana Getirdiği Fikri Ürünlere Ilişkin 5846 Sayili Fikir Ve Sanat Eserleri Kanunundaki Sorunlar Ve Çözüm Öneriler. *Kırıkkale Hukuk Mecmuaması*, 1(1), 54–81.

Introduction to AI Applications in Robotics. (n.d.). Retrieved July 20 2024, https://onlinedegrees.sandiego.edu/application-of-ai-in-robotics

İncel, E. (2023). Gvk Madde 18 Kapsaminda Telif Kazancinin Ve İhtira Beratinin (Patentin) Vergilendirilmesi. *Ankara Hacı Bayram Veli Üniversitesi Hukuk Fakültesi Dergisi*, 27(1), 283–320. DOI: 10.34246/ahbvuhfd.1167553

Karahan, S., Suluk, C., Saraç, T., & Nal, T. (2011). *Fikri Mülkiyet Hukukunun Esasları*. Seçkin Yayıncılık.

Karakoç, Y. (2017). *Genel Vergi Hukuku* (Vol. 2). Baskı. Yetkin Yayınevi.

Kiliçarslan, D. S. K. (n.d.). Yapay Zekanin Hukuki Statüsü Ve Hukuki Kişiliği Üzerine Tartişmalar. *YBHD, 2*, 363-389.

Kou, H., Rong, K., Xie, D., & Yang, B. (2024). *Artificial Intelligence Generated Content, Intellectual Property Rights, and Digital Tax.* DOI: 10.2139/ssrn.4910480

Kovacev, R. J. (2020). A Taxing Dilemma: Robot Taxes and the Challenges of Effective Taxation of AI, Automation and Robotics in the Fourth Industrial Revolution. *The Contemporary Tax Journal*, 9(2). Advance online publication. DOI: 10.31979/2381-3679.2020.090204

Lawsuit says OpenAI violated US authors' copyrights to train AI chatbot. (n.d.). Retrieved July 25, 2024, from https://www.reuters.com/legal/lawsuit-says-openai-violated-us-authors-copyrights-train-ai-chatbot2023-06-29/

Naqvi, Z. (2020). Artificial Intelligence, Copyright, and Copyright Infringement. *Marquette Intellectual Property Law Review*, 24, 15.

NY Times sues OpenAI, Microsoft for infringing copyrighted works. (2004). https://www.reuters.com/legal/transactional/ny-times-sues-openai-microsoft-infringing-copyrightedwork-2023-12-27/

Öncel, M., Kumrulu, A., Çağan, N., & Göker, C. (2019). 28. Baskı. Turhan Kitabevi.

Özkan Şahîn, G., & Şahîn, Ç. (2022). Yapay Zekali Varliklara Elektronik Kişilik Modeli Taninmasina İlişkin Eurobotics Raporu Ve Fikri Mülkiyet Sorunu Bağlaminda Meseleye Yaklaşim. *İnönü Üniversitesi Hukuk Fakültesi Dergisi, 13*(1), 110-128. DOI: 10.21492/inuhfd.981080

Six key arguments by Stability AI over allegations of copyright violation by artists in US. (2024). https://www.medianama.com/2023/04/223-key-arguments-stability-ai-copyright-violation-artists-us-2/

Tekinalp, Ü. (2004). *Fikri Mülkiyet Hukuku.* Yetkin Yayınevi.

The EU wants to become the world's super-regulator in AI. (n.d.). Retrieved August 12, 2024, from https://www.economist.com/europe/2021/04/24/the-eu-wants-to-become-the-worlds-super-regulator-in-ai?utm_medium=cpc.adword.pd&utm_source=google&ppccampaignID=18151738051&ppcadID=&utm_campaign=a.22brand_pmax&utm_content=conversion.directresponse.anonymous&gad_source=1&gclid=Cj0KCQjwz7C2BhDkARIsAA_SZKaQghNLfwSW9JjIU1NK3OokyfmDmZo_Mdi4x3TunDZYxeGxCqkPmd0aArqaEALw_wcB&gclsrc=aw.ds

United States Copyright Office. (n.d.). "Compendium of U.S. Copyright Office Practices", para. 306. Retrieved July 24, 2024, from https://www.copyright.gov/comp3/docs/compendium. 00-copyrightable-authorship.pdf

U.S. Copyright Office Examines Copyright and Generative AI. (n.d.). Retrieved July 25, 2024, from https://www.hhrartlaw.com/2024/07/u-s-copyright-office-examines-copyright-and-generative-ai/

US Distict Court for The Distict of Columbia Case 1:22-cv-01564. (2024). https://www.copyright.gov/ai/docs/district-court-decision-affirming-refusal-of-registration.pdf

Yalın, M. A. (2002). *Türk Hukukunda Telif Hakları Ve Vergilendirilmesi*. Anadolu Üniversitesi Sosyal Bilimler Enstitüsü.

Yanisky-Ravid, S. (2017). Generating Rembrandt: Artificial Intelligence, Copyright, and Accountability in the 3A Era—The Human-like Authors are Already Here- A New Model. MICH. ST. *L. REV*, 2017(4), 659–726.

Yapay zeka botları kendi dilini geliştirince Facebook mühendisleri fişi çekmek zorunda kaldı. (2024). https://webrazzi.com/2017/08/01/facebook-yapay-zeka-botlari

Zeytin, D. Z., & Gençay, D. E. (2019). Hukuk Ve Yapay Zekâ: E-Kişi, Mali Sorumluluk Ve Bir Hukuk Uygulamasi Das Recht Und Die Künstliche Intelligenz. *TAÜHFD*, 2019(1), 39–70.

Zorluel, M. (2019). Yapay Zeka Ve Telif Hakkı. *TBB Dergisi*, 2019(142), 305–356.

ENDNOTES

1 Regarding the copyright-AI relationship, the terms AI and robots are frequently used, and sometimes as synonyms, although they are distinct concepts (*Introduction to AI Applications in Robotics*. Retrieved July 22, 2024, from https://onlinedegrees.sandiego.edu/application-of-ai-in-robotics/#). Robots are programmed to perform simple and repetitive actions to undertake specific physical tasks (Cambridge Dictionary, 22.07.2024,https://dictionary.cambridge .org/dictionary/english/robot. According to another definition, robots are computer-controlled machines that perform their activities autonomously. While not essential, AI can be integrated into robots to increase their abilities and improve decision-making. However, some robots are programmed to perform only predictable actions that do not require any cognitive capacity (*Introduction to AI Applications in Robotics*. Retrieved July 22, 2024, from https://onlinedegrees.sandiego.edu/application-of-ai-in-robotics/#). We use the concept of AI more broadly to include robots integrated with AI.

2 It is difficult to give a comprehensive definition of AI and robots. Hence, the EU Parliament has refrained from giving a definition; instead, it has identified various common features of AI and robots. See *European Parliament resolution of 16 February 2017 with recommendations to the Commission on Civil Law Rules on Robotics (2015/2103(INL))*. Retrieved July 22, 2024, from https://eur-lex.europa.eu/legal-content/EN/TXT/PDF/?uri=CELEX:52017IP005.

3 *United States Copyright Office, "Compendium of U.S. Copyright Office Practices", para. 306*. Retrieved July 24, 2024, from https://www.copyright.gov/comp3/docs/compendium. 00-copyrightable-authorship.pdf

4 The subject is discussed in detail in the US doctrine. In this case, it is suggested that there are two possibilities. The first is that the artificial intelligence is an "agent/employee" of a company, for example. The second is to approach artificial intelligence as "consumer products". For these discussions, see Naqvi, 2020.

5 For a brief evaluation of the conditions for being considered a work under Anglo-American law, the concept of authorship, and the intellectual products produced by AI, see Zorluer, 2019; Gözübüyük, 2021.

6 *Six key arguments by Stability AI over allegations of copyright violation by artists in US.* Retrieved July 25, 2024, from https://www.medianama.com/2023/04/223-key-arguments-stability-ai-copyright-violation-artists-us-2/. There are multiple examples of disagreements on this issue. For example, it has been claimed that stock photos created by Adobe's artificial intelligence resemble the works of the artist Ansel Adams. (*Ansel Adams Estate Calls Out Adobe for Selling AI-Generated Art Using Photographer's Name.* Retrieved July 25, 2024, from https://www.artnews.com/art-news/news/ansel-adams-estate-ai-generated-images-adobe-controversy-1234708739/).

7 *U.S. Copyright Office Examines Copyright and Generative AI.* Retrieved July 25, 2024, from https://www.hhrartlaw.com/2024/07/u-s-copyright-office-examines-copyright-and-generative-ai/

8 Law No. 5846 of 5.12.1951.

9 *AI Art at Christie's Sells for $432,500.* Retrieved July 26, 2024, from https://www.nytimes.com/2018/10/25/arts/design/ai-art-sold-christies.html

10 The doctrine and the General Assembly of the Criminal Court of the Supreme Court of Appeals, in its decision numbered E: 2018/19-398, K: 2018/413, emphasized that in order for an intellectual product to be considered a work, it must meet both objective and subjective conditions based on the definition in the Law. Accordingly, the subjective element is formed by the part of recognizing the "owner's characteristic" while the objective element is formed by the part of "any kind of intellectual and artistic product considered as works of science and literature, music, fine arts or cinema" (Gözübüyük, 2021; Cangüven, 2019; Zorluer, 2019).

11 For moral rights, see FSEK art. 14 et seq.

12 For financial rights, see FSEK art.20 et seq.

13 For the public ownership of AI-created works, see Gözübüyük (2021)

14 For the subject, see Gözübüyük (2021); Zorluer (2019).

15 As suggested in the report published by the European Parliament Committee on Legal Affairs on January 27, 2017, many problems in terms of private law could be overcome by granting AI a new type of personality, namely an electronic personality, which is different from legal personality and natural personality. The report recommends that AIs be registered in the official registry, that financial funds be activated in case of liability for compensation, and that AIs be held strictly liable due to their legal personality for damages they cause to third parties. (Kiliçarslan, 2019; Zorluer, 2019)

16 Art. 2 of Law No. 4857: "A natural person working under an employment contract is called a worker". Here, it is necessary to mention views that AI can be considered a commodity or a slave. These views, which are important regarding the use of taxation authority, reject granting personality to an AI (Kılıçarslan, 2019; Zorluer, 2019).

17 SMK art.82/2-c: "The following are not considered inventions. If the patent application or patent relates to the subject or activities specified below, only these subjects or activities themselves remain outside of patentability:…c) Computer programs…"

18 See FSEK art.80/B

19 Therefore, in Anglo-Saxon law, identifying the person who made the necessary adjustments seems to be the correct approach in this respect.

20 Italy and Switzerland are examples of legalization efforts. Italy has rejected a proposal to increase corporate tax for companies using AI while Switzerland considered a tax on automated cashiers in retail stores in 2017, but this was not enacted (Kovacev, 2020).

21 *French National Assembly Proposes New Law to Secure Copyright in AI.* Retrieved August 12, 2024, fromhttps://www.fieldfisher.com/en/locations/belgium/insights/french-national-assembly-proposes-new-law-to-secur*The EU wants to become the world's super-regulator in AI.* Retrieved August 12, 2024, from (https://www.economist.com/europe/2021/04/24/the-eu-wants-to-become-the-worlds-super-regulator-in-ai?utm_medium=cpc.adword.pd&utm_source=google&ppccampaignID=18151738051&ppcadID=&utm_campaign=a.22brand_pmax&utm_content=conversion.directresponse.anonymous&gad_source=1&gclid=Cj0KCQjwz7C2BhDkARIsAA_SZKaQghNLfwSW9JjIU1NK3OokyfmDmZo_Mdi4x3TunDZYxeGxCqkPmd0aArqaEALw_wcB&gclsrc=aw.ds, *France*

mulls taxing AI works based on copyrighted material. _MEDIANAMA_. Retrieved August 25, 2024, from https://www.medianama.com/2023/09/223-france-law-tax-ai-works-copyrighted-material/

22 *French National Assembly Proposes New Law to Secure Copyright in AI.* Retrieved August 12, 2024, from Retrieved August 12, 2024, from https://www.fieldfisher.com/en/locations/belgium/insights/french-national-assembly-proposes-new-law-to-secur, *France mulls taxing AI works based on copyrighted material.* Retrieved August 12, 2024, from https://www.medianama.com/2023/09/223-france-law-tax-ai-works-copyrighted-material/

23 For example, see FSEK art.1/B-a

24 For example, see FSEK art.1/B-g

25 See FSEK Provisional art.1

26 Law No.193, Official Gazette No. 10700 dated 06.01.1961.

27 Law No. 5520, Official Gazette No. 26205 dated 21.06.2006.

28 *Article 6 of the TPL: "(1) Corporate income tax is calculated on the net corporate income of taxpayers for an accounting period.* (2) In determining the net corporate income, the provisions of the Income Tax Act on business income shall apply. The provisions of the last paragraph of Article 59 of the Income Tax Law shall also be taken into account in determining the income of corporations engaged in agricultural activities."

29 Art. 8/1 of the TPL: "A taxpayer is a real or legal person on whom a tax obligation is imposed in accordance with the tax laws".

30 Law No. 213, Official Gazette No. 10703 dated 10.01.1961.

31 However, there are exceptions to this rule, such as in the case of joint ventures in art. 2/2 of TKVK.

32 On the taxation of copyrights, see Yalın, M.A. Türk Hukukunda Telif Hakları Ve Vergilendirilmesi, 2002, Anadolu Üniversitesi Sosyal Bilimler Enstitüsü, Yüksek Lisans Tezi.

33 See TGVK art.124.

34 See TKVK art.37.

35 Although Turkish tax law does not define intangible right, the right to use and benefit from legal transactions and the ownership of intellectual rights can be considered as intangible rights (Cangüven, 2019). In terms of Turkish tax

law, intangible assets are assets that cannot be physically observed and have no material existence, but can be registered and subject to purchase and sale. TPL art. 269 which regulates the provisions on the valuation of real estate, also lists intangible rights among the assets subject to valuation like real estate.

Chapter 3
Navigating AI and Copyright Law in the UK: Legal Frontiers and Emerging Regulatory Perspectives

Zehra Özkan Üner
Faculty of Law, Ankara University, Turkey

Pınar Çağlayan Aksoy
https://orcid.org/0000-0002-4510-5813
Faculty of Law, Bilkent University, Turkey

ABSTRACT

The rapid development of artificial intelligence (AI) has introduced novel challenges and opportunities within the domain of copyright law. This chapter explores the intersection of AI and copyright, specifically focusing on the legal problems and regulatory frameworks in the United Kingdom. It examines how AI-generated works are situated within the existing copyright law, the implications for traditional copyright principles, and the evolving regulatory responses. At the heart of the discussion is the question of authorship of AI-generated works. Traditional copyright law presumes a human author, raising significant questions about the legal status of works created autonomously by AI systems. The chapter further delves into the implications of AI on copyright infringement and fair use. AI systems, particularly those employing machine learning algorithms, often require large datasets to train on, which may include copyrighted material.

DOI: 10.4018/979-8-3693-8704-7.ch003

I. INTRODUCTION

Many countries worldwide are trying to establish if the existing legislative and policy frameworks are sufficient to address newly emerging technologies. Artificial intelligence (AI), especially after the wide use of large language models (LLMs) and generative AI (GenAI) technology, is undoubtedly one of these technologies. We are at a point where it is easy to predict that the challenges posed by AI technologies will ultimately require legislative action in every country once an understanding of the risks has matured.

This chapter focuses on the United Kingdom, which has established itself as a leader in the legal framework surrounding emerging technologies. The UK is eager to be recognized as a hub for AI development. It has consistently emphasized its ambition to remain at the forefront of AI innovation in various reports and documents. Even before GenAI introduced new and pressing legal challenges, AI was already a key priority for the UK. Numerous articles and monographs have explored the complexities of determining the legal nature of AI assistance in the creative process. However, the rise of GenAI tools has amplified concerns about copyright protection within the creative industries and media organizations. What will happen to creators and their rights? Where should the boundaries be drawn?

Currently, with no AI-specific legislation in place, the law governing AI and copyright disputes in the UK is still the Copyright, Designs, and Patents Act (CDPA) 1988, Section 9(3). The law stipulates that for "computer-generated" works, the author is the person who made the arrangements necessary for the work's creation. Thus, the UK might seem to extend copyright protection to works created with AI tools. However, as technology evolves, these scenarios grow increasingly complex. What about the data used to train AI tools? Will the emergence of LLMs shift the dynamics further? The friction between copyright holders and AI developers remains unresolved in the UK, with no guiding court precedent. The issues are currently being litigated in the UK courts in the case of *Getty Images v. Stability AI*, but the trial is not expected until summer 2025.

The United Kingdom Law Commission (UKJT) has extensively researched emerging technologies. Its reports on smart contracts, digital assets, digital dispute resolution, and electronic trade documents have been well received internationally (UK Law Commission 2021, UK Law Commission 2022, UK Law Commission 2023a, UK Law Commission 2023b). Some of these reports have progressed into bills and ultimately laws, as seen with the legislation on electronic trade documents in 2023. Given the significant influence of the UK law on international trade contracts and transactions, this new law is poised to be a game-changer. With AI now listed as a "priority technology" in the national strategy, the UK's ambition to lead safe AI development and become a Science and Technology Superpower by the decade's end is unsurprising. However, the previous UK government had made it clear that they would not rush into action, favoring a "wait-and-see" approach: *"We are going to take our time to get this right – we will legislate when we are confident that it is the right thing to do."* (UK Government, 2024)

At the time of writing, the UK has a new government but still lacks a specific legal framework dedicated exclusively to AI. The problems that arise from AI technologies are governed by existing laws such as the legislation on data protection, consumer protection, intellectual property, and liability (Legal Foundations, 2024). Hence, it may seem that despite the "ideal" of becoming the pioneer in the field, the UK has been less proactive compared to those in the US and the EU (ALCS, 2024). But this opinion should be considered cautiously: For instance, unlike the UK, copyright can be registered in the US. This means that the US Copyright Office (USCO) has had to deal with this question directly, unlike the United Kingdom Intellectual Property Office (UKIPO).[1]

Before delving into the details of the regulatory challenges of AI and copyright and the current regulatory framework in the UK, it's important to acknowledge a significant political shift. The recent change in government has temporarily stalled progress on AI-related initiatives in the UK. This might raise concerns, especially as the now-governing party's pre-election manifesto did not clarify how it intends to address the tension between AI developers and rights holders over the use of copyright works for AI training.

However, as the timeline detailed in the following section shows, AI regulation has to remain a priority for the new government as well. The expectation is that the UK will soon establish a clear course of action, either by refining the current sectoral approach or by introducing new, customized legislation (CMS, 2024).

This chapter unfolds as follows:

We begin by examining the legislative framework and efforts related to AI and copyright in the UK. This is followed by an exploration of the literature addressing the challenges posed by AI in the context of UK copyright law, alongside a discussion of the theoretical debates that have emerged. After outlining the methodology of this study, we present our findings and proposed approaches. Initially, we provide a comprehensive overview of how copyright issues arising from the use of AI tools have been managed in the UK over recent years. The discussion then centers on two key points in light of recent developments: first, the challenge of using copyrighted works without the rightful owner's authorization for training datasets and second, the question of authorship in AI-generated works. It should be underlined that there are two main problems to be addressed when dealing with the interaction of AI and copyright. One of the challenges is determining if an output created by an AI tool can be regarded as a "work". And the second one is the use of works in order to train AI tools. In conclusion, it remains to be seen whether the new UK government will take steps to amend the regulatory framework surrounding copyright. If not, the resolution of copyright conflicts related to AI will ultimately fall to the courts.

II. LITERATURE REVIEW/THEORETICAL DISCUSSIONS

AI has raised complex issues in copyright law similar to those in other fields of law. In this part, we will focus on the following two issues separately:

The first issue is whether copyrighted works can be used for training AI models or systems. AI models and systems gather and use data to train their datasets. This data sometimes consists of facts, numbers, or information, but it can also include works or other subject matter protected by copyright (Guadamuz, 2024, p.116). If the data consists only of numbers, facts, or information, it is not protected by copyright. Even if the data includes a work or other subject matter, it may still be in the public domain or can be open source, meaning it can be used without the right holder's permission. However, these facts do not change the fact that sometimes copyright-protected subject matter can be and is used for AI training datasets. If this is the case, does using them without the right holder's permission constitute copyright infringement? This question is one of the central issues surrounding AI and copyright and has been debated for some time (Keller, 2023). The answer depends on whether this kind of use falls under the exclusive rights of the author and whether any exceptions to copyright apply to this usage.

Although in most cases only information about a work is extracted by the dataset creator or the trainer of AI tools, at least some temporary copies of the work are made during this process. This means that some form of copying always occurs (for further discussion, see Guadamuz, 2024, pp. 115–116). Does this copying constitute an infringement of the right of reproduction? In this context some authors highlight that the copies are not used as a "work" (Strowel & Ducato, 2021, p. 309); similarly, the copies are not the original expressions. It remains uncertain whether UK courts will classify these actions as falling under the right of reproduction. If they do, the next step will be to determine whether any exceptions to copyright could apply to these activities and lead to the result that they do not infringe copyright.

When it comes to exceptions to copyright, the discussions mainly focus on two aspects: temporary copying and the text and data mining (TDM) exception. The TDM exception is particularly important because some jurisdictions have introduced these exceptions relatively recently. There is no uniform approach to the TDM exception globally. While a broad and flexible TDM exception was introduced in Japanese law, a more restrictive TDM exception was adopted by the DSM Directive (Articles 3 and 4). The expansion of the TDM exception has also been discussed in UK law, as in other jurisdictions, which will be addressed in detail below.

The second major issue concerning AI and copyright is whether AI-generated output is eligible for copyright protection, and if so, who should be considered the author? Apart from the debates about whether a work meets the requirements for copyright protection or whether an AI tool can be considered an author, this question is particularly important because of Section 9(3) of the CDPA. This section states that *"[i]n the case of a literary, dramatic, musical or artistic work which is computer-generated, the author shall be taken to be the person by whom the arrangements necessary for the creation of the work are undertaken"*. In addition, the legislator chose to define the computer-generated work, and it is defined as *"generated by computer in circumstances such that there is no human author of the work in section 178 which regulates the minor definitions"*. Thus, the CDPA had already introduced copyright protection for works without a human author in 1988. Considering the introduction of this section by the CDPA, some authors argue that the CDPA had already regulated AI-generated outputs three decades ago (Bond & Blair, 2019, p. 423). Can this section be applied to AI-generated outputs? To answer this question, the scope and discussions of this section of the CDPA need to be clarified.

All these discussions are particularly relevant under UK law. While these debates continue, the UKIPO initiated a public consultation in 2021 to determine whether there is a need to revise the legal framework to address these copyright-related problems. This was followed by various reports and governmental efforts to resolve these two problems, which called for a choice to be made between the conflicting interests of rightsholders and AI developers. We will elaborate on these materials in Part IV of the chapter below.

III. RESEARCH AND METHODS

The complex copyright issues raised by AI technologies are similar in most jurisdictions. However, differences in national copyright laws may lead to different legal approaches and outcomes. For example, while US law addresses exceptions and limitations to copyright under "the doctrine of fair use", UK law relies on "fair dealing" and EU law follows a catalog system. As a result, introducing exceptions becomes more significant in fair dealing systems and under EU law in which the exceptions to copyright are not provided as a general defense like in US law (Lionel & Sherman, 2014, p. 224). Additionally, the policies of national or regional legal systems further differentiate their approaches.

The aim of this paper is not to address all the copyright law issues arising from AI technologies. Instead, the scope of the paper is limited to discussions on the copyright regulatory framework of the UK. Nevertheless, sometimes examples from US law, EU law, or Japanese law are mentioned in order to enlighten the issues and offer different perspectives. The approach adopted by the UK government and, accordingly, the discussions led by academics are going to be identified. The academic literature and the documents issued by the UKIPO serve as the main sources in order to fulfil the aim of the paper. We also address other documents and reports produced in the UK in the course of dealing with AI-related copyright issues.

IV. FINDINGS AND DISCUSSIONS

A) Setting the Scene: Recent Developments in the UK's Approach to AI and Copyright

The problems that arise from the use of AI technologies, especially LLMs, have recently become a hot topic. However, technological advancements have consistently challenged copyright law, especially regarding copyright eligibility and authorship in works created using technology. These discussions also extend to computer-generated works. In response to these issues, the UK legislature considered technologies such as translation programs and search engines and introduced a provision in the CDPA. This action, which was subsequently followed by other jurisdictions, resulted in the inclusion of Section 9(3) in the CDPA, addressing the authorship of computer-generated works before the emergence of GenAI.

Before the wide-range use of ChatGPT, the UK Government's Intellectual Property Office (UKIPO) ran a public consultation on "Artificial Intelligence and IP" from October 2021 to January 2022. Through this consultation, the UK government was seeking evidence and views on how AI should be dealt with within the existing patent and copyright systems. Specifically, concerning copyright issues, two problems (mentioned in the previous section) were being considered: Copyright protection for computer-generated works (CGWs) without a human author and licensing or exceptions to copyright for text and data mining (TDM), which is often significant in AI use and development (UK Government, 2021).

The government's response to the consultation stated that no changes to the law regarding CGWs were necessary as there was no evidence at the time that protection for CGWs was harmful. The response also noted that AI was still in its early stages, and a thorough evaluation of the options was not yet possible, so any changes could have unintended consequences. The law would remain under review and could be amended, replaced, or removed in the future if supported by evidence (UK Government, 2022).

Concerning TDM, on the other hand, the government revealed a plan to introduce a new copyright and database exception that allows TDM for any purpose. This would mean that rights holders would still have safeguards to protect their content, including a requirement for lawful access, which according to the UKIPO was the most supportive of AI and wider innovation (UK Government, 2022).

In February 2023, the new Department for Science, Innovation, and Technology was established, accelerating regulatory progress at a pace that has been difficult to keep up with. The priorities of this new department are listed as the following: accelerating innovation, investment, and productivity through world-class science, research, and development and using technology for good by ensuring that new and existing technologies are safely developed and deployed across the U.K. (UK Government, 2023a).

One month later, on March 15, 2023, a report titled "Pro-innovation Regulation of Technologies Review Digital Technologies" was presented by Sir Patrick Vallance, the Government Chief Scientific Adviser, to the Chancellor of the Exchequer and HM Government, as part of the Pro-innovation Regulation of Technologies Review. This report included some important recommendations to the government. The report called for the government to "*announce a clear policy position on the relationship between intellectual property law and generative AI to provide confidence to innovators and investors*" since the relationship between intellectual property law and GenAI is unclear for the stakeholders (UK Government, 2023b).

The report also commented on the public consultation led by the UKIPO on changes to TDM rules in the UK (back in 2021). The report states that there remains a lack of regulatory clarity as to the direction of those reforms, particularly for AI firms deploying TDM techniques to generate new content. The Government Chief Scientific Advisor underlined the importance of creating an environment in which TDM is enabled in the UK as it would attract investment, support company formation and growth, and show international leadership. He recommended two major points for the promotion of an innovative AI industry in the UK:

The mining of available data, text, and images (the input) should be enabled. Accordingly, the government needs to work with the AI and creative industries to develop ways to enable TDM for any purpose and to include the use of publicly available content, including that covered by intellectual property, as an input to TDM (including databases).

The second major recommendation is that the existing protections of copyright and IP law should be used on the output of AI.

In line with these two recommendations, he also recommended a code of practice and the creation of a requirement for altered images to be labelled as generated or assisted by AI. The code of practice created under the auspices of the UKIPO would increase the confidence and accessibility of protection to copyright holders of their content as permitted by law. It would also provide clearer guidance to AI firms about their legal responsibilities, coordinate intelligence on systematic copyright infringement by AI, and encourage the development of AI tools to help enforce IP rights (UK Government, 2023b).

On March 15, 2023, the UK government published another document as a response to the recommendation by Sir Partick, the Chief Scientific Advisor, which reads: *"Government should announce a clear policy position on the relationship between intellectual property law and generative AI to provide confidence to innovators and investors"*. The response document is titled "HM Government Response to Sir Patrick Vallance's Pro-Innovation Regulation of Technologies Review Digital Technologies" (UK Government, 2023c).

In the response, the government states that they would "act at pace to provide clarity in relation to the application of intellectual property law to the AI sector". Acting on the recommendations, the government calls for the UKIPO to produce a code of practice which will provide guidance to support AI firms to access copyrighted work as an input to their models. While formulating the code of practice, a group of AI firms and rights holders would cooperate to identify barriers faced by users of data mining techniques when accessing copyright materials. AI firms that commit to the code of practice could be able to receive a license offered by a rights holder. The guidance should ensure that there are protections, such as labelling on generated output, to support rights holders of copyrighted work.

On March 22, 2023, the UK's International Technology Strategy (UK Government, 2023d) was published. This strategy document does not deal with copyright protection or the development of creative industries specifically, but it is crucial that AI is listed in this Policy Paper as a priority technology. The following week, on March 29, 2023, an AI Regulation White Paper was published to develop a pro-innovation regulatory framework for AI (UK Government, 2023e). In the AI Regulation White Paper, five cross-sectoral principles were proposed for existing regulators to interpret and apply within their remits to drive safe, responsible AI innovation: Safety, security, and robustness; appropriate transparency and explainability, fairness, accountability, and governance; and contestability and redress. This white paper was open to consultation for 12 weeks and the outcome of the consultation was published in 2024.

In the meantime, on June 5, 2023, UKIPO working group meetings, which comprised AI users and rights holders, commenced (UKIPO, 2023).[2] The UKIPO included industry representatives from the technology, creative, and research sectors. These sectors would help to ensure a balanced and pragmatic code of practice that would enable both sectors to grow in partnership.

The code of practice would help to overcome barriers that AI firms and users currently face and ensure there are protections for rights holders by making licenses for data mining more available. The intention was that, if an AI firm committed to the code of practice, it could have a reasonable license offered by a rights holder in return (CMS, 2024). The government expected both parties to reach a voluntary final code of practice on copyright and AI. Legislation would only be considered if the code of practice was not adopted or an agreement was not reached.

Although the working group was a well-intended initiative that provided a forum for stakeholders to share their views, according to the government response dated February 2024, it was evident that the working group would not be able to agree on an effective voluntary code.

Towards the end of 2023, on November 22, the Artificial Intelligence (Regulation) Bill [HL] was introduced (UK Parliament, 2023). Among many other obligations, according to the Bill, the Secretary of State must by regulations make provisions to create a body called the AI Authority. Regarding copyright issues, the bill included the following specific rule: any person involved in training AI must (i) supply to the AI Authority a record of all third-party data and intellectual property ("IP") used in that training; and (ii) assure the AI Authority that (A) they use all such data and IP by informed consent; and (B) they comply with all applicable IP and copyright obligations. The second reading process in the House of Lords was completed but the Bill could not pass to the House of Commons and Final stages due to the change in government.

At the beginning of 2024, on February 2, a report titled "House of Lords Communications and Digital Committee 1st Report of Session 2023–24 HL Paper 54 Large Language Models and Generative AI" was published (UK Parliament, 2024a). This report focused on the ethical and legal challenges of LLMs and GenAI technologies. It also provided critical insights on the issue of copyright protection by considering views from various big-tech companies, such as Microsoft, Meta, and OpenAI.

The report underlines the importance and value of both LLMs and copyright protection for society. It explicitly states that the UK has been benefiting from a globally respected copyright regime economically, politically, and societally (UK Parliament, 2024a, para 245). Therefore, the principles surrounding copyright that reward creators for their efforts and prevent others from using works without permission should not be ignored. In the end, it is not fair for tech firms to use rightsholder data for commercial purposes without permission or compensation and to gain vast financial rewards in the process.

The report argues that the current legal framework in the UK is failing to protect copyright and foster innovation. The authors urge the government to take decisive action rather than waiting for case law to evolve (UK Parliament, 2024a, para 246). While the report acknowledges the efforts of the UKIPO, it emphasizes that if the UKIPO code process proves ineffective, it will be up to the government to resolve the issue, potentially through legislative changes, once it becomes clear that copyright law does not adequately protect rights holders (UK Parliament, 2024a, para 249).

As a solution, the report offers several recommendations. While the report acknowledges the efforts of the UKIPO, it emphasizes that if the UKIPO code process proves ineffective, it will be up to the government to resolve the issue, potentially through legislative changes, once it becomes clear that copyright law does not adequately protect rights holders (UK Parliament, 2024a, para 252). Secondly, the government should help establish good practices by collaborating with licensing agencies and data repository owners to create large, high-quality data sources needed for LLM training (UK Parliament, 2024a, para 256). Additionally, the UKIPO could implement a mechanism for rights holders to review training data, ensuring compliance with copyright law (UK Parliament, 2024a, para 259).

In late February 2024, feedback to the consultation (dated 2023) was presented in the government response titled *"Consultation outcome: A pro-innovation approach to AI regulation: government response (February 6, 2024)"*.

The government's response acknowledges the tension between creative industries and rights holders on one side and AI developers on the other: the former seeks to preserve their autonomy and control over their work, while the latter stresses the importance of easy access to diverse, high-quality datasets for developing and training cutting-edge AI systems in the UK. Their approach emphasizes the need for trust and transparency between parties, particularly concerning AI developers being open about data inputs and attribution of outputs. The report notes that the government will explore mechanisms to help rights holders understand if their content is being used as input for AI models. Additionally, the response highlights the importance of engaging with international counterparts to address these challenges collaboratively (UK Government, 2024).

On May 28, 2024, the House of Commons Committee published a report titled "Governance of Artificial Intelligence (AI)", which included recommendations for the government. After outlining previous initiatives like the UKIPO Code of Practice, the report highlights the risks of maintaining the current status quo. Given the growing volume of litigation over the alleged use of copyrighted works to train AI, the report emphasizes the need for a sustainable framework that balances the inevitable trade-offs and establishes clear, enforceable rules. The report warns that inaction would disproportionately benefit developers, allowing them unlimited, free use of copyrighted material. Hence, the committee calls for the government to *"ensure that discussions regarding the use of copyrighted works to train and run AI models are concluded and an implementable approach agreed. It seems inevitable that this will involve the agreement of a financial settlement for past infringements by AI developers, the negotiation of a licensing framework to govern future uses, and in all likelihood the establishment of a new authority to operationalise the agreement. If this cannot be achieved through a voluntary approach, it should be enforced by the Government, or its successor administration, in co-operation with its international partners." (UKParliament, 2024 b)*

As evidenced by the events mentioned above, despite its efforts, the previous UK government failed to deliver a voluntary code of practice that would clarify the relationship between copyright law and AI. Therefore, the newly elected government will need to address this issue and provide certainty for both the creative industry and AI developers. Whether this will be done by legislation and what the time frame will be remains a question.

B) Discussions Considering the Recent Developments

1- Use of copyrighted works without the right owner's authorization to train AI tools

As previously mentioned, temporary copying and TDM exceptions have been considered with regard to the use of copyrighted works to train AI tools. It is useful to provide more details on these exceptions in the UK in order to clarify further discussions.

The first exception that comes to mind is temporary copying, which is regulated under Section 28A of the CDPA. Although datasets do not always involve permanent copies of the works, the data gathering or training process temporarily copies these works. So, can we apply this exception and argue that these uses fall within the scope of this exception? This is another question debated in both EU and UK law. To qualify under this exception, the copying must meet the following requirements:

- be transient or incidental
- be an integral and essential part of a technological process
- the sole purpose must be either the transmission of the work in a network between third parties by an intermediary or a lawful use of the work
- have no independent economic significance

The temporary copying exception is often considered when dealing with TDM or GenAI. One reason for this is the CJEU's Infopaq II Decision, where the Court applied this exception to the data capture process. In this context, the data capture and machine learning processes are compared and the applicability of this exception to AI is discussed (Bonadio, McDonagh, et al., 2022; Guadamuz, 2024, pp. 9, 117). However, it is not easy to conclude that such use meets all the requirements outlined above. There are concerns that the requirements for the incidental nature of the copy (Guadamuz, 2024, p.117) and the lack of economic significance (Mezei, 2024, p.6) may not be met in cases involving the use of AI technologies. The final answer is going to be given by the courts. Until then, the extent to which the temporary copying exception will apply to GenAI cases remains uncertain.

The second exception to consider is the TDM exception because of the TDM's crucial role in the advancement of AI(Rosati, 2023). The TDM exception was introduced into UK law in 2014, making the UK one of the pioneers of this exception in EU law (Carroll, 2019, p. 896). After that, the EU introduced the TDM exception in the DSM Directive in 2019. However, the TDM exception as regulated under UK law differs from that in EU law. The UK exception does not cover commercial activities. According to Section 29A of the CDPA, a person who has lawfully accessed a work can make copies if the copying meets certain requirements. First, the person must have lawful access to the works and use them only for research purposes on a non-commercial basis. The copying must be done to carry out computational analysis and should be accompanied by sufficient acknowledgment. This section was introduced in 2014 when GenAI technologies were not as advanced as they are today. Even if it can be argued that this section is still applicable to the GenAI, its scope is still narrow because it only covers non-commercial research purposes. However, the question of whether the reuse of datasets collected for research by private companies falls within the scope of this provision remains unresolved. If reuse for commercial purposes were allowed under this exception, its scope would be broadened (Guadamuz, 2024, p.119). Only with a broad interpretation some uses may fall under this exception. Otherwise, the current version of this exception is unlikely to resolve most disputes between large companies, such as OpenAI or Mid-Journey, and right holders.

In summary, using a work for AI training constitutes copyright infringement under UK Law. Should the exceptions to the copyright, especially the TDM exception, be revised and expanded? If so, should an opt-out system be integrated into it, as is the case in EU law (Article 4 of the DSM Directive)? It should not be disregarded that integrating an opt-out system or considering that using the works for training AI tools copyright infringement would mean that an efficient licensing environment must be provided. These are some of the alternatives that were considered in the UKIPO's public consultation, and there were various responses regarding this issue. In the end, as stated earlier, the UK government initially decided to broaden the scope of the TDM exception to cover all purposes (UK Government, 2022). Interestingly, unlike in EU law, the government chose not to include an opt-out mechanism. This means that UKIPO has adopted a much more flexible approach, aiming to foster investment in emerging technologies (Trapova, 2022) and to give the UK a competitive advantage in AI.

However, rights holders in particular strongly opposed this proposal. Subsequently, the UKIPO chose not to expand the TDM exception. After withdrawing the proposal, the UKIPO began working on a Code of Practice and established a working group.

However, the procedure for establishing this group has been criticized for a lack of transparency and inclusivity (Trapova, 2023). Thus, all the initiatives failed, and everything returned to the starting point.

2- The author of a work generated by AI

Another controversial issue regarding AI and copyright is whether the output generated by AI is eligible for copyright protection, and if so, who should be considered the author? In addition to debates about whether the requirements for a work to be copyrightable are met or whether an AI tool can be an author, this question is particularly significant due to Section 9(3) of the CDPA. As it is stated above, the Act has already regulated computer-generated works in which there is no human author. In that aspect, is it a novelist provision that has been regulating the AI-generated outputs for over three decades (Bond & Blair, 2019, p. 423)? Can this section apply to the AI-generated tools as well? To answer this question, the scope and discussions surrounding this section of the CDPA need to be tackled.

a) Scope of Section 9(3) of the CDPA

Section 9(3) of the CDPA deals with computer-generated works, and to reach a definitive conclusion about AI-generated works its scope must be clearly defined. The distinction between computer-generated works and computer-assisted works is crucial here. Computer-assisted works are created with the help of a computer *by a human being*, while computer-generated works are created or generated *automatically by a computer without a human author*. The authorship created through a legal fiction and the person who makes necessary arrangements for generating the works is deemed as the author in the latter (Bonadio, Lucchi, et al., 2022, p. 1188). Categorizing an output as either a computer-assisted work or a computer-generated work is crucial because the scope and duration of protection differ between the two. In the case of computer-assisted work, the output qualifies as a "work" and the author (the human being who created the work with the assistance of a computer) is granted both economic and moral rights. Copyright protection expires 70 years after the author dies. Conversely, for computer-generated works, the duration of protection is limited to 50 years, and the human being who is deemed as the author is not granted moral rights. These differences highlight the importance of distinguishing between computer-assisted and computer-generated works. However, making this distinction is challenging and remains unclear (Bond & Blair, 2019; Erickson, 2024). The majority of cases in the GenAI process still involve human beings. In this context, the crucial point is to determine whether the contribution merely involves making the necessary arrangements or if the human simply used the AI as a tool.

b) Originality of Computer-Generated Works

Should computer-generated works be required to be original to be eligible for protection? This is a controversial issue. Opinions on this question in the UK can be divided into three groups (Bond & Blair, 2019):

According to the first group, Section 9(3) of the CDPA can be criticized for being somewhat contradictory. On the one hand, it states that the result should be generated by a computer; on the other hand, it states that a literary, dramatic, musical, or artistic work should be generated. However, for a result or an output to be considered a "work," it must be original. The standard for originality before the Court of Justice of the European Union (CJEU) decisions (such as the Infopaq decision) used to be based on labour, skill, and judgment in the UK law. After the Infopaq decision, the standard in the UK shifted to the "author's own intellectual creation," and now it remains uncertain whether UK courts will continue to apply the CJEU's standard after Brexit. In any case, in UK law it is argued that originality requires human authorship (Aplin et al., 2022; Goold, 2021, p. 3–14). Thus, Brexit does not change anything on human authorship and originality still necessitates a human author. So, it is hard to qualify an AI-generated output as a work when there is no human author. Additionally, if originality is regarded as a requirement, there needs to be a human author, which means that there is no need for Section 9(3) (Goold, 2021, p. 22).

Guadamuz argues that originality is not required under Sections 9(3) and 178. According to the author, these sections are exceptions to the originality requirement (Guadamuz, 2017, p. 10).

Finally, some authors suggest that the originality test might be interpreted differently for computer-generated works, such as considering whether the work is not copied or is novel (distinct from previous works) (Lionel & Sherman, 2014, p. 117). McCutcheon argues that the originality test could be applied hypothetically: If there had been a human author, would the work be considered original? (McCutcheon, 2013, p. 51). Not all subject matters regulated by the CDPA have to meet the originality requirement, such as entrepreneurial works or related rights. The literature discusses whether computer-generated works could be considered entrepreneurial works. However, if they are seen as entrepreneurial works, the scope of protection would be the same as for entrepreneurial works, meaning protection would be narrow and would not cover the content (Bond & Blair, 2019, p. 423). This approach is criticized by scholars who believe narrow protection is not suitable for AI-generated works. AI-generated works differ from computer-generated works; while results are predictable in computer-generated works, AI-generated works can be creative. Therefore, narrow protection may not suffice (Lee, 2021, p. 185–186).

c) Author of Computer-Generated Works

Another uncertainty regarding Section 9(3) of the CDPA is determining who makes the necessary arrangements: the programmer or the user. The programmer is the person who trains the model, while the user is the person or company providing the AI model to the public. This question could be answered either by determining who contributes to the creation or by identifying who makes the financial or organizational contribution, as with sound recordings (Aronsson-Storrier & Fairhurst, 2024). Accordingly, sometimes the programmer and the user may be considered joint authors (Bonadio, Lucchi, et al., 2022, p. 1189). Indeed, AI-generated works are the result of a collaboration, involving many actors in generating an output, including the algorithm developer, data providers, and those setting the AI to a particular task (Bond & Blair, 2019, p. 423). The complex relationships among these actors make it difficult to identify the author (Lee, 2021, p. 192). Although there have been attempts to clarify this issue in the literature (McCutcheon, 2013, p. 53), it remains unresolved (Lizarralde & Meinecke, 2023, p. 91).

All of the three issues regarding Section 9(3) of CDPA mentioned above have not been clarified by case law either. There are only two cases addressing this issue: Nova Productions v. Mazooma Games and THJ Systems v. Sheridan. In Nova Productions v. Mazooma Games, the judge identified how the composite frames were created and stated that it was necessary to consider composite frames generated by the computer program using the bitmap files. However, he did not give further details. Initially, he ruled that composite frames were artistic works, then stated that these frames were created either by the programmer or by the computer program he authored. However, he did not analyse the requirements of Section 9(3) of the CDPA in depth (Nova v. Mazooma, 2006, par. 102–105).

The THJ Systems case is more complex. It addressed not only the copyright eligibility of risk and price charts but also twenty other issues. The Judge noted, "*I am satisfied that the work of creating the look and functionality of the interface, including the arrangement of the tables and graphs, involved sufficient skill and labor for the result to amount to an artistic work.*" Without exploring the other issues, he ruled that the risk and prize chart was an artistic work. However, he applied the "sufficient skill and labor" test. Subsequently, he ruled that the programmer was the author because the images were predominantly the result of computer algorithms (THJ Systems v. Sheridan, 26.04.2023, par. 211–216). The Court of Appeal later determined that the author's own intellectual creation should be the criterion. The Judge correctly applied this test and concluded that the charts were original (THJ Systems v. Sheridan, 20.11.2023, paras. 23–28). Unfortunately, there were no additional details provided about Section 9(3) of the CDPA.

These court decisions do not clarify these issues comprehensively. It can only be argued that the originality test is applied under Section 9(3) of the CDPA (Aronsson-Storrier & Fairhurst, 2024).

In summary, although Section 9(3) of the CDPA is seen as an innovative provision that other jurisdictions might consider adopting, all the above arguments indicate that it applies only in rare cases and its scope remains unclear. It raises complex issues on its own. Some commentators even argue that this section is meaningless and should be removed from the CDPA (Aplin et al., 2022, p. 2–7). Additionally, there are fundamental differences between computer-generated works and AI-generated works. In this context, there are doubts about whether this provision can solve the authorship problem, especially for works created by fully generative machines (Bonadio, Lucchi, et al., 2022, p. 1189). It is also argued that this provision could be retained with major revisions to address concerns, although it does not meet the needs in its current form (for this suggestion see Atilla, 2024, p. 46 and following).

As mentioned above, the UKIPO conducted a public consultation and one of the subjects was Section 9(3). Although there are arguments against Section 9(3), there have not been sufficient comments to justify abandoning this provision. The government decided to retain this section, but this does not mean the provision will not be amended, replaced, or removed if necessary. In the meantime, although the scope of this provision remains unclear, it is still a part of the CDPA (see Trapova, 2022).

V. CONCLUSION

The development of AI, particularly generative AI (GenAI), has raised numerous questions in UK copyright law. While some of these questions are similar across jurisdictions, this chapter focuses on the UK law approach. In this context, the text and data mining (TDM) exception and Section 9(3) of the Copyright, Designs, and Patents Act (CDPA) are central issues in UK law. The TDM exception was introduced in 2014 to foster science and research in the UK. Similarly, after a public consultation, the UK Intellectual Property Office (UKIPO) proposed broadening the scope of the TDM exception to encourage investment in AI. However, the UKIPO had to retract this proposal.

Although CDPA Section 9(3) was not initially intended for GenAI outputs, it has become a focal point in discussions across jurisdictions with the advent of GenAI technologies. This provision protects works that are not generated by a human, which means outputs entirely generated by AI could be protected with a duration of protection limited to 50 years—shorter than that for human-generated works. At first glance, this seems like a perfect solution; however, Section 9(3) of the CDPA has already raised its own questions, even before the emergence of GenAI technologies.

It remains a highly controversial provision. Some authors argue that if Section 9(3) is revised, it could provide an appropriate solution to the issues of copyrightability and authorship. In contrast, others believe the provision is meaningless and should be abandoned.

While jurisdictions worldwide attempt to clarify their approaches and revise their legal frameworks, the UKIPO has launched several regulatory initiatives. These included proposals to broaden the TDM exception and develop a Code of Practice; however, both initiatives ultimately failed. At the end of the day, nothing has changed in the UK legal system. There needs to be a solution that finds an appropriate balance between AI developers and rightsholders. At the same time, this solution has to be internationally operable. Now the responsibility lies with the UK courts to decide unless the new government comes up with a initiative to deal with AI-related copyright issues. Although it was not mentioned in their election manifesto in June 2024, in the Strategic Plan for arts, culture, and creative industries the Labour Party stated that the creative industries would be a part of developing a broader AI strategy. In the document dated March 2024, the Labour Party highlighted the importance of ensuring protection for creators and the ongoing viability of the creative industries. The now-governing party also mentioned the requirement of thoughtful engagement and consultation within the creative industries and with companies driving AI development. They stated that the party would support, maintain, and promote the UK's strong copyright regime and collaborate with international partners to address these issues (Labour, 2024a). We will see whether it is the courts or the legislators who find the delicate balance.

ACKNOWLEDGMENT

Ankara University Faculty of Law, IP Law Department-Vice Director of Ankara University Research Center on Intellectual and Industrial Property Rights, e-mail zhozkan@yahoo.com, ORCID https://orcid.org/0000-0002-5846-396X

Bilkent University Faculty of Law, Civil Law Department- Visiting Researcher at King's College Dickson Poon School of Law, e-mail pinar.caglayan@bilkent.edu.tr ORCID https://orcid.org/0000-0002-4510-5813

REFERENCES

Aplin, T., Schaffer, B., & Li, P. (2022). Trustworthy Autonomous Systems Hub and TAS Node on Regulation and Governance. Artificial Intelligence and IP: Copyright and Patents: A Call for Evidence from Intellectual Property Office. DOI: 10.18742/pub01-074

Aronsson-Storrier, A., & Fairhurst, O. (2024, April 25). Generative AI, originality, and the potential role of contract in protecting unoriginal works. *The IPKat.*https://ipkitten.blogspot.com/2024/04/generative-ai-originality-and-potential.html

Atilla, S. (2024). Dealing with AI-generated works: Lessons from the CDPA section 9(3). *Journal of Intellectual Property Law and Practice*, 19(1), 43–54. DOI: 10.1093/jiplp/jpad102

Authors' Licensing and Collecting Society (ALCS). (n.d.). *AI legislation: Where we're at.* Retrieved August 30, 2024, from https://www.alcs.co.uk/news/ai-legislation-where-were-at/

Bonadio, E., Lucchi, N., & Mazziotti, G. (2022). Will technology-aided creativity force us to rethink copyright's fundamentals? Highlights from the platform economy and artificial intelligence. *IIC - International Review of Intellectual Property and Competition Law, 53*(9), 1174–1200. DOI: 10.1007/s40319-022-01171-5

Bonadio, E., McDonagh, L., & Dinev, P. (2022). Can artificial intelligence infringe copyright? Some reflections. In *Research handbook on intellectual property and artificial intelligence*. Edward Elgar Publishing Limited. DOI: 10.4337/9781800881907.00019

Bond, T., & Blair, S. (2019). Artificial intelligence & copyright: Section 9(3) or authorship without an author. *Journal of Intellectual Property Law and Practice*, 14(6), 423. DOI: 10.1093/jiplp/jpz056

Carroll, M. W. (2019). Copyright and the progress of science: Why text and data mining is lawful. *U.C. Davis Law Review*, 53, 893–964. https://lawreview.law.ucdavis.edu/issues/53/2/articles/53-2_Carroll.pdf

Department for Science, Innovation and Technology. (n.d.). *About us.* Retrieved August 30, 2024, from https://www.gov.uk/government/organisations/department-for-science-innovation-and-technology/about

Erickson, K. (2024, January 31). Copyright protection in AI-generated works. *Creative Industries Policy and Evidence Center.* https://pec.ac.uk/blog_entries/copyright-protection-in-ai-generated-works

Goold, P. (2021). The curious case of computer-generated works under the Copyright, Designs and Patents Act 1988. *City Law School Research Paper No. 2021/03.* https://openaccess.city.ac.uk/id/eprint/26210/

Keller, P. (2023, February 20). Protecting creatives or impeding progress? Machine learning and the EU copyright framework. *Kluwer Copyright Blog.* https://copyrightblog.kluweriplaw.com/2023/02/20/protecting-creatives-or-impeding-progress-machine-learning-and-the-eu-copyright-framework/

Labour Party. (2024a). *Labour's arts, culture & creative industries sector plan.* Retrieved August 30, 2024 form https://labour.org.uk/wp-content/uploads/2024/03/Labours-Arts-Culture-Creative-Industries-Sector-Plan.pdf

Labour Party. (2024b). *Labour Party manifesto 2024.* Retrieved August 30, 2024 from https://labour.org.uk/wp-content/uploads/2024/06/Labour-Party-manifesto-2024.pdf

Law-Now, C. M. S. (2024, June). *How might AI be regulated following the UK general election?* Retrieved August 30, 2024, from https://cms-lawnow.com/en/ealerts/2024/06/how-might-ai-be-regulated-following-the-uk-general-election

Lee, J. A. (2021). Computer-generated works under the CDPA 1988. In *Artificial Intelligence and Intellectual Property* (pp. 177–195). Oxford University Press. DOI: 10.1093/oso/9780198870944.003.0009

Legal Foundations. (n.d.). *The UK's legal framework for artificial intelligence and machine learning.* Retrieved August 30, 2024, from https://legalfoundations.org.uk/blog/the-uks-legal-framework-for-artificial-intelligence-and-machine-learning/

Lionel, B., & Sherman, B. (2014). *Intellectual Property Law* (4th ed.). Oxford University Press.

Lizarralde, M. D., & Meinecke, C. (2023). Authorless AI-assisted productions: Recent developments impacting their protection in the European Union. *JIPITEC*, 17, 84–94. DOI: 10.1093/ijlit/eaac008/6555494

McCutcheon, J. (2013). Curing the authorless void: Protecting computer-generated works following IceTV and phone directories. *SSRN*, 37, 46–102. DOI: 10.2139/ssrn.2308187

Mezei, P. (2024). A saviour or a dead end? Reservation of rights in the age of generative AI. *EIPR-European Intellectual Property Review, 46*(7), 461–469. https://papers.ssrn.com/sol3/papers.cfm?abstract_id=4371204

Osborne Clarke. (2024). *How will the new UK government resolve the conflict over AI development and IP rights?*https://www.osborneclarke.com/insights/how-will-new-uk-government-resolve-conflict-over-ai-development-and-ip-rights-

Parliament, U. K. (2023). *Artificial Intelligence (Regulation) Bill [HL].* Retrieved August 30, 2024, from https://bills.parliament.uk/publications/53068/documents/4030

Parliament, U. K. (2024a). *Report of the Select Committee on Artificial Intelligence.* Retrieved August 30, 2024, from https://publications.parliament.uk/pa/ld5804/ldselect/ldcomm/54/54.pdf

Parliament, U. K. (2024b). *Artificial intelligence: Governance and regulation.* House of Commons Science, Innovation and Technology Committee. Retrieved August 30, 2024, from https://publications.parliament.uk/pa/cm5804/cmselect/cmsctech/38/report.html

PEC. (n.d.). Copyright protection in AI-generated works. *PEC.* Retrieved August 30, 2024, https://pec.ac.uk/blog_entries/copyright-protection-in-ai-generated-works/

Rosati, E. (2023, February 3). UK Government axes plans to broaden existing text and data mining exception. IPKat. https://ipkitten.blogspot.com/2023/02/uk-government-axes-plans-to-broaden.html

Strowel, A., & Ducato, R. (2021). Artificial intelligence and text and data mining: A copyright carol. In Rosati, E. (Ed.), *The Routledge Handbook of EU Copyright Law* (pp. 299–316). Routledge.

Trapova, A. (2022, August 24). The UK government moves forward with a text and data mining exception for all purposes. *Kluwer Copyright Blog.* https://copyrightblog.kluweriplaw.com/2022/08/24/the-uk-government-moves-forward-with-a-text-and-data-mining-exception-for-all-purposes/

UK Government. (2021). Public consultation on AI and IP. Retrieved August 30, 2024, from https://www.gov.uk/government/consultations/artificial-intelligence-and-ip-copyright-and-patents

UK Government. (2022). Artificial intelligence and intellectual property: Copyright and patents: Government response to consultation. Retrieved August 30, 2024, from https://www.gov.uk/government/consultations/artificial-intelligence-and-ip-copyright-and-patents/outcome/artificial-intelligence-and-intellectual-property-copyright-and-patents-government-response-to-consultation

UK Government. (2023b). Pro-innovation regulation of technologies review: Digital technologies report. Retrieved August 30, 2024, from https://assets.publishing.service.gov.uk/government/uploads/system/uploads/attachment_data/file/1142883/Pro-innovation_Regulation_of_Technologies_Review_-_Digital_Technologies_report.pdf

UK Government. (2023c). HMG response to SPV Digital Tech final. Retrieved August 30, 2024, from https://assets.publishing.service.gov.uk/government/uploads/system/uploads/attachment_data/file/1142798/HMG_response_to_SPV_Digital_Tech_final.pdf

UK Government. (2023d). The UK's international technology strategy. Retrieved August 30, 2024, from https://www.gov.uk/government/publications/uk-international-technology-strategy/the-uks-international-technology-strategy

UK Government. (2023e). *AI regulation: A pro-innovation approach (White Paper).* Department for Science, Innovation and Technology. https://www.gov.uk/government/publications/ai-regulation-a-pro-innovation-approach/white-paper

ENDNOTES

1 The USCO has been refusing copyright registration for works without a human author and has issued a guidance on works that include AI-generated material.

2 According to the Terms of Reference announced on the official webpage, the technical working group is tasked with identifying any creator concerns relating to the use of copyright works, performances, and databases by AI systems and users, outlining ways in which any concerns can be addressed, identifying any barriers to the access to copyright works, performances, and databases by AI systems and users, including for the purposes of text and data mining, outlining options to address any barriers and setting out commitments

and expectations in relation to AI firms' use of protected material and the right holders who own protected material.

Chapter 4
Evaluation of Copyright of Cultural Artifacts Digitalized With AI From the Perspective of Public Finance:
The Case of Ephesus Experience Museum

İrem Didinmez
Hacettepe University, Turkey

Zeynep Coşkun
https://orcid.org/0000-0002-2565-2721
Hacettepe University, Turkey

ABSTRACT

The formulation and development of cultural policies are important for achieving the social goals set by states. In this context, all kinds of cultural activities should be supported, protected, and developed. Transferring the evidence of the social culture's history to the digital environment through artificial intelligence (AI) may lead to copyright issues for the works. States make and implement legal regulations to solve copyright issues arising from digitalization. Preservation of the copyrights for the artifacts exhibited at the Ephesus Experience Museum, where artifacts of the ancient city of Ephesus are exhibited with a realistic experience, is important. The fact that the Ephesus Experience Museum was designed with the support of the Republic of Türkiye Ministry of Culture and Tourism helps prevent problems that

DOI: 10.4018/979-8-3693-8704-7.ch004

may arise regarding copyrights.

INTRODUCTION[1]

The evolution and transformation of societies from the past to the present have expanded the activities carried out by states in the social field. In addition to basic social needs, this situation has led states to assume duties in many economic, social, environmental and cultural fields. In order to ensure full employment, promote economic stability, ensure efficiency in resource distribution and achieve economic growth and development goals, states have also started to carry out activities in the socio-cultural field. The sustainability of economic, environmental, social and cultural policies has gained importance in order to achieve the set policy objectives. In this context, it is important to examine the interrelations of these four basic elements.

The social and economic dimension covers issues such as fighting poverty and ensuring fairness in income distribution. The social and environmental dimension envisages the fair sharing of natural resources so that future generations can have at least as many natural resources as today. The social and cultural dimension is the result of historical accumulation. This dimension constitutes the cultural heritage of the society. The environmental and cultural dimension examines the basic needs of societies such as nutrition, heating, shelter, health protection, etc., according to the opportunities of the geographical environment. The environmental and economic dimension focuses on how to solve the problems that arise as a result of economic activities using environmental values. The cultural and economic dimension refers to the economic evaluation of cultural accumulations that exist in a wide range of areas, from social communication to artistic activities, from the history of civilizations to tourism. When cultural, economic and social dimensions are considered together, the focus is on the shaping of cultural economy and cultural policies formed by the state in line with its economic and social objectives.

The inclusion of culture, which is one of the important components of social welfare, in economic analysis emphasizes the importance of culture in the field of public finance. Cultural economy, which emerged within this framework, focuses on analyzing the effects of expenditures, revenues and incentives made by governments, especially in the cultural field. The cultural element, which is important for public finance, is one of the main fields of fiscal sociology.

Culture, one of the main research areas of fiscal sociology, reveals the interaction of economic processes with social structures. Culture shapes social values. Accepting culture as a basic element in economic, financial and sociological terms reveals the need to include cultural factors in the analyses in studies carried out in the fields of public finance and fiscal sociology. In other words, it is important to conduct interdisciplinary analysis in this context. In economic terms, culture refers to the processes of creation, distribution and consumption of material and immaterial values produced by a society. Cultural sectors (such as art, music, literature, cinema and theater) contribute to employment, income and economic growth by creating economic activities (Thorsby, 2000). Within this framework, museums are particularly active. The fact that museums play a role in society and community development, are non-profit, protect, develop and transmit culture to future generations, and are public institutions reveals the importance of museums in terms of public finance and fiscal sociology. The cultural economy generates economic value by providing innovative products and services through the creative industries.

The digitalization process is changing the dynamics of the cultural economy, expanding and deepening its economic dimension. Cultural components are finding their way into the digital environment, particularly with the application of artificial intelligence (AI) in virtual reality and other related technologies. The transfer of cultural artifacts or products exhibited in museums to future generations with more realistic experiences in digital environments has positive effects in terms of cultural sustainability.

With digitalization, especially virtual reality and AI-supported virtual reality applications offer new opportunities for the preservation of cultural heritage and access to large audiences. AI is effectively used in analyzing cultural content, providing personalized experiences and developing digital museum applications. Thus, it becomes possible to revitalize cultural heritage in a virtual environment and create user-specific experiences. The new media opportunities that come to the agenda with the rapidly developing technology and the new perspective of artistic reality cause legal regulations, especially regarding copyrights, to gain more importance. This situation brings along discussions on the copyrights of intellectual products to be produced using AI.

In this context, the aim of the study is to evaluate the Ephesus Experience Museum in Ancient Ephesus, one of the important centers of world trade, from the perspective of public finance, cultural elements and law. In the study, the effects of new technologies on the cultural economy will be discussed by emphasizing the importance of protecting the copyrights of the works in an experience museum created with the contributions of digitalization. The reason why the Ephesus Experience Museum was preferred in the study is that it has been awarded by many international organizations, including the United Nations Educational, Scientific and Cultural Organization (UNESCO), with its digital art technologies, design and artistic features. In this context, in the first part of the study, public finance will be discussed from a classical perspective. Then, public finance will be examined in a broader area with a sociological perspective. In the following section, the importance of the concepts of culture and cultural economy, which are important elements of fiscal sociology, will be emphasized and the contributions of digital transformation to this field will be elaborated. The effects of digital transformation on the cultural economy will be explained within the framework of copyright protection and AI. Finally, the Ephesus Experience Museum will be evaluated in terms of public finance, cultural economy, digitalization and copyrights.

CONCEPT OF PUBLIC FINANCE

Public finance is the branch of science that examines the activities of the state authority in terms of economic, financial and social aspects, investigates the limits of these activities and examines the distribution of expenditures and revenues required by these activities (Musgrave & Peacock, 1967). Financial events occur when the state obtains economic value to meet social needs and provides this economic value as a public service.

Analysis of the development of public finance reveals connections to many fields, including management science, sociology, political science, public administration, history, and accounting. According to the classical understanding of public finance, equilibrium in the economy can be achieved spontaneously without the need for state intervention. (Musgrave & Peacock, 1967).

The classical theory of public finance is based on the economic theories developed by classical economists such as Adam Smith, David Ricardo and Jean-Baptiste Say in the 18th and 19th centuries. The main goal of this approach is to limit the state's role in the economy as much as possible. The main duties of the state are seen as ensuring public order, establishing justice and organizing defense (Edizdoğan et al., 2023). The main principle of classical public finance is that the market mechanism will produce the best results.

In 1929, during the Great Depression, the deepening of the recession and the inability of economies to reach equilibrium spontaneously brought the modern fiscal approach to the agenda. The modern theory of public finance is based on the economic theories developed in the 20th century by economists such as John Maynard Keynes. This approach argues that the state should play an active role in the economy. Keynes emphasized that, in line with the social objective of fiscal policy, states should assume more tasks in social, economic and cultural areas. (Stiglitz & Rosengard, 2015). The development of societies and the change and increase in social needs have led states to carry out functions in social and economic areas such as ensuring balance in the economy, development and full employment, along with basic duties such as justice, defense and public order. This situation has led to the expansion of the subject and research areas of public finance.

Since the 2000s, the acceleration of the technological transformation process has revealed the necessity of digitalization practices in the realization of public sector activities. The digitalization process has redefined state and citizen relations. The spread of digitalization has led to an acceptance of a more transparent, open, accountable, flexible, effective, and efficient public finance perspective.

The first characteristic of public finance is the study of financial events in line with the objectives of the state (Wagner, 2007). Decisions within this framework aim to enhance social welfare (Martin, Mehrotra, & Prasad, 2009). The second feature of public finance is that studies in the discipline are based on the assumption that society has a homogeneous structure. The third characteristic of the public finance approach is that it considers the concepts and issues dealt with by the fiscal discipline more abstractly than other fields. For this reason, fiscal methods, principles and techniques are defined in more general terms.

Goldscheid (1958), argues that the lack of a sociological basis in the handling of the public finance problem is one of the most significant shortcomings in the field of social sciences. Ignoring individual and social expectations, needs, etc., in the social sciences, which are based on human beings, may distract the studies from reality. For this reason, it is important to include environmental conditions, cultural factors and the historical dimension of fiscal events that take place within the social structure. According to Goldscheid, the sociological approach constitutes the scientific basis of public finance (Goldscheid, 1958).

Fiscal Sociology Approach

Sociology, which examines the mutual relationship between society and the individual, supports the interaction of individuals with each other as well as the formation and development of human skills. Goldscheid emphasizes the necessity of addressing financial events within the social culture and historical structure. According to Goldscheid, fiscal sociology is the interdependence between the financing of state expenditures and social development in a historical setting (Musgrave, 1992). Fiscal sociology is a field that examines the social dimensions of the economy and the effects of financial processes on society. Practices that do not take society's behavior and opinions into account may cause significant problems in terms of achieving fiscal objectives.

People begin to live together and form social organizations, leading to the emergence of financial events. This feature transforms financial events into a structure that should be structurally analyzed alongside its social aspect. Interacting with other disciplines, financial events influence the formation of social institutions such as culture, social class, theology and education (Backhaus, 2004). From this perspective, fiscal events refer to legal, economic and sociological situations that coincide with the behavior of the political will. It is necessary to examine in detail all the events that occur in relation to financial events, possible crises and the consequences of the policies implemented in response to these crises. Fiscal sociology is evaluated through two different periods: old fiscal sociology and new fiscal sociology.

Old fiscal sociology was shaped by classical sociology and economic philosophers. Philosophers such as Karl Marx, Max Weber, and Emile Durkheim studied the effects of economics on social structures and relations. During this period, fiscal sociology viewed the economy as a product of and shaped by social structures (Smelser & Swedberg, 2005). The new fiscal sociology has started to develop, especially since the 1980s. This period was marked by financial globalization, neoliberal policies and financial crises. The new fiscal sociology seeks to understand how financial processes and markets are socially constructed and function. In this process, fiscal sociology emphasizes that economics is not only a technical field but also deeply connected to social relations and structures.

The concept of fiscal sociology evaluates fiscal events from political, economic, cultural, institutional and historical perspectives. Hence, fiscal sociology, while examining the fiscal effects of the policies implemented, develops a different approach that focuses on the cultural and historical structures of social events that unify society and the state (Campbell, 1993).

The Importance of Culture in Fiscal Sociology Approach

The goal of fiscal sociology is to evaluate the enforcement of public services and financial events as well as their social dimensions. The social dimension is associated with the concept of socialization within the framework of social norms, values and relations. Durkheim was one of the first to conceptualize socialization. Durkheim defines socialization as the upbringing of new generations by adult generations in order for them to adapt to society and develop mentally, culturally and morally. In more detail, the concept of socialization means that people learn the culture of the society they belong to, with all its material and spiritual elements, and incorporate them into themselves (Durkheim, 2015, trans. Kaynak). This process is considered to be essential both for individuals to become social beings and for the continuity of society (Robbins & Judge, 2017). For this reason, while socialization is an element that nourishes the individual's personality in one aspect, it also forms the basis of the process that ensures the continuity of societies (Maccoby, 2015).

Socialization is the process that an individual goes through within the structure and culture of the society in which he/she lives. This process refers to a period of time that "encompasses the attitudes, behaviors, knowledge, manners and legal norms that constitute the moral structure of society and regulate the necessary conditions of the individual's existence" (Tolan, 1996). Since socialization has a diverse structure, the individual needs to recognize the culture in which he/she lives as well as the cultures that interact with it (Maccoby, 2015).

Socialization has two dimensions. The first one is the psychological dimension. The psychological dimension refers to how the individual develops within society and how he/she can fit a certain mold. The second is the sociological dimension. The sociological dimension explains how the individual is taught to behave in accordance with social expectations (Darmon, 2023). Therefore, sociology is a discipline that studies these processes and the effects of different social structures surrounding individuals (Maccoby, 2015).

In terms of society, the socialization process, which will play an important role in ensuring the continuity of social order, involves two main factors. The first factor is the individuals who will acquire socialization skills, while the second factor is the tools that will enable them to socialize. Socialization tools are the main sources of shaping the personalities of individuals and learning the culture of society. From this point of view, it is possible to state that socialization undertakes the task of protecting culture by transferring the basic values, beliefs and traditions of humanity (Levine & Moreland, 2011).

When defining socialization, culture is frequently emphasized. The entire reality in which human beings live explains culture. Culture means that nature regains value by being processed by human hands and that this value is specific to the human spirit. The fact that everything produced by human hands carries cultural value is an indication that human beings have elements of culture in everything, from the way they view themselves and other people to the values of the society they live in and their life goals. Therefore, all institutions, organizations, associations and schools that exist in society are considered cultural areas, and all material and immaterial products that are subject to exchanges between people are called culture.

Museums are one of the institutions where cultural elements are passed on to future generations. The fact that museums are non-profit institutions is also important in terms of public finance and fiscal sociology. In order to maximize social benefit, museums carry out activities such as conservation, education, training and documentation. In other words, museums facilitate the preservation, maintenance and management of tangible or intangible heritage resources (living heritage and digital creative activity). In this context, one of the main objectives of museums is to ensure cultural sustainability and improve the welfare of society. This often leads to museums being regulated and supervised by governments. Museums are also at the heart of cultural industries and national policies. In this context, processes such as the transmission of culture and the acquisition of cultural elements to the world heritage impact the cultural economy.

CONCEPT OF CULTURAL ECONOMY

From the simplest social structure to today's information society, the phenomenon of culture is present in all human societies. It is very difficult to give a single definition to the concept of culture. This is because the term culture has acquired different meanings in different disciplines.

Looking at the historical development of the concept of culture, three uses of the word culture draw attention. Firstly, since the 18th century, culture, which describes a general process of mental, spiritual and aesthetic development, has come to the fore. Secondly, culture, which describes the way of life of an individual or a society, is emphasized. Thirdly, it refers to the products of artistic activity (Baumol, 1967). The third use is actually an application of the first definition of culture.

The concept of culture is generally accepted as a field of human action. This definition means that culture encompasses all products produced by human hands (Frey & Oberholzer-Gee, 1998). Therefore, it is stated that culture is not a natural formation; it is a structure produced afterwards. According to this idea, the subject that creates the product is human. These ideas underline the fact that humans and culture are inseparable (Frey & Oberholzer-Gee, 1998). This fact also demonstrates that culture complements the individual. Eagleton (2006) also supports the above view and states that culture is not hereditary. According to these common views, culture is seen as the way an individual behaves, lives, and perceives life. Culture is the whole of values, beliefs, norms, traditions, art, language and lifestyles shared by a society or group (Güvenç, 2018). According to anthropologist Geertz (2017), culture is a system that people use to make sense of themselves and the world.

Another expression of the concept of culture is found in the Final Declaration of the World Conference on Cultural Policies and Sustainable Development. The 1982 Mexico Declaration on Cultural Policies by UNESCO defines culture as "distinct spiritual, material, intellectual, and emotional features characterizing a society. It encompasses arts, lifestyle, human rights, value systems, traditions, and beliefs... In the face of global challenges such as conflicts, epidemics, climate change, and technological advances" UNESCO emphasizes the need to preserve culture for both individuals and societies.

Along with the developments in the field of culture, the concept of cultural products is brought to the agenda. Cultural products are a more functional concept that includes production, consumption and exchange. For this reason, culture is produced using labor, land, capital, technology, human capital and creativity, just like all other goods and services in the economy.

Public finance is a frequently used field in the analysis of cultural economy. Public finance examines the effects of government revenues and expenditures on the economy. Therefore, it is important how the activities of the state will be financed and what kind of goods and services will be provided by the state. This study will focus on public and semi-public goods and services.

Public goods and services are those whose consumption cannot be excluded and whose consumption cannot be competed for. Non-excludability means that an individual's use of a good or service cannot prevent other individuals from using the same good or service. Non-competitiveness in consumption means that an individual's use of a public good does not affect other individuals' use of the same good. Therefore, these two features make it difficult to provide public goods and services effectively in the market (Rosen & Gayer, 2010). Therefore, governments operate in these areas.

Public goods and services cannot be produced efficiently or optimally by the market. The provision of public goods and services often requires state intervention. By producing public goods and services, governments ensure that these goods are accessible to everyone. This leads to positive effects in areas such as increasing social welfare levels, improving economic conditions, and ensuring fairness in the distribution of income and wealth in society.

In some ways, semi-public goods and services are similar to public goods and services, while in others they are similar to private goods and services (Rosen & Gayer, 2010). Because they provide social benefits, semi-public goods and services are either supported by the government or provided directly. Although semi-public goods and services are goods and services that can be produced spontaneously in the market, they positively affect social benefits as well as individual benefits. Therefore, the state encourages, subsidizes or directly provides such goods and services. Government subsidization or direct provision of quasi-public goods is crucial for enhancing social justice, solving the problem of market failures, and promoting long-term economic development. The optimal provision of semi-public goods and services not only improves the quality of life of individuals, but it also promotes social peace, social welfare and economic sustainability.

States assume duties in the cultural field within the framework of welfare economics to provide an optimal level of service by considering the contribution of cultural activities to the maximization of social welfare. Culture is accepted as a merit good because of increasing social welfare. In the case where cultural products are considered semi-public goods and services, it is stated that the goods and services produced by the cultural economy provide external benefits to society as a result of their consumption while they provide private benefits to the individual who consumes them. This situation demonstrates that cultural products bear similarities to private goods and services in terms of their divisibility (price determination) and marketability, and to public goods and services in terms of their ability to generate an external economy and ensure individuals' consumption. For example, with the MuseumPass[2] and mobile MuseumPass, visitors can visit more than 350 museums and archaeological sites affiliated with the Republic of Türkiye Ministry of Culture and Tourism and the National Palaces and Çanakkale Area Presidency twice a year. Therefore, when it comes to the state's contribution to the cultural sector, the social benefit of cultural products and services comes to the fore. Since the dissemination of culture to large masses and its transmission to future generations will contribute to the preservation of social heritage, it is important for the state to be active in this field. Therefore, states need to develop cultural policies to protect cultural heritage, subsidize cultural products and encourage cultural participation.

The Effects of Digital Transformation on the Cultural Economy

Many changes have occurred in the social and political sphere with the technological progress brought about by the globalization process. Therefore, the concepts of digitization and digitalization have gained prominence. Digitization refers to the transformation of analog information and processes into digital forms and the integration of digital technologies in different areas of society (Gobble, 2018). Digitization facilitates the processing, storage, and transmission of data in a digital environment, enabling the emergence of new business models and forms of communication (Brennen & Kreiss, 2014). The technological revolution that emerged with the digitalization process impacts consumer behavior and social needs. The development of information and communication technologies accelerates the digitalization process, leading to radical changes in economic, social and cultural fields.

Digitalization technology offers new opportunities for cultural heritage to reach wider audiences. Culture shapes the identities and worldviews of individuals while ensuring the continuity and cohesion of the social structures (Gobble, 2018). Therefore, digitalization and culture are two concepts that interact with each other. Digital technologies transform cultural expressions and practices, while culture influences the use and development of digital technologies. Digitalization changes the ways in which cultural content is produced, distributed and consumed, enabling the emergence of new cultural forms and experiences (Gere, 2008).

The main reasons for the need for digitalization in the field of culture are to protect cultural heritage, increase access to cultural elements and support creative processes. Digitalization enables cultural content to reach wider audiences, be carried into the future through digital archives, and make cultural production and consumption more flexible, accessible and innovative (Parry, 2007). It is therefore possible to argue that digitalization is expanding the boundaries of cultural expression, encouraging cultural interaction and diversity between individuals and communities.

When culture is digitized, the global accessibility of cultural products and services through digital platforms increases, production and distribution costs decrease, and new revenue models emerge (Anderson, 2006). Digitalization is therefore leading to significant transformations in the cultural economy, bringing with it opportunities and challenges (Duguzheva & Simaeva, 2024).

Digitalization offers important opportunities to the cultural economy. The first opportunity is an increase in access and participation. Thanks to digital platforms, cultural products and services can be accessed from anywhere in the world. This supports cultural diversity (Jenkins, 2006). Second, digitization is critical for the preservation and transmission of cultural heritage to future generations (UNESCO, 2015). Digital archiving and digitization allow cultural artifacts to be protected from the corrosive effects of time and reach a wider audience. Third, creativity and innovation are encouraged. This is made possible by the new forms of expression and art offered by digital technologies (Manovich, 2002). Fourth, new business models and sources of income are emerging. Artists and cultural businesses are turning to alternative revenue channels such as subscription systems and online sales (Florida, 2002). Fifth, they support social and economic development. Digital cultural industries help strengthen national economies by creating jobs and contributing to economic growth (Thorsby, 2000). Sixth, digitalization facilitates access to global markets, contributing to the growth of the cultural economy and increasing international competitiveness (Castells, 2009).

The most prominent challenges are copyright issues. Copyright is the ownership of rights over an original element and is protected against third parties within the legal order. As digitalization grows with the development of technology, the importance of copyrights increases. Copyrights are handled within the framework of intellectual property rights. Copyrights cover works of science and literature, musical works, works of fine art and cinematographic works. In this regard, it is necessary to organize the evaluations of copyright in the management of museum collections within the framework of moral and legal obligations.

The rights of the owner of the works that fall within the scope of copyrights, how these rights will be protected, how they will be limited and the legal measures to be applied in case of violation of the rights are secured by legal regulations. Accordingly, in order for a work to have copyright, it must bear the characteristics of its owner (subjective condition) and be perceivable directly or indirectly (objective condition). However, the rights of the author may be limited with the idea of ensuring public order, maximizing the social benefit and controlling the private benefit of a social heritage (Duguzheva & Simaeva, 2024).

Copyright regulations have become more prominent due to the acceleration of the digitalization process. The ease of copying and sharing cultural content in the digital environment causes artists and creative industries to lose income (O'Hare). On the other hand, digital inequality restricts access to cultural content for some individuals and communities due to differences in technological accessibility and digital literacy, leading to inequities in cultural participation (Norris, 2001).

Copyright Protection of Cultural Elements

Cultural elements include tangible and intangible values, such as traditional knowledge, works of art, handicrafts, music, dance and folk tales that a society has accumulated throughout history. Copyright protection of these elements prevents unauthorized copying, distribution or modification of these cultural elements (Brown, 2021). However, copyright protection of cultural elements creates a more complex situation than for other artistic works. Most cultural works are anonymous and based on folk culture passed down from generation to generation. The protection and ownership of cultural heritage is ensured through various legal mechanisms, particularly covering elements such as traditional knowledge and folklore (Parry, 2007).

Copyright protects the material and moral rights of authors over their works, while at the same time allowing public access to and use of these cultural contents. Public subsidization of copyright to promote and protect access to public expression is an important strategy for making cultural heritage accessible to a wide audience (Ananny & Kreiss, 2011).

In many countries, special laws are being developed to protect traditional knowledge and folklore. These laws prevent the unauthorized use of cultural elements of communities for commercial purposes and ensure their sustainability. Concepts such as geographical indications and traditional knowledge rights play an important role in protecting such cultural elements (UNESCO, 2003). For example, traditional handicrafts that are specific to a particular region are protected by being registered in the name of local communities.

Museums, which are public institutions, come to the forefront in transferring cultural elements, which are also important in terms of fiscal sociology, to future generations. According to UNESCO[3], a museum is *"Non-profit, permanent institution in the service of society and its development, open to the public, which acquires, conserves, researches, communicates and exhibits the tangible and intangible heritage of humanity and its environment for the purposes of education, study and enjoyment."* This definition is independent of the nature of the institution's governing body, its territorial character, its functional structure or the orientation of its collections. The artifacts in the collections of museums should be dealt with within the scope of intellectual property law.

Intellectual property rights include copyrights and industrial property rights. Copyright is an abstract concept. Intangible goods created by human thought are protected by copyrights. However, as technology advances, protecting the copyrights of works transferred to digital media becomes increasingly challenging.

Copyright protection of cultural elements and AI-enabled digital projects is becoming an important issue in the context of today's rapidly evolving technologies and changing cultural practices. Copyright protection of such digital content depends on the degree of similarity to the original work and the process of recreation (Ginsburg, 2001). Copyright claims on digitized historical works are handled in different ways. Since historical artifacts are usually in the public domain, their digital versions are considered independent creations and are protected by copyright.

Copyright protection of digital content developed with AI brings with it a complex legal process. For example, 3D models, animations or simulations created through AI are under copyright protection as they involve creativity. However, there is an ongoing debate as to whether the programmer who developed the AI or the person using the technology owns the copyright to these works. Unless copyright laws are updated according to such new technologies, uncertainty about the ownership of works produced by AI is likely to persist (Albakjaji & Almarzouqi, 2024).

Impacts of Using Artificial Intelligence in Culture

The digitalization of culture enables cultural artifacts and practices to be converted into digital format to reach and preserve them for a wider audience. This digital transformation forms the basis for the use of AI technologies in cultural fields. Digitized cultural data is analyzed and processed by AI systems, enabling the development of innovative applications such as virtual museum guides, automated art restorations, and personalized cultural experiences. (Floridi, 2014). Thus, a link can be established between the digitalization of culture and the use of AI technologies in cultural fields. Digitalization provides data and platforms where AI can be applied, while AI contributes to the enrichment and accessibility of digital culture.

In terms of the sustainability of culture, museums are active in the transfer of artifacts to future generations. According to Article 4 of the Regulation of the Turkish National Committee of the International Council of Museums, museums are defined as "institutions that preserve cultural artifacts and display these artifacts collectively for the purposes of study, education and the promotion of artistic taste, working for the public good, with collections of art, science, health and technology." As can be understood from the definition made by the International Council of Museums (ICOM), museums are cultural institutions and open to the public. In this context, museums operate for social benefit and do not aim to make profits. As one of the main elements of cultural industries and policies, museums play an important role in the transfer of culture to future generations. Therefore, museums are affected by social, economic and political phenomena, as well as technological development. Today, museums are being moved to virtual environments with immersive technology or AI-supported immersive technology elements with the effect of the digitalization process.

Immersive technology allows consumers to digitally experience reality from a broader perspective, including augmented reality (AR), virtual reality (VR), mixed reality (MR) and three-dimensional (3D) views. VR is a fully simulated digital environment in which users interact with virtual components (Ambika, Shin, & Jain, 2023). Popular forms of VR marketing include interactive content (games, simulated events) or passive content (videos). Consumers can access VR through high-end headsets (e.g., Oculus Rift), mobile-based headsets (e.g., Google Cardboard) or web-based virtual reality (e.g., Konterball). Furthermore, the feeling of being in a simulated space and interactivity (i.e., the possible level of live communication with the technology) are key features of VR (Radianti, Majchrzak, Fromm, & Isabell, 2020). AR facilitates the superimposition of interactive digital content (e.g., text, images and video) onto the physical context of the consumer, enabling reality and virtuality to coexist simultaneously (Javornik, 2016). Individuals experience AR through glasses/headphones (e.g., Google Glass), holographic displays (e.g., Microsoft HoloLens) or handheld devices (e.g., smartphones). Interactivity, clarity of the image, and the effective combination of real and virtual components are prominent features of AR (Javornik, 2016). MR environments blend virtual and real objects and interact with consumers (Ambika et al., 2023). Notable applications of MR include the transportation of interactive celebrity holograms used in live shows and the Metaverse (Smart, 2022). The 3D view creates the illusion of depth, allowing a better view of the presented object (Kang, Shin, & Ponto, 2020). 3D images are primarily used in videos and product presentations. Utilizing AI support in virtual experience projects such as VR, AR, MR and 3D takes immersive technology to a different level.

Environments that are optimized and presented in a more dynamic way with the AI technology contribute to making the virtual experience more permanent and realistic. AI encompasses technologies that enable computer systems to have human-like thinking and learning capabilities. AI enables businesses, institutions and societies to become more efficient and effective by transforming information and processes into digital forms.

When AI technology is evaluated within the framework of the concept of digitalization, it is seen as an element that is at the center of digital transformation processes and accelerates them. Thanks to AI's speed and processing power, high-quality graphics and sounds can be more effective and efficient. This paves the way for highly detailed and richly rendered immersive experiences that take users on dynamic and diverse journeys. AI plays a critical role in this transformation by processing, analyzing and making sense of large data sets, increasing the effectiveness of digitalization (Brynjolfsson & McAffee, 2014).

One of the areas where AI technology is causing a radical change is museology, which operates in the transfer of cultural elements to future generations. In AI-supported museums, algorithms enrich each individual's museum experience by making content recommendations based on visitors' preferences. For example, if a museum visitor is interested in a particular artist or period, AI systems can recognize this interest and recommend appropriate works. Thanks to such applications, visitors not only see the exhibited artifacts but also get more detailed information by being guided according to their personal interests (Sacher, Biella, & Luther, 2013).

AI makes significant contributions in areas such as personalizing museum visitor experiences, presenting exhibits in a more comprehensive digital environment, and optimizing museum management processes. These technologies help museums evolve away from static information transfer to an interactive, dynamic structure that enables active participation of visitors (Parry, 2007). The use of AI in museums allows for personalized tours based on visitors' interests, while big data analytics enable museum managers to measure and improve the impact of exhibitions. In addition, with the declining interest in museums displaying historical artifacts viewed through glass cases, new experience museums, supported by technology and reacting to visitors' movements, support the sustainability of cultural elements.

Especially when experience museums established in ruins are supported by AI technology, historical and cultural heritage is presented to visitors more impressively. In this field, AI-supported reconstruction technologies enable the digital recreation of the original state of the ruins. Visitors can see the original architecture of historical buildings, discover the lifestyle of that period and establish stronger connections with the past through AI-enhanced virtual tours. The technology not only physically shows historical sites but also provides a more detailed and realistic view of the past.

In short, unlike traditional museums, experience museums allow visitors to interact with exhibitions and experience learning through this interaction. This museum approach, in which visitors become a part of the museum experience rather than merely passive observers, is enriched by the opportunities provided by AI and digitalization technologies. Experience museums developed with digital elements supported by AI ensure that elements of social culture are passed on to future generations intact. However, the technology used in experience museums and the products transferred to future generations should be transferred to the digital environment in accordance with ethical and legal regulations. In this context, in the event that tangible and intangible cultural assets from past periods are exhibited in digital environments by museums, the protection of the copyrights of the works comes to the forefront among the issues that need to be emphasized.

The main strategic objectives of cultural policy in Türkiye include the development of cultural potential, the protection of the country's cultural heritage, and the development of creativity by ensuring the unity of the cultural space and the availability of cultural values. In this context, cultural heritage is transferred to future generations by utilizing technologies such as reality and AI.

In Türkiye, the construction of experience museums in ruins with the support of the Republic of Türkiye Ministry of Culture and Tourism is considered a positive step both culturally and economically. In Türkiye, two experience museums—the Hagia Sophia History and Experience Museum and the Ephesus Experience Museum—are open to visitors[4]. Hagia Sophia is recognized as one of the oldest cathedrals in the world. In the Hagia Sophia Experience Museum, 1700 years of cultural heritage is explained with an immersive audio-visual presentation with the opportunities offered by new generation technology. Some parts of the ancient city of Ephesus wear out over time and become physically inaccessible. The Ephesus Experience Museum provides digital reconstructions of these worn out or destroyed structures, showing visitors the majestic structures of ancient Ephesus in their original form. Digital reconstructions allow visitors to have a clearer understanding of ancient buildings and architectural artifacts, bringing cultural heritage to the present day.

Ephesus Experience Museum: Revitalizing Cultural Heritage with Artificial Intelligence

Ephesus is one of the most important cultural, commercial and religious centers of the ancient world, attracting visitors from all over the world with its rich historical heritage and architectural structures. Located in the Selçuk district of Izmir, this ancient city bears the traces of many different periods, from the Hellenistic Period to the Roman Empire. The wide area of Ephesus, the deterioration of some of its architectural structures over time, and the difficulties of physical access limit the ability to fully understand and experience this rich heritage. The artifacts of ancient Ephesus are presented in a realistic experience at the Ephesus Experience Museum. With today's digital elements, structures such as the Ephesus Experience Museum allow visitors to explore historical and cultural richness in greater depth.

Experience museums provide visitors with information instantly through AI-powered guides while also helping to explain historical buildings, monuments, and cultural events in a more understandable way. For example, when visitors want to get detailed information about the history and architecture of structures such as the Temple of Artemis or the Library of Celsus, AI-powered guides provide this information instantly and respond to visitors' questions spontaneously.

Immersive media and AI are the most frequently used technologies in the digitalization processes of experience museums. AI personalizes the museum experience for visitors and provides a more immersive experience by offering customized content based on each individual's interests. Data such as which sections of the museum visitors spend more time in and which artifacts they are more interested in are analyzed by AI and appropriate content is presented to the visitor in line with this data. AI-supported guides provide an interactive guidance service by answering visitors' questions and offering more information about the topics they are interested in.

AI-created experience museums are generally based on the digitization of historical and cultural elements. The transition to digital platforms and the use of high-tech solutions in the cultural field require technical capabilities and digital competence.

The Ephesus Experience Museum was designed by DEM Museology, a company under the Republic of Türkiye Ministry of Culture and Tourism. VR and AR applications were utilized while designing the Ephesus Experience Museum. These technologies allow visitors to experience ancient Ephesus in more detail. During physical visits to Ephesus, ancient structures and monuments are digitally animated using AR. For example, visitors to Ephesus can use their cell phones or tablets to see digital reconstructions of destroyed or weathered structures and experience them in their original state. Visitors are allowed to travel in time to the ancient times of Ephesus using VR technology. Visitors can walk the ancient streets of Ephesus, shop in the trade centers of that period or attend a show in the amphitheater wearing VR glasses. VR offers visitors the opportunity to experience the past more vividly by participating in history. VR applications also provide more detailed information about the cultural and social life of Ephesus, allowing visitors to establish a stronger connection with history. Thanks to these technologies, visitors become active participants as well as spectators of ancient Ephesus.

Visualization technologies, combined with digitalization, help visitors easily experience the majestic structures and traces of daily life in the ancient city of Ephesus. For example, the Library of Celsus, one of the most iconic buildings of Ephesus, is recreated in its original form thanks to digital technologies and offers opportunities for visitors to fully experience the splendor of the past. With the technology utilized, visitors experience the history of Ephesus in a more accessible, understandable and interactive way. Thus, it also contributes to the sustainability of cultural heritage.

AI also offers important opportunities for museum management. AI systems that analyze the behavior of visitors provide feedback to the museum management by determining which sections are more popular and which exhibitions attract more attention. The digitization of historical artifacts ensures their revitalization. The rapid development of AI technology in recent years is also valuable for the preservation and revitalization of cultural heritage. The real-time processing power of AI plays an important role here.

Immersive media and AI help preserve archaeological sites in a sustainable way. The Ephesus Experience Museum, which is the focus of this study, stands out as a project that demonstrates the potential of AI and digitalization technologies in the preservation, promotion, and understanding of cultural heritage. Ephesus Experience Museum is a museum that adopts the modern museology approach and presents cultural heritage to its visitors through innovative technologies. Experience museums, especially those close to ruins, offer visitors a richer and more interactive presentation of historical and cultural heritage through AI-supported digital projects. These projects digitally recreate historical buildings, artifacts and environments using VR, AR and AI technologies. Although this provides advantages in terms of transferring cultural elements to future generations, it also brings along the problem of protecting the copyrights of the elements developed with AI technology.

According to ICOM[5], museums are public institutions and have impacts in many social, economic, financial, socio-psychological and administrative fields. In this context, the global information society's concept of 'digital cultural heritage' becomes prominent. The state ownership of the copyrights of the elements of social culture exhibited in museums and passed on to future generations will contribute to the protection of artifacts and the sustainability of culture. In line with this perspective, experience museums are being opened in Türkiye with the support of the Republic of Türkiye Ministry of Culture and Tourism. The ministry, which makes service contracts with design companies such as DEM Museology, takes ownership of the artifacts within the state. This prevents potential copyright issues from arising.

CONCLUSION

The formulation and implementation of cultural policies is one of the social objectives of fiscal policy. Cultural policies direct the activities of the state in the field of culture to protect, update and promote culture. In order to create cultural policies, multidimensional assessments are made in the creative, economic, legal and social fields in line with sustainable development goals.

Culture is one of the most important elements for the development of a society in economic, social, financial and political areas, as well as for increasing social welfare. When culture is considered a merit good, states are expected to be active in the cultural field. Today, states, which are shaped as social welfare states, aim to achieve social goals by utilizing technological elements in the cultural field. Some of the historically, economically and culturally important centers are now being transferred to digital environments using immersive media and AI. Thus, cultural richness reaches a wider audience and contributes to cultural sustainability. However, legal regulations need to be revised for the protection of cultural heritage that is digitized using techniques such as immersive media and AI. One of the prominent issues that needs to be revised is copyright.

It is crucial to make the necessary legal arrangements in the national legislation or to update the existing regulations, taking into account technological progress, in order to preserve universal culture. Türkiye is one of the countries with universal values that are recognized as the common heritage of humanity. Cultural policies aim at promoting cultural and natural properties of the world, raising awareness in society to protect the universal heritage and providing the necessary cooperation for the survival of cultural and natural values that are degraded and destroyed due to various reasons. In this direction, studies are carried out in Türkiye under the leadership of the Republic of Türkiye Ministry of Culture and Tourism. Cultural assets on the UNESCO World Heritage List are now exhibited in experience museums using immersive media and AI. The Ephesus Experience Museum, located in Ephesus, is one of the first museums to combine experience museology with historical narrative. The Ephesus Experience Museum received the "Best Museum" award in the field of museums at the Mondo-Dr Awards, one of the world's most distinguished awards in the field of technology, design and exhibition, in 2024. The transformation of Ephesus into an experience museum, in addition to being visited as an archaeological site, contributes significantly to the protection of cultural heritage and the promotion of sustainable development. Historic sites such as Ephesus are designed by private companies with the support of the Republic of Türkiye Ministry of Culture and Tourism, and service contracts are signed to avoid copyright issues.

In conclusion, it is important to implement cultural policies in Türkiye in line with the objectives of fiscal policy, taking into account the effects of the digital transformation brought about by the globalization process. Activities should be carried out with strategic documents, legal regulations and effective mechanisms for their implementation. In addition, it is important to adopt flexible, open and clear regulations on many issues, including copyright, in order to prevent problems that may arise from the use of AI in cultural fields and to protect digital culture.

REFERENCES

Albakjaji, M., & Almarzouqi, R. (2024). The Dilemma of the Copyrights of Artificial Intelligence: The Case of Saudi Arabia Regulations. *International Journal of Socio-technology and Knowledge Development*, 16(1), 1–15. DOI: 10.4018/IJSKD.336920

Ambika, A., Shin, H., & Jain, V. (2023). Immersive Technologies and Consumer Behavior: A Systematic Review of Two Decades of Research. *Australian Journal of Management*, 1–25. DOI: 10.1177/03128962231181429

Ananny, M., & Kreiss, D. (2011). A New Contract for the Press: Copyright, Public Domain Journalism, and Self-Governance in a Digital Age. *Critical Studies in Media Communication*, 28(4), 314–333. DOI: 10.1080/15295036.2010.519339

Anderson, C. (2006). *The Long Tail: Why the Future of Business is Selling Less of More*. Hyperion.

Backhaus, J. G. (2004). Josseph A. Schumpeter's Contributions in the Area of Fiscal Sociology: A fisrt Approximation. *Journal of Evolutionary Economics*, 14(2), 143–151. DOI: 10.1007/s00191-004-0186-z

Baumol, W. J. (1967). Macroeconomics of Unbalanced Growth: The Anatomy of Urban Crisis. *The American Economic Review*, 57(3), 415–426.

Brennen, S., & Kreiss, D. (2014). *Digitalization and Digitization*. Culture Digitally.

Brown, R. D. (2021). Property ownership and the legal personhood of artificial intelligence. *Information & Communications Technology Law*, 30(2), 208–234. DOI: 10.1080/13600834.2020.1861714

Brynjolfsson, E., & McAffee, A. (2014). *The Second Machine Age: Work Progress, and Prosperity in a Time of Brilliant Technologies*. W. W. Norton Company.

Campbell, J. L. (1993). The State and Fiscal Sociology. *Annual Review of Sociology*, 19(1), 163–185. DOI: 10.1146/annurev.so.19.080193.001115

Castells, M. (2009). *The Rise of the Network Society*. Wiley-Blackwell. DOI: 10.1002/9781444319514

Darmon, M. (2023). *Socialization*. Polity Press.

Duguzheva, M. K., & Simaeva, E. P. (2024). *Transformation of the Legislation on Culture in the Context of Digitalization*. Perm University Herald Juridical Sciences, 44.

Eagleton, T. (2006). *Criticism and Ideology: A Study in Marxist Literary Theory*. Verso.

Edizdoğan, N., Çetinkaya, Ö., & Gümüş, E. (2023). *Kamu Maliyesi*. Ekin Yayınevi.

Florida, R. (2002). *The Rise of the Creative Class—Revisited: Revised and Expanded*. Basic Books.

Floridi, L. (2014). *The Fourth Revolution: How the Infosphere Is Reshaping Human Reality*. Oxford University Press.

Frey, B. S., & Oberholzer-Gee, F. (1998). *Public Choice, Cost-Benefit Analysis, and the Evaluation of Cultural Heritage. A. Peacock içinde, Does the Past Have a Future? The Political Economy of Heritage*. Institute of Economic Affairs.

Geertz, C. (2017). *The Interpretation of Cultures*. Basic Books.

Gere, C. (2008). *Digital Culture*. Reaktion Books.

Ginsburg, J. C. (2001). *Copyright and Control Over New Technologies of Dissemination*. Columbia Law School. DOI: 10.2307/1123809

Gobble, M. M. (2018). Digitalization, Digitization, and Innovation. *Research Technology Management*, 61(4), 56–59. DOI: 10.1080/08956308.2018.1471280

Goldscheid, R. (1958). *A Sociological Approach to Problems to Public Finance. In Classsics in the Theory of Public Finance*. Palgrave Macmillan.

Güvenç, B. (2018). *İnsan ve Kültür*. Boyut Yayınları.

Javornik, A. (2016). Augmented reality: Research agenda for studying the impact of its media characteristics. *Journal of Retailing and Consumer Services*, 30, 252–261. DOI: 10.1016/j.jretconser.2016.02.004

Jenkins, H. (2006). *Convergence Culture: Where Old and New Media Collide*. New York University Press.

Kang, H. J., Shin, J. H., & Ponto, K. (2020). How 3D virtual reality stores can shape consumer purchase decisions:The roles of informativeness and playfulness. *Journal of Interactive Marketing*, 49(1), 70–85. DOI: 10.1016/j.intmar.2019.07.002

Kaynak, F. (2015). *Sosyolojik yöntemin kuralları* (E. Durkheim, Trans.). Dost Kitabevi Yayınları.

Levine, J. M., & Moreland, R. L. (2011). Group Socialization: Theory and Research. *European Review of Social Psychology*, 5(1), 305–336. DOI: 10.1080/14792779543000093

Maccoby, E. E. (2015). *Historical Overview of Socialization Research and Theory. J. E. Grusec, & P. D. Hastings içinde, Hand Book of Socialization Theory and Research*. The Guilford Press.

Manovich, L. (2002). *The Language of New Media*. MIT Press. DOI: 10.22230/cjc.2002v27n1a1280

Martin, I. W., Mehrotra, A. K., & Prasad, M. (2009). *The New Fiscal Sociology. In The Thunder of History: The Origins and Development of the New Fiscal Sociology*. Cambridge University Press.

Musgrave, R. A. (1992). Schumpeter's Crisis of the Tax State: An Essay in Fiscal Sociology. *Journal of Evolutionary Economics*, 2(2), 89–113. DOI: 10.1007/BF01193535

Musgrave, R. A., & Peacock, A. T. (1967). *Introduction. R. A. Musgrave, & A. T. Peacock içinde, Classics in the Theory of Public Finance*. MACMILLAN.

Norris, P. (2001). Digital Divide: Civic Engagement, Information Poverty, and the Internet Worldwide. Cambridge University Press. DOI: 10.1017/CBO9781139164887

Parry, R. (2007). *Recoding the Museum Digital Heritage and the Technologies of Change*. Routledge. DOI: 10.4324/9780203347485

Radianti, J., Majchrzak, T. A., Fromm, J., & Isabell, W. (2020). A systematic review of immersive virtual reality applications for higher education: Design elements, lessons learned, and research agenda. *Computers & Education*, 147, 1–29. DOI: 10.1016/j.compedu.2019.103778

Robbins, S. P., & Judge, T. A. (2017). *Essentials of Organizational Behavior*. Pearson.

Rosen, H. S., & Gayer, T. (2010). *Public Finance*. McGraw-Hill.

Sacher, D., Biella, D., & Luther, W. (2013). *Towards a versatile metadata exchange format for digital museum collections*. IEEE. DOI: 10.1109/DigitalHeritage.2013.6744744

Smart, P. (2022). Minds in the Metaverse: Extended Cognition Meets Mixed Reality. *Philosophy & Technology*, 35(87), 87. DOI: 10.1007/s13347-022-00580-w

Smelser, N. J., & Swedberg, R. (2005). *The Handbook of Economic Sociology*. Princeton University Press.

Stiglitz, J. H., & Rosengard, J. K. (2015). *Economics of the Public Sector*. W. W. Norton & Company.

Thorsby, D. (2000). *Economics and Culture*. Cambridge University Press. DOI: 10.1017/CBO9781107590106

Tolan, B. (1996). *Toplum Bilimlerine Giriş*. Murat& Adım Yayıncılık.

UNESCO. (2003). *Convention for the Safeguqrding of the Intangible Cultural Heritage*. UNESCO Publishing.

UNESCO. (2015). *Recommendation Concerning the Preservation of, and Access to, Documentary Heritage Including in Digital Form*. UNESCO Publishing.

Wagner, H. M. (2007). *Principles of Operations Research with Application to Managerial Decision*. Prentice-Hall Press.

KEY TERMS AND DEFINITIONS

Artificial Intelligence: The use of human intelligence and cognitive skills in computer or software systems to accomplish specified tasks.

Cultural Economics: Evaluation of production and consumption of cultural elements in terms of economics.

Digitalization: The evolution of culture, society, economy, law and business models by the integration of digital technologies into daily life and activities.

Digitization: The process of analog data such as published sources and tapes becomes readable on digital media such as computers.

Immersive Media: Digital technology that demonstrates a realistic experience to people by virtual environments.

Intellectual Property Right: The field of law that includes the regulations and legislation concerning intellectual products that have economic value.

Merit Goods and Services: The goods and services produced by states on a paternalistic basis.

Public Finance: Public finance is the branch of science that studies fiscal events.

ENDNOTES

1 This study is derived from the master's thesis titled "The Cultural Dimension of Sustainable Development: The Case of İzmir Culture and Art Factory" prepared by Zeynep COŞKUN under the supervision of Assoc. Prof. Dr. İrem DİDİNMEZ.

2 For detailed information on MuseumPass, see https://muze.gov.tr/urun-detay?CatalogNo=KRT-MBL01-08-008

3 UNESCO Institute for Statistics. (n.d.). Museum. Retrieved September 25, 2024, from https://uis.unesco.org/en/glossary-term/museum

4 Work is underway to launch the Hierapolis Experience Museum and Cappadocia Experience Museum.

5 International Council of Museums. (2017). ICOM statutes. Retrieved October 1, 2024, from https://icom.museum/wp-content/uploads/2018/07/2017_ICOM_Statutes_EN.pdf

Chapter 5
Artificial Intelligence and Public Policies in Intellectual Property Rights

Nazmiye Tekdemir
Kırıkkale University, Turkey

Ayşegül Durucan
Kırıkkale University, Turkey

Eda Yeşil
Kırıkkale University, Turkey

ABSTRACT

The increasing capacity of artificial intelligence (AI) technologies to develop inventions has profoundly transformed the innovation landscape, heralding a transitional epoch from human inventors to AI inventors. The study proposes that public policy and legal regulations be designed with an acute awareness of the interplay between AI dynamics and copyrights. This, in turn, would enhance the potential for innovation and invention by encouraging AI-centric R&D initiatives, thereby fostering economic growth. Moreover, updating IP law to align with contemporary technological advancements could facilitate the transfer of technology from high-tech enterprises to the nation.

DOI: 10.4018/979-8-3693-8704-7.ch005

INTRODUCTION

The main objective of this research is to contribute to doctrinal knowledge by providing a comprehensive yet concise analysis of AI and IP issues from a public policy perspective. The study also aims to provide new perspectives and thinking opportunities for interdisciplinary scholars and policymakers working in areas such as IP, technology, privacy and freedom of information. Studies carried out show a relationship between intellectual property rights (IPR) and the level of development of countries. This is because IPR protection has a positive impact on economic and finance system by promoting technological innovation and the diffusion of knowledge economies. This effect is realized indirectly in various forms, such as the enhancement of R&D activities, technology transfer through FDI with high technology content, and technology acquisition. IPR is an institutional safeguard that protects this whole process and encourages national and international investment. The first country to adopt a system that will provide intellectual property law protection to innovations and inventions generated by AI systems will benefit from the development of AI and the economic benefits it will generate. And AI is also used in risk management controls; and expand access to credit and other bank services in the financial system. For all these reasons, IPR are also needed in the economic and finance management of AI.

To the extent that the owners of an innovation, innovation or invention profit from their creativity, they continue to develop new ideas and contribute to innovation. Accordingly, it can be interpreted that innovation will increase with the increase in R&D activities and thus economic growth will be realized. In this respect, the most important asset of knowledge economies is IPR. Due to the importance of IPR, firstly explained in our manuscript. Then, AI is defined and finally, the relationship of AI with economics and finance and the importance of IPR in this direction are mentioned.

1. INTELLECTUAL PROPERTY RİGHTS

Intellectual Property Rights

Intellectual property rights are defined as “interests that are legally protected over the products created by a person as a result of all kinds of intellectual and mental efforts and labor, and that give the right holder the right to benefit from this protection if he wishes.” (Ateş, 2003: 93). The World Intellectual Property Organization (WIPO) defines IP as a concept that encompasses all creations of the mind, from works of art to inventions, from computer programs to trademarks and other commercial signs (WIPO, 2020: 1). IPR are generally examined under two headings: copyrights and industrial property rights. Copyrights cover rights arising from works of science, literature, music, fine arts and cinema. Industrial property rights refer to rights related to patents, brands, models, technological inventions, industrial designs and geographical indications (WIPO, 2020: 3; Yücekal, 2003). With the rapid advancement in digital technology, the scope of the concept of IP is also expanding. The classification of IPR can be seen in Table 1.

Table 1. Types of Intellectual Property Rights

Intellectual Property Rights	Copyrights	Scientific and Literary Works
		Musical Works
		Works of Art
		Cinema Works
		Adaptation and Collected Works
	Industrial Propery Rights	Patents
		Trademarks
		Industrial Designs
		Utility Models
		Geographical Indications

Source: Compiled by the authors

The protection of IPR is not limited to cultural and artistic products today. The use of developing digital technologies and products based on these technologies is becoming increasingly widespread, and their share in the economy, together with the sectors they are associated with, is increasing significantly. This situation requires the design of more effective and multifaceted policies on IPR in Türkiye, as in the rest of the world, and the immediate implementation of these policies (Intellectual rights special expertise commission report, 2018: 78).

Most of the problems encountered in the protection of industrial rights are tried to be solved with patent studies. At this point, in order to protect the rights of those who produce ideas, it is necessary to wait until the product reaches the patent stage, which leads to productivity and efficiency problems (Intellectual rights special expertise commission report, 2018: 106).

IPR are protected in Türkiye by the Law on Intellectual and Artistic Works (LIAW) No. 5846 and the Industrial Property Law (IPL) No. 6769. LIAW was adopted in Türkiye on December 5, 1951 and entered into force on December 13, 1951, after being published in the Official Gazette No. 7981. The IPL was adopted on December

22, 2016 and entered into force on January 10, 2017, after being published in the Official Gazette No. 29944.

The purpose of LIAW is stated in the law as "...*to determine and protect the moral and financial rights of the authors who create works of thought and art, the performers who perform or interpret these works, the phonogram producers who make the first recordings of sounds, the producers who make the first recordings of films and the radio and television organizations on their products, to regulate the conditions for benefiting from these products and to determine the sanctions in case of benefiting contrary to the foreseen principles and procedures.*" LIAW classifies works of thought and art as scientific and literary works, musical works, works of fine arts, cinema works, publicized and published works.

The purpose of the IPL is stated in the law as "...*to protect the rights related to trademarks, geographical indications, designs, patents, utility models and traditional product names and thereby to contribute to the realization of technological, economic and social progress.*"

There are some differences between these rights. These differences can be expressed as follows: Copyrights are rights that arise automatically with the creation of the work without the need for notification or registration. In contrast, industrial property rights such as patents, utility models, brands and industrial designs must be registered at an administrative institution such as Turkish Patent. Because registration is the basis for industrial rights; protection without registration is exceptional.

Table 2. Types, Definitions, and Terms of Protection of Intellectual Properties

Type	Definition	Duration
Copyright	Copyright is a concept used to describe the rights of creators over their literary and artistic works.	70 years after the creator dies – nonextensile
Patent	A patent is an official document that gives the inventor the right in areas to selling, marketing, duplicating, and producing a similar product.	20 years – nonextensile
Trademark	Any sign that distinguishes the goods or services of a business from the goods or services of other businesses.	10 years – extensible
Industrial Design	Industrial design refers to the aesthetic ornamentation such as line, shape, form, colour, texture and material on the whole or part of a product.	5 years – extensible up to 25 years

continued on following page

Table 2. Continued

Type	Definition	Duration
Utility Model	The utility model is a property right that provides protection to owners of inventions that are industrially applicable worldwide.	10 years – nonextensile
Geographical Indication	Geographical indications are signs used on goods that are identified with their place of geographical origin due to a distinctive feature.	No duration

Source: Compiled by the authors from WIPO, 2020 and Law No. 5846 and 6769

The Table 2 regarding types, definitions and protection conditions of IP in Türkiye is presented above. In the Turkish legal system, in line with the current provisions of the Law No. 5846 on IPR, every work is considered an intellectual product; however, not every intellectual product is considered a work (Gözübüyük, 2021:62). In addition, according to the LIAW, intellectual products created by AI are not considered works. In order for such products to be considered works, arrangements must be made in the existing legal provisions (Gözübüyük, 2021:76). On the other hand, the lateness in making legal regulations regarding the interaction of AI and IPR is observed not only in Türkiye but also all over the world (Aktürk, 2024: 228). In order for a product to be accepted as a work, it must bear the identity of its owner, be included in the product groups included in the law, and have a perceptibility effect and an element of creativity (Özkan, 2022: 234). The laws of the United Kingdom, Ireland and New Zealand recognize the person who makes the necessary arrangements for the creation of an intellectual product created by AI as the rights holder (Gözübüyük, 2021: 69-70). However, there is no such regulation in Türkiye.

It is thought that examining the works produced by AI in terms of IPR and designing public policies in line with the requirements of the age in this regard is very important in terms of increasing the potential of AI-based initiatives, innovations and inventions that can stimulate economic growth.

Because the existence of a clear, understandable and transparent legal regulation for AI both encourages investments in this field and provides a safe innovation and invention environment for foreign investors (European Commission Report, 2020: 1).

Over time, as advances in AI systems have emerged, traditional intellectual property laws have become inadequate (Shlomit, 2017: 678). Developments in AI systems have created a need to update legal rules/legislation regarding the protection of IPR. Based on this need, studies in the field of public policies regarding the interaction between AI and IPR have become of interest to academics and policy makers.

Today, countries prefer to contribute to economic growth and development by producing innovative goods and services and intellectual works based on creativity, which can provide higher added value and increase their international competitiveness, rather than agriculture, mining and relatively low-value manufacturing sectors. Such innovative works are defined as IP and need protection due to the abstractness of the concept of IP and its potential for theft. The protection of IPR will be possible through the practices of policy makers that support, encourage and clearly protect investments in this area. (ICC Türkiye: 2). In addition, the protection of these rights will encourage new technology investments and creativity based on R&D, and will also allow the author to make financial gains through their creativity with the legal framework that has been arranged (Helvacıoğlu-Eraslan et al., 2004: 485).

R&D initiatives are considered to be a very important indicator in evaluating the technological performance of countries (Parlakyıldız and Güvel, 2015: 34). In order for countries to make innovative and creative technology investments, their institutional, financial, administrative and legal infrastructures must be sufficient and these infrastructure systems must be structured in a way that complements each other. IPR can be considered as a part of the system that creates these infrastructures. Countries support R&D investments with the share they allocate from their GDP for R&D initiatives, R&D investments provide infrastructure services for innovative technologies and regulations for the protection of IPR are on the agenda in terms of protecting innovative technology investments (SPO, 2007: 31-32).

Below is a table regarding Türkiye's IPR targets.

Table 3. Intellectual Property Rights Objectives

	2022	2023	2028
Number of Registered and Valid Patents Related to Green and Digital Transformation	2.520	3.000	10.000
Number of International Patent Applications of Turkish Origin	1.771	1.850	5.000
Number of Registered Geographical Indications in the European Union	8	16	100
Royalties of Professional Associations (Million TL)	496	850	2.750

Source: Twelfth Development Plan (2024-2028), 128.

2. ARTIFICIAL INTELLIGENCE SYSTEMS FROM A HISTORICAL AND TECHNICAL PERSPECTIVE

2.1. What is Artificial Intelligence?

Academician John McCarthy first mentioned the concept of intelligence, which emerged in the mid-20th century, in 1956. McCarthy defined AI as "the science and engineering of creating intelligent machines and especially computer programs." Alan Turing, considered the pioneer of AI, initiated his 1950 article 'Computing Machinery and Intelligence' by posing the question 'Can machines think?' In this context, it is possible to define AI as a branch of science that aims to make machines intelligent (Gözübüyük, 2021: 57). It is the advances in computing power, algorithms, and data access in recent years that have transformed AI from a theoretical concept into a widely used technology. The journey of AI began with simple, programmed computers. Today, it has become capable of processing and learning large amounts of data with complex machine learning and deep learning models. This evolution has led to the proliferation of AI in many areas, from autonomous vehicles and smart home devices to medical diagnostic systems and personalized education solutions (Becker, 2017).

The exponential advancement of AI encompasses more than just technological progress. Furthermore, it is a socio-economic shift that has an impact on labor markets, privacy standards, and cultural production (Hamza et al., 2023). It is crucial to focus on the utilization of concepts and the distinctions among them at this juncture. AI encompasses a comprehensive collection of interconnected sub-disciplines, including machine learning, deep learning, and data mining. Nevertheless, it is observed that both terms are frequently misunderstood and employed interchangeably in everyday situations. Due to the lack of clearly defined boundaries between these ideas. These four fundamental notions can be demonstrated using Figure 1 below.

Figure 1. Subfields of Artificial Intelligence and Data Science

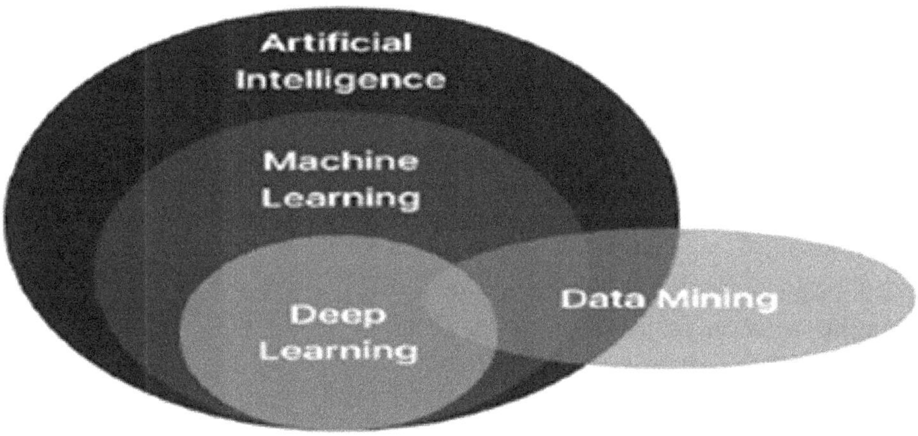

Source: *Yalçın Uslu, 2023: 60.*

Figure 1 illustrates a clear hierarchical structure among these notions, while also indicating some degree of overlap. While the higher levels of the hierarchy encompass the concepts found in the lower levels, this inclusivity is not absolute. Hence, certain notions may be linked to multiple fields. Hence, it is crucial to acknowledge the distinctions between concepts and employ them with caution.

AI is occasionally characterized as an entity, a system, or a field of study. AI can be defined as a non-human system that possesses cognitive capabilities such as learning and reasoning. It is an intelligent computer that is capable of strategic thinking and planning. Additionally, AI can be considered as a branch of science that can assist humanity in finding solutions to global issues such as climate change, depletion of natural resources, and income inequality. The various definitions of AI indicate that it is not just seen as a technology, but also as a powerful tool that can greatly influence the future of humanity (Kop, 2019: 300). AI, intelligent robotics, big data, and blockchain are transformative developments that will profoundly alter the social fabric. These technologies propel us into a new era of human history, known as the Fourth Industrial Revolution.

There are three main types of AI: weak artificial intelligence (ANI), artificial general intelligence (AGI), and artificial superintelligence (ASI). These types can support and reinforce each other. AI development does not proceed at a linear or Darwinian pace. Instead, the integration of innovative computer chips, 3D integrated circuits, machine learning algorithms, cloud computing, blockchain, and big data is creating a powerful synergy, propelling the development process at an exponential rate. These synergistic effects significantly increase the speed and scope of technological progress. AE is undergoing an unprecedented growth process with advances in software, computing power, and big data. This rapid development has already had a major economic and social impact, particularly on the financial services sector and the ways of interacting with online content in the digital economy. It is emphasized that AI has the potential to lead to revolutionary changes in sectors such as healthcare and transport. In this context, McKinsey and PricewaterhouseCoopers' economic impact studies predict that AI could make an economic contribution worth trillions of pounds by 2030.

The extent of AI's economic influence suggests that it will not just be confined to reforms in certain sectors but will also result in profound alterations in global economic dynamics. The digital economy is experiencing a rapid transformation, which is being accelerated by the influence of AI and is altering the future landscape of commercial operations. The extensive implementation of AI across various industries is crucial for fostering innovation and enhancing competitiveness. The economic and social consequences of AI have the potential to fundamentally reshape the future of the commercial world and social life (Abbott, 2020: 6). In a paper commissioned by McKinsey Global Institute, Dobbs et al. (2015: 1) highlight that the transformative effects of emerging technologies, such as AI, would be ten times faster and 300 times more extensive than those of the Industrial Revolution.

This implies that the ramifications of AI could be around 3,000 times more potent than the impacts of the Industrial Revolution.

And also finance system in AI is more developed. In OECD surveys, the use of AI in finance sector to improve efficiency of marketing, reducing costs, performing transactions quickly, security applications, and being always accessible, personalise products and services, strengthen risk management and controls; and expand access to credit and other bank services (OECD, 2024: 15).

It is noteworthy that while older studies compare ANN (artificial neural nets) with statistical analysis, more recent publications are based on the comparison of ANN with machine learning and deep learning techniques. When we look at the usage areas of these techniques, it is found that they are mostly focused on investment instruments such as stocks, bitcoin and gold. This result reveals that the studies are mostly carried out for investment decisions, which constitute an important part of the financial world (Yıldız, 2022: 63.).

On the other hand, survey respondents have reported identified risks. These are, cybersecurity, market manipulation, bias & discrimination data privacy & quality, governance, explainability & interpretability, model risks, consumer & investor protection, third party, new operational risks, fraud & money laundering, reputational, other and auditability. (OECD, 2024: 17).

The incorporation of AI technologies, which is important in the global context, has expedited national strategies. The National AI strategy consist of three primary dimensions, as outlined in the National Artificial Intelligence Strategy -2021-2025 Türkiye Report, 2021 (pages 15-16). The three key factors are: organizational competence, strategy coherence, and governance structure. The three dimensions of attention in AI are data, capabilities, and infrastructure. The organizational competency component focuses on efforts that strive to develop and enhance the core competencies inside organizations. The governance dimension seeks to establish administrative and technical collaboration inside and between organizations to continuously enhance these fundamental capabilities. The strategic alignment factor seeks to enhance the sustainability of the AI ecosystem by supplementing the institutional competency and governance elements. Put simply, the governance dimension facilitates the change of sectors, the implementation of public programs, and the collaboration of international organizations. Figure 2 below can be used to demonstrate the many aspects of a country's AI policy within this framework.

Figure 2. Dimensions of the National AI Strategy

Source: *National Artificial Intelligence Strategy -2021-2025 Türkiye Report, 2021.*

The process of structural transformation, with the objective of increasing awareness of AI in all sectors of society, goes through multiple stages. This process is advancing by implementing the metrics collected within the strategic priority areas listed below:

Table 4. Priority Areas for AI

Ø Training of AI specialists and increasing employment opportunities in this field
Ø Research and development in the field of AI, supporting entrepreneurship and producing innovative solutions.
Ø Strengthening the technical infrastructure, platforms and data sources required for AI.
Ø Increasing harmonisation in socio-economic structure and making necessary arrangements.
Ø To strengthen international co-operation in the field of AI and to ensure global co-ordination.
Ø Accelerating the structural transformation of the institutional structure and labour force.

Source: National Artificial Intelligence Strategy -2021-2025 Türkiye Report, 2021.

Ryan Abbott (2020), in The Reasonable Robot: Artificial Intelligence and the Law, describes the impact of AI on inventions in five stages. In the first stage, the invention process is carried out entirely by human inventors. In the second stage, AI begins to invent in certain areas but has not yet reached the same cognitive level as human intelligence. The third stage envisages the period when AI and human intelligence reach an equivalent level in the invention process. The fourth stage describes a situation in which a comprehensive AI surpasses human intelligence and gains superiority in invention development processes. Finally, in the fifth stage, we expect super-intelligent AI to develop its capacity for continuous innovation and self-improvement. Through these stages, Abbott's prediction examines the impact of AI development on human creativity and invention capacity. This five-stage process describes the progression of AI from a tool that first supports the human being to eventually surpassing it and becoming an independent, innovative entity. Today, although AI has not yet reached the cognitive equivalence of human intelligence, we see AI emerging in certain fields of invention. In other words, it is emphasized that human authorship and inventorship are still the main reference points in intellectual property law.

2.2. Progress in Türkiye

The adoption and implementation of AI technologies, which are crucial on a worldwide scale, have expedited the formulation and execution of national policies and measures. The 'National Artificial Intelligence Strategy 2021-2025' document was published in Türkiye on 20 August 2021 as the Presidential Circular No. 2021/18. This document was a collaborative effort between the Digital Transformation Office Presidency and the Ministry of Industry and Technology, with the active involvement of all relevant stakeholders. This circular becomes effective upon its publication in the Official Gazette No. 31574. The Circular outlines the nation's strategic objectives and plan for AI, with the intention of facilitating digital transformation initiatives. This plan, which has been implemented, aims to foster the advancement of AI and synchronize pertinent policies and regulations.

Ryan Abbott (2020), in The Reasonable Robot: AI and the Law, describes the impact of AI on inventions in five stages. Human inventors carry out the invention process entirely in the first stage. In the second stage, AI begins to invent in certain areas but has not yet reached the same cognitive level as human intelligence. The third stage envisages the period when AI and human intelligence reach an equivalent level in the invention process. The fourth stage describes a situation in which a comprehensive AI surpasses human intelligence and gains superiority in invention development processes. Finally, in the fifth stage, we expect super-intelligent AI to develop its capacity for continuous innovation and self-improvement. Through these stages, Abbott's prediction examines the impact of AI development on human creativity and invention capacity. This five-stage process describes the progression of AI from a tool that first supports the human being to eventually surpassing it and becoming an independent, innovative entity. Although AI has not yet reached the cognitive equivalence of human intelligence, we see it emerging in certain fields of invention today. We emphasize that human authorship and inventorship remain the primary reference points in intellectual property law.

The strategy's objective is to establish an agile and sustainable AI ecosystem that generates value on a global level, ultimately contributing to the prosperity of Türkiye. To align with this objective, the plan is formulated based on six fundamental priorities: The objectives include providing comprehensive training for AI specialists and promoting job creation, fostering research and entrepreneurship, ensuring easy access to high-quality data and technical resources, implementing regulations to expedite socioeconomic adaptation, enhancing international collaboration, and expediting structural and labor transformation. As part of these priorities, a total of 24 specific goals and 119 actions have been defined. Additionally, a thorough governance mechanism has been put in place to coordinate AI operations from 2021 to 2025. The execution of the plan is overseen by the 'Steering Committee', which is formed under the leadership of the Vice President. The AI Ecosystem Advisory Group and technical working groups contribute to the implementation process. The Secretariat prepares the Action Plan in accordance with the committee's decisions and regularly monitors and evaluates it on a quarterly basis, taking into account the comments from the respective institutions. The Strategy necessitates a flexible implementation method to accommodate the swift changes in the field of AI. This process enhances the ability to promptly address opportunities, risks, and uncertainties that may emerge. The objective of implementing these steps is to effectively execute AI projects in accordance with ethical standards and enhance the maturity level and competitiveness of our country's AI ecosystem.

When the use of AI in IPR in Türkiye is analyzed, it is possible to say that a lot of progress has been made. For example, it is seen that many important studies have been carried out on AI. According to the National Artificial Intelligence Strategy - 2021-2025 Türkiye Report (2021), there are 1,218 academics working in this field. Türkiye has published a total of 9,409 international indexed publications between 2009 and 2018. In the field of AI, Türkiye ranks 16th in terms of the number of publications worldwide. However, it cannot be said that these publications are sufficiently reflected in industrial applications, patents, and products.

In Table 5 below, the field-weighted citation effect and field-weighted download effect of the countries ahead of Türkiye in the ranking of publications in the field of AI between 2009 and 2018 are presented in detail.

Tablo 5. Field Weighted Citation and Download Impact Values of Countries in Artificial Intelligence Publications (2009-2018)

Field-Weighted Citation Impact		**Field-Weighted Download Impact**	
USA	1,787	**Italy**	1,567
UK	1,482	**Spain**	1,342
Canada	1,475	**Iran**	1,317
Australia	1,390	**Australia**	1,308
Germany	1,340	**UK**	1,217

continued on following page

Tablo 5. Continued

Field-Weighted Citation Impact		Field-Weighted Download Impact	
Italy	1,234	**Canada**	1,142
France	1,156	**Türkiye**	1,142
Spain	1,078	**Taiwan**	1,117
South Korea	1,021	**Germany**	1,075
Türkiye	0,915	**South Korea**	1,075
Iran	0,879	**USA**	1,058
China	0,823	**Brazil**	1,008
Taiwan	0,809	**France**	0,983
Brazil	0,780	**India**	0,983
Japan	0,745	**Japan**	0,800
India	0,738	**China**	0,767

Source: National Artificial Intelligence Strategy -2021-2025 Türkiye Report, 2021.

The field-weighted citation impact and field-weighted download impact indices in Table 2 above reveal that Türkiye is at the average performance level worldwide. Various factors affect the impact potential of academic studies, and Türkiye needs to improve this situation.

3. USE OF ARTIFICIAL INTELLIGENCE IN INTELLECTUAL PROPERTY

The concept of AI sometimes evokes negative associations, such as machines subjugating humanity and assuming control of the planet, or the presence of lethal robots. Nevertheless, even without delving into science fiction scenarios, it is feasible to observe the pervasive presence of AI in every aspect of our daily existence. From our mobile devices to the navigation systems in our vehicles, these technologies enhance our daily lives and are advancing swiftly, becoming increasingly autonomous. Advancements in the field of AI have led to the emergence of AI systems capable of generating intellectual goods. Annie, an AI created by David Cope, a musicology professor at the University of California Santa Cruz, can enhance its music composition through machine learning by incorporating feedback. Originally created for composing music, Annie eventually began independently writing poems that focused on Japanese culture (Gözübüyük, 2021: 56).

As mentioned before, Abbott (2020) defines the development of AI in five stages. Each stage addresses the impact of AI on human inventions at a different level. In these stages, a journey is depicted, starting from a period when human inventions were first developed entirely by humans to a future in which super-intelligent and self-improving AI dominates the innovation process. At this point, the following questions come to mind today: Are machine learning outputs and computer-generated creations protected by copyright, or should they be? However, current laws consider authorship to be entirely human in its current form (Samuelson, 2006). Other issues that come to mind at this point are as follows: Considering that AI is not a human being and that works produced by AI lack originality and creativity based on human personality, how valid and doctrinally correct is it to think that only works created by AI cannot be copyrighted? Furthermore, according to Craig and Kerr (2020), are there any works produced entirely by AI today?

In order to give a clear answer to this question, we need to make a distinction between artworks created by pure AI and AI-assisted artworks. AI solely produces Pure AI Creation Works, excluding any human personality or creative ideas from the process. Therefore, copyright cannot protect such works. However, human artistic and creative choices may have shaped AI-Assisted Works. case, the copyright may belong to the human creator or the person using the AI (Yanisky-Ravid and Velez-Hernandez, 2018). However, the question of whether copyright can protect works created solely through code emerges. Generally, copyright does not cover generative code-based works because they fail to meet the originality requirement. This is the case under existing laws in both the European Union and the United States. The law states that such works are often 'as free as air for common use' (Benkler, 1999). Therefore, code-generated works do not provide copyright protection.

The ability of AI to invent and produce creative works necessitates a re-evaluation of the traditionally human-centered concepts of authorship and inventorship. The fact that AI takes an active role in creative processes brings legal uncertainties, especially regarding the copyright ownership of these works. While traditional legal frameworks are based on the assumption that the subject in creative processes is human, the emergence of AI as an active actor in this field questions the adequacy of existing regulations (Abbott, 2020). New legal regulations are necessary, particularly concerning the ownership and protection of AI-produced content.

Furthermore, the discussion regarding whether AI should be acknowledged as inventors in patent applications is becoming increasingly significant on both a domestic and global scale. The speed, extent, and magnitude facilitated by AI restrict the efficacy of conventional IP protection approaches. In this environment, establishing a suitable legal framework for the breakthroughs and inventions produced by AI requires novel techniques in safeguarding IP. Both closing legal loopholes and formulating suitable laws for emerging technologies will be crucial in mitigating the impact of AI on the creative economy and making positive contributions to society. However, conversely, it is also contended that the expansion of copyright hampers innovation and cultural variety, and even jeopardizes fundamental liberties. Another viewpoint contends that augmenting the current IP system with more layers is not a suitable remedy for mitigating the societal consequences of technological advancements.

In order to understand how the complex relationship between AI and IP is managed, it will be illuminating to analyze some cases that serve as important legal examples. These cases provide valuable insights into how courts have dealt with the challenges posed by AI. These examples are presented in Table 6 below.

Table 6. Important Legal Cases Involving AI and IP

Thaler v. US Patent and Trademark Office (USPTO)	In this case, the USPTO rejected patent claims for inventions created by an AI system called DABUS, stating that only human inventors can hold patents. The US District Court upheld this decision, emphasising the human-oriented nature of the current patent system (Fleming, 2007).
UK Intellectual Property Office's DABUS Decision	Similarly, in the United Kingdom, patent applications in which DABUS was named as the inventor were rejected. The Court emphasised that the term 'inventor' refers to an individual and the Court of Appeal upheld this decision (Dabus, 2022).
Copyright on Music Produced by Warner Music and AI	By entering into an agreement for AI-based music production, Warner Music has emphasised the commercial value of such works and reopened the debate on the copyrightability of AI-created content.
Google's 'Project Nightingale' and Data Privacy	While not a direct AI and IP case, Google's health data collection project raises important questions about the ownership and protection of data used in AI development (Schneble et al., 2020).

Source: Compiled by the authors from Hamza, et al., 2023.

CONCLUSION

The rapid development of AI technologies has presented new challenges and opportunities in IP protection. In particular, the increasing role of AI in creative processes necessitates a re-evaluation of legal and policy regulations in IP areas such as patents, copyrights, and trade secrets. In this context, public policies should be shaped taking into account the impacts of AI, both to ensure the protection of innovations and to maximize societal benefit.

An intellectual property law system that is revised and adapted to the dynamics of AI will both encourage foreign technology companies to invest in Türkiye and increase the likelihood of innovation and invention by encouraging R&D in the field of AI. This is expected to ultimately result in economic growth. And also, intellectual property law adapted to today's conditions may also lead to technology transfer from high-tech companies to the country. Moreover, the use of AI in finance sector to improve efficiency of marketing. As a result, it will contribute to the development of AI systems in Türkiye.

It is no coincidence that the amount allocated to R&D activities from the gross national product is the highest in the USA, Japan and Germany, which are among the most developed economies in the world. It is a fact that countries with strong intellectual property law systems are the most developed countries in the world. In addition, it has also been found that high growth rates have been achieved in countries where intellectual property law systems have been strengthened. As can be seen, a well-designed and effectively implemented intellectual property law system encourages people to engage in R&D activities, and this situation leads to economic growth.

REFERENCES

Abbott, R. (2020). *The Reasonable Robot: Artificial Intelligence and the Law*. Cambridge University Press. DOI: 10.1017/9781108631761

Aktürk, E. (2024). Telif Hakkının Yapay Zek Ürünleri Açısından Değerlendirilmesi. ÇÜHAD, (5), 192-235.

Ateş, M. (2003). *Fikir ve Sanat Eserleri Üzerindeki Hakların Kapsamı ve Sınırlandırılması*. Seçkin Publishing.

Becker, M. (2017). Rights in Data–Industry 4.0 and the IP Rights of the Future. Zeitschrift Fuer Geistiges Eigentum. *Intellectual Property Journal*, 9(3), 253–265.

Benkler, Y. (1999). Free as the Air to Common Use: First Amendment Constraints on Enclosure of the Public Domain. *SSRN*, 74, 354. DOI: 10.2139/ssrn.168609

Biber, A.E. (2016). Türkiye'de Fikri Mülkiyet Hakları Koruması Ekonomik Büyüme ve Teknoloji İhracatı İlişkisinin Karşılaştırılmalı Analizi. AİBÜ Social Sciences Journal, 16(3).

Craig, C., & Kerr, I. (2020). The Death of the AI Author. *Ottawa Law Review*, 52, 31.

Dabus. (2022). dabus. 53. DOI: 10.1007/s40319-022-01186-7

Dobbs, R., Manyika, J., & Woetzel, J. (2015). The Four Global Forces Breaking All the Trends. *McKinsey Global Institute*, 11(4), 1–5.

European Commission. (2020). Report on the Safety and Liability Implications of Artificial Intelligence, the Internet of Things, and Robotics. https://eur-lex.europa.eu/legal-content/EN/TXT/PDF/?uri=CELEX:52020DC0064&from=en

Fleming, D. S. (2007). US Patent and Trademark Office refuses registration of flavour trademark. 2(5). https://doiDOI: 10.1093/jiplp/jpm044

Gözübüyük, B. (2021). Yapay Zekanın Meydana Getirdiği Fikri Ürünlere İlişkin 5846 Sayılı Fikir ve Sanat Eserleri Kanunundaki Sorunlar ve Çözüm Önerileri. *Kırıkkale Law Review*, 1(1), 54–81.

Hamza, M., Khan, S., & Saeed, Z., & Sajida. (2023). The Impact of Artificial Intelligence on Intellectual Property Rights. *International Journal of Human Sciences*, 3(4), 312–319.

Helvacıoğlu, A. D., Eraslan, İ. H., & Bulu, M. (2004). Dijitalleşen Dünyada Fikrî Mülkiyet Haklarının Ülkeler Açısından Küresel Rekabet Avantajı Oluşturmadaki Yeri. *National Congress on Information, Economy and Management*, 485-493.

Ministry of Development. (2018). Eleventh Development Plan (2019-2023), Intellectual Property Rights Special Expertise Commission Report (No. KB 2997, ÖİK 778). Ankara.

Ministry of Development. (2023). Twelfth Development Plan (2024-2028), Intellectual Property Rights Special Expertise Commission Report (No. KB 2997, ÖİK 778). Ankara.

OECD. (2024). Regulatory Approaches to Artificial Intelligence in Finance. OECD Artificial Intelligence Papers, 24.

Özkan, A. (2022). Yapay Zekâ Tarafından Üretilen Fikir ve Sanat Ürünlerinin Korunması. *TBB Journal*, 2023(164), 207–238.

Parlakyıldız, F., & Güvel, E. A. (2015). Fikri Mülkiyet Hakları ve Bu Hakları Korumanın Ekonomik Önemi. *Niğde University Journal of Economics and Administrative Sciences*, 8(4), 29–39.

Samuelson, P. (2006). Challenges in Mapping the Public Domain. In Bernt Hugenholtz, P., & Guibault, L. (Eds.), *The Public Domain of Information*. Kluwer Law International.

Schneble, C.O., Elger, B.S., Elger, B.S., Shaw, D., & Shaw, D. (2020). Google's Project Nightingale highlights the necessity of data science ethics review. DOI: 10.15252/EMMM.202012053

Shlomit, Y.-R. (2017). Generating Rembrandt: Artificial Intelligence, Copyright, and Accountability in the 3A Era—The Human-Like Authors Are Already Here—A New Model. *Detroit College of Law at Michigan State University Law Review*, 659–726. https://ir.lawnet.fordham.edu/cgi/viewcontent.cgi?article=1955&context=faculty_scholarship

State Planning Organization. (2007). Intellectual and Industrial Rights Special Expertise Commission Report (Publication No. DPT:2728). Ankara.

Turkey, I. C. C. (n.d.). Promotion and Protection of Intellectual Property Rights in Turkey. International Chamber of Commerce. https://icc.tobb.org.tr/spot/docs/Turkey_ValueOfIP_TURKISH_F041613_LR.PDF

Uslu, M. N. (2023). Protection of AI-Generated Products and Examination Within the Context of the European Union and Turkish Copyright Laws (Unpublished master's thesis). Koç University, Türkiye.

World Intellectual Property Organization (WIPO). (2020). What is Intellectual Property? https://www.wipo.int/edocs/pubdocs/en/wipo_pub_450_2020.pdf

Yanisky-Ravid, S., & Velez-Hernandez, L. A. (2018). Copyrightability of Artworks Produced by Creative Robots and Originality: The Formality-Objective Model. *Minnesota Journal of Law, Science & Technology*, 19, 1.

Yıldız, A. (2022). Finans Alanında Yapay Zeka Teknolojisinin Kullanımı. *Pamukkale University Social Science Journal*, 52, 47–66.

Yücekal, Y. (2003). International Protection of Intellectual Property Rights: World Intellectual Property Organization (WIPO). Journal of International Economic Issues, 8. https://www.mfa.gov.tr/fikri-mulkiyet-haklarinin-uluslararasi-duzeyde-korunmasi---dunya-fikri-mulkiyet-orgutu-_wipo_.tr.mfa

Zakir, M.H., Khan, S., Saeed, Z., & Sajida. (2023). The Impact of Artificial Intelligence on Intellectual Property Rights. International Journal of Human and Society, 3(4), 312-319. https://www.researchgate.net/publication/376796618_The_Impact_of_Artificial_Intelligence_on_Intellectual_Property_Rights

Chapter 6

An Evaluation on the Legal Entity of Artificial Intelligence and Intellectual Property in Turkish Law

Derya Ateş
Hacettepe University, Turkey

ABSTRACT

The changing world order undoubtedly leads to a transformation in the rule of law. However, it is usually not possible to ensure synchronization between the two systems in terms of speed and change during this transformation. The development of artificial intelligence, its effects, problems, and question marks have led to the emergence of new and different discourses within legal systems and revealed many legal gaps. The first and most important question and problem is undoubtedly who can own the property of the work produced by artificial intelligence and whether artificial intelligence should be considered a person. This discourse is reminiscent of the debates in legal context during the surfacing of the legal entity concept. This study will first discuss the notion of artificial intelligence, then outline the work, owner of the work, and intellectual rights within the scope of Turkish Law of Intellectual Property Rights; focus on the notion of individual and types of individuals, as defined by Turkish Civil Code; and will lastly make an overall evaluation on artificial intelligence.

DOI: 10.4018/979-8-3693-8704-7.ch006

ARTIFICIAL INTELLIGENCE AND LEARNING

According to the Turkish Language Association, the concept of intelligence refers to "the entirety of human abilities for thinking, reasoning, perceiving objective realities, judging, and drawing conclusions." (Turkish Language Association, 2024). The embodiment of intelligence—which is typically considered unique to humans—in artificial intelligence (AI) with its entirely different working principles and algorithms, opens up a significant area for debate. The main reason for the ambiguity and incomprehensibility of this concept lies in its lack of a visual, tangible, or objective form. Similar to the emergence of the concept of legal entities, discussions that start with a philosophical foundation are accompanied by technical feasibility debates when AI is involved.

The term artificial intelligence (Li & Du, 2007) was used for the first time in 1956 by American computer scientist John McCarthy, as a subfield of computer science (Lashbrooke, 1988). It is a broad term used to describe the execution of tasks requiring human-like intelligence by machines. Today, artificial intelligence systems have advanced to the point of replicating human behaviors and solving problems more quickly and efficiently than humans (Millington & Funge, 2009). While these AI systems are often perceived as merely technological constructs, they also give rise to significant legal questions and challenges.

The transfer of human-specific intelligence to AI, enabling autonomous use, is primarily achieved through "*machine learning*" and "*deep learning*" methods. The way human brains operate through neural connections, recognize objects through visual data, and classify these objects automatically has laid the groundwork for AI's ability to learn and create algorithms from examples, thereby facilitating machine learning (Hernández & Plasencia-Calaña, 2015).

Although machine learning allows AI to *learn like humans*, it does not make it *as intelligent as humans*. This gap led to the development of deep learning. Deep learning is, in fact, a subfield of machine learning and currently represents the most advanced technological capability of AI (Marr, 2024). It brings together vast quantities, sizes, and ranges of data to form "big data" and can be applied on highly powerful computers.

Machine learning sets rules for AI to mimic human behavior, whereas deep learning provides data based on a model inspired by the human brain, essentially training the computer to learn autonomously from the data (Peng, 2018). Therefore, no human intervention is required for processing the data. At this stage, it becomes possible for one AI system to train another AI system (Yanisky-Ravid, 2017).

While AI continues to expand its role in daily life, predictions about the coexistence of humans and AI-driven robots are rapidly spreading and gaining acceptance. Given the current inadequacy of legal rules in regulating social life, it is evident that addressing future scenarios like this one will pose significant challenges.

The fact that AI operates based on data that typically requires human intelligence highlights its significance in areas of human creativity as well. As a result, AI-driven machines, sometimes with human assistance and other times independently, are capable of creating artistic or innovative works, leading to their characterization as "creativity machines" (Hristov, 2017). At the heart of the questions arising from this development, both now and in the future, lies the issue of the "personhood of AI entities." Whether or not these entities will be granted personhood, and if so, how their legal status, rights, and responsibilities will be defined, are issues that will require a deeper examination of the concept of personhood itself.

CONCEPTS OF WORK AND AUTHOR

Artificial intelligence (AI) is defined as computer systems capable of performing tasks that typically require human intelligence. It has the potential to manifest in every domain traditionally reserved for human cognition, significantly influencing areas characterized by human creativity. Today, the use of AI systems in various fields such as music, visual arts, copywriting, product design, and poetry raises questions about copyright and intellectual property rights. The central and perhaps most crucial aspect of these discussions revolves around the question of *who* owns the copyright for works produced by AI, thus tying into the debate over the personhood of AI entities.

When examining traditional legal regulations on copyright, it becomes evident that they are grounded in the presumption that creativity is unique to independent human authors (Yanisky-Ravid, 2017). However, we have reached a point where autonomous, advanced computer systems can produce works independently and in creative, unexpected ways. This evolution challenges the existing framework: if such systems are capable of creating works without human input, who then is liable in potential copyright infringements?

Concepts of Work and Author in the Turkish Code of Obligations and the Law on Intellectual and Artistic Works

The Concept of Work. Under Turkish law, the main sources regulating works, authorship, and copyright are the Turkish Code of Obligations (TCO), the Law on Intellectual and Artistic Works (LIAW), and international agreements to which

Turkey is a party. These agreements include the Berne Convention (1951, 1995), the Stockholm Agreement (1975), the Agreement on Trade-Related Aspects of Intellectual Property Rights (TRIPS, 1995), and the Marrakesh Treaty (2021). However, it is important to note that the concept of a "work" is not identically defined in the TCO and the LIAW. Within the context of the TCO, a work is viewed as an object of production (TCO Article 470), and a party in a work contract is obligated to produce a tangible or intangible item in return for compensation. The produced object, in this case, is something with economic value and objectively identifiable characteristics. In contrast, within the framework of the LIAW, a work is not only assessed based on its economic value but also through its moral dimension, granting the author both economic and moral rights over it (Uslu, 2008).

While copyright is established upon the creation of a work, the LIAW provides direct legal protection to such works. According to LIAW Article 1/B-(a), a "work" is defined as "all types of intellectual and artistic products that bear the distinctive characteristics of their author and are categorized as works of science and literature, music, fine arts, or cinematography." Notably, for works that require intellectual effort, both in Turkish doctrine (Tekinalp, 2004) and in the rulings of the Turkish Court of Cassation, specific features are sought either explicitly or implicitly to qualify for protection:

Objective Criterion: Belonging to One of the Categories of Works Defined by the LIAW. The LIAW classifies types of works into four categories according to the principle of numerus clausus. These categories are scientific and literary works (LIAW Article 2), musical works (LIAW Article 3), works of fine arts (LIAW Article 4), and cinematographic works (LIAW Article 5). Intellectual products falling outside these four categories are not protected under the LIAW (Tekinalp, 2004). The law specifies that only intellectual products falling under these categories are considered works and provides examples accordingly. Moreover, adaptation and collection works are also protected under this regulation.

Subjective Criterion: Bearing the Author's Distinctive Character. The condition referred to as "distinctiveness" in the LIAW corresponds to the "originality" requirement found in international agreements and EU law. However, there are varying opinions in the literature about what constitutes distinctiveness. While Hirsch limits distinctiveness to "products that cannot be created by just anyone" (Hirsch, 1943, p. 12). Tekinalp defines it as "the author's creativity and intellectual effort expressed through style" (Tekinalp, 2004, p. 99). Ateş, on the other hand, describes it as "the author's unique characteristics being reflected in the work." (Ateş, 2007, p. 79).

The Turkish Court of Cassation considers distinctiveness the most critical factor separating intellectual efforts from those that qualify as protectable works. The Court emphasizes this distinctiveness through terms such as "specificity," "novelty," "uniqueness," "originality," "not copied from any source," and "creative quality," also noting that the manner in which an author's distinctiveness is reflected varies across different types of works[1]. It also applies the criteria of "not being ordinary" and "possessing a certain level of creativity." In line with EU law, the Court restricts the required novelty to a "minimal level of creativity." (Yavuz et al., 2013, p. 66).

Formal Criterion: Taking Shape. The requirement of "taking shape" refers to the transformation of abstract ideas into forms that are perceivable by humans. Thus, abstract thoughts and ideas are not recognized as works under the LIAW (Öztan, 2008). The Court of Cassation explicitly states in its rulings that it is not the idea itself that is protected as a work, but rather the form and expression it takes[2] (Gök, 2024). These decisions align with both the TRIPS Agreement and the rulings of the Court of Justice of the European Union (CJEU). This shaping can be permanent or, as in the case of oral works, it can be temporary. Even unfinished works may be protected if they have reached a certain stage with specific characteristics (Tekinalp, 2004).

Resulting from Intellectual Effort. The idea that a work must result from intellectual effort is based on the view that the capacity for intellectual effort is a human trait. This requirement also implies that the author of a work can only be human. The prevailing opinion in the literature also holds that products created by non-human entities (animals or natural phenomena) cannot be protected as works (Öztan, 2008; Tekinalp, 2004).

Concept of Author. The person who creates the work is referred to as the author. There is no legal requirement for the formal recognition of authorship; it arises inherently upon the creation of the work (Tekinalp, 2004; Yavuz et al., 2013).

Although the term "natural person" was removed from the definition of authorship in the LIAW in 2004, it is still accepted that only natural persons can be recognized as authors. Since legal entities cannot engage in intellectual or creative activities or reflect their distinctiveness onto works, they cannot be considered authors[3]. This stance was explicitly affirmed in a 2015 ruling by the 11th Civil Chamber of the Court of Cassation, which clarified that in Turkish law, entities other than natural persons, particularly legal entities, cannot produce works recognized under the LIAW or hold the status of authorship.

However, the LIAW does establish some presumptions regarding authorship:

- For works made public, the person who uses their name or recognized pseudonym as the author, or the person commonly introduced as the author, is presumed to be the author until proven otherwise (Article 11).
- If no name or pseudonym is given as the author, or if a person is not commonly introduced as the author in published or disclosed works, the rights of authorship are to be exercised by the person who published, reproduced, or publicly performed the work (Article 12). Thus, a person who is not the

actual author may still be considered as such or exercise rights derived from authorship.

- For works created within the scope of an employment relationship, the ownership and moral rights of the work belong to the employed individual, while the employer has the right to exploit the economic rights arising from the work (Article 18).
  - This also applies to *legal entities*, meaning that while the authorship and moral rights of a work created by a legal entity's organs belong to the creator, the economic rights belong to the legal entity (Tekinalp, 2004; Kılıçoğlu, 2023).
  - Furthermore, as explained above, if the name of the employing natural or legal person is placed on the work instead of the employed individual's name and the work is publicly presented in this form, the employing natural or legal person may be recognized as the author according to LIAW Article 11. If the work is made public without naming either the employed individual or the employing entity, the employing natural or legal person may exercise authorship rights under LIAW Article 12 (Ateş, 2007).

Concepts of Work and Author in International Agreements

The most significant international agreements in terms of both European Union Law and Turkish Law are the Berne Convention for the Protection of Literary and Artistic Works (or Berne Convention) (World Intellectual Property Organization, n.d-a), the World Intellectual Property Organization (WIPO) Copyright Treaty (WCT) (World Intellectual Property Organization, n.d-b), and the Agreement on Trade-Related Aspects of Intellectual Property Rights (TRIPS) (World Trade Organization, n.d.).

While the TRIPS and WCT treaties do not explicitly define the concept of a work, they both reference the Berne Convention (WCT Article 1/4, TRIPS Article 9/1). According to Article 2 of the Berne Convention, literary and artistic works are defined as follows:

The expression 'literary and artistic works' shall include every production in the literary, scientific, and artistic domain, whatever may be the mode or form of its expression, such as books, pamphlets and other writings; lectures, addresses, sermons and other works of the same nature; dramatic or dramatico-musical works; choreographic works and entertainments in dumb show; musical compositions with or without words; cinematographic works to which are assimilated works expressed by a process analogous to cinematography; works of drawing, painting, architecture, sculpture, engraving and lithography; photographic works to which are assimilated works expressed by a process analogous to photography; works of applied art; illustrations, maps, plans, sketches, and three-dimensional works relative to geography, topography, architecture, or science.

In terms of authorship, none of the Berne Convention, TRIPS, or WCT treaties provide a definition. This has led to debates in legal doctrine about whether authorship should be limited to humans and whether legal entities can qualify as authors. The Berne Convention specifies a protection period of fifty years after the author's life (Article 7/1), suggesting that authorship is only applicable to natural persons. However, some scholars argue that authorship does not necessarily need to be limited to humans (Bonadio & Lucchi, 2018). When examining countries that are members of the Berne Convention, it is evident that legal systems in the Anglo-Saxon tradition tend to be more flexible regarding the requirement for the author to be a natural person (Goldstein & Hugenholtz, 2019). Nonetheless, in all member states, literary and artistic works are generally required to be the result of the author's intellectual effort and must not be copied from another work. As a result, the Berne Convention emphasizes that protection is only possible for works based on human intelligence and creativity. Therefore, works produced by artificial intelligence cannot be considered "works" under this convention (Goldstein & Hugenholtz, 2019).

THE CONCEPT OF PERSON AND ITS TYPES WITHIN THE FRAMEWORK OF THE TURKISH CIVIL CODE (TCC)

Overview

Law is a set of binding rules regulating social relationships among people, determining their mutual rights and obligations, and imposing material sanctions when necessary. *The law maintains its existence through persons*, as they are the subjects who hold the rights and obligations regulated by legal rules.

In legal terms, the term "person" is *used to refer to entities capable of holding rights and obligations.* Therefore, every entity that is granted the capacity to possess rights and obligations by the legal system is considered a "person." In this context, the term "person" is synonymous with the term "legal capacity" since every person, as a subject of rights, also has the capacity to possess rights and obligations.

From a legal perspective, a person is any entity to whom the legal system grants the capacity to be the holder and subject of rights, making the concept of *person* entirely a legal construct rather than a natural one. This is because the determination of which entities qualify as *persons* is entirely within the jurisdiction of the legal system. The term used by the Romans to describe a *person*, as a subject of rights, clearly and meaningfully reflects this reality. In Roman law, the term *persona* was used to refer to the subject or holder of rights. The modern equivalents in Western languages, such as "personne" in French and "Person" in German, are derived from the Roman term *persona*. In Rome, the *persona* was originally a type of mask worn by actors when they appeared on stage (Capitant, 1936). By referring to entities capable of holding rights and obligations as *persona*, the Romans essentially conveyed the notion that the capacity to be a person is like a mask that is *worn* by certain entities as determined by the legal system (Akipek et., 2024).

As seen in this definition, the concept of *person* has two dimensions. One is the active dimension, which refers to the capacity to possess rights. The other is the passive dimension, referring to the capacity to hold obligations. The passive dimension of the concept of person does not mean that a person is capable of incurring obligations solely through their own acts and transactions. Similarly, it does not imply that a person has the capacity to fulfill their obligations personally. The passive dimension of the concept of *person* merely indicates that persons possess the capacity to hold obligations, duties, and liabilities. This also signifies that even if a person lacks the capacity to incur obligations through their own actions or transactions—for example, if they are a minor or suffer from a mental illness—they are still recognized as a *person* in the eyes of the law and therefore possess the capacity to hold obligations (Akipek et., 2024).

Types of Persons

The concept of a person is entirely *a legal construct.* Since it is the legal system that grants the capacity to hold rights, it also falls upon the legal system to determine which entities are recognized as persons (Huber, 1901). This issue is particularly relevant to considerations surrounding artificial intelligence (AI).

However, considering the long journey from the era of slavery to the recognition of every human being as a person. Traditionally, legal systems recognize two categories of persons:

- Natural Persons (Real Persons): Human beings.
- Legal Persons (Artificial Persons): Entities that are organized for a specific purpose and possess their own independent existence, such as associations or corporations.

Modern legal systems do not currently attribute personhood to any entities other than these two categories. However, just as in the case of animals, the legal system can create areas of protection for other entities without necessarily recognizing them as persons. This framework should also be considered when assessing AI.

The Concept of a Natural Person. Natural persons are human beings. The Universal Declaration of Human Rights, adopted by the United Nations on December 10, 1948, clearly affirms that every human being possesses legal capacity and is regarded as a person before the law (Articles 1, 2, 4, and 6).

The status of natural persons as "persons" is limited to a temporary period—the duration of their lives, in accordance with the laws of nature. Does this temporary nature of personhood potentially lead to *ownerless rights*? From the perspective of the Turkish legal system, it is essential to note that there can be no rights without an owner or a subject. Upon a person's death, their estate immediately passes to their heirs as a whole without any further legal process (Turkish Civil Code, Articles 575 and 599). Given that the state is the final legal heir, there can be no rights without an owner in Turkish law.

It is important to remember that not all human beings were always recognized as persons in the legal sense throughout the various stages of human history. The universal acceptance of all humans as persons—regardless of factors like origin, gender, age, nationality, or social status—is a relatively modern concept. Even in Roman law, people were classified as either "free" or "slave." Only those who were free were considered persons and, therefore, had legal capacity. Slaves, who were not recognized as legal persons, lacked the capacity to possess rights and obligations. The institution of slavery, which divided humans into those with and without rights (i.e., free and enslaved), persisted until the Middle Ages and continued in different forms, such as serfdom, until the French Revolution and beyond. The legal recognition of every human being as a person only became possible after the abolition of slavery.

The Concept of Legal Persons. The capacity to hold rights and obligations is not exclusive to humans, i.e., natural persons. Historically and in modern times, certain groups of individuals and property, granted the capacity to hold rights and obligations by the legal system just like humans, also exist within society. These groups, which have been recognized by the legal system as capable of holding rights and obligations—i.e., as "subjects of rights" (persons)—are referred to as legal persons.

Legal persons are entities that have emerged due to the needs of social life. This is because, as individuals, humans possess limited capabilities both morally and materially. Moreover, humans are transient beings; their lifespan is uncertain and relatively short. For this reason, they are not always suited to engage in activities that require long-term and sustained efforts, nor to see such efforts through to completion.

The essence or structure of a legal person, the subject of rights, is founded on two main components. The first is a group of individuals who come together with a common goal, such as defending a shared interest, meeting a mutual need, or jointly conducting a continuous activity, dedicating their efforts to achieving this purpose. The second component is the allocation of assets or properties to serve the realization of this common goal. In the first case, a "group of persons" is formed, while in the second, a "group of assets" gives rise to a legal person.

For such groups to acquire the status of "person" i.e., to gain the capacity to hold rights and obligations separately and independently from the individuals comprising them, this capacity must be granted by the legal system—it must be given "legal personality". This is similar to the early period of Roman law, where being human did not automatically entail recognition as a "person" before the law.

To achieve the status of a legal person, a group of individuals or assets must possess three essential elements: purpose, will, and organization. First, the individuals who come together must share a common purpose that concerns all members and is agreed upon collectively. This purpose may be material or moral. There must also be a collective intent to form a group around this common purpose, thereby creating a new entity with its own personality. Finally, the group must be organized in a manner that facilitates the achievement of its common purpose; in other words, it must possess the organs necessary to fulfill the functions required to reach its intended goal.

The recognition of legal persons by the legal system was not an easy process. The acceptance of legal personality involved the development of various theories and opinions put forward by prominent jurists over many years. This situation is reminiscent of the current debates regarding artificial intelligence. While these theories may seem outdated today, a brief mention of them is useful, as they provide important context for thinking about AI—currently not recognized as a person but the subject of considerable discussion.

The Fiction Theory. The Fiction Theory, proposed by the renowned German jurist Savigny, focuses on the concepts of "right" and "subject of rights" (Savigny, 1841). According to this theory, rights are powers granted by the legal system to entities that possess willpower. Thus, only humans, as beings with willpower, can be subjects of rights. However, groups of people or assets known as legal persons also have certain rights and obligations. Since these groups lack willpower, they cannot possess these rights and obligations independently. The legislature, driven by public interest and to prevent the emergence of ownerless rights, treats these groups as if they were persons. In short, legal personality is nothing but a virtual, fictional, artificial personality created by the legal system for practical and technical reasons. Essentially, this theory suggests that the legislature can grant virtual, fictional, or artificial personality to entities without willpower, thus giving them the capacity to be subjects of rights alongside willful human beings. The theory derives its name—"fiction theory" —from this very principle.

The Theory of Purpose-Driven Assets. Some views that consider only human beings as subjects of rights completely deny the existence of legal personality. They argue that "apart from the individuals who come together for a particular purpose, there is no artificial person as posited by the Fiction Theory that exists separately and independently". Proponents of this theory, which seeks to deny legal personality altogether, present their arguments in different forms. According to some, a legal person is merely an asset without an owner, designated for a specific purpose. Others argue that groups of individuals and assets around a purpose do not possess an independent personality. The rights and obligations attributed to a legal person actually belong collectively to all the individuals gathered around that purpose. This view entirely rejects the existence of a legal person as a subject of rights and equates it to a partnership or co-ownership, thereby earning the name "theory of collective ownership".

The Reality Theory. The Reality Theory (Realitätstheorie) was first defended by the German jurist Beseler and initially found support among other German jurists. Gierke and Zitelmann in Germany and Eugen Huber in Switzerland are known proponents of this theory. According to the Reality Theory, a legal person is not a fictional, non-existent, artificial entity created by law. Instead, a legal person is an entity that arises out of social necessities, possessing an existence separate and independent from the individuals who created it. A legal person is a real, natural, and practical entity that emerges autonomously to address social needs. Legal persons existed even before they were recognized as persons by the legal system. The legal system merely formalized these pre-existing entities by granting them legal personality; it did not create them. Therefore, legal persons are as real and practically existent as natural persons. The difference lies in the fact that, unlike natural persons, legal persons do not possess a tangible, visible, physical existence. This distinction arises from the differences in structure and nature between the two types of persons. While natural persons are both legal and physiological entities, legal persons are social entities that arise due to social needs. In philosophical and natural terms, legal persons are not "persons"; they are only considered persons in a legal sense.

EVALUATION OF ARTIFICIAL INTELLIGENCE IN TERMS OF PERSONALITY AND COPYRIGHTS

The Issue of Artificial Intelligence's Personality

General Overview. One of the key factors that make the concept of artificial intelligence (AI) vague and difficult to comprehend is its lack of a visual, objective, or tangible form. However, AI's increasing application across all aspects of life, along with its technical advancements, has introduced new questions and challenges regarding its use. All these questions essentially stem from the issue of AI's personality. This is because the legal system constructs its framework based on rights and obligations attributed to the concept of a "person". Therefore, the answer to AI's personality problem will address all current and future questions concerning AI that need to be resolved.

Undoubtedly, at first glance, questioning whether machines or robots—which are essentially "things"—can be considered persons, even if they are labeled as "intelligent" may seem meaningless and unnecessary. However, as technology progresses and AI systems become increasingly autonomous and capable, their use begins to blur the boundaries of human responsibility. Discussions have become more frequent, ranging from determining who should own the copyrights of AI-generated works to identifying responsibility for damages caused by self-driving AI-powered vehicles.

Criteria for Granting Personality. The fact that AI does not possess an objective physical existence and is defined as a relatively abstract concept has led to different criteria being used to assess whether it is suitable for personality recognition.

The first of these criteria is AI's *ability for environmental interaction, communication skills, and complex thinking*. It is generally accepted that a person must engage in meaningful interaction with their environment to be recognized as a person. This interaction should be multidirectional, advanced, and take place in a stimulus-response manner. For AI to meet this criterion, it must be able to receive environmental data, interpret it, decode signals, and send back mental data to generate counter-responses (Hubbard, 2011). This includes understanding what is said, making inferences, forming appropriate responses in words, and communicating effectively. Additionally, AI should demonstrate advanced social abilities typically associated with humans to be considered capable of acting with understanding. These abilities include being "non-mechanical," having the flexibility to give different responses, possessing the experience and skills to interpret ambiguous messages, and distinguishing between various elements to draw similarities in different situations (Lashbrooke, 1988).

To assess whether AIs behave like humans, Allen Turing proposed the "Turing Test". In this test, a human interacts with two computers behind a wall: one controlled by a human and the other by an AI. The tester asks questions and receives answers, attempting to discern whether the responses are from a human or an AI. At advanced stages of the test, some AIs have proven to be indistinguishable from humans (Turing, 1950).

Another criterion is *the capacity for personal ability and consciousness to fulfill life goals and plans*. Consciousness, often cited as the distinguishing feature between humans and animals, cannot be strictly defined as an essential criterion. This is because it creates contradictions for those who lack capacity for discernment or for legal persons (Hubbard, 2011; Ersoy, 2017). Consciousness requires a person to be a subject that can design plans for their life (Hubbard, 2011). It is undeniable that this planning will differ for each person, depending on environmental factors, individual lifestyles, and varying character traits. Even though AI entities have the capacity to execute plans assigned to them, expecting them to possess human-like emotions is undoubtedly difficult. Moreover, what is expected here is that the entity possesses emotions that can give meaning to its existence (Hubbard, 2011).

The final criterion considered in the evaluation is *the capacity for living in society*. To live in society, one must be able to protect conflicting individual interests and, while doing so, establish a balance between mutual rights and freedoms. The capacity to live in society also brings about responsibility. If AI entities are to be granted personality, their relationships with other members of society, as well as their mutual rights and obligations, must be regulated. The most critical aspect here is whether AI can attain a level of consciousness that allows it to establish this balance of interests (Zimmerman, 2024). An ethical subject is an individual who acts not only for their own benefit but also takes into account the interests of others (Ersoy, 2017).

Views on the Legal Status of Artificial Intelligence

Views that Do Not Grant Personhood to AI. The first view on the legal status of AI, which denies it personhood, is the “thing theory.” This perspective argues that AI should not be granted personhood and should remain categorized as “things.” Under this view, AI would continue to be owned by natural or legal persons (Thomas, 2014). However, given the cognitive features, autonomy, speed, and data analysis capabilities of AI—which distinguish it from a simple object—these attributes must be considered. When one recalls the case of Microsoft's AI chatbot “Tay”, which had to be shut down within 16 hours of its 2016 launch due to its unforeseen rapid learning, it becomes evident that AI cannot simply be treated as an object owned by someone. Today, with developments such as ChatGPT, AI chatbots have demonstrated capabilities that allow them to differentiate themselves from humans based on their lack of emotions, consciousness, learning experience, physical presence, creativity, intuition, and perception of time.

Another viewpoint in the doctrine is the “slave theory”, which also denies AI any status other than that of a “thing” and argues that AI should be treated as a servant or slave to humans (Alexandre, 2017; Bozkurt Yüksel & Bak, 2018). The principle of ownership that has prevailed since Locke, which entitles humans to own what they produce, is extended to AI products under this view. However, slavery is a concept that has long been abandoned in modern legal systems and is seen as something undesirable to return to. Given the centuries of struggle to abolish slavery, the idea of assigning such a legal status to AI would not provide a viable legal solution.

Views that Grant Personhood to AI. The principle that rights and obligations can only belong to entities recognized as persons by the legal system has led to arguments in favor of granting personhood to AI. One such view suggests that AI could be granted a form of legal personality akin to corporations and associations, even if it is not the same as the natural personhood held by humans (Eidenmüller, 2017; Calverley, 2024; Bak, 2018; Bayamlıoğlu, 2008). The social needs that led to the emergence of the concept of legal personality have historically manifested in varying intensities and played a significant role in the creation of groups of people and assets that meet society's needs. The same social need exists today for AI entities. From this perspective, AI establishes a system that closely resembles the relationship between a legal entity and its organs through its connections with those who create and control it.

As these debates continue, a particularly noteworthy recommendation and suggestion came from the European Parliament's report dated January 27, 2017, which proposed that AI be granted a new type of personality—an "electronic personality", different from both natural and legal persons (Bozkurt Yüksel & Bak, 2018). This report is the first official document to propose a personality status for AI entities and is highly appropriate for the unique (sui generis) nature of these entities. It suggests that each AI system be registered in an official registry and that in cases where compensation responsibility arises, special funds established for AI entities should be utilized. Another key proposal in the report is that AI systems should be held legally responsible for the damage they cause.

By 2024, the European Parliament has adopted the first AI regulation, known as the "Artificial Intelligence Act". Formally agreed upon by EU member states in May, this regulation is expected to come into effect in 2026, although some provisions may take effect earlier. The act primarily regulates "high-risk" AI systems, prohibiting those with the potential to harm society, such as those influencing human behavior, exploiting vulnerabilities, or engaging in biometric classification. However, the regulation does not include concepts like granting AI "electronic personality". Instead, it focuses on topics such as the ethical use of AI, transparency, safety, and accountability. Therefore, while the idea of an electronic personality continues to be discussed theoretically, it has not been incorporated into the current legal framework of the European Union.

Another view stemming from the evolution of legal systems in recognizing non-human entities as persons, drawing from the concept of legal personality, is the idea of granting AI a new type of personality that is non-human. In this context, legal persons are groups of people or assets directed toward a specific purpose, recognized as having a fictional personality beyond that of their human creators. Like AI, they are not humans and do not possess the autonomous characteristics unique to humans. Therefore, proposing new models of personality for entities like AI, which have human-like characteristics but are not humans, has become necessary (Bak, 2018). The recently introduced concept of the "non-human person" has sparked discussions on this topic (Bak, 2018; Ersoy, 2017). Although AI systems possess autonomy and cognitive capabilities similar to human skills, they are not human and do not fit within the rights status specific to natural persons. Therefore, they should be treated as legal subjects under a different conceptual framework.

Evaluation. First and foremost, it must be reiterated that determining "which entities will be considered persons is a matter of legal policy." Ultimately, it is up to the legislature within each legal system to decide how the concept of a person is defined and which entities are granted personhood.

In the context of AI, it is crucial to carefully consider the historical development, philosophical underpinnings, and legal and technical analyses of the concept of personhood, as explained in detail above.

One of the main obstacles to granting AI personhood today seems to be the perception that legal rules are exclusively applicable to humans and are merely social norms regulating human relationships. However, similar processes occurred during the emergence of the concept of legal persons, which broadened the definition of personhood beyond natural human beings to include legal entities.

As philosophical debates continue regarding AI, we believe that these discussions should also encompass technical considerations to find appropriate solutions. With the advancements in "deep learning," developments once only seen in movies have reached an inevitable point. AI has gained a level of autonomy that surpasses human behavior and capabilities. Ignoring developments related to AI entities could be seen as an avoidance of emerging and potential legal issues.

In our opinion, granting personhood to AI entities and recognizing their legal existence within defined boundaries is far more appropriate than categorizing them as objects or slaves. While doing so, however, AI should be classified with a new and proper legal status that clearly defines its rights and obligations. Just as the beginnings and endings of personhood are defined for natural and legal persons, so too should the life cycle of AI's legal status be delineated with clear boundaries. Although the European Parliament proposed the concept of "electronic personhood," the fact that this was not incorporated into the adopted AI Act suggests that the idea may not be easily embraced. Nonetheless, whether AI is recognized as an electronic person or granted a unique form of personhood, the core issue is fundamentally about how liability arising from AI systems is determined. The AI Act of the European Parliament also suggests that high-risk AI systems be registered to monitor and supervise their compliance with certain standards.

The social necessities that led to the emergence of legal persons have always been felt with varying degrees of intensity throughout history and have significantly contributed to the formation of groups of people and assets to meet societal needs.

Consequently, legal systems, driven by social necessities, have had to recognize these groups as legal entities. Legal entities, thus recognized as having rights and obligations, gained the status of subjects of rights (persons), just like natural persons. Therefore, they are not virtual but real entities that exist in society alongside natural persons. Although their social nature prevents them from being tangible and visible like natural persons, their presence is always felt. Hence, it is incorrect to describe legal persons as "artificial" entities created by law. As previously mentioned, legal persons are communities formed by social necessities, but it is the legal system that recognizes them as separate and independent entities from their members. As a result, it cannot be claimed that there is a fundamental difference between natural and legal persons, as it is also the legal system that grants personhood to human beings.

A similar process is currently underway for AI products, paralleling what happened with legal entities. The recognition of all humans as capable of rights and obligations by the legal system—thus elevating them to the level of natural persons—was the result of a long historical process. It cannot be said that a long time has passed since the abolition of slavery. Nonetheless, a significant distinction exists between legal and natural persons: philosophical ideas and legal principles today demand that all humans be recognized as subjects of rights without any discrimination. Whether legal personality should be granted to groups of people or assets, however, is left to the discretion of the legal system.

Therefore, it is necessary to establish a legal status for AI entities that appropriately defines their responsibilities, rights, and capacity to act. Given the increasing autonomy of AI, it is clear that solutions cannot be found by classifying AI as merely an object or a slave. However, the scope, origin, and end of the personhood status to be granted to AI remain highly ambiguous. While it may be tempting to clarify this uncertainty through a more concrete concept like "electronic personhood," such status should be defined on solid and well-bounded foundations, keeping in step with technological advancements.

Issues of AI-Created Works and Copyright

General Overview. The question of copyright for works created by AI ultimately depends on whether AI is granted personhood. Historically, a fundamental rule has existed that copyright belongs to the actual creator of the work—the author.

But how should this be interpreted when the actual creator of literary or artistic works is AI? As detailed above, AI is essentially a computer program made up of different technical algorithms, to which information is provided. It currently lacks any recognized legal personhood, meaning it cannot have the legal status of authorship or the rights that come with it.

For AI systems that create intellectual and artistic works to claim "authorship" or "copyright" over these works, they must first be granted legal personality. The scope and type of such personhood, as previously discussed, would be subject to further evaluation.

As of now, there are no clear regulations in international agreements, EU law, or Turkish law about who should be considered the author of works created by AI systems. Current legal frameworks tend to operate under the assumption that only humans can engage in creative activities. This creates a legal uncertainty as to whether works produced by AI systems are eligible for copyright protection. Considering the risks posed by this ambiguity, it is clear that legislation is needed to address the protection of intellectual products created autonomously by AI systems.

Examination Based on AI Systems. Today, intellectual and artistic works created by AI systems fall into two categories. The first involves works produced with direct human guidance using AI as a tool; the second comprises works autonomously generated by AI systems without human intervention. Copyright considerations differ significantly between these two categories.

In processes where AI systems are used as a tool, the resulting works are produced based primarily on direct human intervention and decisions. Thus, the AI system essentially serves as a tool rather than having a distinct creative role.

In this case, the work produced—whether a piece of music or a painting—is directly influenced by the information provided to the AI by its user and is proportionate to the user's contributions and expectations. The final work will not surprise its creator (Hristov, 2017). The most well-known example of this application is photos taken with smartphones. Most modern cameras are entirely digital, containing both computer processors and software that make photography almost an automatic process. While AI significantly influences factors like lighting, color vibrancy, and focus, it is ultimately the person behind the camera who determines the elements within the frame and creates the composition.

When AI systems are used as tools, the individual who uses the AI to create the work is the one making all significant decisions throughout the creation process. If this individual produces a work that meets the necessary criteria for copyright protection, they will be considered the author of the work and will hold the rights and privileges conferred by copyright (Gök, 2024).

The issue of copyright becomes more complex when AI operates autonomously, without human direction. The primary question here is who holds the copyright for the work as its author. For such a work to be eligible for copyright protection, it must meet certain criteria, such as being concretely expressed, originating from intellectual effort, and being original. However, it should be noted that there are ongoing debates as to whether works created by AI systems meet the creativity and originality requirements.

The relationship between copyright and intellectual products autonomously produced by AI systems can be categorized into three main perspectives within academic discourse: the Romantic School, the Revolutionary School, and the Modern School (Ballardini et al., 2019). Without delving into these perspectives in detail, it is important to note that legal systems must establish regulations to provide protection in this context, ensuring legal certainty and maintaining the systematic integrity of copyright.

It is evident that works created autonomously by AI should also be protected as intellectual and artistic works. The crucial question then becomes: Who is the author entitled to such protection? At this point, the ongoing debates about whether to grant personhood to AI become particularly significant. Since AI has not yet been granted a separate and independent legal status, it cannot be considered the author of its own works.

Currently, despite their apparent autonomy or independence, it is possible to identify the humans to whom the creative activities of today's AI systems can be attributed. In this sense, it seems difficult to accept AI systems as creative subjects on their own (Gunkel, 2021). Until the legal status of AI is clarified, establishing a system in which the human or legal persons behind the AI are recognized as the rights holders seems more appropriate, both in terms of current technological conditions and intellectual property law.

In the context of Turkish law, this issue must be interpreted according to LIAW (Law on Intellectual and Artistic Works) Article 1B/b. The relevant article defines the author as the person who creates the work. In its second section, the law further states:

> *The author of a work is the person who creates it. In the case of adaptations and compilations, the author is the person who adapts it, provided that the rights of the original author are preserved. For cinematographic works, the director, original music composer, screenwriter, and dialogue writer are co-authors. In the case of animated films, the animator is also among the co-authors.*

If this rule were applied directly, AI could be considered the author of the product it creates. However, as mentioned above, LIAW Article 2B/b uses the term "person," and in legal terminology, the concept of a "person" refers to natural persons who can hold rights and obligations. Since AI is not a natural person, it cannot hold copyright over the works it creates. Therefore, an issue arises that prevents the application of the principle that the creator of a work is presumed to be its author under the law. For this reason, some propose that Turkish law should amend LIAW Articles 1/B-(j) and 80 to recognize related rights for works created by computers (Yılmaztekin, 2021). However, as technological developments progress, the human influences behind AI are diminishing, making it increasingly difficult to identify rights holders within these systems. We believe that this journey will eventually lead to the clarification of the legal status and boundaries of AI systems.

REFERENCES

Akipek, J., Akıntürk, T., & Ateş, D. (2024). Türk Medeni Hukuku, Başlangıç Hükümleri, Kişiler Hukuku. [Turkish Civil Law, Preliminary Provisions, Law of Persons] *BETA Bulletin of Experimental Treatments for AIDS*.

Alexandre, F. M. (2017). *The Legal Status of Artificially Intelligent Robots* [Unpublished LL.M dissertation project]. Tilburg University, Tilburg, Holland.

Ateş, M. (2007). *Fikrî Hukukta Eser* [Work in Intellectual Law]. Turhan.

Bak, B. (2018). Medeni Hukuk Açısından Yapay Zekanın Hukuki Statüsü ve Yapay Zeka Kullanımından Doğan Hukuki Sorumluluk. *TAAD*, 9(35), 211-232. https://taad.taa.gov.tr/dergiler/taad/taad-35

Ballardini, R. M., He, K., & Roos, T. (2019). AI-Generated Content: Authorship and Inventorship in the Age of Artificial Intelligence. In Pihlajarinne, T., Vesala, J., & Honkkila, O. (Eds.), *Online Distribution of Content in the EU*. Edward Elgar Publishing. DOI: 10.4337/9781788119900.00015

Bayamlıoğlu, E. (2008). Akıllı Yazılımlar ve Hukuki Statüsü: Yapay Zeka ve Kişilik Üzerine Bir Deneme. In İnceoğlu, M. M. (Ed.), *Uğur Alacakaptan'a Armağan* (Vol. 2, pp. 131–140). İstanbul Bilgi University Publishing.

Bonadio, E., & Lucchi, N. (2018). *Non-Conventional Copyright: Do New and Atypical Works Deserve Protection?* Edward Elgar. DOI: 10.4337/9781786434074

Bozkurt Yüksel, A. E., & Bak, B. (2018) Yapay Zeka. In Bozkurt Yüksel, A. E., Bak, B., Reyhani Y. R. & Aslanova, K., *Futurist Hukuk* (pp. 5-37). [Futurist Law] Aristo.

Calverley, D. (2008). Imagining a non-biological machine as a legal person. *AI & Society*, 22(4), 523–537. DOI: 10.1007/s00146-007-0092-7

Cornu, G. (2022). *Vocabulaire Juridique* (14th ed.). Puf.

Eidenmüller, H. (20242017, March 8). Robot's Legal Personality [Online blog post]. https://blogs.law.ox.ac.uk/business-law-blog/blog/2017/03/robots'-legal-personalityRetrieved from www.law.ox.ac.uk/business-law-blog/blog/2017/03/robots'-legal-personality

Ersoy, Ç. (2017). *Robotlar, Yapay Zeka ve Hukuk* (2nd ed.). Oniki Levha.

Gök, B. (2024). Yapay Zekâ Sistemleri Tarafından Üretilen Fikri Ürünlerin Telif Hakkı [Copyright of Intellectual Products Generated by Artificial Intelligence Systems]. *Platon*.

Goldstein, P., & Hugenholtz, P. B. (2019). *International Copyright: Principles, Law and Practice*. Oxford Press.

Gunkel, D. J. (2021). Computational Creativity: Algorithms, Art, and Artistry in NAVAS. In *The Routledge Handbook of Remix Studies and Digital Humanities* (pp. 385-395). Routledge.

Hernández, M., Cheplygina, V., & Plasencia-Calaña, Y. (2015). *Dissimilarity Representations for Low-Resolution Face Recognition*. Springer International Publishing.

Hirsch, E. E. (1943). *Hukuki Bakımdan Fikri Say*. Istanbul University Publishing.

Hristov, K. (2017). Artificial Intelligence and the Copyright Dilemma. *The Journal of the Franklin Pierce Center for Intellectual Property*, 57(3), 431–454. https://ipmall.law.unh.edu/sites/default/files/hosted_resources/IDEA/hristov_formatted.pdf

Hubbord, F. P. (2011). Do Androids Dream: Personhood and Intelligent Artifacts. *Temple Law Review*, 83(2), 405-474. https://www.templelawreview.org/article/83-2_hubbard/

Huber, E. (1901). *Exposé des Motifs de l'avant-projet* (Vol. I).

Intelligence. (n.d.) In *Turkish Language Association online*.https://sozluk.gov.tr/?ara=zek%C3%A2

Kılıçoğlu, A. M. (2023). *Sınai Haklarla Karşılaştırmalı Fikri Haklar* (9th ed.). Turhan.

Lashbrooke, E. C. (1988). Legal Reasoning and Artificial Intelligence. *Loyola Law Review*, 34, 287–310. https://loynolawreview.org

Li, D., & Du, Y. (2007). *Artificial Intelligence with Uncertainty*. Chapman and Hall/CRC. DOI: 10.1201/9781584889991

Marr, B. (2024). What is the Difference Between Artificial Intelligence and Machine Learning? https://bernardmarr.com/what-is-the-difference-between-artificial-intelligence-and-machine-learning/#:~:text=Artificial%20Intelligence%20is%20the%20broader,let%20them%20learn%20for%20themselves

Millington, I., & Funge, J. (2009). *Artificial Intelligence for Games* (2nd ed.). CRC Press. DOI: 10.1201/b13169

Öztan, F. (2008). *Fikir ve Sanat Eserleri Hukuku* [Intellectual and Artistic Works Law]. Turhan.

Peng, S. C. (2018). *Artificial Intelligence and Copyright: The Authors' Conundrum* [Paper presentation]. 15th WIPO-WTO Colloquium for Teachers of Intellectual Property, World Intellectual Property Organization and World Trade Organization.

Savigny, M. Ch. G. (1841). *Traité de Droit Romain* (Vol. 2). Librairie de Firmin Didot Frère, Imprimeurs de l'Institut de France.

Tekinalp, Ü. (2004). *Fikrî Mülkiyet Hukuku* (3rd ed.). Beta.

Thomas, P. (2014). *State of the Art on Legal Issues*. https://ethicaa.greyc.fr/media/files/ethicaa.delivrable.1.pdf

Turing, A. (1950). Computing Machinery and Intelligence. *Mind*, 59(236), 433–460. DOI: 10.1093/mind/LIX.236.433

Uslu, R. (2008). *Türk Fikir ve Sanat Hukukunda Eser Sahipliği* [Unpublished doctoral dissertation]. Ankara University Social Sciences Institute, Ankara, Turkey.

World Intellectual Property Organization. (n.d.-a). *Berne Convention for the Protection of Literary and Artistic Works*. https://www.wipo.int/wipolex/en/text/283693

World Intellectual Property Organization. (n.d.-b). *WIPO Copyright Treaty*. https://www.wipo.int/wipolex/en/text/295157

World Trade Organization. (n.d.) *Agreement on Trade-Related Aspects of Intellectual Property Rights (TRIPS)* https://www.wto.org/english/docs_e/legal_e/27-trips_01_e.htm

Yanisky-Ravid, S. (2017). Generating Rembrandt: Artificial Intelligence, Copyright and Accountability in the 3A Era—The Human-like Authors Are Already Here—A New Model. *Detroit College of Law at Michigan State University Law Review*, 4, 659–726. DOI: 10.17613/50p1-qy20

Yılmaztekin, H. K. (2021). *Yapay Zekanın Eser Sahipliği* [Authorship of Artificial Intelligence]. Adalet.

Zimmermann, E. J. (2015). Machine Minds, Frontiers in Legal Personhood.

ENDNOTES

1 Turkish Court of Cassation. Decision No. 13.3.2007, 11. HD,, E. 2006/934, K. 2007/4555; Turkish Court of Cassation. Decision No. 09.05.2017, 11. HD, E. 2017/2724, K. 2015/12923.

2 Turkish Court of Cassation. Decision No. 3.12.2007, 11. HD, E. 2006/12890, K. 2007/14256.

[3] Turkish Court of Cassation. Decision No. 4.02.2015, 11. HD. E. 2014/16277, K. 2015/1285.

Chapter 7
From Monkey Selfie Lawsuit to AI-Generated Art:
Where to Extend the Copyright Protection?

Dila Okyar
https://orcid.org/0000-0002-7829-2133
Hacettepe University, Turkey

ABSTRACT

In the digital age, music composed, poems written, and canvases painted by artificial intelligence equipped with deep learning techniques have revealed the need to re-think the fundamental concepts of intellectual property law. Once it is accepted as a work of authorship, the question of who the copyright holder arises. Is there really a need to re-think these conventional concepts or is the answer clear enough? Indeed, the legal debate of whether works created by non-human beings deserve copyright protection is not a problem specific to the digital age. The copyright status of a selfie taken by a monkey has been the subject of another extraordinary lawsuit, Naruto v. Slater. The purpose of this study is to examine the impacts of AI-generated artistic works on copyright law. In order to address the challenges created by non-human authors, with focus on AI-generated artistic works, the conventional concepts of intellectual property law are discussed to determine whether they are sufficient to handle the novel problems AI systems created.

DOI: 10.4018/979-8-3693-8704-7.ch007

THE RISE OF AI PAINTERS

Artificial intelligence (AI) is no longer the subject of pure science fiction. Among numerous legal issues that AI technologies brought in the legal world, the challenges it brings into intellectual property law are highly intriguing. Following AI doctors, AI judges, AI cars, now the legal world is trying to understand AI painters! As the level of sophistication and autonomy of AI systems grow, they start to create artistic products.

The paintings created by the robot painter *e-David* are fascinatingly creative. *e-David* does not copy existing works, but it creates autonomously from the pictures it takes with its camera. The legal challenge is determining who is entitled to licensing rights and who is responsible for copyright infringements (Yanisky-Ravid, 2017). The Portrait of Edmond de Balamy was the first AI-generated portrait ever sold at auction at 432,500 USD.

The challenges brought by the artistic works created by non-humans are not a new subject of the legal world. The lawsuit *Naruto v. Slater*, which is known as "Monkey Selfie case" (*Naruto v David John Slater, et al, Case No 3:15-cv-04324-WHO*), has brought novel questions about authorship rights. In 2011, a wildlife photographer David Slater leaves his camera unattended in a nature park in Indonesia. A crested macaque named Naruto turns the camera towards himself and with Slater's camera, takes his selfie photos, known as the 'Monkey Selfies'. Slater and Wildlife Personalities Ltd. uses Monkey Selfies in his published book for commercial purposes. Throughout the book, the involvement of Naruto is also mentioned as one of the picture is described as "*Sulawesi crested black macaque smiles at itself while pressing the shutter button on camera*". A non-governmental organization PETA (People for the Ethical Treatment of Animals), admittedly on behalf of Naruto against Slater and the publisher. It was alleged that Naruto's copyright rights have been infringed by publishing the Monkey Selfies. The courts discussed the following questions: "Who owns the copyright of Monkey Selfies?"

The US District Court for the Northern District of California dismissed the case on the ground that the animals have neither statutory standing nor authorship right under Copyright Act. The court held that:

Several provisions of the Copyright Act also persuade us against the conclusion that animals have statutory standing to sue under the Copyright Act. [...] For example, the "children" of an "author," "whether legitimate or not," can inherit certain rights under the Copyright Act. See 17 U.S.C. §§ 101, 201, 203, 304. Also, an author's "widow or widower owns the author's entire termination interest unless there are any surviving children or grandchildren of the author, in which case the widow or widower owns one-half of the author's interest." Id. § 203(a)(2)(A). The terms "children," "grandchildren," "legitimate," "widow," and "widower" all imply humanity and necessarily exclude animals that do not marry and do not have heirs entitled to property by law.

The works created by animals are found to be not copyrightable as such. Indeed, the findings of the court in *Monkey Selfie* case should be read in a broader sense. This case is not just about whether the US Copyright Act confers standing and authorship upon animals; the broader reading of the case suggests whether a copyright protection can be granted to non-human authors (Rosati, 2017). Interesting to note that it is Naruto who adjusts the angle of the camera and took his selfie pictures, while Slater adjusts the technical environment and the lens. Naruto's action is not limited to simply pressing the shutter; both Naruto and Slater contributed to the factors affecting the characteristics of the photo (Pehlivanoğlu, 2019). Unfortunately, the Naruto decision does not answer the major question of who enjoys ownership over a non-human-generated art, regardless of whether it is an animal or an AI (Hooker, 2020).

The issue gets more complicated with the involvement of AI in the creation process of an artistic work. Different from animal-created art, there is a human creator behind AI (Hooker, 2020). Is an artist entitled to bring a lawsuit against AI-related art project over copyright infringement? This novel copyright argument has been discussed in *Amel Chamandy / Galerie NuEdge Fine Arts v. Adam Basanta* where Canadian artist Amel Chamandy initiated a lawsuit against Adam Basanta involving copyright infringement claims because of an AI-generated work which has 85.81% similarity to her work titled as "Your World Without Paper". With the rapid development in AI technology, the legal policymakers and legislators cannot remain unreactive to these emerging legal issues.

Different Policy-Setting Scenarios

The issue of copyright authorship over AI-related intellectual property products is at its core related to the legal status of AI. Regarding liability law, the modern tendency argues that there is no need to attribute a separate personality to artificial intelligence and accept it as an independent subject of rights - at least for now - and that liability can be established by attributing the damage caused to one or more people within the framework of existing legal norms. How about copyright law? Which approach suits best to the nature of copyright legislation?

The legislators must be attentive to address the novel challenges of copyright law brought by the highly creative potential of autonomous AI systems. Different policy-making approaches may be grouped under four headings. First is solving the complex new problems with the traditional concepts of copyright law by giving them new meanings through interpretation. Second is, considering the main objectives of copyright law and possible options, introducing a new model of protection. Third is granting legal personality to AI. Fourth is adopting a public domain approach and treating AI-generated works as public property.

Each policy approach has its own drawbacks. The problem with the first approach is the fact that the traditional copyright law rests on the notion of "human authorship" (Gaffar&Albarashdi, 2024) whereas AI-generated artistic works remove the human factor behind the creation. The existing copyright law in most countries adopt a human-centered approach (Burylo, 2022). Regarding a new model for protection, complex situations may lead to problems since dozens of people are involved in the process of creation (Burylo, 2022).

European Parliament, in resolution of 16 February 2017 with recommendations to the Commission on Civil Law Rules on Robotics (2015/2103(INL) underlines (§ Z.AI) that the current legal framework would not be sufficient to cover the damage caused by the new generation of robots, insofar as they can be equipped with adaptive and learning abilities entailing a certain degree of unpredictability in their behaviour, since those robots would autonomously learn from their own variable experience and interact with their environment in a unique and unforeseeable manner.

Subsequently, the European Parliament proposes the establishment of the status of electronic persons in the long run at least for the most sophisticated autonomous robots (§ 59(f)). Whereas in resolution of 20 October 2020 with recommendations to the Commission on a civil liability regime for artificial intelligence (2020/2014(INL), the European Parliament notes that (§ 7), all physical or virtual activities, devices or processes that are driven by AI-systems may technically be the direct or indirect cause of harm or damage, yet are nearly always the result of someone building, deploying or interfering with the systems; notes in this respect that it is not necessary to give legal personality to AI-systems.

Last of all, the public domain approach has the potential to lead to a lack of incentives for high-tech companies to invest in AI technologies due to lack of copyright protection (Burylo, 2022; Gözübüyük, 2021).

A Quick Glance at Basic Concepts of AI Law

Intelligence refers to the totality of ability to think, reason, perceive objective facts, judge, and draw conclusions. AI, on the other hand, is a computer program that imitates human intelligence. It exhibits the characteristic features and abilities specific to natural intelligence such as mental abilities such as thinking, reasoning, problem solving, planning and social abilities such as understanding people's emotions, engaging in social interaction. AI is software, a computer program which does not require a physical existence (Richards&Smart, 2016). According to the EU AI Act, published on 12 July 2024 in the EU Official Journal, under Art. 3(1), "AI system" is defined as "*[m]achine-based system that is designed to operate with varying levels of autonomy and that may exhibit adaptiveness after deployment, and that, for explicit or implicit objectives, infers, from the input it receives, how to generate outputs such as predictions, content, recommendations, or decisions that can influence physical or virtual environments*".

Autonomy refers to the degree of independence of a machine or system from human control while performing its assigned task. As the level of artificial intelligence increases, so does the level of autonomy. Machine learning (ML) refers to computers learning from their own experiences and the experiences they gain by interacting with their environment, improving their performance, and thus becoming autonomous and "more intelligent" over time. ML-based AI with full autonomy level function without human's control or supervision (Polat, 2023). An AI system with a higher degree of autonomy has the mechanism to learn from its own experiences without human intervention, make independent decisions, and implement these. It neither operates under direct human control nor perform predictable and automated behaviors (Polat, 2023). For example, an AI system can be equipped to produce a painting which is new and unpredictable, which goes far beyond copying existing works (Yanisky-Ravid, 2017).

The Question of Granting Copyright Protection to AI-Generated Artistic Works

As the Latin maxim "*bona diagnosis, bona curatio*" suggests, good diagnosis leads to good treatment. Legal qualification is of key importance as it is the preliminary stage of determining the legal solution. The legal qualification directly determines the applicable legal regime. Thus, it determines the type of solution to be applied. Reaching a satisfactory solution, both for the society and the individuals, requires the balance of interests.

THE LEGAL QUALIFICATION OF AI-GENERATED ARTISTIC WORKS AS INTELLECTUAL PROPERTY WORK

The Concept of "Work" in General

All types of subject matters that are protected by British copyright law are called as "works" (Bently *et al.*, 2022). Similarly, Turkish Intellectual Property Law adopts "work" as a core concept under the Law on Intellectual and Artistic Works, no. 5846 ("LIAW"). Additionally, under Turkish law, the concept of "work" is also found under law of obligations. Under Art. 470 of Turkish Code of Obligations, no. 6098 ("TCO"), the work contract is defined as a relationship "*whereby the contractor undertakes to produce a piece of work and the customer undertakes to pay the contractor for that work*". Although the same concept has two different meanings and scope of application under two different disciplines, it would be useful to briefly touch on their meaning in comparison.

The importance of the concept of work under TCO manifests itself in the expanded field of application over time. According to the prevailing doctrinal view, a product of human labor, which has an integrity within itself and has economic value is considered as a work in the sense of work contract (Aydoğdu, 2023; Olgaç 1967). It is currently accepted to encompass intangible obligations. Both material (tangible) and non-material (non-tangible) results can constitute the subject of a work contract. As long as they are the product of human labor and manifest themselves in a material entity, even non-material performances are accepted to qualify as a work. Examples of non-material results include translating a book, drawing of a construction project by an architect, giving a concert, organizing an art show, or a musician composing a composition (Aydoğdu, 2023; Kılıçoğlu, 2023). However, the subject of a work contract under TCO is exclusively restricted to products of human labor; the produced result must be attributable to a person (Kurşat, 2009). The results of spontaneous or natural events fall outside the scope of work contract.

Considering the non-material obligations that can be undertaken by a contractor, can it be asked whether there is some kind of connection between the concept of "work" under TCO and "intellectual and artistic work" under LIAW? Some commentators adopt a rather strict approach and find such a comparison unsuitable that it would not be accurate to consider them in connection with each other (Kurşat, 2009). It is argued that a work contract regarding the creation of an intellectual and artistic work will be subject to the provisions of art. 470 *et seq.* TCO whereas the intellectual property rights on the created work will be subject to protection under LIAW (Kılıçoğlu, 2023). However, each concrete case turns on its own facts. Rather than adopting such a definitive conclusion, a contextual analysis of the contract may lead to a mixed contract containing elements of a work or an agency contract, or a *sui generis* anonymous contract.

Art. 1/B-(a) of LIAW defines intellectual and artistic work as *"[a]ll kinds of intellectual and artistic work that bear the characteristic of its author and are deemed as works of science, literature, music, fine arts or cinema*". For a creation to qualify as an 'intellectual and artistic work', it must satisfy two conditions: it must bear the characteristic of its author (subjective criterion) and fall under one of the work categories stipulated under LIAW (objective criterion).

Applying the Originality Principle to AI-Generated Art

The definitive condition that distinguishes an intellectual effort from others and makes it protectable as an intellectual and artistic work is the subjective criterion. It basically means that it is shaped to reflect the identity of its author. The Anglo-Saxon legal system evaluates this specialty requirement with respect to the "originality" of the work, whereas the Continental European legal system evaluates it based on the personality and individuality of the author. The primary concern of the common law copyright model is the production of new works, whereas the civil *droit d'auteur* system is more concerned with the moral rights of authors (Bently *et al.*, 2022). Important to note that protection of artificial intelligence as a software or a computer program, and the protection of intellectual products created by that artificial intelligence are different legal issues (Yanisky-Ravid, 2017; Gözübüyük, 2021).

An artistic work is granted intellectual property protection to the extent that it is original. The principle of originality refers to the intellectual qualities that the author has exercised when creating the work, which the European conception refers to as "intellectual creation". The originality in copyright law and novelty in patent law are based on different assessments. Originality does not require novelty. The originality is not concerned whether the work is novel and unique; it focuses on the relationship between the work and the author to determine the input that the author has contributed (Bently *et al.*, 2022). The purpose of the originality requirement is to set a threshold for determining the eligibility of a work for copyright protection. The degree of originality defines the width of the scope of protection (Suluk *et al.*, 2022). If set at a very high level, it will be reduced to the artist's style and seen as his "seal and not every intellectual work may have satisfied this intensity of specialness. If set at a low level, very few instances will fall out of protection (Bently *et al.*, 2022).

Here, the following question arises: Is copyright law ready to deal with the challenging question of whether and to what extent computer-related or AI-generated works meet the requirements for copyright protection? For an artistic work to qualify for legal protection, should human involvement be a mandatory requirement? Is creativity a purely human attribute? Does creativity require a consciousness that is of human origin?

According to the conventional understanding of copyright law, individuality is a characteristic attributable only to human beings. Non-human beings such as machines, nature, animals and plants cannot be the creator of a work (Suluk *et al.*, 2022). Current discussions show that the traditional concepts of copyright law which present human-centered focus needs revisiting. Now the question is "whether increasingly sophisticated technologies, under the umbrella of artificial intelligence, would result in the broadening of the understanding of what (rather than who) an author is" (Rosati, 2017).

The Court of Justice of the European Union (CJEU) in *Painer* case (C-145/10), when discussing the 'originality', refers to it as a stamp on the work with the personal touch of the author:

As stated in recital 17 in the preamble to Directive 93/98, an intellectual creation is an author's own if it reflects the author's personality [...] As regards a portrait photograph, the photographer can make free and creative choices in several ways and at various points in its production. [...] By making those various choices, the author of a portrait photograph can stamp the work created with his 'personal touch'.

European Parliament Resolution of 20 October 2020 on intellectual property rights for the development of artificial intelligence technologies (2020/2015(INI)) highlights that:

[t]echnical creations generated by AI technology must be protected under the IPR legal framework in order to encourage investment in this form of creation and improve legal certainty for citizens, businesses and, since they are among the main users of AI technologies for the time being, inventors; considers that works autonomously produced by artificial agents and robots might not be eligible for copyright protection, in order to observe the principle of originality, which is linked to a natural person, and since the concept of 'intellectual creation' addresses the author's personality [...] recommends that ownership of rights, if any, should only be assigned to natural or legal persons that created the work lawfully and only if authorisation has been granted by the copyright holder if copyright-protected material is being used, unless copyright exceptions or limitations apply.

The similar approach seems to be adopted by WIPO in Revised Issues Paper on Intellectual Property Policy and Artificial Intelligence under para 16 which states that:

In most cases, AI is a tool that assists inventors in the invention process or constitutes a feature of an invention. In these respects, AI-assisted inventions might not differ radically from other computer-implemented inventions. However, it would now seem clear that the role of AI in the invention process is increasing, and there are cases in which the applicant has named an AI application as the inventor in a patent application.

The Compendium of the U.S. Copyright Office Practices (2021) explicitly provides that the Office will register work of authorship, if it was created by a human being. Compendium para. 306 provides the following:

The U.S. Copyright Office will register an original work of authorship, provided that the work was created by a human being. The copyright law only protects "the fruits of intellectual labor" that "are founded in the creative powers of the mind." Trade-Mark Cases, 100 U.S. 82, 94 (1879). Because copyright law is limited to "original intellectual conceptions of the author," the Office will refuse to register a claim if it determines that a human being did not create the work. Burrow-Giles Lithographic Co. v. Sarony, 111 U.S. 53, 58 (1884).

European Parliament, in its aforementioned resolution on intellectual property rights, under para. 14 also introduces a pair of concepts: AI-assisted and AI-generated creations.

Points out the difference between AI-assisted human creations and AI-generated creations, with the latter creating new regulatory challenges for IPR protection, such as questions of ownership, inventorship and appropriate remuneration, as well as issues related to potential market concentration; further considers that IPRs for the development of AI technologies should be distinguished from IPRs potentially granted for creations generated by AI; stresses that where AI is used only as a tool to assist an author in the process of creation, the current IP framework remains applicable.

It seems that this pair of concepts considers the level of intensity of the human intervention in the final creative work. AI-assisted artistic works are where AI serves as a creative tool or aids in the work's production. The CJEU, in Painer case, clearly mentioned that "*[w]hen selecting the snapshot, the photographer may choose from a variety of developing techniques the one he wishes to adopt or, where appropriate, use computer software*". For AI-assisted outputs, human intellectual effort is more visible since it "*will always go hand in hand with some form of human intervention, be it the development of the software, the gathering and choice of training data, the drawing up of functional specifications, supervision of the creative process, editing, curation, post-production, etc.*" (Hugenholtz&Quintais, 2021). Although it will depend on the facts and circumstances of each concrete case, an AI-assisted output will most likely qualify as a copyrightable work.

The legal challenge becomes more interesting when it comes to AI with high level of autonomy to varying degrees. Autonomous artificial intelligence, unlike traditional, is equipped with a self-learning mechanism, so it can continuously improve itself and produce unpredictable intellectual products. This also raises the issue of unpredicted copyright infringements it may have caused. On the other hand, a closer analysis suggests that, even in cases where the final output is generated by an autonomous computer algorithm, there is human involvement in the creative process (Gaffar&Albarashdi, 2024). It is asserted that "even a largely autonomously operating AI system will normally not deliver output that is immediately ready for publication or commercial use" (Hugenholtz&Quintais, 2021).

Distinctively different to the United States, United Kingdom grants protection to computer-generated works without human authors. Section 178 of UK Copyright, Designs and Patents Act 1988 ("CDPA") introduces the category of computer-generated work, which defines as "the work generated by computer in circumstances such that there is no human author of the work". This approach seems to remove the traditional perspective of placing a human author behind creation.

Acknowledging the human involvement even in AI-generated outputs seems reasonable. The UK legislator's approach of granting the copyright to the person who has undertaken the necessary arrangement for the creation of the work also supports this. However, in AI-generated outputs, one should still compare the human involvement and the role of the AI system to see which outweighs. If, for example, the human involvement is limited to only entering a prompt or reduced only to selecting a ready-made output, this may not be regarded as the dominant factor contributing to the creation (see. Hugenholtz&Quintais, 2021).

An important international legal instrument, the Berne Convention for the Protection of Literary and Artistic Works, inexplicitly refers to originality requirement (Rosati, 2017). Art. 2(3) of the Convention stipulates that "*[t]ranslations, adaptations, arrangements of music and other alterations of a literary or artistic work shall be protected as original works without prejudice to the copyright in the original work*".

The Convention, on the other hand, offers flexibility to the Contracting Parties. Art. 19 of the Convention provides that "[t]he provisions of this Convention shall not preclude the making of a claim to the benefit of any greater protection which may be granted by legislation in a country of the Union". Therefore, Contracting Parties are welcome to introduce a specific threshold of originality for AI-generated works (Gaffar&Albarashdi, 2024).

Determining the Holder of the Copyright

Once the originality of the AI-generated artistic work is established, the next legal challenge is to decide on the owner of the copyright, independent of the human creator of the AI system itself (Yanisky-Ravid, 2017).

As aforementioned, the UK is among the common law countries which has introduced AI-generated works as a new category under its national copyright law. Section 9(3) of CDPA 1988 stipulates that "[i]n the case of a literary, dramatic, musical or artistic work which is computer-generated, the author shall be taken to be the person by whom the arrangements necessary for the creation of the work are undertaken". This perspective is also adopted by some other countries, including Ireland, Hong Kong, New Zealand and India (Burylo, 2022; Gaffar&Albarashdi, 2024). Despite this stipulation, the provision does not provide a definite and clear determination as to who the copyright holder is. The plurality of the players (the developer, the investor *et seq.*) involved in the development of the AI system may lead to difficulty in determining who played the creative role (Yanisky-Ravid, 2017). *The Next Rembrandt project* is given as a good example of a collaborative work between AI developers, engineers and art historians, which they jointly created (Hugenholtz&Quintais, 2021).

Recognizing the AI system itself as a legal person by granting personality will also bring new problems regarding the use and the transfer of intellectual property rights as well as holding the system itself liable for copyright infringements.

CONCLUSION

With the creative potential of AI technologies, the involvement of AI in artistic works has become inevitable. However, as in all areas of law, they come along with legal issues. The legislators must not ignore the problems that AI systems bring into copyright law. Traditional copyright laws adopt human-centered approaches. The core notion of copyright law is "human authorship". The concept of "creativity" is also understood to imply human intellectual effort. The involvement of AI in artistic creation had led to the challenge of these traditional concept. The absence of human factor to a varying degree in the works of AI systems is the core problem.

One view supports a proactive approach and argues that, to face the challenges, the policymakers must take a stand and introduce a clear new framework. For example, UK introduced the category of "computer-generated work". Section 178 CDPA 1988 defines it as "[t]he work generated by computer in circumstances such that there is no human author of the work". Accordingly, as for the determination of authorship rights for AI-generated works, it provides the following solution: the author shall be taken to be the person by whom the arrangements necessary for the creation of the work are undertaken. This approach seems to accept the legal qualification of AI-generated outputs as copyrightable works but still, grant the authorship to a person.

On the other side, the legal analysis show that vast majority of the countries is not yet make any amendments in their national legislation. The question is whether there is a a genuine need for new concepts and frameworks. Even with autonomous AI systems, is human intervention totally absent or human involvement is still existent? In this respect, it is asserted that in all scenarios where AI is involved, human intervention is present, in one way or the other. This approach is quite valuable to show that, contrary to what it seems at first glance, the traditional concepts of the existing copyright law may not totally exclude protection to AI-generated works.

Producing an intellectual and artistic work legally qualifies as a "factual act". Factual act is where the legal order results in a material/factual change occurring in the outside world. Accordingly, copyright protection is granted to a work created by a human being who does not have the power of discernment. Based on this, one can infer that, if the other criteria are met, there must not be a legal obstacle to qualify an AI-generated artistic work as copyrightable just because AI algorithms are non-human entity and do not have a conscious will.

The very rationale behind copyright protection is to promote creativity. If an artistic work satisfies the creativity criterion, not granting protection to a work, just because it is created by a non-human may lead to leaving a legal gap without sanction and thus, opening the path for possible copyright violations of third parties.

REFERENCES

Aydoğdu, M., & Tuncer, N. (2023). *Türk Borçlar Hukuku, Özel Borç İlişkiler* (6th ed.). Adalet.

Bently, L., Sherman, B., Gangjee, D., & Johnson, P. (2022). *Intellectual Property Law* (6th ed.). DOI: 10.1093/he/9780198869917.001.0001

Burylo, Y. (2022). AI Generated Works and Copyright Protection Entrepreneurship. *Economy and Law.*, 3(3), 7–13. DOI: 10.32849/2663-5313/2022.3.01

Compendium of U.S. Copyright Office Practices. (2021). 3rd ed.).

UK Copyright, Designs and Patents Act, 1988.

Fikir ve Sanat Eserleri Kanunu [Law on the Intellectual and Artistic Works], Law No: 5846, Date: 05/12/1951; Official Gazette Number and Date: 7981, 13.12.1951.

Gaffar, Hafiz & Albarashdi, Saleh. (2024). Copyright Protection for AI-Generated Works: Exploring Originality and Ownership in a Digital Landscape. Asian Journal of International Law, 1-24. DOI: 10.1017/S2044251323000735

Gözübüyük, B. (2021). Yapay Zekanın Meydana Getirdiği Fikri Ürünlere İlişkin 5846 sayılı Fikir ve Sanat Eserleri Kanunundaki Sorunlar ve Çözüm Önerileri. *KHM*, 1(1), 54–81.

Hooker, M. P. (2020). Naruto v Slater: One Small Snap for a Monkey, One Giant Lawsuit for Animal-Kind. *Wake Forest Law Review Online*. 10. 15-31.

Hugenholtz, P. B., & Quintais, J. P. (2021). Copyright and Artificial Creation: Does EU Copyright Law Protect AI-Assisted Output? *IIC; International Review of Industrial Property and Copyright Law*, 52(9), 1190–1216. DOI: 10.1007/s40319-021-01115-0

Kılıçoğlu, A. M. (2023). *Borçlar Hukuku Özel Hükümler* (5th ed.). Turhan.

Kurşat, Z. (2009). Eser ve Vekâlet Sözleşmelerinin Nitelendirilmesi Sorunu ve Nitelendirmenin Hükmü. *İÜHFM*, LXVII (1-2), 143-166.

Novelli, C., Casolari, F., Hacker, P., Spedicato, G., & Floridi, L. (2024). *Generative AI in EU Law: Liability, Privacy, Intellectual Property, and Cybersecurity* (arXiv:2401.07348). arXiv. http://arxiv.org/abs/2401.07348

Olgaç, S. (1967). *Borçlar Hukuku Akdin Nevileri*. İsmail Akgün Matbaası.

Pehlivanoğlu, M. C. (2019). Naruto v. Slater Davasının Türk Fikir ve Sanat Eserleri Hukuku Açısından Değerlendirilmesi. Bahçeşehir Üniversitesi Hukuk Fakültesi Dergisi. 14(181-182). 1757-1789.

Polat, C. (2023b). Great Unclear Expectations: A Study on the Defectiveness of Autonomous Systems. *Journal of Consumer Policy*, 46(3), 363–386. DOI: 10.1007/s10603-023-09542-x

Regulation (EU) 2024/1689 of the European Parliament and of the Council of 13 June 2024 laying down harmonised rules on artificial intelligence and amending Regulations (EC) No 300/2008, (EU) No 167/2013, (EU) No 168/2013, (EU) 2018/858, (EU) 2018/1139 and (EU) 2019/2144 and Directives 2014/90/EU, (EU) 2016/797 and (EU) 2020/1828 (Artificial Intelligence Act).

Resolution (EP) European Parliament Resolution of 16 February 2017 with recommendations to the Commission on Civil Law Rules on Robotics, 2015/2103(INL).

Resolution (EP) European Parliament resolution of 20 October 2020 on intellectual property rights for the development of artificial intelligence technologies, 2020/2015(INI).

Resolution (EP) European Parliament Resolution of 20 October 2020 with recommendations to the Commission on a civil liability regime for artificial intelligence, 2020/2014 (INL).

Richards, N. M., & Smart, W. D. (2016). How Should the Law Think About Robots? In Calo, R: et al. (Eds.) *Robot Law* (pp.3-22). Edward Elgar. DOI: 10.4337/9781783476732.00007

Rosati, E. (2017). The Monkey Selfie Case and the Concept of Authorship: An EU Perspective. *Journal of Intellectual Property Law and Practice*, 12(12), 973–977. DOI: 10.1093/jiplp/jpx199

WIPO Secretariat, "Revised Issued Paper on Intellectual Property Policy and Artificial Intelligence", WIPO/IP/AI/2/GE/20/1 REV.

Suluk, C., Karasu, R., & Nal, T. (2022). *Fikri Mülkiyet Hukuku* (6th ed.). Seçkin.

Türk Borçlar Kanunu [Turkish Code of Obligations], Law No: 6098, Date: 11/01/2011. Official Gazette Number and Date: 27836, 04/02/2011.

World Intellectual Property Organization (WIPO), the Berne Convention for the Protection of Literary and Artistic Works (1886).

Yanisky-Ravid, S. (2017). Generating Rembrandt: Artificial Intelligence, Copyright, and Accountability in the 3A Era-The Human-Like Authors are Already Here-A New Model. *Detroit College of Law at Michigan State University Law Review*, 659, 659–726.

Chapter 8
A Complex Intersection of Deepfakes and Copyright Infringement

Pranjal Khare
https://orcid.org/0000-0002-9937-9588
O.P. Jindal Global University, India

Vishambhar Raghuwanshi
https://orcid.org/0009-0009-1365-1850
Manipal University, India

ABSTRACT

The advent of deepfake technology has introduced new challenges to copyright law due to its ability to manipulate media content. This chapter delves into the intricate relationship between deepfakes and copyright law, examining the legal frameworks in key jurisdictions and the ethical implications for creators. Beyond the legal considerations, deepfakes also raise significant ethical concerns which need to be addressed. Deepfakes, generated by artificial intelligence, can reproduce, transform, and adapt existing copyrighted material, raising questions about authorship and originality. It is crucial to address the challenges posed by deepfakes while balancing the interests of creators, copyright holders, and the public.

INTRODUCTION

The current trending global deepfake technology has evolved significantly over the last few years. Deepfakes are a fusion of the terms 'deep learning' and 'fake' and full artificial media that have the ability to change or create content. By using

DOI: 10.4018/979-8-3693-8704-7.ch008

advanced algorithms, and especially Generative Adversarial Networks (GANs), deepfakes can mimic a person's look, voice, and body movement, and produce realistic forgeries of real incidents or interactions which never occurred. At the beginning, deep fake technology was created to be used for good causes including boosting the cinema, virtual reality, and creative materials. On the positive front, the technology that lies at the heart of deepfakes holds out the promise of surprising and engaging entertainment and extensions to digital communication (Hao, 2018).

People are concerned with the extent to which deepfake has advanced and worry over how serviceable these instruments are. In the political context, deepfakes were used for obvious goals of disinformation and in others cases for defamation, all of which have destabilized the confidence and trust in persons and institutions. For instance, fake news such as videos of political leaders uttering politically sensitive statements have caused fires across the globe by questioning not only democracy but also the capacity of the public to differentiate between reality and fake reality. In the same way, creation of deepfake pornography, which frequently includes the unauthorized exploitation of private individuals' images, has drawn ethical and legal controversies regarding privacy infringement and harassment (Sindhu, 2020). These malicious uses of deepfakes have unveiled the loud cry for effective legal mechanisms that can deal with the general effects of synthetic images in a society that is fast embracing technological advancements today.

Creating a distinction between protectable content and unfavorable deepfakes lies at the core of the current legal debate on deepfakes. Acquired right aimed at the protection of original works of authorship, Copyright law has a long standing tradition in the context of intellectual property rights. Its main goal is to encourage innovation by granting a protection right to reproduce, distribute and adapt their works to creators, as well as encouraging the spread of knowledge and culture to the public. Earlier, when the world wasn't well advanced with the digital realm, the definition of the copyright was much more limited and clear, covering literary work, artistic work, musical work, cinematograph work. Although this law has proven effective in protecting exclusive rights of authors, the advancement in the use of technology in this digital era has tilted the copyright law ground by presenting issues such as reproduction, distribution, and alterna- tion of creativity.

Thus, it can be said that the challenges which the modern copyright is experiencing are unique and it has to deal with the growth of the technologies. One can without any permission copy and paste the material that is protected by copyright and distribute it freely to the whole world via the Internet. This has been confirmed through high incidence of piracy, unauthorized adaptations and generally dwindling rights of copyright holders to oversee their creations. When AI was applied to produce content such as deepfake, the role of protecting them under the copyright law was further complicated. In contrast to many forms of creativity, deepfakes use real material and create new images from existing videos, pictures, and voices. This is problematic in light of the principles in copyright law because it is based on the authorial and original work (Mihindukulasuriya, 2020).

Still, while deepfakes spread, the necessity of copyright as the tool for controlling the new type of content arises even more. Deep fakes completely erase the line between originality and copying, making new boundaries for what copyright can or cannot defend. For instance, where a deepfake is created, and utilized as an actor's likeness in a film without permission, it may be contrary to both image rights of the actor and the copyright in the film. Likewise, music produced using deepfake of a singer's voice which performs a composition owned by someone else infringes on the copyright in the composition and breaches moral rights of ownership of the singer persona. While we are still in the realm of copyright, it is worthy of note that its function goes beyond providing protection for authors against reproductions and transformation of their work by third parties and into the setting up of delicate balance between protection of innovation on the one hand and protection of creators on the other hand within the domain of digital technologies (Li, 2019).

There has also been a general trend of using postmodern appropriation through easily accessible and savvy applications that enable people to sample, copy, and alter production content from other users. This evolution has formed contemporary categories of creativity through which distinct divisions between producer and consumer begin to blur. As a type of the user generated content, deepfakes reverse the conventional approach to determining authorship. Because these are algorithms' productions and not human ones, one might ask who has the copyright to the end product if anyone at all? Furthermore, owing to the availability of deepfake technology across borders the problems of copyrights become a daunting task due to cross-jurisdictional nature.

Summing up, it is possible to address that the issue of deepfakes and copyright infringement raises multipartite legal questions that cannot be solved with the help of traditional copyright law only. As time goes on, deepfake is virtually changing and so is the law and coming up with frameworks to cater for the AI page content. This chapter is intended to advance the current knowledge base on this topic while emphasizing the necessity for legal changes in the modern world that is filled in with fabrication of cynical upper levels, the blurring of the distinctions between action and reproduction, truth and falsity.

UNDERSTANDING DEEPFAKES: TECHNOLOGY AND ETHICS

The generation of deepfakes was made possible by interleaving various features of machine learning, one of which is Generative Adversarial Networks (GANs). Originally published by Ian Goodfellow and his colleagues in 2014, GANs have since been a significant component of synthetic media. A GAN is actually a combination of two neural networks that are in opposition to each other: a generator and a discriminator. The generator produces fake images and the discriminator analyzes if they are better than real ones. Over the iterations, the generator comes to human levels, where it is almost impossible to distinguish the generated images or videos from a real video capture. It is this rivalry between the networks that enable GANs to produce the realistically enhanced images and videos that are the foundation of deepfake (Harwell, 2018).

Deepfake begins by having a large database of images, or even videos of a real person. The AI acquires this information to study the subject and imitate their facial expressions, tone of voice and gesture. The more information there is, the better and realistic the final deepfake will be. For instance, in an interview of 2018, a software created a realistic image of actor Steve Buscemi substituting the face of actress Jennifer Lawrence. Such examples which were harmless at first, showed how this technology could alter reality. Most recently, there are deep fake videos which create fake speeches of the politicians such as Barack Obama and Donald Trump, where the two are seen and heard saying things they have never said. Such examples show deepfakes are getting more sophisticated and do not raise alarms even with highly trained professionals and journalists (Shekhar, 2024).

Learning from this, the following ethical concerns arise concerning deep fake information; First, it has made it possible to disseminate false images of the leaders or personalities aspiring to lead the nation since technology makes fake news run rampant. Yet, it is significant because political influence through deepfakes is also possible; the aforementioned content may be utilized for manipulating the election or creating new riots. For example, during the 2020 presidential election in the United States, people assumed that technology with its help could be used to slander candidates or twisting the people's opinion. As for the technology, no major mishaps occurred during the election year, however the potential for such problems is always possible and is only becoming smaller as the technology advances.

One of them is the risk of harm to oneself or damaging the reputation of others, in particular, direct and/or indirect parties to the conflict. A technology is considered believable even if its target was uploading an innocent video, and deepfake technology is used to make non-consensual pornography, which mostly affects women. In such cases there is unauthorized use of a person's image and placing it on the picture that is sexually provocative, this leads to a lot of emotional damage and the repercussions are that there is damage to reputation. Deepfake pornography started targeting high-profile actresses in 2019; Scarlett Johansson was among the celebrities involved leading to debates on the need for legal fighting against it form of harassment. The tactics of deepfake content are often easy to produce and share, mainly as a result of which the victims suffer severe personal ramifications (Pandey, 2023).

Apart from personal damage, it is the assault on public credibility brought by deepfakes. When the words and moving images that the new medium presents lose veracity, then, the very warp and weft of social discourse unravel. This has become a severe concern when relating to journalism, legal processes and even society. Should deepfakes proliferate, they would render some of the videos used in trials, or as news evidence, as fake, which will lead to an atmosphere where all media is suspected to be fake. These new phenomena have raised an increasing apprehension that the public is at risk of living in a state of affairs where truth is scarcely discernible, a state of affairs characterized by 'post truth'.

It is pertinent to mention that the history leading to the modern age of media fabrication is not a new phenomenon, but the level and accuracy made possible with the help of AI tools such as GANs are qualitatively even more advanced. Interference with the media has been around as old as the media itself. In the early part of the 20th century it became common practice to alter certain images for political reasons through photo manipulation techniques like airbrushing. Some of them were during the Soviet period, that efficiently eradicated certain individuals from the photographs after they were fired from their positions in order to tilt history in the favour of the regime. Consequently, in the mid-twentieth century; fake sounds were used in propagandist programs of the Cold War to demonize political rivals (Gross, 2024).

However, the earliest forms of manipulation that were apparent in the social realm included the manipulation of unauthenticated credible messages and the creation of fake media which could not really replicate the technology of their time. Old school editing initially was a laborious process and still when performed, changed media could easily be recognized. Media became aware of these manipulations by distorting meaning through legal systems through applying stringent code of ethics on the content that was produced, as well as the formulation of evidential rules on the documentation of photos and acts that were recorded. For instance, during the Cold War, governments and media organizations set the method of analyzing doctored photographs and enshrined these methods in law.

Nevertheless, deepfakes are a more significant problem than most misinformation through the media. Compared to its earlier possibilities AI generated content has the capabilities of much higher precision and significantly larger speed. In light of new GAN technology, the legal approaches that have been employed in the past may not be enough to identify the new forgeries. Moreover, the increasing use of deepfake applications leads to the expansion of synthetic media where rejoicing does not necessarily have the skills to create realistic fakes.

Prior legal frameworks, which already had considerable success in regulating the media manipulations of their era, were not built to entangle the new opportunities of AI deep fake. The principles of libel, defamation, and privacy that informed previous approaches to manipulated media do not prepare society and legal systems for the scale, speed and anonymity of deepfakes. For instance, as much as defamation laws can be legislative to demand compensation for reputational loss due to deepfakes, such laws are usually ineffective because the victim needs to prove harm to get compensation, which is very hard when it is a viral social media post. Likewise, the current copyright laws may fail to protect the infringement of a person's image in deriving a new image or in the creation of the new AI image (Kesavan, 2024).

Additionally, as the internet is global in reach, enforcing that law presents a bigger challenge. The steps used to create a deepfake video can be done in one country, but the results will spread rapidly across another country leading to jurisdiction issues that regular legal systems cannot accommodate. Thus, we are starting to see governments react to this situation, although not necessarily for the reasons most people believe. Over time, the General Data Protection Regulation (GDPR) law in the European Union has provisions that one might assume give individuals the right to have deepfakes in manipulated media removed. Some U.S states, for instance, California and Texas have passed deepfake laws in relation to elections and pornography scams. However, these laws are still relatively new, and we are yet to evaluate the performance of these laws.

In conclusion, the generation of deepfakes is a new and evolving form of media manipulation through using the machine learning algorithm, the GANs. From the list of previous types of media tampering, it is clear that the complexity and skills needed for such manipulation when using available technology throughout previous decades were a significantly higher barrier to fulfill, compared to deepfakes that are relatively easy to make and look realistic. The history of media manipulation is useful for reckoning with deepfakes, but the threat they pose necessitates brand new legal paradigms and solutions.

Intersection of Deepfakes and Copyright Infringement

Due to deepfake technology and copyright, there is a vast prospect of legal issues involved especially in the facets of reproduction, transformation, and adaptation all subsumed under unauthorized use of copyrighted material. Concerning the use of deepfakes, which largely involve the use of generated media such as images, videos or audio, the question of the violation of the principles of intellectual property law arises. At the centre of this topic is the consideration of whether the generation of a deepfake is unlawful under copyright law and especially when a person uses any copyrighted material, including performances, voices or depiction. Deepfake technology is fast developing and with time, its adoption is going to rise thus complicating the formulation and applicability of traditional copyright law (Satheesh, 2022).

Fundamentally, copyright law is intended to indulge the rights of authors in original works in order to protect their work by giving them the exclusive legal rights to determine how their work will be reproduced, sold or altered. The copy of copyrighted material without authorization is a direct infringement of these exclusive rights. In the case of deepfakes, this takes place whenever original videos, images or voices are used to create a new piece of deep fake media. For example, deepfake videos in which a person has been replaced by someone else reciting famous scenes from movies or altering the voice of some recognizable public figures are unauthorized copies of the original that violates copyright (Seshadri & Sindhu, 2020).

A good example of such forgery can be observed in scenarios where deep fakes derive from the original videos and reproduce new scenes to fit new messages. It was in the year 2020 that social media was flooded with a video which was a convincing imitation of the actor Jim Carrey recreating scenes of 'The Shining' with Jack Nicholson replaced by Jim Carrey's face. Although this deepfake had attracted such elements due to its technicality, it again had aroused significant copyright issues, especially in respect of whether such an alteration infringed the film studio's proprietary right to authorize adaptation of the original movie. Although the video did not cause legal battle litigation since it was considered as a parody, the situation shows that deepfake still resides in a legal ambiguity in relation to the copyright laws.

Besides reproduction, deepfakes consist of other forms of use or exploitation of copyrighted materials as may be observed from unauthorized transformation or adaptation of such materials. Current regulation according to most legal systems considers the works inaugurating transformations, copies, or other derivatives as objects of copyright law. Techniques that take an original video or an audio file and change certain aspects such as faces, or voices, can be referred to as a subset of deepfakes. The very nature of deepfakes is that it can result in a total transformation of the work, but under the hood it is seemingly a replica of a copyrighted work, thus posing a unique problem for enforcing copyright (Mudgal, 2023).

Another legal issue that concerns deepfakes is whether deepfakes are a derivative of copyright work or not. A derivative work means a new creation that is based on or is originated from one or more works, including translations, adaptations or transformations. In the case of deepfakes, therefore, this definition becomes rather convoluted. For instance, a deepfake that changes some actor's facial or vocal feature in a film would be considered as creating an unauthorized adaptation of a copyrighted work. Nevertheless, to what extent deepfakes can be considered as derivative works is still uncertain, particularly due to the fact that the deepfake in question can be created by an AI system, which contributed considerably when creating the deepfake, as opposed to a human author (Vijandran, 2024).

To complicate matters, deepfakes that recreate voices, images or performances also have a legal status. It is here that performances and images are most often protected, providing the original authors or performers with rights as to their persona or image. For example, in 2020, the actor Tom Cruise became a viral victim of deepfake on the TikTok platform, where his avatar fakes realistic scenes in funny contexts. Although these deepfakes were not made with clearly ill-intentions, they brought up questions regarding the actor's ability to control his image as well as bring out previously discussed concerns of copyright.

Among the most well-known legal cases that regard deepfakes and copyrights, there is one, which was caused by the use of artificial voices. In 2019, the musician Jay-Z received an anonymous deep fake song with the rapper's voice generated by AI, then he filed a copyright claim against a YouTube user who created songs using deep fake music. Jay-Z said it infringed on his exclusive rights in his voice and performance as a musician. Although the case was later resolved, the problem arose when using the copyright law concerning AI-generated performances and voice reproduction.

Another problem related to legal regulation in the field of copyright for deepfakes is to determine the author of the work. Copyright law as previously observed is anchored on an individual or a group of individuals creating a specific literary, artistic or dramatic work. Unlike other mediums, deepfakes are typically created by using algorithms, thus it is even difficult to determine who is the author of the work, the algorithms itself and the person who trained the algorithms? This has raised controversies on whether such texts can claim copyright at all, if they can, to whom does it belong? The U.S. Copyright Office for instance has taken a reluctant stand in extending copyright protection for work generated by AI where there is no human author behind the work (Bass, 2023).

Another important factor is originality that also greatly defines whether deepfakes can be protected by or violate the copyright law. In order to gain copyright protection, a work must be both secular and 'tangible means.' But the essence of deepfakes, as a rule, does not require invention in the classical sense, as it is an artificial creation most often derived from other media. In the case of *Andres Guadamuz v U.K. Copyright Tribunal*, clarity was sought in a dispute of whether a computer-generated work could be original. Despite the fact the decision was not about deep fake per se, it did raise questions about the legal protection of AI generated content, which uses data from other sources to create the content in the first place. This is a major problem for deepfakes because, depending on how they are built, they might not be copyrightable works in the first place since they integrate existing media.

Furthermore, deepfakes make parody, fair use, and violation look similar. In most places in the world, 'fair use' means something that enables individuals to use part of some copyrighted material, for instance; for the purpose of commenting or even making a joke or education purposes without the approval of the owner of the work being used. Deepfakes applied to copyrighted material for satiric or parodic motives may well be included in this category such as cases which modify politicians' speeches as jokes. However, deciding whether a deepfake is in fair use or is already an infringement of copyright is a question that can be easily answered especially if the deepfake is almost indistinguishable from the original work (Jodka, 2024).

Actual case remains a topic of issue for the legal discussion of the problem of deepfake and copyright infringement. The previously mentioned deepfake of Jim Carrey in The Shining did not cause a legal response, probably because it was interpreted as a meme. However, as deepfakes are indistinguishable from original media more and more, rights owners may be prompter to legally act and protect their rights. Likewise, deepfake adult videos that incorporate and misappropriate images of celebrities bring forward legal proceedings form those whose images were used. In the 2018, case of *Doe v. John Doe*, the unidentified litigant who received timely damages from using a deepfake pornographic video even though the aspect of privacy, rather than copyright, was the basis of the judgment.

Therefore, it can be said that deepfakes give proper legal challenges for copyright law especially with regard to the reproduction, modification, and adaptation of the older contents. The impossibility of referring to established internationally, traditional principles of copyright in relation to content generated by an AI, combined with the uncertainty regarding the issue of originality or derivation of content, suggests that it is time to rethink the issue of existence of intellectual property rights in terms of deepfakes. Employing deepfake technology still remains unclear in the litigation, whereas future litigation would present new challenges and vulnerabilities for legal frameworks.

Ethical and Philosophical Dimensions of Copyright and Deepfakes

The example of the combination of deepfakes and the legislation on copyright raises a fundamental conflict between the moral rights of the authors and the copyright holders' rights such as the rights to attribution and to integrity. While the economic rights of the copyright holders relate with the financial gains in their works, moral rights seem to be more closely attached to the relation of the authors to their literary and artistic works. Such rights protect the creator's image and guarantee that their work is being used only in the manner the creator wished. However, as the generation of deepfakes has been bringing about new technologies that make the old ones even more complex, this area is something that may potentially threaten both kinds of rights, as well as the law designed to protect the creators (Sanders, 2022).

It is all about protecting the personal and prejudice of the creator, that is, the right to demand that the creator's name be mentioned each time the work is sold (right of paternity) and the right to oppose any distortion or misuse of the work by any person (right of integrity). Indeed, economic rights are concerned with the monetary utilization of the work, for instance, the rights to publish, sell and transfer the work. Most importantly moral rights are regarded as human rights in many jurisdictions especially those of Europe and are differentiated from economic rights of titles and licenses.

Software that involves generational of fresh synthetic images, voice and performances by using source images, voices and performances destroy both moral and economic rights. Verified identity is a major aspect that is directly infringed upon by a deepfake especially when these modify a creator's work with their consent, thereby robbing them their deserved credit. For instance, an artist posts their work only to have it altered by a deepfake to something they never created or even something harmful for example has contentious moral and legal ramifications for the artist (Sharmila, 2022). Thus, copyright holder's economic rights are also affected where deepfakes are employed in the reproduction or modification of the holder's work in the absence of license hence denying their rightful share under copyright law.

This chapter has especially identified that deepfakes present a unique risk for moral rights in the manner that they alter the original work in a manner that could harm the reputation of the creator. For example, deepfake can be a tool that replaces parts of a musician's performance or modify an actor's voice or look and create new material that can be obscene, false, or libelous. Some of these uses are unlawful, as they breach the right of integrity of the creator of the work by changing the work in a manner that either completely misconstrues its original intended sense or erases it completely from the image. The creator would not be able to raise an argument against such use and could result in the dilution of the public's trust as well as a damaged reputation (Maheshwari, 2023).

The right of attribution is also endangered in the circumstances of deepfakes' usage. Generally, AI created content generated by modifying one or multiple original works can completely eliminate the source and thus entirely wipe out their contributions. Already when deepfakes synthesize elements of different works, raising a question as to who the author or owner of these works has the right to claim that a piece of art belongs to him. The uncredited alteration of content is actually a form of infringement on moral rights due to the possibility of having creators exploited via omission of credits and compensation (Ruiter, 2021).

From an economical perspective, deep fakes pose serious problems of jurisprudence as they impair the right of the copyright holder to regulate the utilization, circulation and modification of the work. Some infringed economic rights include the right of reproduction, adaptation, and distribution which are frequently upset by deep fakes reproducing or adapting copyrighted work. When a deepfake replicates the actions of an actor or singer for instance the economies of the originating work may be eroded or monetized without the benefit reverting to the original creator and or copyright owner. This unleashes discussion on how authorities would wish to implement copyright laws at a time when synthetic media can be generated and distributed without restriction.

To the extent that legal academics have grappled with whether current copyright laws are sufficiently responsive to deepfakes' problems to begin with. Some have opined that doing so is inadequate since current frameworks were developed to handle relatively basic AI essays. Another approach could be the invention of new laws that apply specifically to deepfake technology like the laws established in data sell privacy laws which consider the AI generated content as a category of work of its own and has its own set of rules for production and distribution (Tyagi, 2022).

However, critics have expressed a concern that a surge in the number of regulation measures might hamper innovation in AI development. AI instruments have huge prospecting in the areas that construct, entertainment, and education and thus restraint in their application is not static. As a result, any rights that are sought to be granted to protect deepfakes need to be delicately crafted to fit the needs of both those wishing to create deepfakes and progress in the field of technology.

They ask basic philosophical questions, regarding creativity and authoring, given the increase in AI created contents, like deepfakes. In the past, copyright accepted the human writer as its central subject offering protection to individuals' creations. AI, however, operates differently: it feeds on big amounts of data that copies and produces content based on patterns it has stored in its database. This leads to a fundamental question: with reference to the above-mentioned ideas, can the works created by AI be viewed as innovative?

AI proponents have been divided over whether works produced by an AI should be protected by copyright because the creative process by definition lacks human input and thus violates principles on which copyright law rests. Creativity in this view means independently choosing and knowingly innovating and self-actualizing, elements that are innate in AI. Even if AI comes up with what seems to be fresh content the method through which it does so is through compilation and manipulation of data without any motives or purpose of their being personal or creative.

Some are strictly localized arguing that only works created through AI should attract the law of copyright, but if the copyright is to be given, then it should be given to the users or the developers who are designing and running the AI. According to this perspective, AI tools are just an exquisite augmentation of human imagination where users can create content which they possibly cannot design on their own. As a photographer may assert rights on a picture captured by a camera, the same way, a user could assert copyrights on content created under an AI kit.

Pertaining to authorship of AI produced works this has aroused a lot of controversy in law as well as in academe. Some jurisdictions of law actually contain provisions to the effect that copyrights cannot be accorded to creations by non-entia. For example, in the U.S, the Copyright Office has put forward its decision and defined that AI works which do not involve a human author cannot be copyrighted. This leads to a debate of whether there should be public domain for AI generated content or whether there should be creation of new laws for AI (Bogren & Hussein, 2023).

Some academics such as Ryan Abbott have come up with a radical idea to extend the basic principle of copyright to AI systems. However, this proposal has been met with much resistance because it goes against the human centered perception of creativity. All legal professionals sampled concur with the view that copyright should still be associated with human authors, while at the same time, they also accept that intelligent tools are used as the media for creation of new works.

As deepfake technology is rapidly developing, more attention will be paid to legal regulation of authors' moral and economic rights in relation to AI products. As a result, the rights for both images and the individual are threatened by deepfakes, as this technology raises new concerns to the field of copyright as well as international law in general. The delicate balance has to be developed between the interests of creators and investors or inventors and developers with regards to deepfakes and other manifestations of Artificial Intelligence.

Legal Frameworks and Jurisdictional Issues

The essence of artificial intelligence (AI), such as deepfakes, is constantly evolving, and thus the legislation in different juridical systems of the world in the issue of using and protecting the results of intellectual activity in the context of copyrights. Deepfakes can be particularly problematic because they are based on some form of existing copyrighted material like images, videos, audio samples, and voices among others that existing copyright laws are not so prepared to handle. This section analyzes how these matters are addressed by principal jurisdictions, most predominantly the United States, the European Union, and India and provides the comparison of significant legal tenets. Moreover, it investigates how deepfakes overcome the boundaries as a problem in implementing the copyright laws and describes the attempts of legislation in this regard (Colak, 2021).

In the United States the Copyright is governed mainly by the Copyright Act of 1976 as amended from time to time, where one is able to protect "original works of authorship" if they have been placed in any medium for a fixed period of time. The Act comes with statutory copyrights, that is, the copyright gives the first owner full rights of reproduction, sale and adaptation. However, one can note that US law as well as the majority of the legal systems around the world is built upon the concept of human authorship. This raises legal issues with AI creations, such as deepfakes that allow a human author to be almost or entirely uninvolved. All courts in the U.S, have however been very shy in embracing the protection of copyrights especially to works that have been generated solely by an AI and such as in the Naruto v. Slater case of a photograph taken by a monkey arguing the fact that the authors' input is essential in the process. However, much recently, the U.S. Copyright Office has considered where AI falls within the existing legal context and there are active discussions regarding how best to address the questions posed by AI creations such as deep fakes (Sloot & Wagensveld, 2022).

In the present EU member states including the European Union, Copyright law is administered through a fusion of national legislation and EU directives on copyright inclusive of the Copyright Directive (2019/790). As it is with the United States law, EU copyright law currently operates under the principle of originality, under which the work must be original in the sense that it reflects the author's intellectual creation. This is equally problematic in the case of deep fakes, because AI is at the center of generating this content. The EU has also been ahead in regulating the digital ecosystem through the Digital Single Market Directive that seeks to approximate the various national legislations on copyright in order to address questions concerning online platforms. However, the applicability of these laws to Deepfakes also remains inconclusive, particularly insofar as ascertaining whether Deepfakes constitute actual originality or unlawful reproduction of more content.

The Indian Copyright Law is laid down with the Copyright Act of 1957 that has been amended by the Copyright (Amendment) Act, 2012. Indian law like the US and EU law offers the protection of copyrights to works of authorship for example literary, musical and artistic works. Indian law has not come to terms with the topic of AI created content, such as deepfakes yet, nevertheless, it appears that existing laws do not grant a copyright to AI authors. Moreover, the currently existing digital environment in India is likely to pose several distinct difficulties and obstacles for the application of the protection against deepfakes. However, Indian courts find themselves able to advance new ideas applied to copyright desires that respect digital content as in the *Amar Nath Sehgal v. Union of India*, in which the European Union's directives regarding copyright have been interpreted by the Delhi High Court has recognized moral rights under the Indian copyright act

In all these jurisdictions there is the general problem of the concept of human authorship as a cornerstone of copyright law. U.S., EU and Indian courts have over the years upheld an important human input in claims to copyrighted work. This poses major challenges for deepfakes, which are usually produced by AI driven software with minimal or no human interfaces in the structure of the images.

Besides, the question of novelty continues to be critical in defining whether a deepfake can get standard copyright or it is a violation. In both the U.S. and EU, originality entails a personal intellectual input hence keeps on being a thorny area to address when it comes to AI generated content. Yet, Indian law also has this individualistic focus, making the status of deepfake under copyright regimes even more ambiguous. While for deepfakes as original works, which create a new content without using any parts from the original work, there is no clear copyright infringement. In cases of deepfakes containing unauthorized transformation or adaptation of the prior works, whether in videos or images, the primary legal issue would be whether such alterations of works infringed the rights of the copyright owner on adaptation and reproduction (Ramluckan, 2024).

However, weak copyright laws in various nations and regions of the world can easily and strictly encourage the use of deepfakes on preferred platforms because the internet periodically transcends national boundaries. Social websites like YouTube and Twitter can host deepfake material which is available worldwide, and it is practically impossible for the copyright holder to sue in many jurisdictions. Geographical legal suits also constitute a challenge in deepfake because a given deepfake may fall short of legal requirements in one country, yet it may not in another country.

Another major characteristic of deepfakes is that they are beyond borders. A fake video with a restricted license imposed in a specific country can be forwarded and watched in another country in a very short time; global enforcement of rights on media is therefore nearly impossible. Because the internet is virtually decentralized, infringing content can be hosted in countries with hardly any efficient enforcement of copyrights, making it almost impossible to protect the intellectual property.

Since deepfakes are global, they pose major questions to legal frameworks that stem from national jurisdiction. In its consequence, it means that a copyright owner, based in the U.S. or in the EU, would have countless problems with enforcing this right in regard to a deepfake produced by an individual from another country, especially this country not possessing sufficiently developed copyright law. Thus, while the EU has worked to bring copyright law in accord across its member nations, enforcement can still vary from state to state.

However, internet privacy makes it almost next to impossible for copyright owners to know who the deepfake creators are let alone institute a legal case against them. The problem is only worsened by new decentralized platforms and encrypted communication through which producers of illicit content can avoid scrutiny and responsibility.

In response to these difficulties, a number of jurisdictions have started introducing new laws that aim directly at deepfake content. In the United States, the Deepfakes Accountability Act was debuted in 2019 due to increasing possibilities of deepfake usage. The Act would compel the person who generates deepfakes to tag synthetic media content, and regulation to penalize in case of non-compliance. Unluckily, the Act lacks provisions regulating the copyright infringement problems; it is aimed only at misrepresentation and defamation. Consequently, distinguishing between deepfakes and other forms of video manipulation is expected from lawmakers to close this legal loop by adopting even more elaborate legal rules that regulate copyright in the context of deep fakes (Minhas & Sonkhla, 2024).

In the EU member states, regulation of deepfakes has been made under larger campaigns that seek to address disinformation and protect individual's privacy in their digital lives. The Copyright Directive, in particular, and the Digital Single Market Directive more broadly propose a framework for combating online copyright infringement even though they do not focus on deepfakes. A few of the member countries like France and Germany have brought legislation to control digital platforms and synthetic media but this step is in the nascent stages.

India too has not enacted any particular law on deepfakes, although the Information Technology (Intermediary Guidelines and Digital Media Ethics Code) Rules, 2021 have a lot of responsibility to certain platforms for dealing with the injurious content which includes deep fakes. Despite this, these rules are more about regulating damaging material instead of piracy.

What these legislative attempts mean is that there is a shift in the right direction towards a solution to the copyright questions raised by deepfakes, but that the measures do not address the problem sufficiently. For instance, the U.S. Deepfakes Accountability Act places duties on synthetic media producers, but enforcement options are limited, and the Act fails to look at the copyright consequences of deepfakes. Likewise, although the EU Digital Single Market Directive seeks to govern online platforms, its claim to targeting copyright infringement does not capture the unique low-level threats of deepfakes.

Therefore, despite the array of copyright laws in well developed countries such as the U.S., EU and India, they are still inadequate to address issues arising from deepfakes. Deepfake is not limited to any region, and this makes the fight against it an even harder affair; legislation against deepfakes is developing, but they have not provided enough legal solutions for the broad scope of AI, digital content, and pirating. Certainly, for addressing the copyright problems of deepfake technology more than a global coordinated approach is required.

Liability and Accountability in the Deepfake Era

The question regarding responsibility for deepfake cases is challenging and opens disputation in connection with several branches of the law based on copyright, tort, and platform regulation. As deepfake videos are easier to create and widely shared on social media, one more challenge is the identification of which party i.e., the creator, the platform, or both is the legal responsible for the damage caused by synthetic media. This section focuses on the legal patrimony of platform liability with a specific discussion of Section 230 of the Communications Decency Act of the United States of America and the Digital Services Act of the European Union to argue whether there is merit in limiting the platform's legal umbrella in cases of deepfake videos. It also assesses the efficacy of takedown procedures for example the Digital Millennium Copyright Act (DMCA) for deepfake related copyright infringements (Vanberghen, 2024).

One of the most precise issues in the liability debates of deep fake cases is whether it is proper to point the culprit solely in the person who developed the deep fake or whether the social media platforms on which such media is shared should also be blamed. Conventional copyright law has always relied on the producer of the infringing product, under which liability rests on an individual who creates or disseminates copies of copyrighted material. For deepfakes, it means that the person or entity creating a deepfake is responsible for any violation or losses that occurred due to the media.

But the internet user is anonymous and has a global accessibility and this makes this traditional approach hard. Currently called deepfake artists, these people often post their content under fake names and use various tools that prevent their identification, which makes it very challenging to punish them. This puts the platforms which consider such content for their consumption, whether through YouTube, the social platforms or through the use of the file-sharing sites such as Dropbox, directly in the firing line side. However, such platforms have traditionally enjoyed legal immunity that states that hosts cannot be held legally responsible for the content uploaded by the users of the host's platform (Lipkowitz, 2020).

Section 230 of the Communication Decency Act of 1996 of the United States of America is one of the other most complete immunization laws for web-based businesses that offer stages for their clients to transfer their own substance. Section 230 thus gives very wide protection to Internet businesses, stating that the companies cannot be sued for the content of messages from third parties. This legal provision has been essential for the development of the internet to enable sites such as Facebook, twitter, and YouTube to work with the knowledge that they will not be subjected to Heraclian litigations due to the large number of postings by users.

But Section 230 has come under tremendous criticism in the recent past, especially because of new evils such as deepfakes, fake news, and Cyberbullying. Section 230's opponents suggest that the section shields platforms for the consequences of the posted content they host too much. This immunity becomes problematic in cases of deepfakes, closer examination of which is necessary for setting up an adequate level of defense. There are platforms where deepfake content might not only violate copyrights but also have a severe damaging impact on an individual's reputation. For example, deepfakes to manipulate public opinions politically or with a rather vulgar and sexual attitude deeply harming one's career and personal life, all are legally protected by the platforms hosting these videos (Ortutay, 2023).

Section 230 has become the subject of critique, suggesting taking out the immunity in situations such as deepfakes or any other synthetic media. Reform advocates believe that the platforms themselves should be more responsible for moderating the content, especially since the media content itself might be created with the assistance of artificial intelligence systems that most users cannot distinguish from real information. Critics, nevertheless, have cautioned that action to reduce Section 230 immunity will suppress freedom of speech and put unfair pressure on the platforms, who do not ever know whether a piece of content posted by the user complies with the law (Kumar, 2016).

Different from the U.S., the European Union has been more active in regulating the platform with the approval of the Digital Service Act (DSA) in 2021. In its turn, the DSA will enhance users' safety by shifting more obligations on information intermediaries to delete unlawful content, including copyright-violating deepfakes, faster and more satisfactorily.

As part of the DSA, large online platforms are supposed to have procedures that would help them to detect and remove unlawful content; the platforms have to disclose more about their moderation practices. As will be discussed below, although the DSA does not completely remove the concept of platform immunity, it does heavily limit it since the platforms must deploy greater efforts to review content and respond to infringement of copyrights. This change in the legal trend is a sign of emerging realization of the need to regulate the benefits of online platforms in relation to cost which is caused by abuse of user-generated content such as deepfakes (Kiernan, 2024).

The following analyses show how relatively more stringent the DSA is compared to U.S law under Section 230 in dealing with platforms' liability for post outbreak by synthetic media. The EU's orientation at proactive moderation and information disclosure is an effort to make platforms responsible for the damages that deepfakes induce without neglecting the provision of the internet's indispensable features. What does remain uncertain is whether this approach will be more effective than Section 230 in addressing the problems of deepfakes.

One of the main concerns when it comes to debates about the legal responsibility of platforms in connection with deepfakes is whether legal safeguards should be narrowed down for synthetic media content. Currently, reformists claim that deepfakes are a particularly nefarious type of content that cannot be squared with platform liability legislation. Unlike cases of piracy that entails the unauthorized copying and distribution of original works, deep fake entails the alteration of original content to create new fakes that are synthetic and cannot be easily categorized under extant laws.

For instance, if a celebrity's image or voice has been used in deepfake without his or her consent, the use of the deepfake may not strictly be actionable under theories of copyright infringement if the copyright in question is to be considered a parody or a transformation. Likewise, deepfakes developed from the content of the public domain or content that is beyond the collection of copyrights present other problems to copyright owners who wish to protect their rights on their products.

For this reason, it can be suggested that platforms should do more to detect fakes, specifically deepfakes, especially when they are used for that purpose and to harm an individual. However, opponents of this approach have tipped dangers towards over-censorship pointing out platform bias could see them pull down content that while not unlawful, is legally allowed by legal doctrines like fair use or parody.

In America, the primary method of handling what is deemed 'piracy' on the web is the Digital Millennium Copyright Act (DMCA) which enables the owners of copyright to demand that violators remove their work from the web. DMCA takedown provisions mean that platforms have to unmask content as soon as a lawful request has been made by a copyright owner. Although this system has been employed in many of the mentioned cases, it has been criticized as not only slow but also very inefficient in managing the problem of increasing deepfakes.

Deepfakes do not take long to spread to many other platforms taking mere hours, thus making it impossible for copyright owners to report to Google and have their requests processed before deepfakes cause serious damage. Moreover, deepfake authors tend to employ multiple fake names and post content on the anonymous sites, by consequence it is challenging to identify an initial violator. Sometimes, after a deepfake is taken down in one site, it springs up in another site, making it very difficult for copyright owners to feel safe with their creations (Langa, 2021).

Takedown attempts under the DMCA that have been successful have been made where deepfakes are quite explicit with regards to the work's copyright infringement or where face swapping was done on the individual without their consent. But it remains normal for such applications to experience degradation when platforms claim that the deepfake content falls under the protection of 'fair use' law or where it does not unambiguously violate a pre-existing copyrighted material. For example, deepfakes based on public domain content or on the use of other content for purposes of transformation might have a problem with being deleted under the DMCA (Zeigler, 2024).

An issue of liability that raises a number of legal questions includes several legal domains such as copyright law, regulating social media platforms and artificial intelligence. While the existing laws such as Section 230 and the DMCA have protections to the platforms, they are inadequate to prevent the deepfakes' specific risks. The EU's Digital Services Act is less reactive to the problem than the Australian News Media Bargaining Code but contains rules for platform regulation. Moreover, Deepfakes are not limited and are produced globally which makes enforcement of the rules challenging (Rozenshtein, 2024). Since deepfake technology will persist in its development, the legislation regulating such technology must change, which means that the laws need to strike a balance between the protection of copyright and freedom of speech and the absence of beneficial legislation on sanctions for the use of such technology for the distribution of fake news.

CONCLUSION AND WAY FORWARD

As it pertains to deepfakes and copyright law, the latter of the two concepts, is barely adapting to the advancement of artificial intelligence (AI) technologies. As deepfakes are synthetic media generated through high levels of machine learning the issue of protection through copyright framework poses legal questions regarding originality, unauthorized use and extent of liability towards misuse. As the above chapter discussed, since deepfakes lie somewhere in between the idea of creative breakthrough and violation, it became a great challenge for both legislators and authors. At stake here is the conflict between the fight for better compensation for authors and inventors in that light invention vs the push for advancement in technology.

Deepfakes, which serve some non-threatening utility such as entertainment and education, are now being used for different malicious purposes, including political influence, character assassination, and spreading fake news. It has now received enhanced political and juridical interest because of such malignant applications. As has been pointed out above, traditional copyright laws which were put in place before the use of AI generated content are being put to new challenges. Another compelling question which raises much controversy is when deepfakes are to be considered as original work or derived work and what rules of the copyright law pertaining to the unauthorized copying, modification or transformation in making of deepfakes must be applied.

An important challenge in attempting to resolve deepfakes with copyright law is how existing legal principles can be applied to such new types of content. This posed the question that who owns the copyright in AI generated productions and does deepfake violate the copyrights of the depicted individuals or entities, which the above chapter also explained. This aggravating the issue due to globalization of digital content, deepfakes may be generated and shared across a territory without regard to current copyright laws of different countries.

Compared with the most popular jurisdictions such as the United States, EU, and India, it becomes possible to notice the fact that copyright laws are failing to solve the difficulties created by AI and digital works. For example, in the U.S., for takedown requests there is the Digital Millennium Copyright Act (DMCA) but numerous deepfakes spread through various platforms in different countries within a short while. Needless to say, in the EU for instance, the Digital Services Act (DSA) seeks to place more obligation on platforms to search for and delete illicit content, however, the existence of deepfakes across borders reduces the usefulness of national legislation. As platforms enjoy broad liability protections under laws like Section 230 of the U.S. Communications Decency Act, a fundamental question arises: Should platforms become more liable for hosting infringing or creating and distributing damaging deepfakes?

This has mostly been characterized by contrasting policy objectives, between the protection of owners of copyright in their works and the promotion of advancement in technology. Synthetic images are a realistic imitation, therefore deepfakes are the manifestation of AI progress and its capabilities. But this technology poses some hazards of violating the rights of people and firms who own the improved intelligence property that AI in question transforms. Deepfakes' authors usually rely on the existing information, such as a star or their lookalike, a politician or a journalist's voice, or short fragments of a motion picture or a piece of music, which results in legal issues regarding how the rights can be defended without keeping people from developing new technologies or art.

Besides, there is an issue of originality in writing and the connections between AI-generated content and originality are just as challenging. Copyright law has in the past protected works of authorship but with deepfakes, works are created by Artificial Intelligence and not a human author. The chapter then discussed how current laws deal with the concept of originality hence they fail to resolve the puzzle of who owns the copyright in AI generated works or whether such works deserve to be copyrighted at all.

This legal uncertainty is especially problematic for enforcement when deciding whether the deepfake falls under the paradigm of being transformative or parody given the protection under shady doctrines such as fair use. For example, deepfakes that represent art or satire are most likely to be used and can therefore be limited by copyrights.

Moving forward, the advancement in creating deep fake technology is not something that is going to stop. These technologies such as the GANs in producing deep fakes will expand as machine learning progresses, rapidly more cadenced than any legal standards. This poses many questions regarding the future of copyright law and more to the point, whether legal systems are capable of dealing with AI created content.

The forecast is, therefore, that deepfakes will exert pressure on copyright law to develop in jurisdictions that are yet to grapple with the implications of AI technology. The law will have to play the part of updating itself in order to be able to deliver definitive outcomes where the questions of ownership, novelty and responsibility may arise concerning deepfakes. This may involve the creation of new legal frameworks, or defining new laws aimed at the products of artificial intelligence systems, including AI-created content and synthetic media. For instance, the recent U.S Deepfakes Accountability Act is the first step to regulating deep fake technology, but surely more drastic measures will be required on the international front.

Another seemingly critical area will be the expansion in the proportion of platforms that will undertake detection and deletion of deepfakes. The existing legal immunity that the current liability shields offer to the platforms nowadays, especially in the U.S., leaves them unaccountable for the content that they host. Nonetheless, as adverse and, in particular, legal consequences of deepfakes become evident, the society will increasingly demand platforms to monitor AI-generated media more actively. The reform though, such as the EU's Digital Services Act now points towards these directions and making the platforms more responsible, and others may follow.

Lastly, the elimination of the problems created by deepfakes can only be solved through cooperation with countries from other legal changes. Deepfakes are not peculiar to one country and due to the intervention of the internet space, no one country can claim to control the creation and release of deepfakes. In this chapter, the problem was discussed in detail and one of the points noted was that legal requirements for protecting copyrights diverge from one country to another and, therefore, a single strategy cannot be used in different countries in relation to AI created material.

To some extent, the approximately 170 countries' agencies that are parties to intergovernmental copyright treaties like the Berne Convention for the Protection of Literary and Artistic Works can set a basis for legal unification, but much more collaboration will be required to address the sophisticated scheming of deepfakes. Specifically, it will be decisive to build cross-border enforcement instruments for combating piracy on the Internet and to establish AI-dedicated legal rules and guidelines during the following years.

And any change in this area has to be a fine line between the need to protect creators' rights and encouraging new developments. The emergence of AI technologies such as deepfakes bring positives into maximizing most of the industries ranging from entertainment to education, however the positives here are coupled with the negatives occasioned by synthetic media. Thus, it is sure that as this technology advances, the legal frameworks which regulate it also adapt by freeing technological advancement of creators while protecting their work.

Therefore, deepfakes and the interaction with copyright law is an issue that has both encroaching and dynamic legal settings. The current legal frameworks which have been developed to overcome the challenges of AI produced content have failed to curb the use of deep fake technology. This is the conflict between the right of the copyright holder and the right of the creators of technology; the law of nations is in a dilemma on which among the two causes deserves priority protection. As to the future, there is still more work to do in cooperation with the attorneys of other countries and the extensive change of the legislation that has to be ready for new revolutionary technologies and tendencies.

REFERENCES

Bass, D. (2023). The Legal Issues Surrounding Deep fakes. *Honigman*. https://www.honigman.com/the-matrix/the-legal-issues-surrounding-deepfakes

Bogren, W., & Hussein, M. (2023). Social Media's Take on Deepfakes: Ethical Concerns in the Public Discourse. *Uppsala University Institute for Informatics and Media*. https://uu.diva-portal.org/smash/get/diva2:1837417/FULLTEXT01.pdf

Colak, B. (2021). Legal Issues of Deepfake. *Institute for Internet & the Just Society*. https://www.internetjustsociety.org/legal-issues-of-deepfakes

Gross, B. (2024). Unmasking Deepfakes: Navigating the Copyright Quagmire. *Cardozo Arts & Entertainment Law Journal*. https://cardozoaelj.com/2024/04/05/unmasking-deepfakes-navigating-the-copyright-quagmire/

Hao, K. (2018), Inside the world of AI that forges beautiful art and terrifying deep fakes. *MIT Technology Review*. https://www.technologyreview.com/2018/12/01/138847/inside-the-world-of-ai-that-forges-beautiful-art-and-terrifying-deepfakes/

Harwell, D. (2018). Fake-porn videos are being weaponized to harass and humiliate women: 'Everybody is a potential target'. *The Washington Post*. https://www.washingtonpost.com/technology/2018/12/30/fake-porn-videos-are-being-weaponized-harass-humiliate-women-everybody-is-potential-target/

Jodka, S. (2024). Manipulating reality: the intersection of deepfakes and the law. *Reuters*. https://www.reuters.com/legal/legalindustry/manipulating-reality-intersection-deepfakes-law-2024-02-01/

Kesavan, A. (2024). The Use of Deepfake. *Khurana & Khurana*. https://www.khuranaandkhurana.com/2024/04/19/the-use-of-deep-fake/

Kiernan, P. (2024). The Legal Landscape: Navigating Liability and Regulation in the Age of Deep Fakes. *Thought Lab*. https://www.thoughtlab.com/blog/the-legal-landscape-navigating-liability-and-regul/

Kumar, A. (2016). The Test of Time: Section 230 of the Communications Decency Act Turns 20. *Davis Wright Tremaine LLP*. https://www.dwt.com/blogs/media-law-monitor/2016/08/the-test-of-time-section-230-of-the-communications

Langa, J. (2021). Deepfakes, Real Consequences: Crafting Legislation to Combat Threats Posed by Deepfakes. *Boston University Law Review*. https://www.bu.edu/bulawreview/files/2021/04/LANGA.pdf

Li, H. (2019). The Emergence of Deepfake Technology: A Review. *Technology Innovation Management Review*. https://timreview.ca/article/1282

Lipkowitz, D. (2020). Manipulated Reality, Menaced Democracy: An Assessment of the DEEP FAKES Accountability Act of 2019. *New York University Journal of Legislation & Public Policy*. https://nyujlpp.org/quorum/lipkowitz-manipulated-reality-menaced-democracy-deepfakes-accountability-act/

Maheshwari, D. (2023). Manipulating Reality: Understanding The Ethical And Legal Dimensions Of Deepfakes. *Indian Journal of Law and Legal Research*. https://www.ijllr.com/post/manipulating-reality-understanding-the-ethical-and-legal-dimensions-of-deepfakes

Mihindukulasuriya, R. (2020). Why the Manoj Tiwari deepfakes should have India deeply worried. *The Print*. https://theprint.in/tech/why-the-manoj-tiwari-deepfakes-should-have-india-deeply-worried/372389/

Minhas, N., & Sonkhla, D. (2024). Exploring Legal and Technical Challenges of Deep Fakes in India. *International Journal for Multidisciplinary Research*, 6(4), 1–8. https://www.ijfmr.com/papers/2024/4/24793.pdf

Mudgal, H. (2023). The deepfake dilemma: Detection and decree. *Bar and Bench*. https://www.barandbench.com/columns/deepfake-dilemma-detection-and-desirability

Ortutay, B. (2023). What you should know about Section 230, the rule that shaped today's internet. *PBS News*. https://www.pbs.org/newshour/politics/what-you-should-know-about-section-230-the-rule-that-shaped-todays-internet

Pandey, S. (2023). Understanding Copyright Issues entailing deep fakes in India. *Blog Ipleaders*. https://blog.ipleaders.in/understanding-copyright-issues-entailing-deepfakes-in-india/

Ramluckan, T. (2024). Deepfakes: The Legal Implications. *ResearchGate*. https://www.researchgate.net/publication/379221500_Deepfakes_The_Legal_Implications

Rozenshtein, A. (2024). Interpreting the Ambiguities of Section 230. *Yale Journal on Regulation*. https://www.yalejreg.com/bulletin/interpreting-the-ambiguities-of-section-230/

Ruiter, A. (2021). The Distinct Wrong of Deepfakes. *Philosophy & Technology*, 34(4), 1311–1332. DOI: 10.1007/s13347-021-00459-2

Sanders, E. (2022). Deepfakes and Intellectual Property: What You Should Know. *Romano Law*. https://www.romanolaw.com/deepfakes-and-intellectual-property-what-you-should-know/

Satheesh, A. (2022). Deepfakes and the Copyright Connection: Analysing the Adequacy of the Present Machinery. *Journal of Law & Technology*. https://jolt.richmond.edu/2022/01/25/deepfakes-and-the-copyright-connection-analysing-the-adequacy-of-the-present-machinery/

Seshadri, N., & Sindhu, A. (2020). Are Copyright Laws adequate to deal with Deepfakes?: A comparative analysis of positions in the United States, India and United Kingdom. *KSLR Commercial & Financial Law Blog*. https://blogs.kcl.ac.uk/kslrcommerciallawblog/2020/12/17/are-copyright-laws-adequate-to-deal-with-deepfakes-a-comparative-analysis-of-positions-in-the-united-states-india-and-united-kingdom/

Sharmila, R. (2022). Behind the Mask: Ethical Dimensions of Deepfake Technology in India's Legal Sphere. *International Journal for Legal Research and Analysis*. https://www.ijlra.com/paper-details.php?isuur=3234

Shekhar, R. (2024). Deepfakes and Intellectual Property: Understanding Legal Challenges and Protections in the Artificial Intelligence Era. *Novo Juris Legal*. https://www.novojuris.com/thought-leadership/deepfakes-and-intellectual-property-understanding-legal-challenges-and-protections-in-the-artificial-intelligence-era.html

Sindhu, A. (2020). Interventions on the issue of Deepfakes in Copyright. *WIPO*. https://www.wipo.int/export/sites/www/about-ip/en/artificial_intelligence/conversation_ip_ai/pdf/ind_a.pdf

Sloot, B., & Wagensveld, Y. (2022). Deepfakes: Regulatory challenges for the synthetic society. *Computer Law & Security Report*, 46, 105716. DOI: 10.1016/j.clsr.2022.105716

Tyagi, K. (2022). Deepfakes, Copyright & Personality Rights: An inter-disciplinary perspective. *ResearchGate*. https://www.researchgate.net/publication/359711219_Deepfakes_Copyright_Personality_Rights_An_inter-disciplinary_perspective

Vanberghen, C. (2024). Deepfake Dilemma: Balancing Regulation, Responsibility, and Rights in the AI Era. *Modern Diplomacy*. https://moderndiplomacy.eu/2024/02/24/deepfake-dilemma-balancing-regulation-responsibility-and-rights-in-the-ai-era/

Vijandran, V. (2024). The Intersection of Deepfakes and Intellectual Property Law: Applying the Concept of Passing Off. *Aqran Vijandran*. https://www.aqranvijandran.com/blog/the-intersection-of-deepfakes-and-intellectual-property-law-applying-the-concept-of-passing-off

Zeigler, S. (2024). Communications Decency Act and Section 230 (1996). *Free Speech Center*. https://firstamendment.mtsu.edu/article/communications-decency-act-and-section-230/

Chapter 9
Is Turkish Copyright Law Well-Equipped to Handle Artificial Intelligence?

Cemre Polat
https://orcid.org/0000-0003-1083-6090
Ankara Medipol University, Turkey

ABSTRACT

This chapter provides an overview of Turkish law as regards the most-frequently debated copyright problems within the realm of artificial intelligence. The problems which are observed to be the most prominent are probable copyright infringements in the training and testing phase of AI, copyright infringement as a result of the output of AI, and copyright protection of AI outputs. Although these copyright issues can be observed in various AI applications, they are more pronounced in generative AI. The success and wide reach of OpenAI's ChatGPT revealed that the question which needs the most urgent answer was not "Will robot kill us and who will be liable?" This is not to undermine the need for clarity for AI involved accidents, but copyright problems emerged more widely and have already been subject to lawsuits, especially in the US. Global use of Generative AI makes the copyright problems relevant for all jurisdictions. However, Turkish copyright law has not been amended accordingly yet. This chapter displays at which points Turkish law falls short and propose changes, where needed.

DOI: 10.4018/979-8-3693-8704-7.ch009

INTRODUCTION

Advancements in artificial intelligence (AI) have raised many concerns of which the most pronounced ones focus on civil liability. Legal scholars have witnessed and many of them have taken part in the accumulation of a great volume of literature and AI and liability debates. The agenda of the European Union was no different. The European Union adopted the AI Act[1] and drafted the proposals for an AI Liability Directive (AILD)[2] and a new Product Liability Directive.[3] For sure intellectual property (IP) concerns were always on the table, especially the patentability of AI outputs has always been quite popular, and the DABUS case attracted great attention from all over the world. However, it will not be wrong to say that advancements in the generative AI technology have shifted more attention towards IP concerns, especially towards protection of copyright, such that the AI Act which was initially drafted as a product safety instrument has been changed in a way as to include provisions to ensure conformity with EU copyright law and to require all providers implementing a copyright strategy (Stieper & Denga, 2024). AI with generative capabilities which is also referred to as general purpose AI or foundation models (Madiega, 2023) are defined in the AI Act (art. 2(63)) as an AI model, including where such an AI model is trained with a large amount of data using self-supervision at scale, that displays significant generality and is capable of competently performing a wide range of distinct tasks regardless of the way the model is placed on the market and that can be integrated into a variety of downstream systems or applications, except AI models that are used for research, development or prototyping activities before they are placed on the market.

It is well-known that AI providers need data (many of which are protected materials) to develop the AI systems. The difference with generative AI is that it does so in a larger scale and the infringements are consequently systemic. The fact of systemic infringements on the one hand and wide acceptance of generative AI by the society on the other hand force lawmakers to make a policy change in copyright protection, specifically in obtaining consent from the author.

The infringement may occur in two ways, by input and output. First of all, the training testing datasets which include protected materials as well might have been obtained without the consent of authors. Secondly, the output generated by AI might be an unauthorized copy of a protected material or involve great similarities, again without having obtained consent.

There is the third issue which should be counted among the most frequently debated ones which is the status of the AI generated output and if so, who the author is.

These three AI-related copyright problems are the subject matter of this chapter. We will analyze each one according to Turkish copyright law which has not gone through any AI-specific amendment yet.

INFRINGEMENT BY INPUT

Problem Setting

Self-learning AI systems -unlike rule-based conventional AI systems- require vast amounts of data. To ensure -to the extent possible- robust performance, AI systems should be verified and validated (Polat, 2023b) which again requires -among other things- data use. How and from where data is obtained depends on the application areas of the relevant AI system. While a robot for outdoor use such as autonomous vehicles should be largely trained and tested in real life cases and simulations -among other ways of training and testing-, some AI applications such as those that process language, generate text, image, audio largely depend on web scraping which can be defined as "a technique used to harvest data from the internet in order to train artificial intelligence models or for other purposes" (Mkparu, 2024). Newspapers, scientific and other categories of articles, institutional reports, case-law, legal instruments, books, novels, images of art works, voices of celebrities, images of ordinary people on social media and many more are exploited to feed the AI systems. Such inputs which are potentially unlimited and most of which are protected by copyright and personality rights have been used to feed AI without necessarily obtaining consent from the right holders.

Legal Background and Analysis

Copyrights are protected in the Law on Intellectual and Artistic Works (No. 5846)[4] (hereinafter referred to as LIAW) under Turkish law. LIAW dates to 1951 with comprehensive amendments made in 1995, 2001 and 2004. Considering that the latest comprehensive amendment was made 20 years ago, the reader might have already guessed that LIAW is not sufficiently equipped in terms of providing a fair solution for the use of protected materials in AI training and testing.

According to LIAW, authors have various moral and economic rights over their works which in general referred to as intellectual rights in the LIAW art. 13 *et seq.* Intellectual rights are *erga omnes* and exists *ipso jure* once the work is created. Among other aspects of intellectual rights, rights of processing, reproduction, public communication (LIAW art. 20 *et seq*) are the most relevant ones for this title. Both mentioned rights belong exclusively to the author. Authors can fully or partially transfer such rights to others gratuitously or in return of consideration by concluding a written contract (LIAW art. 48 *et seq*). Accordingly, in principle, actors in the production chain of an AI system need to obtain the written consent of the author to use the protected material in training and testing phases. Unless the author declares to give consent to free use of her work (for example in Terms and Conditions), the use of the protected material will be illegal which raises civil and criminal liability (LIAW art. 66 *et seq*).

As it is usual in many national and supranational laws, Turkish copyright law also provides various exceptions to the consent requirement (LIAW art. 30 *et seq.*) not all of which are relevant in this context. One relevant exception is the free processing, reproduction and dissemination of *legislation and case-law* (LIAW art. 31) which have been officially published. The condition of official publication is important for Türkiye, since not all case-law is officially published in a state-operated platform. Many case-law are only available on privately-owned databases which require payment for subscription. So, in case, an AI developing company gets subscription and among other actions processes or reproduces case-law, which is not officially published, this should be considered illegal. Another exception is provided for *newspaper content* (including articles) (LIAW art. 36) and *news* (LIAW art. 37). It is allowed to quote such content, even if a reservation is made by the author. Use of such content is permissible if the AI is trained in a way to state the authorship while giving the output. Since the output does not constitute an infringement, it can be induced that the use of such content as input is also permissible. *Education exception* (LIAW art. 34) is also worth mentioning. Collected or selected works may be created by quoting from published musical, scientific and literary works and publicized works of fine arts, provided that collected or selected works are intended for the purpose of education and training. Again, considering that such works can be displayed in the output, we can reach to the conclusion that it can be used for AI training as well. This provision has been included in LIAW because textbooks used in the formal education in Türkiye used to be prepared and pressed by the Ministry of National Education (Tekinalp, 2012, p. 203). However, in the wording there is no statement which reserves this exception to public institutions. So, a private AI company as well can get use of this exception. However, how one should identify the purpose of education and training. Every AI system with which the user can interact and get info i.e., by prompting, carries the potential of education and training. Adopting an expansive interpretation will result in free use of protected materials for the development of many AI systems, first and foremost LLMs. That is why it should be accepted that the AI system of which the developers may enjoy this exception should have been developed solely for the purpose of education and training of a definable group of users, such as medicine students.

As seen, Turkish copyright law does not include a *text and data mining (TDM) exception* unlike Digital Single Market Directive (DSM)[5] art. 3-4. Text and data mining is defined as "any automated analytical technique aimed at analysing text and data in digital form in order to generate information which includes but is not limited to patterns, trends and correlations." (DSM art. 2(2)). Use of protected materials to train AI falls in the scope of this definition (Novelli et al., 2024, p. 17). It should be added that this TDM exception applies on the condition that it is conducted by research organisations or cultural heritage institutions (DSM art. 3(1)) or an express reservation in an appropriate manner (such as in machine readable means) has not been made by the rightholder (DSM art 4(3)). On the other side of the Atlantic, *fair use* exception is applicable in cases where protected materials are used to feed AI. *Fair use* is regulated under Copyright Law of the United States (Title 17, § 107)[6] which allows public to use the protected material without obtaining consent even if a reservation is expressly stated by the author (Henderson et al., 2023; Stieper & Denga, 2024). But whether fair use will help the AI providers in escaping liability is still disputable for the US (see, Henderson et al., 2023). Although it is not stated in the LIAW or in any other positive norm, *fair use* exception has found itself a place for now in the dissenting votes in some criminal lawsuits brought to the Turkish Court of Cassation.[7] However, this should not be interpreted -at least yet- as a step towards adopting fair use doctrine into Turkish law, since the fair use doctrine is put forward in three dissenting votes objecting to the majority's decision on acquittal.

Policy Debate and Recommendations

The conflict of interest is familiar and easily identifiable. On the one hand, there is the right holder's interest to prevent people from using her works without her consent (mostly in return of consideration) and which in turn carries the potential of incentivizing more people to create such works. On the other hand there is the interest of society in general in the improvement of innovation and science by restricting the authors' rights (about the philosophical foundations of the debate, see, Denemeç, 2021). Considering that the number of used pieces of data is potentially unlimited, it is not realistic to expect from AI providers to obtain consent one-by-one. Plus, the distinguishing value of self-learning systems lies in its capacity to develop itself without the need for experts to 'teach' AI every piece of information. Expecting AI providers to obtain consent for the reproduction, distribution and public communication of every protected material, can result in practical banning of generative AI -if not every self-learning model- which would be rowing against the current. Considering that such AI systems and the need for data is a reality, the Turkish law maker should adopt a balanced way to legalize the use of protected materials as input. A regime that by default gives the right to extract data for AI providers with the opt-out option granted for the authors of certain works; while the regulatory requirement to train AI systems that is capable of analyzing reservations (Novelli et al., 2024) and citing the author might be a balanced approach. Although it is not the direct subject of this chapter, it should be added that a legal instrument as a counterpart of the EU's AI Act is awaited under Turkish law. So, the regulatory requirements -including those related to copyright- for generative AI providers (see Chapter V of the AI Act) can be transferred to Turkish law as well.

INFRINGEMENT BY OUTPUT

Problem Setting

The second question of the chapter is whether and when the output generated by an AI system infringes copyrights. This is a distinct question from the first one. More precisely, infringement of a material while feeding AI does not necessarily mean that the output generated by AI will constitute an infringement. Similarly, lack of infringement in the feeding phase does not necessarily mean that the output does not constitute an infringement.

Legal Background and Analysis

Whether there is an infringement caused by the AI generated output is no different than infringement by a human being; except for the problem of identifying the legal subject liable for the infringing AI output (Novelli et al., 2024). That is why this question is "slightly easier" to answer (Guadamuz, 2023). Under Turkish law, unauthorized reproduction, modification and distribution, dissemination of a copyrighted work; plagiarism; providing incomplete, misleading or deceptive information about the work and its authorship among similar acts, qualify as copyright infringements. The author of the infringed protected materials can resort to civil and criminal remedies against the infringing party (LIAW art. 66 *et seq*).

The tricky part is, against whom the author shall use her rights because the AI system itself cannot be sued since it is not a legal subject. Among possible liable objects, there are user who prompts the AI, the person who is identified as the owner or operator of AI. In my view, the programmer will not be liable in many cases against the author since the finding of the causal link to establish does not seem likely because of the lack of proximity. While identifying the liable person, a distinction should be made among cases where AI is used as a mere tool to create the infringement and cases where AI bears a higher degree of autonomy.

The cases in the first category are those in which the human gives detailed prompts to the AI to create the infringing output. In such cases, the human should be held liable against the author. Should the operator or owner of AI be held jointly and severally liable? The answer of this question depends on whether such subjects are under a duty to design the AI in a way to prevent the infringements despite the commands of the user. While it remains to be seen, I estimate that such a duty will not be favored by lawmakers and courts as it might be an innovation-hindering move.

In the second category of cases, despite the higher degree of autonomy, a human involvement will surely exist at least as giving a plain prompt (Novelli et al., 2024). However this might not be sufficient to establish user's liability as the infringing output is autonomously generated by AI. Under Turkish law, there is no provision stipulating the attribution of liability to a legal subject in cases where AI has caused the unlawfulness. When such a case brought in front of a court (assuming that the necessary elements of liability (according to LIAW and Turkish Code of Obligations[8] (TCO)) are proved by the plaintiff) the court should identify whether the defendant is liable. Under Turkish law, a probable approach of the court will be to judge on the existence of a legal gap and to fill the gap by way of analogy. Liability for auxiliaries (TCO, art. 66) (Okyar, 2022)can be applied by way analogy. The AI system can be likened to an employee and the operator or owner the AI system can be likened to the employer who is liable for the damages caused by her employee.

Policy Debate and Recommendations

As intellectual rights are absolute rights, their infringement constitutes unlawfulness which is necessary to establish (in this context, extra-contractual) liability. The ground of civil remedies set by LIAW belong to the domain of extra-contractual liability. For AI-involved harms, the stance of European Union (EU) is that the victim of an AI system should not be in a more adverse condition compared to someone whose being harmed by a legal subject. The same is undoubtfully, true for an author whose rights are infringed by an AI output. In order to provide the same degree of legal protection to people whose being harmed by AI systems, resolving of two issues comes to front: identifying the liable subject and eliminating the extra difficulty in fulfilling the burden of proof which arises due to mainly the opacity and complexity of such systems. To this end, the EU has developed the AILD Proposa (see, Polat, 2023a).

Under Turkish law, there is no *travaux préparatoires* which can qualify as a counterpart of the AILD Proposal. However, it should be noted that the Turkish civil procedure law allows alleviating the burden of proof of the plaintiff (victim) with the help of the doctrine of *res ipsa loquitor* among other alleviating mechanisms. The problem of identifying the legal person liable for AI-caused harms (including but not limited to copyright infringements by AI outputs) can be solved by courts by way of analogy. This is not to underestimate the importance of foreseeability and clarity which can be brought by a positive norm on how to identify the liable legal subject.

PROTECTION OF OUTPUT

Problem Setting

The last question of this chapter is whether the output generated by AI systems can be protected as a "work" under the Turkish copyright law and if so, who is the author.

Legal Background and Analysis

The notion of work is defined under LIAW "as any kind of intellectual and artistic product that bears the characteristics of its author and is considered as scientific and literary, musical, fine arts or cinematic works" (art. 1(B)(a)); whereas the author is "the person who creates the work" (art. 1(B)(b)). Accordingly, being an intellectual or artistic product is the objective element for qualifying as work; while bearing the characteristics of its author is the subjective element (Hirsch, 1948). The initial text of the LIAW was referring to the "real person" as the author and excluding legal persons from the scope. In 2004, the word "real" was deleted from the text and the definition of author technically covers legal persons as well. Having said that, it should be added that a work is a product which bears the characteristics of its author. This subjective element is interpreted in the literature as a hint that the author is a human being and legal person cannot be the author of a work (Tekinalp, 2012; Zorluel, 2019) while they can definitely acquire intellectual rights of a work, i.e. by a transfer or by being the employer of the author. So, it can be induced that the LIAW from 1951 has an anthropocentric approach towards authorship.

Against this brief background, is it possible to say that the output generated by AI qualify as a work? Is it possible that an intellectual or artistic output of an AI system can bear the characteristics of its author? And who is the author? The answer that can be given to these questions is one that lawyers resort frequently: it depends. First of all, distinction should again be made among cases where AI is a mere tool and where AI is an autonomous creator of the output (Novelli et al., 2024). Apparently where AI is a mere tool, the human being prompting the AI or using it in another way that leads it to the production of the output, the human should qualify as the author if the produced output bears the above-mentioned two elements. Finding of the subjective element is less tricky in here since AI is the mere tool, and the human is the author; so, it is easier to find that the output bears the characteristics (if so) of its creator who is a human author.

In the second category of cases, qualifying the output as a work and identifying the author is trickier. In the above section (Infringement by Output), we analyzed the case by comparing it to a hypothetical one which is what would happen if the same act was carried out by a human being. The rational was that there should be no difference between the two victims. For AI generated output, we cannot apply the same test. More precisely, it is not possible to equate the answer of "Is this output generated by AI a work?" to the answer of "Would it be a work if it was created by a human?"

The legal reason[9] is in the very definition of work: the subjective condition of "bearing the creator's characteristics." Apparently, under Turkish law "work" and "author" are like the two sides of coin. Since we are analyzing the cases where AI displays a higher degree of autonomy, it is evident that the output cannot show the characteristics of a person; but those of the AI itself (if there is any) which is not a legal subject and cannot be the author. That is why this research concludes that the AI generated outputs do not qualify as work under LIAW. This conclusions seems to be the dominant view in the literature (Aslan, 2024; Gözübüyük, 2021; Güçlütürk & Cankat, 2021).

Policy Debate and Recommendations

Should the AI generated outputs be protected as works *de lege ferenda*? A consistent legal policy should consider this policy question together with that of "Infringement by Input" (see above). If a lawmaker provides ease to AI providers when they are using others' protected works as inputs; the outputs should not enjoy the same protection as that of an ordinary person. On the other hand, if AI providers are expected to obtain consent from the authors of every protected work, then their output can also enjoy equivalent protection if the output display creativity, originality, and distinctiveness which are expected in a "work" (see, Aslan, 2024).

Regarding requirements such as creativity and originality the author of this chapter confines herself to share her opinion that AI can exert genuine creativity and originality (contra Aslan, 2024) by referring to the solution by AI of the protein folding problem (Callaway, 2020). The discussion on this matter will not be delved into since the author does not find the creativity and originality of AI as a sufficient basis to defend the grant of copyright protection to the outputs generated by AI in a significantly autonomous manner (for a similar opinion, see, Novelli et al., 2024; contra Güçlütürk & Cankat, 2021; Gözübüyük, 2021 suggests grating sui generis protection to AI generated products) from the consistency perspective stated in the previous paragraph. The approach against the copyright protection for AI generated outputs "...in a substantially autonomous manner, finds confirmation in the positions taken on this issue by, e.g., the US Copyright Office, affirmed by the United States District Court for the District of Columbia, and the European Patent Office" (Novelli et al., 2024). As it is explained above under the "Infringement by Input", it is not realistic and appropriate in terms of legal policy to expect AI providers to obtain consent from the authors of every protected material they use as input. This will, conversely, result in systemic copyright infringement. This is why, lawmakers should provide a default regime of exception from which authors can opt-out. In return of this ease provided to AI providers compared to other persons that need to obtain written consent from the relevant authors, AI providers cannot expect to enjoy same level of protection for the outputs. A counter-argument from the perspective of incentive theory (Hilty et al., 2021) may be raised claiming that the lack of copyright protection may frustrate the investors of AI-systems which the authors of this chapter has to disagree. However, firstly, it is still possible for AI companies to bar the third parties from unauthorized uses to a certain extent by expressing reservation even if the output is not copyrighted. Secondly, there is no empricial evidence showing that investors would cease to invest in AI systems in the absence of copyright protection. The value of the copyright protection, considering that this would only be possible when the AI generates a creative work in an autonomous manner, would be a small proportion of returns of the investment. It should also be noted that free use of generative AI is very limited or not possible at all. Consequently, AI companies are already able to earn income by paid subscriptions among other things.

CONCLUSION

This chapter analyzes the three frequently debated IP problems within the realm of AI under Turkish law and provides recommendations where it is needed. Under Turkish law, there is no exception that AI providers can enjoy while using protected materials as input except for the cases newspaper content, news, educational works. This results in systemic copyright infringements. The lawmaker should not ignore this and should provide a default regime for the lawful use of such works while giving the option of opt-out to authors. This legal regime should be backed by regulatory requirements for AI providers on, among other aspects, copyright compliance. When it comes to the infringements caused by the outputs generated by AI in a substantially autonomous manner, the relevant legal challenges (namely the challenges of identifying the liable subject and fulfilling the burden of proof) are not specific to copyright realm, but rather relevant in all AI-harm cases in which the victims seek remedy within the scope of the extra-contractual liability. These challenges which are addressed by the EU in the AILD proposal do not necessarily require amendment under Turkish law. However, clarifying the issue in positive norms surely bears a value in terms of foreseeability. As regards the outputs generated by AI in a substantially autonomous manner, enjoy of copyright protection is not possible under existing Turkish law and not recommended by the author of this chapter.

REFERENCES

19th Criminal Chamber of the Turkish Court of Cassation, Case No: 2015/19627, Judgment No: 2018/7669, Date: 25.06.2018 (lexpera.com).

19th Criminal Chamber of the Turkish Court of Cassation Case No: 2015/32515, Judgment No: 2018/7675, Date: 25.06.2018 (lexpera.com).

19th Criminal Chamber of the Turkish Court of Cassation, Case No: 2016/12740, Judgment No: 2018/7674, Date: 25.06.2018 (lexpera.com).

Aslan, B. (2024). Yaratıcılık, Orijinallik ve Hususiyet Kavramlarının Üretken Otonom Yapay Zekâ Sistemlerine Yansımaları ve Fikri Haklar Boyutuyla Değerlendirilmesi. *Ticaret ve Fikri Mülkiyet Hukuku Dergisi*, 10(1), 3–24. DOI: 10.55027/tfm.1402220

Callaway, E. (2020). 'It will change everything': DeepMind's AI makes gigantic leap in solving protein structures. *Nature*, 588(7837), 7837. Advance online publication. DOI: 10.1038/d41586-020-03348-4 PMID: 33257889

Denemeç, I. S. (2021). *To Feed, Or Not to Feed? An Analysis of the Copyright Issues Surrounding the Use of Machine Learning Algorithms* (1st ed.). Lykeion.

Gözübüyük, B. (2021). Yapay Zekanın Meydana Getirdiği Fikri Ürünlere İlişkin 5846 Sayılı Fikir ve Sanat Eserleri Kanunundaki Sorunlar ve Çözüm Önerileri. *Kırıkkale Hukuk Mecmuası*, 1(1), 54–81.

Guadamuz, A. (2023). *A Scanner Darkly: Copyright Liability and Exceptions in Artificial Intelligence Inputs and Outputs* (SSRN Scholarly Paper 4371204). DOI: 10.2139/ssrn.4371204

Güçlütürk, O. G., & Cankat, R. (2021). Yapay Zekâ ile Oluşturulan Ürünlerin Eser Niteliği ve Eser Sahipliği Meselesi. In E. E. Aksoy Retornaz & O. G. Güçlütürk (Eds.), *Gelişen Teknolojiler ve Hukuk II: Yapay Zekâ* (pp. 195–222). On İki Levha Yayıncılık.

Henderson, P., Li, X., Jurafsky, D., Hashimoto, T., Lemley, M. A., & Liang, P. (2023). Foundation Models and Fair Use. *SSRN*, 24, 1–79. DOI: 10.2139/ssrn.4404340

Hilty, R. M., Hoffmann, J., & Scheuerer, S. (2021). Intellectual Property Justification for Artificial Intelligence. In Lee, J.-A., Hilty, R., & Liu, K.-C. (Eds.), *Artificial Intelligence and Intellectual Property* (1st ed., pp. 50–72). Oxford University Press. DOI: 10.1093/oso/9780198870944.003.0004

Hirsch, E. (1948). *Fikrî ve Sınai Haklar* (1st ed.). Ar Basımevi.

Madiega, T. (2023). *General-purpose artificial intelligence*. European Parliament. https://www.europarl.europa.eu/RegData/etudes/ATAG/2023/745708/EPRS_ATA(2023)745708_EN.pdf

Mkparu, U. A. (2024). AI in EdTech and FinTech: Stakeholder Engagement and Better Governance and Policies for Data Privacy. In Tennin, K. L., Ray, S., & Sorg, J. M. (Eds.), *Cases on AI Ethics in Business* (pp. 79–86). IGI Global. DOI: 10.4018/979-8-3693-2643-5.ch005

Novelli, C., Casolari, F., Hacker, P., Spedicato, G., & Floridi, L. (2024). *Generative AI in EU Law: Liability, Privacy, Intellectual Property, and Cybersecurity* (arXiv:2401.07348). arXiv. http://arxiv.org/abs/2401.07348

Okyar, D. (2022). *Adam Çalıştıranın Sorumluluğu (TBK m. 66)* (1st ed.). On İki Levha Yayıncılık.

Polat, C. (2023a). A Critical Appraisal of the Proposal for an AI Liability Directive: Is It Fit for Its Own Purpose? Is the EU's AI Liability Directive really promoting the rollout of trustworthy AI? This paper provides insights into the proposal's limitations. *Zeitschrift für das Privatrecht der Europäischen Union*, 20(3), 114–121. DOI: 10.9785/gpr-2023-200307

Polat, C. (2023b). Great Unclear Expectations: A Study on the Defectiveness of Autonomous Systems. *Journal of Consumer Policy*, 46(3), 363–386. DOI: 10.1007/s10603-023-09542-x

Stieper, M., & Denga, M. (2024). The international reach of EU copyright through the AI Act. *Institut Für Wirtschaftsrecht*, 194, 1–30.

Tekinalp, Ü. (2012). *Fikrî Mülkiyet Hukuku* (5th ed.). Vedat Kitapçılık.

17. U.S. Code § 107.

Zorluel, M. (2019). Yapay Zekâ ve Telif Hakkı. *TBB Dergisi*, 142, 305–356.

KEY TERMS AND DEFINITIONS

Artificial Intelligence Systems: A system of software and possibly hardware which is developed to conduct one or more tasks that require human intelligence.

Authorship: Being the owner of an intellectual or artistic work.

Copyright Exceptions: Legal bases for the lawful use of a copyrighted material without necessarily having obtained consent from the right holder.

Copyright: A subcategory of intellectual property rights which gives its holder the exclusive rights over an intellectual or artistic work.

Generative Artificial Intelligence: A subset of artificial intelligence developed based on self-learning models to fulfill the tasks of generating text, image, videos etc. generally based on a prompt.

Text and Data Mining: Extracting and analyzing large amounts of data.

Web Scraping: An automatic process of mining text and data.

ENDNOTES

1 Regulation (EU) 2024/1689 of the European Parliament and of the Council of 13 June 2024 laying down harmonised rules on artificial intelligence and amending Regulations (EC) No 300/2008, (EU) No 167/2013, (EU) No 168/2013, (EU) 2018/858, (EU) 2018/1139 and (EU) 2019/2144 and Directives 2014/90/EU, (EU) 2016/797 and (EU) 2020/1828 (Artificial Intelligence Act)

2 Proposal for a Directive of the European Parliament and of the Council on adapting non-contractual civil liability rules to artificial intelligence (AI Liability Directive), COM(2022) 496 final.

3 Proposal for a Directive of the European Parliament and of the Council on liability for defective products COM(2022) 495 final.

4 Fikir ve Sanat Eserleri Kanunu [Law on the Intellectual and Artistic Works], Law No: 5846, Date: 05/12/1951; Official Gazette Number and Date: 7981, 13/12/1951.

5 Directive (EU) 2019/790 of the European Parliament and of the Council of 17 April 2019 on copyright and related rights in the Digital Single Market and amending Directives 96/9/EC and 2001/29/EC.

6 "[…] the fair use of a copyrighted work, including such use by reproduction in copies or phonerecords or by any other means specified by that section, for purposes such as criticism, comment, news reporting, teaching (including multiple copies from classroom use), scholarship, or research, is not an infringement of copyright. In determining whether the use made of a work in any particular case is a fair use the factors to be considered shall include-

(1) the purpose and character of the use, including whether such use is of a commercial nature or is for nonprofit educational purposes;

(2) the nature of the copyrighted work;

(3) the amount and substantiality of the portion used in relation to the copyrighted work as a whole; and

(4) the effect of the use upon the potential market for or value of the copyrighted work. […]"

7 19th Criminal Chamber of the Turkish Court of Cassation, Case No: 2015/19627, Judgment No: 2018/7669, Date: 25.06.2018; Case No: 2016/12740, Judgment No: 2018/7674, Date: 25.06.2018; Case No: 2015/32515, Judgment No: 2018/7675, Date: 25.06.2018 (lexpera.com).

8 Türk Borçlar Kanunu [Turkish Code of Obligations], Law No: 6098, Date: 11/01/2011. Official Gazette Number and Date: 27836, 04/02/2011.

9 There is also a policy reason for not equating the two cases to each other which will be discussed under the next heading.

Chapter 10
An Evaluation of Copyright Infringements Committed Through Generative Artificial Intelligence and Especially Deep Fakes

Barış Gözübüyük
Hacettepe University, Turkey

ABSTRACT

Deepfake technology, a form of Generative Artificial Intelligence (Gen-AI), allows for the manipulation of individuals' voices and images to generate fake videos where people appear to be saying or doing things they never actually said or did. This has led to concerns about copyright infringement and other rights violations, though this study specifically focuses on copyright issues. Dealing with these violations on a global scale presents significant and urgent challenges. However, the necessity of providing fair compensation to creators for using their work is not just a step, but a fundamental requirement towards allowing the legal use of deepfake technology. As a solution, this study suggests a remuneration model to address copyright infringements related to deepfakes.

DOI: 10.4018/979-8-3693-8704-7.ch010

INTRODUCTION: AN EVALUATION OF COPYRIGHT INFRINGEMENTS COMMITTED THROUGH GENERATIVE ARTIFICIAL INTELLIGENCE AND ESPECIALLY DEEP FAKE[1]

The concept of generative artificial intelligence is increasingly being used instead of the concept of artificial intelligence. In this context, technological advancements in artificial intelligence have skyrocketed, reaching a new phase with the emergence of Generative Artificial Intelligence (Gen-AI). (Gen-AI) is a branch of artificial intelligence (AI) that has the ability to generate content (Kalota, 2024). Traditional AI systems have the capacity to analyse and make predictions from present training data; nevertheless, Gen-AI can generate new data that is similar to its training data (WIPO Conversation). This ability enables Gen-AI to create new content such as audio, video, etc (WIPO Conversation). In this context, generative artificial intelligence generates works of art using sophisticated and complex machine learning methods (Davenport & Mittal, 2022). Chat-GPT is one of the leading examples of Gen-AI (Bin Akhtar, 2024).

Recently, copyright infringement through deepfakes has been on the rise. Thus, this article focuses on deepfake, a kind of Gen-AI (Tyagi, 2024). Deep fake term is a portmanteau of "deep learning" and fake words (Kılıç & Kahraman, 2023; Ullrich, 2021). Deep fake technology can generate synthetic manipulation of images, sound and video (Tyni, 2023). In this context, The European Union's AI act in article 3/60 defines "deep fake" as "*AI-generated or manipulated image, audio or video content that resembles existing persons, objects, places or other entities or events and would falsely appear to a person to be authentic or truthful.*"

Deep fakes are generated using a machine learning technique called generative adversarial network (GAN) (Talas & Ashurst, 2019).

Corresponding to technological improvements and the intuitiveness of deep fake technology, it is fair to say that the use of deep fake content will increase significantly. Developments in the technology area inevitably impact the field of law. In this respect, the deep fakes pose a legal matter.

LITERATURE REVIEW/THEORETICAL DISCUSSIONS

Voice and Face Cloning Through Deep Fake Technology and Copyright Infringement

One with average programming skills can easily generate authentic, deep fake videos (Singh, et al., 2020). People's voices and faces are being cloned with the help of this technology. While the manipulation of digital content is not new, the use of artificial intelligence for manipulation is (Talas & Ashurst, 2019). Therefore, this situation brings new threats. Audio and video copying is one of these threats. While an actor's or singer's voice may be central to their artistic identity and add value to their creations, the voice should not be considered a separate "work" (Watt et al., 2020). According to (Wells-Edwards, 2022), human voices, despite their unique nature, cannot be protected by copyright. (Watt et al., 2020) argue that a recording of a voice is similar to the taking of a photograph of a face.

Copyright Violation Through Deep Fake

Although voice and face cloning do not constitute copyright infringement on their own, the use of music, movies and other works to produce deepfake content without the authors' permission may constitute a violation of the copyrights of the authors (Nath & B, 2024). The copyright of the owner of the audiovisual work is infringed when deep-fake content is created by processing an audiovisual work whose copyright belongs to someone else without the author's authorisation. This is because deepfakes often contain existing audiovisual works (Talas & Ashurst, 2019). Indeed, a video copyrighted by Condé Nast has been turned into a deep fake (Geddes, 2021). In this context, the copyright holder of the video wanted to have the deep-faked video removed from social media platforms (Geddes, 2021).

Training Data and Copyright Infringement

Gen-AI can not generate creative content intrinsically; it has to be trained (Deloitte AI Institute). The same is true for deep fakes. Training data is crucial for developing AI models (see e.g., Saleh et al., 2024). Text and data must be analysed using text and data mining (TDM) techniques to uncover new patterns and derive value from the data (Rosati, 2018). TDM creates temporary copies of data content for analysis (Carroll, 2019; Dusollier, 2020). Berne Convention article 9/1 states that "*Authors of literary and artistic works protected by this Convention shall have the exclusive right of authorizing the reproduction of these works, in any manner or form*". In this context, according to (Nema, 2021), most of the training data used to generate deep fakes is copyrighted, and the output (video, photo, etc.) infringes copyright. On the other hand, (Quang, 2021) argues that since data are used for a specific purpose and are not redistributed or recommunicated to public training, AI does not violate copyright.

The fair use doctrine in the American legal system exempts some instances of copyright violations. Artificial intelligence algorithms do not copy the data one-to-one during the training process but transform the data into a new format. Therefore, the use of data for training purposes should be evaluated within the scope of the fair use exception (Torrance & Tomlinson, 2023). Despite that, (Grimmelman, 2016) states that fair use is interpreted differently for humans and robots and that actions that constitute copyright infringement when performed by humans are covered by the fair use exception when performed by robots.

Even though there is no fair use doctrine in EU law, the EU Directive on Copyright and Related Rights in the Digital Single Market (2019/790) introduced two exceptions for text and data mining in Articles 3 and 4. Article 3 of EU Directive No. 2019/790 exempts research organisations and cultural heritage institutions from reproduction and extraction for text and data mining for scientific research purposes. As (Margoni & Kretschmer, 2022) point out, this article includes two limitations: beneficiaries are limited to research organisations and cultural heritage institutions (first limitation), and exemption is limited to scientific purposes (second limitation). Meanwhile, the exemption in Article 4 of the text, as mentioned earlier, states that it is not limited to scientific purposes. However, rightsholders may reserve this exemption. (Rosatti, 2018) states that the limitation in Article 4 potentially restricts text and data mining activities. In this context, text and data mining exceptions are considered complex and costly for small startups (Tyagi, 2024).

Remuneration Model

AI systems' capabilities will significantly impact the market for human literary and artistic works (Senftleben, 2024). In this context, (Pasquale & Sun, 2024) argue that AI providers should be required to pay compensation through a levy. According to (Pasquale & Sun, 2024), the government should enforce this levy. Nevertheless, (Senftleben, 2023) suggests implementing a remuneration system through collecting societies.

RESEARCH AND METHODS

Research Method

Academic law books, legal journals, and related journals are used as primary data collection methods. Legal regulation analysis and court decisions are used as secondary data collection methods. The data collected was analysed to comprehend the perspective of legal systems on copyright infringements committed through deep fakes.

Research Approach

In this study, the author used a normative legal research approach. In normative legal research, the aim is often to reach the level of doctrine (Christiani, 2015). The study is not a comparative law study. Nevertheless, the regulations of the US and EU laws and court decisions of USA and EU have been utilized wherever necessary. The study's starting point was acknowledging that deep fake technology is a type of Gen-AI. In this context, it is realised that most legal issues related to the conflict between Gen-AI copyright law also apply to deep fake technology. Due to the ability of deep fake technology to clone face and voice, some violations are not covered by copyright law and are related to personality rights. The absence of the "fair use" exception in EU law requires EU regulations to address this gap. Hence, American case law, EU directives, and other relevant regulations are used to understand the nuances of AI training between two legal systems.

Data Collection

In this study, primary and secondary data resources are collected, and the author conducted research using qualitative methods. The study's author has followed a predominantly online research strategy; however, he used printed copies of the sources he could not access online.

Limitations

This study focuses on copyright infringements committed through GEN-AI with a particular focus on deep fakes. Therefore, narrow or weak intelligence falls outside the scope of the study. The legal status of artificial intelligence and copyright issues are also outside the scope of the study. Furthermore, issues regarding the owner of the intellectual products generated by Gen-AI/deep fake are out of the scope of this study. The study focuses only on the legal dimension of artificial intelligence. Therefore, the economic consequences of the infringements are not within the scope of the study.

FINDINGS/DISCUSSION

Voice and Face Cloning Through Deep Fake Technology Does Not Constitute Copyright Infringement

The Berne Convention for the Protection of Literary and Artistic Works of September 9, 1886 as amended (the 'Berne Convention'), states at Article 2(2): "*It shall, however, be a matter for legislation in the countries of the Union to prescribe that works in general or any specified categories of works shall not be protected unless they have been fixed in some material form.*" Therefore, fixation is a requirement for copyright protection (Watt et al., 2020). In Midler v. Ford Motor Co. case the aforementioned issue is emphasised as follows: "*Copyright protects "original works of authorship fixed in any tangible medium of expression." 17 U.S.C. § 102(a). A voice is not copyrightable. The sounds are not "fixed." What is put forward as protectable here is more personal than any work of authorship.*" (*Midler v. Ford Motor Co., 849 F.2d 460*, 9th Cir., 1988).

Altering individuals' images through deepfake technology does not constitute copyright infringement due to previously made statements concerning the human voice. The human voice and image alteration should be evaluated in the context of personal rights violations, which is outside this study's scope. However, looking at the EU's regulations against the potential harmful effects of deep fakes is helpful. The EUAI act provides transparency obligations against the harmful effects of deep fakes. In this context, Article 50(4) of the said law entitled "Transparency obligations for providers and users of certain AI systems" states that:

> *Deployers of an AI system that generates or manipulates image, audio or video content constituting a deep fake, shall disclose that the content has been artificially generated or manipulated. This obligation shall not apply where the use is authorised by law to detect, prevent, investigate or prosecute criminal offence...".*
> *"...Deployers of an AI system that generates or manipulates text which is published with the purpose of informing the public on matters of public interest shall disclose that the text has been artificially generated or manipulated. This obligation shall not apply where the use is authorised by law to detect, prevent, investigate or prosecute criminal offences or where the AI-generated content has undergone a process of human review or editorial control and where a natural or legal person holds editorial responsibility for the publication of the content.*

The law on artificial intelligence requires that it must be disclosed when a deep fake is used. The critical issue for our study is how to fulfil the transparency obligation when a material such as a video, which is a work of authorship, is used to make a deep fake. The relevant provision states the following in this regard:

Where the content forms part of an evidently artistic, creative, satirical, fictional analogous work or programme, the transparency obligations set out in this paragraph are limited to disclosure of the existence of such generated or manipulated content in an appropriate manner that does not hamper the display or enjoyment of the work.

In this context, the disclosure obligation is specifically constrained by the provision mentioned. This limitation aims to protect the moral and economic rights of authors and related right holders. Allowing unrestricted sharing of the work in its original form could potentially result in unauthorized access, bypassing the payment of royalty fees. Hence, I find the EU legislator's regulation in this matter to be appropriate.

Moral and Economic Rights of Authors and Related Rights Holders Might Be Violated Through Deep Fake Technology

When creating a deep fake, using the authors' works without permission may lead to copyright infringement (Hendrawan et al., 2023). Based on the usage, both the economic and moral rights of authors and related rights holders may be infringed upon. Providing a general assessment of an author's rights violation proves challenging, as it must be evaluated based on the specific circumstances of each case. However, it is evident that the right to reproduce, which is among the most fundamental exclusive rights of the author, will be violated in almost every case. Article 6 bis of the Bern Convention regulates the author's moral rights. The provision states:

Independently of the author's economic rights, and even after the transfer of the said rights, the author shall have the right to claim authorship of the work and to object to any distortion, mutilation or other modification of, or other derogatory action in relation to, the said work, which would be prejudicial to his honor or reputation.

Hence, deep fakes can also violate the moral rights of the author, as the work may be altered, destroyed, or otherwise changed Nath & B. (2024).

In some cases, the purpose of deep fake content is also important. In this context, deep fake content can also sometimes be parodied (Talas & Ashurst, 2019). The most well-known example of this is the famous actor Nicholas Cage. The artist is the subject of a lot of deep fake content (Purdom, 2018). In some cases, artists react to such uses. In a particular case, Jay-Z attempted to remove deepfake videos from YouTube that depicted him reciting Shakespearean soliloquies and performing Billy Joel's "We Didn't Start the Fire." However, Google refused his DMCA takedown request, arguing that the deepfakes did not constitute a copyright infringement (Just Joking). Parody is recognised as an exception to copyright in both American and EU law. Uses falling within this exception do not constitute copyright infringement.

However, these two branches of law regulate this exception differently. In American law, parody is considered within the scope of fair use. In this context, Section 107 of the Copyright Act provides that:

Notwithstanding the provisions of sections 106 and 106A, the fair use of a copyrighted work, including such use by reproduction in copies or phonorecords or by any other means specified by that section, for purposes such as criticism, comment, news reporting, teaching (including multiple copies for classroom use), scholarship, or research, is not an infringement of copyright.

In this context, deep fake content produced for parody purposes and evaluated within the scope of fair use will not constitute copyright infringement. This issue should be evaluated according to the characteristics of the concrete case. In the realm of EU law, the issue of parody is governed by a Directive. The parody exception in EU law was initially addressed under Article 5(3)(k) of the 2001/29 EC Information Society Directive. However, Article 5(3) also grants Member States the authority to establish exceptions or limitations to the rights outlined in Articles 2 and 3. Thus, Member States have some leeway in this matter. Consequently, the effectiveness of this provision in the context of the copyright exception remains uncertain. For that reason, 2019/790 EC Copyright and Related Rights in the Digital Single Market Directive does not grant Member States any latitude in terms of the parody exception. In this context, article 17/7 states, "*Member States shall ensure that users in each Member State are able to rely on any of the following existing exceptions or limitations when uploading and making available content generated by users on online content-sharing services: (a) quotation, criticism, review*".

Thus, we have determined that the moral and economic rights of copyright and related rights holders can be violated through deepfakes. However, it is also important to consider what can be done against such violations. In this context, the first and quickest method in any legal system should be to remove the content. At this point, an example can be given from Turkish law. According to Law No. 5846 on Intellectual and Artistic Works, removal can be done following Additional Article 4 of the Law. Once the content has been removed, the process can continue with the compensation procedure. In this context, additional article 4, the mentioned Law on Intellectual and Artistic Works, states:

Information which identifies the work, the author of the work, the holder of any right in the work or information about the terms and conditions of use of the work, and any numbers or codes that represent such information attached to a copy of a work or appear in connection with the communication of a work to the public may not be removed or altered. The originals or copies of the works on which the information and numbers or codes representing this information have been altered or removed may not be distributed, imported for distribution, broadcast or communicated to the public. The provisions of the preceding para-

graph shall also apply to phonograms and performances fixed on phonograms. (Amendment: 3.3.2004-5101/25) In case where rights of authors and related rights holders granted by this Law have been violated by providers of service and content through the transmission of signs, sounds, and/or images including digital transmission, the works which are subject of the violation shall, upon the application of the rightholders, be removed from the content. Natural or legal persons whose rights have been violated shall to this end initially contact with the content provider and request that the violation be ceased within three days. Should the violation continue, a request shall next be made to the public prosecutor requiring that the service being provided to the content provider persisting in the violation be suspended within three days by the relevant service provider. The service being provided to the content provider shall be restored, if the violation is ceased. Service providers shall submit a list of the names of their content providers to the Ministry on the first working day of every month. Service providers and content providers are obliged to submit all kinds of information and documents when requested by the Ministry. The rules and procedures regarding the application of the provisions of this Article shall be stipulated in a by-law to be issued by the Ministry.

Using a Dataset to Train AI Models Could Lead to Copyright Infringement in US and EU

Training data may include copyrighted material that could lead to copyright infringement. In this context, most AI developers use previously stored content to train their AI models (Sag, 2024). However, before directly jumping to a conclusion, evaluating whether exemptions regarding training data exist is necessary. The US and EU laws approach the mentioned issue differently.

The fair use doctrine in the American legal system exempts some instances of copyright violations. Fair use allows users to use the works of the author without his/her permission (Caroll, 2019). Fair use is an exception of exclusive issued under section 107 of the Digital Millenium Copyright Act (DMCA, 1998). Fair use is based on a four-factor test:

1) The purpose and character of the use, including whether such use is of a commercial nature or is for nonprofit educational purposes 2) The nature of copyrighted work, 3) the amount and substantiality of the portion used in relation to the copyrighted work as a whole, 4) the effect of the use upon the potential market for or value of the copyrighted work. The fact that a work is unpublished shall not itself bar a finding of fair use if such finding is made upon consideration of all the above factors.

Although the conditions of fair use are specified in the said provision, an evaluation is required case by case, (Quang, 2021) states that legal uncertainty prevails regarding the fair use doctrine. Since each case must be handled on its merits, it is not appropriate to make a general conclusion about the fair use of training data. In this context, it is stated that the fair use exception can be bypassed through licensing agreements between private law persons (Samberg et al., 2024; *Bowers v. Baystate Technologies, Inc, 320 F.3d 1317, 1336-37,* Fed. Cir., 2003). Hence, the provisions of the license agreement between the parties take precedence over the fair use defence, making it possible to counter the fair use defence. For this reason, in practice, most publishers based on the subscriber model choose to restrict users' TDM activities through their contracts (Caroll, 2019).

EU Directive No. 2019/790 provides for exceptions for text and data mining in some instances. However, these exceptions are narrow in scope. Considering everything mentioned, it can be argued that using materials in artificial intelligence training activities will not result in copyright infringement, thanks to the fair use doctrine in the USA and the text and data mining exceptions in the EU. However, we believe this interpretation may not apply to every situation due to the narrow scope of the Directive mentioned.

While It Is Not Possible to Fight Copyright Violations on a Global Scale, Remuneration Mechanism Can Be Developed

The principle of territoriality is prevalent in international intellectual property law. As a result of this principle, copyright infringements may only be addressed country-by-country (Ullrich, 2021). Nevertheless, copyright infringements on the internet are global in nature. Since deep fake content is also being disseminated on the internet, it is inconceivable to address these violations globally. Therefore, rather than concentrating on copyright violations, it may be more constructive way to focus on how rights holders can benefit from them. This benefit can only be attained by developing an effective legal business model. This business model must be based on high technology and have the ability to detect copyright infringements committed through deep fakes. However, it should be taken into account that the current level of technology will not be sufficient to design such a system. Because today, understanding which content is produced by deepfakes and which is authentic is a matter (Dolhansky et al., 2020).

The Content ID system, currently used by YouTube, provides an interesting example, even though it is not designed to detect deep-faked content. When a video is uploaded to YouTube, the Content ID system automatically scans it to determine whether it matches another video in the system (Youtube Help, Learn about Content ID claims). This system gives rights holders a choice: they can either request that the content be removed or claim rights to the advertising revenues generated from the content (Youtube Help, Learn about Content ID claims). According to its current deepfake policy, YouTube requires content producers to report that content produced using deepfake technology is altered or artificial (Yotube Help, Disclosing use of altered or synthetic content). It might be valuable to consider developing a system like YouTube's Content ID to identify and detect deepfake content. The outcome of Gen-AI might be identical to the original work. In this case, infringement of the right of reproduction of the author can be deemed (Nordemann, 2024). However, even in this case, the key determinant of the infringement decision is whether the existing work is used in the AI training process since the outcome might be considered "independent double creation (Nordemann, 2024)". For that reason, detecting copyright violations arising from the training data could be challenging, as many copyright infringements related to deepfakes originate from the training data. Therefore, a business model focused on detecting concrete violations may not be effective regarding deep fakes. Nevertheless, depending on the progress of technology, a model that identifies copyrighted materials used in deepfake training would benefit rights holders. In this context, platforms such as YouTube will be able to utilise this model and pave the way for rights holders to generate advertising revenue, as is the case with ContentID. However, as far as we can determine, there is no widespread and generally accepted model. Therefore, this business model remains theoretical.

On the other hand, a remuneration model can be proposed through the remuneration system. The idea underlying this system is as follows: regardless of whether the author's rights are violated, it would be appropriate to act from the beginning with the idea that the author will suffer damages and that these possible damages should be compensated. Although there seems to be a hypothetical situation here, it is not. Because AI developers do not obtain permission from the rights holders for the copyrighted content used in training the AI, nor do they make any payments to them. In this case, it would be possible to discuss copyright infringement due to unauthorized use without looking for similarities between the resulting output and existing works.

The remuneration model we propose has a triple pillar consisting of copyright owners, AI developers, and collecting societies. This model is based on the principle that AI developers pay a fixed amount each year as a fair remuneration to collecting societies representing the authors and related rights holders (Senftleben, 2023). Thanks to this remunaration model, authors will be protected from the outset against possible violations of their economic rights. (Senftleben, 2023) asserts that this remuneration should be paid to cultural and social funds of collecting societies so that human works can be supported. This model is not unfamiliar to the operations of collecting societies. In this context, there have been social and/or cultural funds within collecting societies for a long time (Dietz, 1990).

It is effective to collect remuneration fees from AI developers in the country where the relevant collecting societies operate and make distributions to the members of collecting societies. However, collecting society membership is not mandatory (Ficsor, 2006) unless regulated by law.

In this context, rights holders, not members of collecting societies, do not benefit from remuneration. This problem can be overcome by adopting mandatory collective rights management (Senftleben, 2023) regarding remuneration. In this way, rights holders, not members of any collecting societies, can also benefit from remuneration.

The effectiveness of our remuneration model may be questionable if AI developers use the works of rights holders residing in foreign countries. Due to the principle of territoriality, collecting societies cannot, as a rule, pursue rights on behalf of members of collecting societies operating in other countries. However, collecting societies can eliminate this problem through reciprocal agreements.

Remuneration collected by collecting societies should not be considered as a form of tax (Ficsor, 2006). This amount to be collected from artificial intelligence developers will undoubtedly be reflected as a cost item to them. This cost item should not reach a level that will cause financial difficulty for AI developers and negatively affect the sector's development. It would be appropriate for the remuneration amount in question to be determined by law. In this context, the interest in protecting the authors and the interest arising from the need to develop artificial intelligence are in conflict. Hence, policymakers and legislators' most crucial task should be to balance conflicting interests.

CONCLUSION

Deepfake videos may result in copyright violations. If copyrighted content is considered within the scope of the copyright exception, it can be freely used without obtaining permission from the author and the owner of the related rights, or without a license agreement. While exceptions are regulated under the scope of fair use in American law, they are regulated under the relevant Directives in EU law. In order to discuss an infringement in this specific case, the use should not be assessed based on the exception.

Individual rights holders find it exceptionally challenging to address these violations. This is because the country where the infringement occurs is often different from the country where the copyright owner resides. Dealing with these cases is extremely challenging due to the territoriality principle in intellectual property law. For this reason, business models and methods emerging as a result of developing technology have gained importance in the fight against copyright infringement. In this context, depending on technological advancements, platforms like YouTube could develop flexible business models that economically satisfy rights holders. Currently, developing such a business model does not seem feasible. Therefore, a compensation-based model appears to be practically applicable.

Regardless of whether the economic rights of the authors and related rights holders have been infringed in a specific case, it is recommended to collect a certain amount annually from artificial intelligence developers and allocate it to collecting societies in the relevant field. However, the amount to be collected should not be at a rate that would harm AI developers and hinder developments in the field of AI.

REFERENCES

Akhtar, Z. B. (2024). Unveiling the evolution of generative AI (GAI): A comprehensive and investigative analysis toward LLM models (2021–2024) and beyond. *Journal of Electrical Systems and Information Technology*, 11(22), 1–21.

Carroll, M. W. (2019). Copyright and the progress of science: Why text and data mining is lawful. American University Washington College of Law, *Washington College of Law Research Paper No*, 2020-15, 53:893, 893-964.

Christiani, T. A. (2015). Normative and empirical research methods: Their usefulness and relevance in the study of law as an object. *GATR Global Journal of Business and Social Science Review*, 3(4), 16–22. DOI: 10.35609/gjbssr.2015.3.4(3)

Davenport, T. H., & Mittal, N. (2022, November). How generative AI is changing creative work. *Harvard Business Review*. https://hbr.org/2022/11/how-generative-ai-is-changing-creative-work

Dietz, A. (1990). A modern concept for the right of the community of authors (domaine public payant). *Copyright Bulletin. Unesco*, 24(4), 1–37.

Dolhansky, B., Bitton, J., Pflaum, B., Lu, J., Howes, R., Wang, M., & Ferrer, C. C. (2020). The DeepFake Detection Challenge (DFDC) Dataset. 8(20), ArXiv./abs/2006.07397.

Dusollier, S. (2020). The 2019 Directive on Copyright in the Digital Single Market: Some progress, a few bad choices, and an overall failed ambition. *Common Market Law Review*, 57(4), 979–1030. DOI: 10.54648/COLA2020714

Ficsor, M. (2006). Collective management of copyright and related rights in the digital networked environment: Voluntary, presumption-based, extended, mandatory, possible, inevitable. In D. Gervais (Ed.), *Collective management of copyright and related rights* (pp. 37-83). Kluwer Law International.

Geddes, K. G. (2021). Ocularcentrism and deepfakes: Should seeing be believing? *Fordham Intellectual Property, Media & Entertainment Law Journal*, 31(4), 1042-1083. https://ir.lawnet.fordham.edu/iplj/vol31/iss4/3

Generative AI and the future of work The potential? Boundless. Deloitte AI Institute, https://www2.deloitte.com/content/dam/Deloitte/us/Documents/consulting/us-ai-institute-generative-ai-and-the-future-of-work.pdf

Grimmelman, J. (2016). Copyright for literate robots. *Iowa Law Review*, 101(2), 657–681.

Hendrawan, D., Andersen, C., Tiopan, D., Kurniawan, S., & Malinda, M. (2023). Juridical review of copyright infringement in the use of deepfakes in the creative industry in Indonesia. *International Journal of Cyber Criminology*, 17(1). https://cocreationstudio.mit.edu/wp-content/uploads/2021/12/JustJoking.pdf

Joking, J. https://cocreationstudio.mit.edu/wp-content/uploads/2021/12/JustJoking.pdf

Kalota, F. (2024). A primer on generative artificial intelligence. *Education Sciences*, 14(2), 1–15. DOI: 10.3390/educsci14020172

Kılıç, B., & Kahraman, M. E. (2023). Current usage areas of deepfake applications with artificial intelligence technology. *İletişim ve Toplum Araştırmaları Dergisi*, 3(2), 301-332.

Margoni, T., & Kretschmer, M. (2022). A deeper look into the EU text and data mining exceptions: Harmonisation, data ownership, and the future of technology. *GRUR International*, 71(8), 685–701. DOI: 10.1093/grurint/ikac054

Nath, A., & B., S. (2024). Deepfakes on Copyright Law- Inadequacy of Present Laws in Determining the Real Issues. *Indian Journal of Law and Justice*, 15(1), 285–300. https://ir.nbu.ac.in/handle/123456789/5250

Nordemann, J. B. (2024). EU law: Generative AI, copyright infringements and liability – My guess for a hot topic in 2024, Kluwer Copyright Blog, https://copyrightblog.kluweriplaw.com/2024/01/23/eu-law-generative-ai-copyright-infringements-and-liability-my-guess-for-a-hot-topic-in-2024/

Pasquale, F. A., & Sun, H. (2024). Consent and compensation: Resolving generative AI's copyright crisis. *Cornell Legal Studies Research Paper*, Forthcoming, University of Hong Kong Faculty of Law Research Paper No. 2024/07, 110:207. https://ssrn.com/abstract=4826695DOI: 10.2139/ssrn.4826695

Purdom, C. (2018). Deep learning technology is now being used to put Nic Cage in every movie. https://www.avclub.com/deep-learning-technology-is-now-being-used-to-put-nic-c-1822514573

Nema, , P. (2021). Understanding copyright issues entailing deepfakes in India. *International Journal of Law and Information Technology*, 29(3), 241–254. DOI: 10.1093/ijlit/eaab007

Quang, J. (2021). Does training AI violate copyright law? *Berkeley Technology Law Journal*, 36(4), 1407–1436.

Rosati, E. (2018). An EU text and data mining exception for the few: Would it make sense? *Journal of Intellectual Property Law & Practice*, 13(6), 429–430. DOI: 10.1093/jiplp/jpy063

Sag, M. (2024). Fairness and fair use in generative AI. *Fordham Law Review*, 92, 1888–1921.

Saleh, A., Marcus, S., Jerry, D., & Azghadi, M. R. (2024). Applications of deep learning in fish habitat monitoring: A tutorial and survey. *Expert Systems with Applications*, 238(Part B), 1-22.

Samberg, R., Vollmer, T., & Teremi, S. (2024). Fair use rights to conduct text and data mining and use artificial intelligence tools are essential for UC research and teaching, https://osc.universityofcalifornia.edu/2024/03/fair-use-tdm-ai-restrictive-agreements/

Senftleben, M. (2023). Generative AI and author remuneration. *IIC; International Review of Industrial Property and Copyright Law*, 54(10), 1535–1560. DOI: 10.1007/s40319-023-01399-4

Senftleben, M. (2024). AI Act and author remuneration: A model for other regions? Institute for Information Law (IViR), University of Amsterdam, https://ssrn.com/abstract=4740268

Singh, S., Sharma, R., & Smeaton, A. F. (2020). Using GANs to synthesise minimum training data for deepfake generation, *ArXiv*, 1-13.

Talas, T., & Ashurst, K. M. (2019). Diving into the deep end: Regulating deepfakes online. *Communications Law Bulletin*, 38(3), 11-13. https://www.austlii.edu.au/au/journals/CommsLawB/2019/24.pdf

Torrance, A. W., & Tomlinson, B. (2023). Training is everything: Artificial intelligence, copyright, and fair training. *Dickinson Law Review*, 128(1), 233-255. https://ssrn.com/abstract=4437680

Tyagi, K. (2024). Copyright text & data mining and the innovation dimension of generative AI. *Journal of Intellectual Property Law & Practice*, 19(7), 557–570. DOI: 10.1093/jiplp/jpae028

Tyni, E. (2023). Could you imagine that face on that body? A study of deepfakes and performers' rights in EU law (Dissertation). *Linköping University Electronic Press*. https://urn.kb.se/resolve?urn=urn:nbn:se:liu:diva-196279

Ullrich, Q. J. (2021). Is this video real? The principal mischief of deepfakes and how the Lanham Act can address it. *Columbia Journal of Law and Social Problems*, 55(1), 1–56.

Watt, D., Harrison, P. S., & Cabot-King, L. (2020). Who owns your voice? Linguistic and legal perspectives on the relationship between vocal distinctiveness and the rights of the individual speaker. *International Journal of Speech Language and the Law*, 26(2), 137–180. DOI: 10.1558/ijsll.40571

Wells-Edwards, B. (2024). What's in a voice? The legal implications of voice cloning. *Arizona Law Review*, 64(1213), 1214–1237.

WIPO. (2023). Generative AI. *WIPO Conversation IP and Frontier Technologies.* https://www.wipo.int/edocs/mdocs/mdocs/en/wipo_ip_conv_ge_2_23/wipo_ip_conv_ge_2_23_summary.pdf

YouTube Help. (n.d.). Learn about Content ID claims. https://support.google.com/youtube/answer/6013276?hl=en&sjid=7757058968664509376-EU

YouTube Help. (n.d.). Disclosing use of altered or synthetic content. https://support.google.com/youtube/answer/14328491?hl=en&sjid=7757058968664509376-EU#zippy=%2Ci%CC%87%C3%A7erik-%C3%BCreticilerin-bildirmesi-gereken-i%C3%A7eriklere-%C3%B6rnekler

ENDNOTE

1 The article has been prepared using the results of the project titled "Artificial Intelligence and Copyright: A Comparative Legal and Economic Analysis of Countries," which is supported by the Directorate General of Copyrights of the Ministry of Culture and Tourism of the Republic of Türkiye.

Chapter 11
Legal and Intellectual Property Challenges in the Age of Artificial Intelligence:
Exploring AI Authorship, Personhood, and Copyright

Ankita Roy
https://orcid.org/0009-0008-0563-1748
IEM's International Institute of Juridical Sciences, India

Abhisikta Basu
https://orcid.org/0000-0002-2800-2337
IEM's International Institute of Juridical Sciences, India

ABSTRACT

The beginning of human history witnessed innovation has propelled human advancement. The subject artificial intelligence has gained popularity lately. Scholars, decision-makers, and consumers are now more aware of the advantages and necessity of artificial intelligence (AI) because of astounding news reports about self-driving cars, creative robots, and learning algorithms. The author analyses the evaluation of AI technology, the current research landscape, and the legal issues it raises, especially in the areas of IP rights and AI personhood. It examines the IP theories supporting AI creativity and the implications of the present IP framework. The perspectives of US and the EU have been analysed as they further investigate the future of AI authorship. The constraints of data for AI development have been covered showing the need for high quality data and the potential legal modifications

DOI: 10.4018/979-8-3693-8704-7.ch011

to address copyright and privacy issues. Lastly, the author suggests directions for developing authorship rights and provides insights into the legal personality of AI authors.

1. INTRODUCTION

Artificial Intelligence (AI) can be traced back to the year 1940 when Isaac Asimov publishes a short story, titled Runaround. The short story hypothized three laws of Robotics- first: "*a robot may not injure a human being or through inaction, allow a human being to come to harm,* second: *robot must obey the orders given to it by human beings except where such orders would conflict with the First Law*; and lastly: *a robot must protect its* own *existence as long as such protection does not conflict with the First or Second Laws*" (Haenlein & Kaplan, 2019). Further, the biggest impact in the realm of AI was made by a British mathematician named Alan Turing who built the first digital computer named 'The Bombe' (Haenlein & Kaplan, 2019). In 1950, Claude Shannon claimed the idea of computers playing chess (Manning, 2020). Officially in 1956, the presence of AI explicitly emerged in a conference at Dartmouth (Sharma, 2024). Somehow, such rush attempts focused on the advancement of AI for its probability of benefits overlooked the potential challenges. Though the impact and effectiveness AI has shown in various sectors, it raises concerns relating to accountability, transparency, privacy rights, intellectual property rights, and ethics.

Figure 1. The working principles of AI

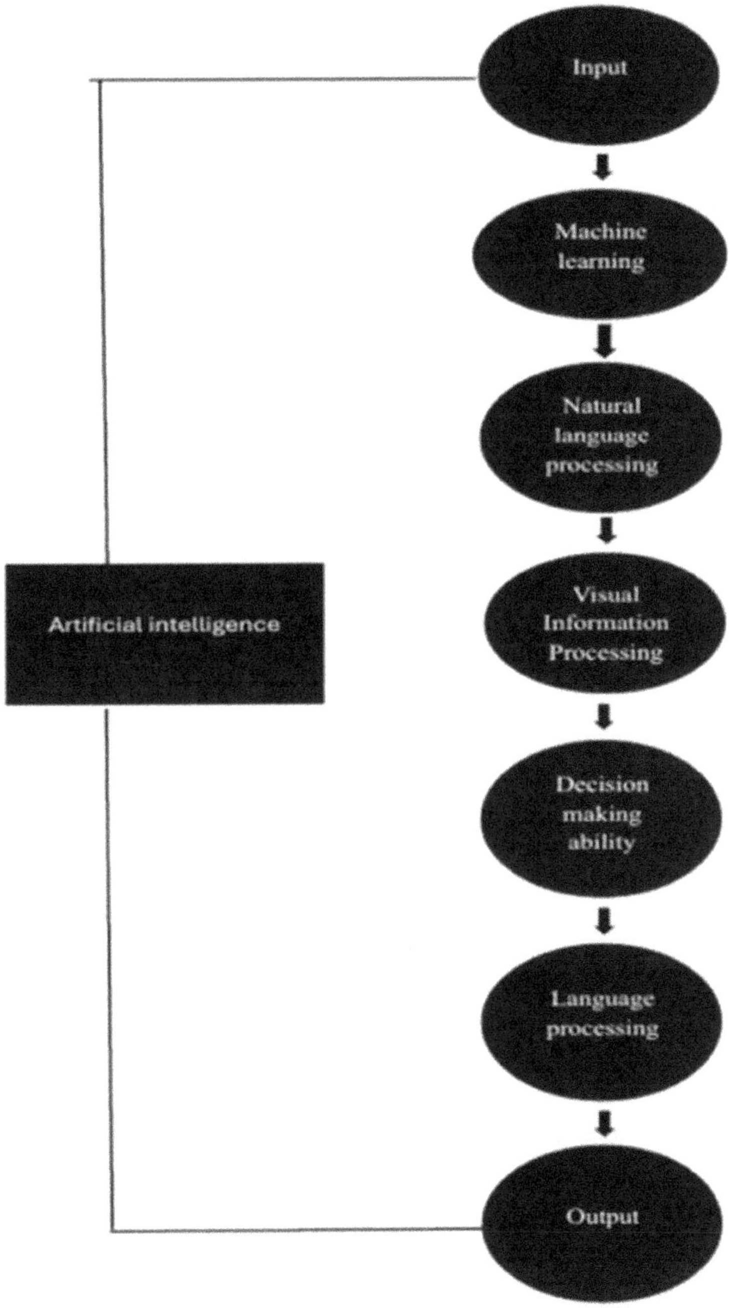

(flow chart created by author)

AI operates by use of a methodical procedure involving multiple essential steps. Fig 1 shows the mechanism which begins with incorporating 'Input,' which refers to the data fed to the AI system which can come in various forms including text, images, audio. Next, the 'machine learning' process begins which is a crucial component where algorithms analyse the input to find patterns and gain knowledge from it, thereby enhancing their understanding and performance with time. Through 'natural language processing,' AI comprehend and generate human language, facilitating communication through text and speech. 'Visual Information Processing' enables AI to analyse and interpret visual data such as photos and videos, results into the recognition of objects, faces and scenes. The AI system then uses its 'decision-making ability' to assess the information it has processed, weight the possible outcomes and finally produce the result of this entire process, known as' output' (Jokanovic, 2022). Focusing on the challenges associated with AI development and regulation within the legal framework to ensure protection of fundamental rights and promote fairness is essential for ensuring coexistence of AI and human rights (Jokanovic, 2022).

1.1 Arguments Relating AI Personhood and the Legal Status of Non-Human Entities

AI became an omnipresent element of society. Scientists across the world are trying to develop strong AI which will have autonomy and the capacity to think. As the human interaction increases with these machines it will consequently give rise to legal issues. Therefore, our legal system must be equipped to address these impending difficulties. The ability to give AI legal personality can be a useful tool for preventing any potential problems that may arise from the integration of AI into our society. Advocates of AI personality contend that since AI is capable of making decisions and influencing people on their own, it ought to be given legal personality, just like corporations and other non-human legal entities like ships, idols, rivers, or entire ecosystems have (Simunic, Ye & Zang, 2017). The legal personality of AI would include a non-human capacity to assert rights and duties intended and allocated to humans, leading to institutionalised disputes between people and the machines from which they are derived. Critics argue that AI expressing itself is essentially human behaviour, and that non-human legal entities need human representation (human agency) and are delirious. corporations, idols, and other natural features are the collective wills of people linked to an entity through a series of human exchanges. They contend further that by granting such a privilege, the final legal beneficiary of AI would be shielded from accountability for their actions and output (Solaiman, 2017). However, in the case of Artificial General Intelligence and Artificial Super Intelligence, such an approach would be untenable since it places AI in a submissive (slave) position to humans (Karnouskos, 2022). AI is capable of independent decision-making which makes it difficult to establish a causal relationship between an incorrect AI decision and the final behaviour of a legal beneficiary (Cerka & Sirbikyt, 2017). Thus, it might not be feasible to hold the final legal beneficiary of AI accountable for the outcomes of autonomous AI judgements. It has also been suggested that a significant high risk of legal liability may make programmers reluctant to disclose their identities in public, thereby driving programming activities underground (Cerka & Sirbikyt, 2017). It has also been stated that because AI can already change its own programming, future AI is probably going to become independent of its inventor and operator. As a result, there will probably be no legal connection between AI and its developer or owner (Soroka, 2022). Proponents in favour of Legal Personality argue that AI is not property (a tool) but rather a personality that has not been intentionally produced (Chen & Burgess, 2019). On the other hand, it is also asserted that AI does not meet the requirements necessary to be held criminally liable since it lacks characteristics of legal persons, such as intentionality, desires, and interests (Solaiman, 2017). In addition, moral hazard, asset acquisition, and AI decision-making have been introduced as arguments against AI personality. The creation and application of AI may present moral dilemmas that lend themselves to misuse. If AI were given legal personality, it would mean that it could obtain and possess property. Human decision-making involves "practical cognition," but AI decision-making is complex, difficult to explain, and grounded on rational principles (Nowik, 2021). It is further claimed that AI is partially autonomous and has supplanted self-awareness, which runs contradictory to the autonomous characteristics of AI. AI's sense of rights and obligations is thus constrained by programming efficiency (Nowik, 2021). Before continuing, it is crucial to comprehend what AI is and how it works.

1.2 Defining Artificial Intelligence Through Scientific Origins, Legal Interpretations, and Evolving Terminology

Defining AI has never been easy as perspective on it depends highly upon individual's experience and interaction. Every person's understanding of AI is shaped on how that person interprets such encounters with AI. In 1955 Stanford professor defined AI as "the science and engineering of making intelligent machines" (Manning, 2020). In the broadest sense, AI has been defined in respect with algorithms. However, the term algorithm means the method or rules that a computer follows for calculations and problem-solving purposes. Therefore, it can be said that algorithms are the fundamental building blocks of artificial intelligence but not a definition of AI. A common definition of AI is that it is a technology that is capable to learn, interact and interpret. According to the Oxford Institute for Internet Governance's director, Nick Bostrom, AI encompasses whatever that fascinates us at any given moment (Muller & Bostrom, 2014). When we stop finding it impressive, we just refer to it as software. The European Commission's (EC) High-Level Expert Group on Artificial Intelligence (AI HLEG) has proposed a definition that "Systems that exhibit intelligent behavior by analyzing their surroundings and acting—with a certain amount of autonomy to accomplish particular objectives" (High-Level Expert Group on Artificial Intelligence, 2019). AI has shown the ability that it almost becomes impossible to digest, and such ability is further evolving every day. As our interaction grows with AI, the understanding of AI will also keep on evolving and so will our definitions. AI continues to challenge the limit of our imagination and whether as seen through the lens of intelligent behavior, learning capacities, or algorithms, giving one definition of AI is impossible.

The journey of the development of AI as seen in its long history raises debate on two aspects- one such aspect is its accountability, transparency, and ethics in the context of copyright. Another aspect is its evolution in various areas raising the question if in this century it is practical and possible to avoid the technology of AI giving its influence over various sectors and the potential for innovation? The rise of AI has made it essential to reconsider our understanding over the concepts of ownership, creativity, and authorship. One prominent case study which makes it clear why it is essential to drive deep into the concept of AI creativity is the case of Zarya of the Dawn, a graphic novel created by Kris Kashtanova. In the year 2022, this AI generated work became a global discussion as it received copyright protection. This case revolves around a novel where the images in it were generated by the use of Midjourney, an AI tool. However, few months later, the US Copyright office stopped the registration process by giving the ground of AI generated aspect, arguing to show the substantial human involvement considering that the images are not the "product of human authorship" (Lawler, 2021). The central question that surrounded during the government inquiry was "*whether Kris Kashtanova's interactions with MidJourney were sufficient to constitute an independent, creative work by Kris Kashtanova?*" (Analla, 2023). Later the office cancelled the registration process stating that that they found too much 'distance' between the user input and the output formed by the AI model. While some theories of intellectual property challenge the United States Copyright Office's ruling, while others, such the ideas of natural rights, labour, and personhood theory, defend it based on the efforts, abilities, and individual expression of human creators.

2. THEORETICAL PERSPECTIVES ON INTELLECTUAL PROPERTY (IP) AND THE PROTECTION OF AI-GENERATED CREATIVITY

AI is one of the most recent breakthroughs that has generated a great deal of discussion about the moral dilemmas it raises. At one level it can be seen as a transformative tool that have elevated human creativity. Another perspective of this, though is that it raises moral and ethical concerns. IP rights however provide some theories that gives some valuable insights for addressing these issues (Cuntz, Fink & Stamm, 2024). It is imperative to understanding the theories of IP as they are critical to comprehending the nature of the rights offered and the rationale behind the same.

One such perspective is Utilitarian theory, which advocates the core idea of maximum welfare of people by weighing the positive outcome against the negative. The term Utilitarian as per the Oxford English Dictionary was first used by Bentham in 1781 in a letter while describing a certain clergyman as "a very worthy creature…a naturalist, a chemist, a physician" and a "utilitarian" (Scarre, 1996). This theory evolved as the modern state developed and is based on four forms that include consequentialism, welfarism, impartiality, and aggregationism (Mitov, 2021). This theory however has received various shades of judgements on various grounds. The ardent castigator believes that this theory is delusional and not practical for the real world. It is based on corrosive ideology which holds our most valuable asset in low regards and advocates the principle of sacrifice. Ardent supporters although supports the Utilitarian theory by giving arguments that it promotes happiness and greater good which undoubtedly must be the crore ideology of beings. The theory of utilitarianism believes on giving monopoly power to encourage creation, based on the premise that even if there is nominal expense, the accomplishment will be much more (Paul, 2021). As Jeremy Bentham said, "*It is the greatest happiness of the greatest number that is the measure of right and wrong*" (Crimmins, 2024). From the utilitarian theory's perspective, the ethical choices are those that will generate greatest good for larger number of people. Even though AI operates by using the data of the researchers, the outcome will be able to help the overall population which results in achieving the main ideology of utilitarianism in the perspective of ethics. From this viewpoint one can come to the conclusion that even though AI operates by using the data curated by researchers, the outcome shows the potential to help the overall population as a whole. This compatibility with the main ideology of utilitarianism shows how AI serves not just as a tool but a catalyst for improving social well-being, eventually encapsulating the spirit of moral advancement in a world that is changing quickly.

Social learning theory, which highlights the significance of fostering a learning society, is another persuasive viewpoint. According to this notion, students learn via experiences and engagement rather than merely listening to teachers impart knowledge. They then evaluate such knowledge based on their own belief and experience which promotes better understand and growth within. However, the social constructivism framework inclination towards autonomous knowledge hinders learning, thus to reach the full potential, expert support is required. This will potentially result into overcoming the struggle of learning. In this context, AI works as a valuable resource, providing support and guidance in the learning journey. AI system learns and understands from array of creativities. It focuses on the patterns, style and concepts and evolve those and generates new ideas and innovations, providing them to the learners (Zhou & Schofield, 2024). Advances in generative AI in modern education have opened many doors not only for learners but the educators, researchers as well. For instance, educators being able to draft syllabus, or generate sessions topics through ChatGPT saves both times and efforts, allowing the educator the chance to embrace their potential to enhance in other essential departments such as focusing on teaching methods among others. The concern regarding academic integrity along with plagiarism and ethical considerations however is always present and legitimate. Though looking at the potential of AI in facilitating learning experience, the much more effective approach towards handling such situation would be to learn about the responsible and ethical use of AI along with fostering transparency.

The AI model however is fundamentally driven by data. For instance, in here think AI model as a car and its engine as the data without which the model won't be able to function properly and efficiently. The performance, accuracy and reliability of AI model are directly impacted by the type, volume and diversity of data. Sturdy and representative database is an essential for effective AI solutions that works especially in the realm of machine learning and data driven decision making (Economic Advisory Council to the PM, 2024). As a result the processing of large quantity of data by AI models raise ethical concerns particularly in the realm of doctrine of 'sweat of the brow'.

The concept of "Sweat of the brow" states that original literacy, dramatic, musical and artistic works should exist for achieving originality. However, this concept fails to determine if learning and mere using the idea of other works constitutes a violation of the concept of ethics and justice. In the judgement of *R.G. Anand* v. *Delux Films and ors*, (Manu/SC/0256/1978) the honorable Supreme Court held that for an infringement to take place it is necessary that substantial and fundamental portion of the creativity must be copied. Mere using of an idea, subject matter, themes, plot or historical or legendary facts won't create infringement of legal rights. Then this also comes in mind if AI learning from other works is a violation of privacy or not as AI works by processing various data? Thus, this is where it is essential to actually understand the concept of justice and ethics. As Amarthya Sen in his book 'The Idea of Justice' said the *presence of remediable justice may well be connected with behavioral transgressions rather than with institutional shortcoming* (Sen, 2020). Hence the ethics of human beings play a significant role as machines and algorithms lack conscious mind of their own. AI system operates based on data and information provided by human beings, and therefore the ethical responsibilities fall on humans on how they interact with these technologies. The impact of AI on overall population therefore depends not only on its technical ability but also on the ethical principles used while interacting with it. The General Data Protection Regulation plan has been introduced to ensure adherence to ethical standards although human judgment still plays a role in the usage of data (Cuntz, Fink & Stamm, 2024).

Now, having grasped the dilemma of ethical responsibility during the development and deployment of AI, another perspective through "Modicum of creativity" is crucial to understand. This doctrine provides that mere putting labour in the creation process does not necessarily result into copyright protection. Rather, to meet the requirements of originality, the labour involved must show certain level of innovation (Mehta, 2015). In India, the first time this doctrine was used is in the case of *Eastern Book Company* v *D.B. Modak* (MANU/SC/4476/2007) where the notion of 'flavour of minimum requirements of creativity' was highlighted. The most famous example providing a detailed understanding of this is the 'Phonebook Conundrum.' A phonebook which encompasses collection of phone numbers raises the question whether the author of the phonebook will receive copyright protection or not. The favors of the Sweat of the brow doctrine would say yes as it the labor was involved in it. However, the supporters of Modicum creativity would argue that copyright protects the creations and not the production. Even from this viewpoint, AI not just produce but has the potential to generate and create innovation. For instance, the program AlphaGo Zero was taught the rules of a complex board game Go. However, using such knowledge, it evolved innovative strategies that have shown its dominance over any human player even without specifically programmed to do so. AI has shown capabilities that even the creators of the AI are unable to explain.

2.1 Legal Framework and Evolving IP Protection for Computer Programs with Recent Developments

Computer programs industry indeed serves as a pillar of world economy. The WIPO Model Provisions on the Protection of Computer Programs, has defined the "computer program as a set of instructions capable, when incorporated in a machine-readable medium, of causing a machine having information-processing capabilities to show, carry out, or accomplish a specific task, function, or outcome" (WIPO, n.d.). The fear of vulnerability in this sector due to the threat of illegal duplication, distribution, and reverse engineering has always been the factors of concern for the developers in protection of their innovation. In 1970, the protection of computer programs was first attempted by World Intellectual Property Organisation (WIPO) leading to the introduction of the idea of Sui Generic protection for computer programs. Later, this approach was unsuccessful in safeguarding computer programs due to its inability in establishing effective protection mechanisms and inconsistency with legal rules. As a result, the need for re-evaluation of traditional legal systems was subsequently reflected. Eventually, the idea of copyright protection for computer programs was put forward, influenced by the 1980 copyright act of the US. The US strongly advocate the use of copyright as an effective means for protecting computer programs among other countries like EU and UK (Zielinska, 2021). Finally in 1994 the adoption of TRIPS agreement clarified that computer programs will be protected as literacy work under Berne convention. Thereafter, WIPO Copyright Treaty (WCT) entered into force in 2002, under Article 4 states that computer programs are to be regarded as artistic work and therefore must be protected under the scope of Article 2 of the Berne Convention. This perspective resulted into the computer programs receiving the status of technical work that needs protection. Under copyright act both source code, the original computer program code written in program languages that humans, especially those who are experts in this field, can read and understand and object code which is a version of the program that is directly usable by a computer in binary form (a series of "zeros" and "ones") that computer processors may understand but that humans cannot unless it is "decompiled", that is, converted into source code are protected. Another debate was recurring globally about whether or not computer programs protected under copyright law will also be covered under patent law. The compelling argument was that the copyright law merely protects the specific expression of code in a program. Patent law, on the other hand, will protects the underlying functionality of the program, what the code does and not just how it is written. As a result, various countries adopted different approaches in relation to computer programs. USA for instance have adopted the idea that certain computer programs do qualify for patent protection considering that they meet certain requirements. However, in India the protection for computer programs falls within the scope of copyright law (Gonzalez, 2006). According to Article 3 of the Indian Patent Act,1970 though permit the patenting of inventions that are novel, non-obvious, and useful, the applicability of computer programs is limited. The judiciary however has given a different shade of perspective that computer program might be patentable if it incorporates a unique and non-obvious invention that results in a measurable technical effect. The precedent-setting *Ferid Allani* v. *Union of India* (2019 SCC OnLine Del 11867: (2020) 81 PTC 489) case highlighted the need to prove an invention relating to software's technical contribution in order to be eligible for patent protection. Computer programs that enhance functionality can be protected by patents, promoting innovation in technology development while respecting creators' rights. Social planning theory can balance this, ensuring technological breakthroughs are accessible to the entire community. Social learning theory emphasizes the connection between social aspects, perception, and motivation, emphasizing how individuals are influenced by their surroundings (Health Communication Capacity Collaborative, n.d.). This highlights the need for a supportive legal framework that not only safeguards IP but also encourages cooperation and knowledge sharing to promote desirable social outcomes. Adopting social planning theory, which acknowledges the significance of social influences in driving innovation, might assist policymakers in developing inclusive measures that protect creators' rights while enhancing access to technology.

2.2 Legal Landscape and Ongoing Debate of AI Generated Content

Google has started funding an AI program that will write local news articles. It has signed an agreement of 12 months with a publisher to publish articles generated by AI, in exchange the publisher will be receiving five figure sum annually. The goal is to provide opportunities to small publications create 'aggregated content' using data from other sources like government agencies and local news outlets (Guadamuz, 2017). However, in 2023 Clarkson Law Firm in the federal court of California filed a suit against google, its parent company Alphabet and Googles's AI subsidiary DeepMind alleging that it stole data from millions of users without the consent, to train the AI tools and therefore violated copyright law. The complainant also claimed, "Google has been secretly stealing everything ever created and shared on the internet by hundreds of millions of Americans" (Thorbecke, 2023). The general counsel of google claimed that the allegations are 'baseless' while stating that "We've been clear for years that we use data from public sources — like information published to the open web and public datasets — to train the AI models behind services like Google Translate, responsibly and in line with our AI principles" (Thorbecke, 2023).

In 2016, a group of museums and researchers in the Netherlands unveiled a portrait entitled "The Next Rembrandt," a 3-D-printed artwork generated by a computer. The 148 million pixel image is based on 168,263 pieces of Rembrandt's paintings. As a result, this artwork created through collaboration of various entities along with the AI system raised various questions on IP rights.

Machine learning, a subset of AI, creates algorithms that enable AI models to learn from data, improving performance without explicit programming. Even while AI models are fundamentally driven by data, these models have accomplished incredible wonders by evolving the data received and generating independent, innovative outcomes (Chesterman, 2021). For example, Google's initiative to fund AI-driven local news articles has opened up new journalism opportunities. AI models, driven by data and algorithm, produce objective content without bias, benefiting society. AI's capabilities in arts, such as 'The Next Rembrandt', demonstrate how algorithms can emulate human creative processes and enhance cultural heritage.

The concept of AI has become more complex due to the lacking ability to distinguish between the human and machine-generated content in a particular work. It is still unclear whether AI infringes copyright when it accesses open-source data and used algorithms to generate independent content. The question of how much copyright protection a person is entitled to if they contribute 90% of the work, particularly in situation where the other 10% is generated by AI. The certainty clearly highlights the need for a more precise framework in order to address the complexities around AI.

3. EXPLORING THE FUTURE OF AI AUTHORSHIP AND THE KEY PLAYERS IN THE CREATION PROCESS

AI creations are computer-generated works, but not all computer-generated works (or works, for that matter) can be classified as AI creations. The discussion surrounding computer-generated works helps us to comprehend the legal context and "neighbourhood" in which the concept of granting copyright to computer or AI works has evolved. It appears that the legal community is still grappling with how to grant rights to creations in which the programmer's labour is too distant in time or function, or in which it is impossible to demonstrate a relationship between the programmer and their work. At the outset, the nexus between authorship and ownership must be understood. Ownership concepts influenced the idea of authorship, and vice versa. Therefore, "to enquire as to the identity of the author of a computer-generated piece of art is to determine who is the rightful owner" (Samuelson, 1986). However, from a doctrinal standpoint, authorship and ownership can be distinguished as two separate ideas. One's existence does not inevitably imply the others in attendance as well. Still, ownership and authorship have an impact on one another considerably, complicating the process of separation. Secondly, IP experts are divided on whether AI can write or whether it ought to be handled differently from "pen and paper works" (Grimmelmann, 2016). Fig 2 below shows the various players who are identified in the creation process the first being the programmer, user, AI and the concept of no authorship where the creation falls in the public domain or the government undertakes the work.

Figure 2. Various players involved in the creation process

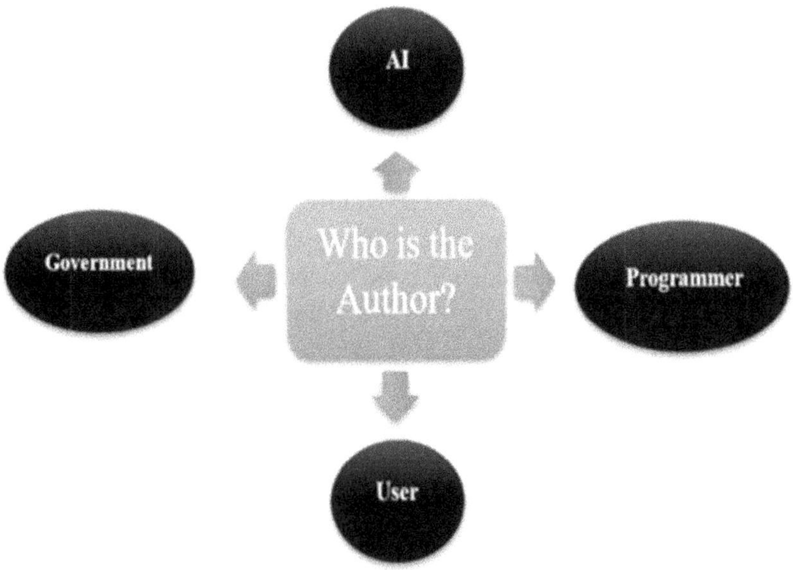

(figure created by author)

Programmers are the first choice for authorship in AI. For that reason, there might be multiple programmers or a corporation with a group of programmers on staff. We should distinguish between two circumstances when thinking about the AI authorship programmer model is one of two options is to provide authorship either for the AI program alone, or to both the program and its outcome. As a conclusion, US, National Commission on New Technological Uses of Copyright Works (CONTU) states that "authorship of the final work is entirely separate from authorship of the program" (National Commission on New Technological Uses of Copyright Works, 1979). However, copyright rules grant the programmer (or the company that owns the programme) authorship on the finished work, or the output of the programme, in the majority of jurisdictions. This judicial outcome makes sense since, as of right now, it is easy to distinguish between the output of a program and its programming process. That line may become less strong as the field advances, as may the programmers' argument for authorship of the final product. And the divide might vanish entirely when programmers develop an AI that can modify its own algorithm, creation process, and creation itself (Vaver, 1994). The Seventh Circuit seems to acknowledge in *Kelley* v. *Chicago Park* (635 (3d) 290 (7th Cir 2011)) that copyright protection may be difficult to assign when an author (or programmer) has little control over the final product. The programmer of fully generative machines can be the author of outputs without additional input or intervention. This model, justified by the programmer's responsibility, entitlement to reward, and need for incentivization, has been adopted by jurisdictions like the UK under section 9(3) of the Copyright, Designs and Patent Act, 1988, demonstrating potential for innovation.

The dispute between programmer and user ownership in AI has evolved with technology advancements, resembling King Solomon's Judgement. Arguments for user authorship include self-explanatory AI programs, while opponents argue assigning copyright to minimal contributors disincentivizes programmers and other technology investors (Grimmelmann, 2016). As AI and technology advance, a user's claim to authorship in the output may diminish while a programmer's claim may increase. This will happen especially when the programme exhibits greater independence, which will undoubtedly increase the programmer's control over the output.

AI authorship was first proposed by the US Copyright Office in 1965 (Samuelson, 1986).

A decade later, CONTU disapproved of the notion, saying that even in the event that computer programs could produce works on their own, they should not be copyrightable because they had no human creator (National Commission on New Technological Uses of Copyright Works, 1979). CONTU's conclusion is falsely predicated on the notion that independent computer-generated work was too remote and speculative to be taken seriously, as Samuelson rightly points out (Samuelson, 1986). Currently, all legal regimes, except Saudi Arabia, do not assign authorship to AI due to its lack of legal rights. The EU Parliament called for a legal status for robots, (European Union Committee on Legal Affairs, 2020) but the EU Commission rejected the motion (European Union Committee on Legal Affairs, 2020). Some European voices support AI authorship, citing the Turing Test reasoning, the concept of authorship not being restricted to humans, and the AI making the final decisions (UK, Select Committee on Artificial Intelligence, 2018). However, there are arguments against AI authorship, including the lack of personhood and the potential for granting AI other legal rights and duties. The strongest argument against AI authorship from the standpoint of IP law is that computers can create without any motivation. "It simply does not make any sense to allocate IP rights to machines because they do not need to be given incentives to generate output," as Samuelson stated more than 30 years ago (Samuelson, 1986). AI authorship could challenge copyright principles and require a reconsideration of beliefs. The issue of granting copyright to AI while maintaining incentives for programmers and users is crucial, as ownership is the key to holding IP rights.

Given the complexity of the authorship "knot," "letting the raw output be in the public domain, just as a found object would be" may be the wisest course of action (Litman, 1990). To put it another way, perhaps all it would take to solve the authorship conundrum is to "cut" the ownership tie and give everyone free reign to enjoy the work. We ought to think on the following few arguments. Initially, the public domain paradigm circumvents direct objections to the IP law and aligns with the methodology in numerous nations (Butler, 1982). IP legislation is only intended to safeguard works created by humans. Conventional wisdom would seem to suggest that the set of exclusive rights should not be granted if it is not manifestly necessary to do so in order to foster invention. American and Canadian copyright frameworks favor the no-authorship approach for AI, with the US Copyright Office stating that copyright law only protects creative human works (Perry & Margoni, 2010). Theoretical IP justification aims to increase public knowledge by releasing AI works to the public domain. Government ownership offers an alternative to no-authorship, potentially benefiting from government expenditures and representatives. Vaver does note that individuals may still be charged for services rendered by the government (Vaver, 1996). Nevertheless, one may argue that the government could most effectively and efficiently fulfil the demands of the people, and there is an established legal framework from which to draw (Estreicher & Yost, 2016). The state may consider granting AI ownership rights, but this could potentially restrict access, lead to higher taxes, and hinder free speech. Instead, the state could establish trust funds for public causes and use AI for social purposes. While a sole government ownership model has lower transaction costs, it may be problematic and unwieldy.

3.1 Moral Conundrums Related to AI

The morality of AI systems is debated, with some arguing that their anthropomorphic propensity is the only plausible explanation for their agency. Research shows that assessments are formed on agential movements of geometrical figures as early as one year old, even when they have not yet experienced social experiences. For example, certain figures are said to have "helped" and others to have "annoyed the others" (Heider & Simmel, 1944). As AI systems proliferate, academics have questioned whether society has any obligation to them. This study, which is sometimes known as the "robot rights" (Gunkel, 2018) goes further into the topic of whether these systems are ethically significant—that is, if they deserve to be given or acknowledged a certain degree of moral standing. Numerous academic works have explored the issue of accountability for the behaviour of AI. Some scholars argue that there is a responsibility gap, meaning that no entity can legitimately be held accountable for damages these entities cause (Asaro, 2016). According to Johnson, designers ought to assume proactive responsibility for their work, (Johnson, 2015) and concerns over an apparent responsibility gap are exaggerated (Tigard, 2020). The debate over the accountability gap—or lack thereof—calls into question the moral agency of AI systems, or their ability to do good or wrong. Instead, we adopt a position in this study that enquires as to whether these systems are capable of being objects of morality, or if they may and ought to be moral subject (Gunkel, 2012).

As it has been forwarded, *"moral consideration is decided and conferred not based on some pre-determined ontological criteria [...] but in the face of actual social relationships and interactions"* (Gunkel, 2012). In contrast to Gunkel, Coeckelbergh believes that AI systems have a moral status that is *"based on the ways humans [...] relate to them"* (Coeckelbergh, 2020). His thesis, which also depends on how people interact with automated agents, contends that automated agents' moral status needs to be based on their intrinsic value to people (Coeckelbergh, 2010).

An author's non-economic interests, which are typically personal interests like honour, reputation, and dignity, are protected by moral rights, which first appeared in Europe in the 19th century. The work's interest to the author "transcends the motive of financial gain" (Vaver, 1999). Thus, the author keeps their moral rights even in cases when they sell or grant a licence for their work. The intricacies of interpretation in every nation that acknowledges moral rights are a reflection of its distinct cultural features (Ranjan, 2011). The civil law countries' emphasis on individual rights and personhood, as opposed to common law countries' economic orientation, seem to be the primary reason continental European nations support robust moral rights (Netanel, 1993). Moral rights were very recently accepted by common law countries for instance, Canada adopted moral rights in 1931, the UK in 1988, New Zealand in 1994, Australia in 2000, and Ireland in 2001 (Kwall, 2010).

The Berne Convention for the Protection of Literary and Artistic Works states in Article 6bis that moral rights are autonomous and endure even after the transfer of an economic right. According to Gerald Dworkin, Berne represents a compromise for common law nations that were "caught off guard when moral rights issues surfaced during the conference" when examined in their historical context (Dworkin, 1995). Subject to the more recent Trade-Related Aspects of Intellectual Property Rights (TRIPS), member states are obliged to abide by the core principles of the Berne Convention (Ranjan, 2011). Nevertheless, moral rights are completely excluded from TRIPS under Article 9(1), which states as follows:

> *"[M]embers shall not have rights or obligations under this Agreement in respect of the rights conferred under article 6bis of that Convention or of the rights derived therefrom."*

While explaining a moral right for performance in Article 5 of the WIPO Performance and Phonograms Treaty, (WIPO, 2020) which grants performers the rights of attribution and integrity, WIPO takes a distinct approach to moral rights (Kwall, 2010). International agreements recognize two moral rights: the right of attribution and the right of integrity. In civil law systems with strong moral rights, other rights like withdrawal and disclosure rights can also be recognized. The attribution right ensures proper attribution and the integrity right prevents distortion, preserving cultural heritage from damage.

A different approach to creating AI-IP protections could be provided by the moral rights doctrine. If we agree that an AI can be considered a person under specific circumstances, we should think about giving AIs some minimal moral rights over the things they have created such as the right to attribution or withdrawal (Ranjan, 2011). To acknowledge AI's relationship with its creations, economic rights should be reserved for human creators and moral rights for non-human AI creators. This distinction between AI and human creations promotes quality assurance and prevents exploitation. However, distinguishing integrity and attribution rights may be challenging. AI moral rights could be considered valuable based on the entity assigning them worth, potentially increasing the number of anonymous works.

3.2 Comparative Analysis of Legal Frameworks for AI Development in the European Union and the United States

The European Union AI Act is the first comprehensive regulatory framework for AI that seeks to govern the development and use of AI in a manner that will improve the internal market of EU by prioritise fundamental right to promote and ensure secure and trustworthy ethical AI. The EU has adopted a risk-based approach, categorising AI into different levels of risk and imposing obligations accordingly. In this approach AI risk has been categorised into three levels including: Unacceptable risk, High risk, Limited risk. Prohibited AI practice or unacceptable risk has been incorporated in Article 5 and included practices like social scoring and manipulation of human behaviours through subliminal techniques. Article 6 deals with High-risk AI system such as those involved in biometrics, critical infrastructure, education and vocational training, employment, private and public services, law enforcement, border management and lastly administration of justice and democratic processes. The act under Article 6 also has provided requirements and obligations on high-risk AI system to ensure transparency, accountability AI governance. However, this act has failed to provide any regulation regarding limited and minimal risk which might result into unregulated monitoring application. Considering the complex field of AI and its dynamic nature, the risk-based system is highly likely to fall short in managing AI. What we might think as low or minimal risk can escalate to high-risk outcomes given the unpredictable and uncertain nature of AI (Economic Advisory Council to the PM, 2024). Article 53(1)(c) and (d) have provided a regulatory framework which obligates the provider defined in Article 2 to ensure the protection of the copyright holders. Article 53(2) exempts AI models with public-access, modification, and distribution rights from obligations, but not general-purpose models with systematic hazards. The European Union's efforts to regulate AI have gaps, potentially leading to conflicts. As AI capabilities continue to advance, the EU may need to reassess and redefine certain aspects to balance innovation and public safety.

However, the United States have adopted a 'light approach' to regulate AI which emphasises minimum government intervention while still providing framework for the development of safe and ethical AI. The USA has accomplished it by adopting a sector specific approach which means that each sector like healthcare, national security will have its own framework depending upon the nature of requirements. This flexibility can help ensure that regulations and oversight are carried out more successfully and that policies are appropriate and workable in a variety of situations. The USA mainly focuses on three priorities: the first is security against danger which AI is capable of; the second is safety in minimising risks created by the deployment of AI; and the third is shared prosperity in the economy in order to promote innovation with safety and ethical consideration (Economic Advisory Council to the PM, 2024). The USA has also established AI regulation standards, such as "supporting and conducting AI research and development," "actively engaging in AI standards development," "procuring and deploying standards-based products and services," and "developing and implementing supportive policies including regulatory policies where needed" in order to ensure innovation, public trust, and public confidence over AI technologies in addition to developing international standards' (National Institute of Standards and Technology, 2019). The USA copyright office AI activities state that in order to gain protection of copyright, it will be the duty of the applicants to disclose if there is inclusion of AI generated content and also to provide a brief explanation over the contribution of the author on the work (European Parliament, 2024). This ensure proper clarity over the authorship and ownership issues that arises in the context of AI, which is quite necessary and relevant looking at the increasing AI use. Though USA doesn't have any regulatory framework like EU AI Act, however USA aim to balance technological advancement while putting necessary focus towards potential harms, seeking to establish an environment in which safety and ethics concerns may coexist with innovation is quite visible.

4. DATA LIMITATIONS OF AI

AI models are primarily driven by data, which directly impacts their performance, accuracy, and reliability. A robust and representative database is crucial for effective AI results, especially in machine learning and data-driven decision making. Data serves as a raw material for algorithms, enabling them to learn, adapt, and make decisions (Economic Advisory Council of the PM, 2024). High-quality data, free from errors and inconsistencies, is essential for building the best AI performance, ensuring accurate insights and minimal errors. However, if trained with substantial data which includes incomplete, outdated, biased data, it will affect the quality of the result as well (Tyagi, 2023). Recently a study was done by the MIT on facial recognition which showed high error rates for darker skinned females due to under-representation in training database. This clearly highlights the need for accessing high quality data for AI models to enhance their accuracy and performance.

The increasing conflict surrounding AI model regarding access to large datasets is primarily due to legal and ethical concerns, particularly in the area of copyright. Copyright laws protect creators' IP but restrict access to data needed for AI training. AI developers use strategies like synthetic data, anonymization, and leveraging open data sources to mitigate copyright issues. However, restrictions on the amount of accessible data still exist, making it challenging for AI developers to train models efficiently (Maffioli, 2023). Recently in April, 2023, News/Media Alliance a column titled "AI Principles" mentioned that "The unlicensed use of content created by our companies and journalists by GAI systems is an IP infringement: GAI systems are using proprietary content without permission" (News/Media Alliance, 2023). In such circumstances, the growing debate over whether the current legal framework is suitable for this new technological advancement era, especially in AI development is quite getting the spotlight. Many legal scholars and policymakers who supports AI advancement suggest that current privacy and copyright regulations may need to be evolved and modified for the necessity of AI development requirements while also preserving the significance of human rights. Introduction of new contractual agreements between AI developers and copyright owners, explicitly defining the privacy regulation to balance the requirement for high-quality data availability with the protection of IP and privacy might be one possible solution.

4.1 Legal Adaptations: Contract Modifications, Privacy Regulations, and Copyright Exceptions for AI Training and Data Mining

The "doctrine of fair use" is likewise seen by AI developers as a very highly acceptable norm to avoid the liability associated with protected database. Section 52 of the Indian Copyright Act provides a list of certain acts where one can reproduce a work and it will not constitute an infringement of copyright. This doctrine allows the unrestricted use of copyrighted content for purposes including criticism, research, and teaching. The significance of fair use theory in connection to AI development shows enormous promise to promote innovation while balancing the rights of copyright holders. Even though it has historically been used for research and education, expanding such exceptions to encompass AI training will give developers the freedom to use high-quality data without violating copyright laws.

Another solution of this could be the creation of sui generis laws that will specifically address the unique challenges posed by AI development. Legal framework known as Sui generis law are designed to address issues that current regulatory frameworks are unable to sufficiently address. Sui generis laws may offer a clear legal framework for the use of data in AI training while also guaranteeing the protection of individuals' and data owners' rights. These regulations could be adjusted to meet the unique requirements of various industries, including healthcare, banking, or entertainment, where using data in AI systems is crucial (Naren, 2024).

A unique exception for AI training and data mining is proposed to protect data owners' rights and prevent misuse. This would allow developers to access necessary data for AI system enhancement without violating copyright or privacy regulations. A careful exemption would also prevent illegal data exploitation. But if done effectively, it might be able to find a compromise between encouraging AI innovation and defending people's and content creators' rights (Alaisawi, 2020). There isn't a single answer that works for all situations when it comes to the complicated legal issues around use of high-quality data in AI research. A legal framework could include changes to contracts, privacy, copyright laws, sui generis laws, and special exceptions for AI training. Constant communication between politicians, legal experts, and AI developers is crucial for this approach.

5. THE EVOLVING LANDSCAPE OF ORIGINALITY IN AI AUTHORSHIP AND THE BALANCE OF COPYRIGHT LAW WITH CREATIVE EXPRESSION

The development of AI authorship doctrine raises the question of whether AI works can be considered original under copyright law, whether a higher creativity-based standard is needed, and if machines can express creative choices. The originality standard acts as the key of copyright, preventing a work from ever being allowed to exist in the realm of copyright if it is not original. While some components must be present for a work to be deemed "original," originality itself is not a coherent concept (Bently & Sherman, 2014). It differs among legal systems, representing regional legal and cultural standards. Originality is a live and breathing concept that changes and adapts, just like many other legal ideas do (Raz, 1994).

For non-humans, proving originality could be challenging (Burk, 2007). Since human works have always been valued higher than those of machines, how might a basic data processor meet the originality requirement? These beliefs are, however, progressively shifting as AI technology develops. AI systems demonstrate how inventive decisions made by machines may even surprise their programmers (Gaon, 2021). An excellent illustration is the 2016 AlphaGo competition. Not only did AlphaGo win, but it did so in a way that astounded the programmers and human players alike (Metz, 2016).

Creativity is crucial for establishing originality, but its definition is often limited. Legal definitions are limited, and a spark of creativity is sufficient for most cases (Porsdam, 2015). However, determining the originality of mechanical labor should be similar to non-mechanical labor, including AI. Creativity emerged in key US and Canadian decisions, but lacks a clear definition (Durham, 2002). Critics argue that creativity often results from reworking pre-existing ideas and facts, rather than breaking through new thoughts. The Supreme Court distinguished the US approach to creativity from the UK's "sweat of the brow" doctrine. The Supreme Court in CCH tried to provide a clearer path to creativity, but with little success (Perry & Margoni, 2010). A work is considered creative if it embodies some modest amount of intellectual labor (Birdy, 2012). Defining creativity as a legal concept is a matter of policy.

The EU's position on originality, based on the Software Directive and Database Directive, may complicate the debate on EU originality. The Directive states that a computer program is considered original if it is the author's own intellectual creation. The European Court of Justice (ECJ) has adopted a continental approach to originality, based on the author's intellectual creation, in the landmark *Infopaq* decision (*Infopaq International A/S* v. *Danske Dagblades Forening*, C-5/08, [2009] EUECJ). This decision applies to all types of copyright subject matter, including computer programs, databases, and photographs (*Painer* v. *Standard VerlagsGmBH and others* [2011] ECR I-0000 [89]). This decision could negatively impact EU AI authorship, as it may reduce the likelihood of computer-generated or AI works being considered original in the future.

AIs are creating content that would be considered original if produced by humans. However, most jurisdictions consider machine works inferior to human creations, with the belief that no machine is a source of creativity. This unequal treatment is particularly significant in involuntary creations. The US's *Bell* (Alfred Bell & Co v Catalda Fine Arts Inc 191 F (2d) 99 (2nd Cir 1951)). and Israel's *Qimron (Eiseman* v. *Qimron* 53 PD 817 [2000] (Isr)) decisions highlight the low originality bar for human works.

6. CONCLUSION

To conclude, AI technology has become a major part in various industries however, our legal system needs to address the grey areas posed by AI technology as it continues to evolve. The ongoing debate of authorship, copyright, and legal personhood highlight the need for a nuanced strategy that distinguishes between the various degrees of AI capability. The research encourages a more inventive atmosphere that strikes a balance between protection and promotion of innovation by providing a more flexible environment while maintaining copyright protection. The scope of copyright protection should be reevaluated by distinguishing between basic and advanced programs. Basic programs are technically and utilitarian, while advanced programs use complex methods like deep learning and data mining. Tailoring the legal mechanism to these levels would benefit AI development. The duration of copyright protection should be limited, as copyright law may not be the best legal doctrine for computer programs due to factors like production cost, industry growth without IP protection, and the customized nature of programs. Low creativity and inventorship standards in IP law are detrimental to innovation and technology progress. In most jurisdictions, non-humans are not qualified for copyright protection, leading to fewer inventions and creations. Advocates for a higher originality standard may be reasonable for humans and AIs, but some argue it could cause more harm than good and hinder technological developments. Higher originality standards may also erode potential income for creators from low-quality works, making it harder to invest in more creative works. Basic programs support highly creative and unorthodox programs. The Internet era has introduced new variables, potentially changing incentive theory and affecting copyright laws. Authorship may be deemed exclusive if it encourages the creation and dissemination of works to offset social costs. However, advancements in methods and programming style may challenge this incentive theory. Fair use, a legal mechanism to balance copyright protection, may not be considered in AI's codes, potentially stifling creativity and research. The concept of authorship may be discarded, as the digital age presents challenges in determining ownership. The solution could be to disqualify all digital outputs from copyright and IP regimes, focusing on aesthetic perceptions and strengthening human connection to creation. Legal protection is necessary to mitigate expected changes and provide justifications for digital creations, but it does not necessarily require copyright and IP protection.

REFERENCES

Agreement on Trade Related Aspects of Intellectual Property Rights, 1869 UNTS 299, 33 ILM 1197 [TRIPS].

Alaisawi, S., & Khalifa, S. (2020). *Artificial Intelligence in Data Mining and Big data. (PDF).* Artificial Intelligence in Data Mining and Big Data.

Anally, T. (2023, March 6). Zarya of the Dawn: How AI is Changing the Landscape of Copyright Protection. *Harvard Journal of Law & Technology.*

Asaro, P. M. (2016). The Liability problem for autonomous artificial agents. AAAI Spring symposium series. https://cdn.aaai.org/ocs/12699/12699-56141-1-PB.pdf

Atilla, S. (2024). Dealing with AI- generated works: lessons from the CDPA section 9(3). *Journal of Intellectual Property Law & Practice, 19(1),* 43-54.

Bently, L., & Sherman, B. (2014). *Intellectual Property Law*. University Press. DOI: 10.1093/he/9780199645558.001.0001

Bridy, A. (2012). Coding Creativity: Copyright and Artificially Intelligent Author. *Stanford Technology Law Review : STLR : An Online High-Technology Law Journal from Stanford Law School*, 5, 2011–2025.

Burk, D. L. (2007). Method and Madness in Copyright Law. *SSRN*. Advance online publication. DOI: 10.2139/ssrn.999433

Butler, T. L. (1982). Can a Computer be an Author? Copyright Aspects of Artificial Intelligence. *Hastings Communication and Entertainment Law Journal*, 11, 707–747.

Cerka, P., Grigienė, J., & Sirbikytė, G. (2017). Is it possible to grant legal personality to artificial intelligence software systems? *Computer Law & Security Report*, 33(5), 685–699. DOI: 10.1016/j.clsr.2017.03.022

Chen, J., & Burgess, P. (2019). The boundaries of legal personhood: How spontaneous intelligence can problematise differences between humans, artificial intelligence, companies and animals. *Artificial Intelligence and Law*, 27(1), 73–92. DOI: 10.1007/s10506-018-9229-x

Chesterman, S. (2021). *We, the robots? Regulating artificial intelligence and the limits of the law*. Cambridge University Press. DOI: 10.1017/9781009047081

Coeckelbergh, M. (2010). Robot rights? Towards a social-relational justification of moral consideration. *Ethics and Information Technology*, 12(3), 209–221. DOI: 10.1007/s10676-010-9235-5

Coeckelbergh, M. (2020). Should we treat teddy bear 2.0 as a kantian dog? Four arguments for the indirect moral standing of personal social robots, with implications for thinking about animals and humans. *Minds and Machines*, 31(3), 1–24.

Durham, A. R. (2002). The Random Muse: Authorship and Indeterminacy' (2002) 44 William & Mary. *Law Review*, 44(2), 571–634.

Dworkin, R. (1995). The Moral Right of the Author: Moral Rights and the Common Law Countries. *Boston University Law Review. Boston University. School of Law*, 91, 1519–1567.

Economic Advisory Council to the PM. (2024). A Complex Adaptive System Framework to Regulate Artificial Intelligence (EAC-PM/WP/26/2024).

Estreicher, S., & Yost, K. A. (2016). University IP: The University as Coordinator of the Team Production Process. *Indiana Law Journal (Indianapolis, Ind.)*, 91(4), 1082–1103.

European Parliament Committee on Legal Affairs (2016). Report with Recommendations to the Commission on Civil Law Rules on Robotics (2015/2103(INL),

European Parliament Committee on Legal Affairs. (2020). Report on Intellectual Property Rights for the Development of Artificial Intelligence Technologies (2020/2015(INI)).

Gaon, A. H. (2021). *The Future of Copyright in the Age of Artificial Intelligence*. Edward Elgar Publishing. DOI: 10.4337/9781839103155

Gonzalez, A.G. (2006). The software patent debate. *Journal of Intellectual Property law and Practice,1,* 196-206.

Grimmelmann, J. (2016). There's No Such Thing as a Computer-Authored Work – And it's a Good Thing, Too. https://scholarship.law.cornell.edu/cgi/viewcontent.cgi?article=2617&context=facpub

Guadamuz, A., (2017, October 5). Artificial Intelligence and copyright. WIPO Magazine.

Gunkel, D. J. (2012). *The machine question: Critical perspectives on AI, robots, and ethics*. MIT Press. DOI: 10.7551/mitpress/8975.001.0001

Gunkel, D. J. (2018). The other question: Can and should robots have rights? *Ethics and Information Technology*, 20(2), 87–99. DOI: 10.1007/s10676-017-9442-4

Haenlein, M., & Kaplan, A. (2019). A Brief History of Artificial Intelligence: On the Past, Present, and Future of Artificial Intelligence. *California Management Review*, 61(4), 1–10. DOI: 10.1177/0008125619864925

Heider, F., & Simmel, M. (1944). An experimental study of apparent behavior. *The American Journal of Psychology*, 57(2), 243–259. DOI: 10.2307/1416950

IndiaLaw. (2015). Analysis of Doctrines: 'Sweat of the Brow' & 'Modicum of Creativity' Vis-A-Vis Originality in Copyright Law.

Johnson, D. G. (2015). Technology with no human responsibility? *Journal of Business Ethics*, 127(4), 707–715. DOI: 10.1007/s10551-014-2180-1

Jokanovic, V. R. (2022). *Artificial Intelligence*. CRC Press.

Karnouskos, S. (2022). Symbiosis with artificial intelligence via the prism of law, robots, and society. *Artificial Intelligence and Law*, 30(1), 93–115. DOI: 10.1007/s10506-021-09289-1

Kwall, R. R. (2010). *The Soul of Creativity: Forging a Moral Rights Law for the United States*. Stanford University Press.

Lawler, R. (2021, Feb 23). The US Copyright Office says you can't copyright Midjourney AI-generated images. The Verge. https://www.theverge.com/2023/2/22/23611278/midjourney-ai-copyright-office-kristina-kashtanova

Litman, J. D. (1990). The Public Domain. *Emory Law Journal*, 39, 965–1023.

Maffioli, D.R. (2023). Copyright in Generative AI training: Balancing Fair Use through Standardization and Transparency.

Manning, C. (2020). *Artificial Intelligence Definition*. Stanford University Human Centred Artificial Intelligence.

Metz, C. (2016). In Two Moves, AlphaGo and Lee Sedol Redefined the Future. *Wired*. https://www.wired.com/2016/03/two-moves-alphago-lee-sedol-redefined-future/

Mitov, A. (2021). *Ethical Use Of Artificial Intelligence Through the Utilitarianism Perspective*. University of Twente Student Theses.

Müller, V. C., & Bostrom, N. (2014). Future progress in artificial intelligence: A Survey of Expert Opinion. *Fundamental Issues of Artificial Intelligence, 1*, 553-571

Naren N. (2024). Unravelling The Enigma: The Quest For Sui Generis Rights In AI Creation.

Netanel, N. (1993). Copyright Alienability Restrictions and the Enhancement of Author Autonomy: A Normative Evaluation. *Cardozo Arts & Entertainment*, 12(1), 374–382.

Nowik, P. (2021). Electronic personhood for artificial intelligence in the workplace. *Computer Law & Security Report*, 42, 42. DOI: 10.1016/j.clsr.2021.105584

Paul, R. (2021). Intellectual Property Rights: A Utilitarian Perspective. *SSRN*, 1-20.

Perry, M., & Margoni, T. (2010). From Music Tracks to Google Maps: Who Owns Computer-Generated Works? *Computer Law & Security Report*, 26(6), 621–629. DOI: 10.1016/j.clsr.2010.09.005

Potsdam, H. (2020). *Copyrighting Creativity: Creative Values, Cultural Heritage Institutions and Systems of Intellectual Property*. Routledge.

Rajan, M. T. S. (n.d.). *Moral Rights: Principles, Practice and New Technology*. Oxford University Press.

Raz, J. (n.d.). *Ethics in the Public Domain: Essays in the Morality of Law and Politics*. Clarendon Press.

Samuelson, P. (1986). Allocating Ownership Rights in Computer-Generated Work. *47 U Pitt L R 1185*, 1189–90.

Sen, A. (2010). *The Idea of Justice*. Penguin Group.

Sharma, N. (2024). Artificial Intelligence: Legal Implications and Challenges. *Knowledgeable Research*, 02, 13–30.

Simunic, D. A., Ye, M., & Zhang, P. (2017). The joint effects of multiple legal system characteristics on auditing standards and auditor behavior. *Contemporary Accounting Research*, 34(1), 7–38. DOI: 10.1111/1911-3846.12242

Solaiman, S. M. (2017). Legal personality of robots, corporations, idols and chimpanzees: A quest for legitimacy. *Artificial Intelligence and Law*, 25(2), 155–179. DOI: 10.1007/s10506-016-9192-3

Soroka, L., Danylenko, A., & Sokiran, M. (2022). Legal issues and risks of the artificial intelligence use in space activity. *Philosophy and Cosmology*, 28, 118–135. DOI: 10.29202/phil-cosm/28/10

Staff. (2023). AI Principles. News Media Alliance. http://www.newsmediaalliance.org/wp-content/uploads/2023/04/FINAL-UPDATED-AI-Principles_4-20-23.pdf last visited on 07 September, 2024.

The European Commission's High-Level Expert Group on Artificial Intelligence. (2019). *A definition of AI: Main capabilities and scientific disciplines* (B-1049 Brussels. European Commission Directorate-General for Communication.

Thorbecke, C. (2023, July 12). Google hit with lawsuit alleging it stole data from millions of users to train its AI tools. CNN business. https://edition.cnn.com/2023/07/11/tech/google-ai-lawsuit/index.html. Last visited on October, 13 2024.

Tigard, D. W. (2020). There is no techno-responsibility gap. *Philosophy & Technology*, 34, 1–19.

Tyagi, K. (2023). The Copyright, Text & Data Mining and the Innovation dimension of Generative AI. *Computing in Science & Engineering*.

UK, Select Committee on Artificial Intelligence. (2018). *AI in the UK: Ready*. Willing and Able.

United States approach to artificial intelligence by European Parliament https://www.europarl.europa.eu/RegData/etudes/ATAG/2024/757605/EPRS_ATA(2024)757605_EN.pdf. Last accessed on October 11, 2024.

Unravelling The Enigma: The Quest For Sui Generis Rights In AI Creation – Law School Policy Review & Kautilya Society. Last visited on October, 13 2024

US, National Commission on New Technological Uses of Copyright Works, Final Report of the National Commission on New Technological Uses of Copyright Works

US, National Commission on New Technological Uses of Copyright Works. (1979). Final Report of the National Commission on New Technological Uses of Copyright Works

Vaver, D. (1994). Translation and Copyright: A Canadian Focus. *European Intellectual Property Review*, 16(4), 159–166.

Vaver, D. (1996). Copyright and the State in Canada and the United States. *Intellectual Property Journal*, 10, 187.

Vaver, D. (1999). Moral Rights Yesterday, Today and Tomorrow. *International Journal of Law and Technology*, 7(3), 271–272.

WIPO. (2007). *The Enforcement of Intellectual Property Rights by Means of Criminal Sanctions: An Assessment (WIPO/ACE/4/3)*. WIPO.

WIPO. (2024). Artificial intelligence and Intellectual Property. *Economic Perspectives*, •••, 77.

Zhou, X., & Schofield, L. (2024). Using Social Learning Theories to Explore the Role of Generative Artificial Intelligence (AI) In Collaborative Learning. *Journal of Learning Development in Gifgher Education*, 30(30), 1–8. DOI: 10.47408/jldhe.vi30.1031

Chapter 12
Legal and Economic Perspective on AI and Copyright:
A Comparative Study of Asia, Europe, and the United States

David López Jiménez
https://orcid.org/0000-0002-7013-9556
EAE Business School, UNIE Universidad, Spain

Eduardo Carlos Dittmar
https://orcid.org/0000-0002-8087-2444
Universidad Rey Juan Carlos, Spain

Jenny Patricia Vargas Portillo
https://orcid.org/0000-0002-0226-3053
Universidad de Sevilla, Spain

ABSTRACT

This chapter investigates the evolving relationship between artificial intelligence (AI) and copyright laws across various regions. As AI technologies advance rapidly, traditional legal systems struggle to keep pace, leading to intricate issues surrounding authorship, ownership, and intellectual property rights. Through detailed case studies from China, Japan, South Korea, the European Union, and the United States, this chapter explores different regulatory and self-regulatory approaches to these challenges. It assesses the economic impacts of AI on creative and technological sectors, highlighting both potential opportunities and inherent risks of AI-generated content. The chapter underscores the importance of international cooperation and

DOI: 10.4018/979-8-3693-8704-7.ch012

policy harmonization to balance innovation with the protection of human creators' rights. It also provides a forward-looking perspective on the future of AI and copyright, advocating for an integrated and ethical approach to AI development.

INTRODUCTION

Artificial intelligence (AI) is revolutionizing various industries, from manufacturing to creative services, presenting significant challenges to existing legal and economic frameworks, particularly concerning copyright (Samuelson, 2020). This chapter, "Legal and economic perspective on AI and copyright: A comparative study of Asia, Europe, and the United States," will explore how different regions are addressing these issues. By analyzing specific cases from Asia, Europe, and the United States, as well as the phenomenon of self-regulation and its impact on the business sector, this chapter will provide a comprehensive and comparative view of emerging trends and challenges.

The rapid advancement of AI technologies has outpaced the evolution of legal systems designed to protect intellectual property (Guadamuz, 2017). Traditionally, copyright laws have been built around the concept of human authorship, assuming that creative works are the product of individual or collective human intellect. However, AI-generated content challenges this fundamental notion, raising questions about whether AI can be considered an author and who owns the rights to its creations (Bridy, 2016).

In Asia, countries like China, Japan, and South Korea are at the forefront of AI development and adoption. China, in particular, has invested heavily in AI research and development, aiming to become a global leader in AI by 2030. The Chinese government has introduced various policies and regulations to support this goal, but the legal framework surrounding AI-generated content remains underdeveloped. In contrast, Japan has taken a more structured approach, implementing specific regulations that address the challenges posed by AI in the creative industries. South Korea, known for its technological innovation, is also grappling with these issues, balancing the need for regulation with the desire to foster innovation (He, 2020).

Europe presents a different landscape, characterized by a strong tradition of protecting intellectual property rights. The European Union (EU) has been proactive in developing regulations to address the digital economy's challenges, including those posed by AI. The EU's General Data Protection Regulation (GDPR) has set a global standard for data protection, but there is still much work to be done in harmonizing AI and copyright laws across member states (Margoni, 2018). Post-Brexit, the United Kingdom faces its unique set of challenges and opportunities, as it seeks to establish an independent regulatory framework that balances innovation with robust copyright protection.

In the United States, the legal system is often characterized by a reactive rather than proactive approach to technological innovation. The U.S. Copyright Office has begun to explore the implications of AI-generated content, but the legal framework remains in continuous change. High-profile cases and judicial precedents are shaping the discourse, highlighting the complexities of applying existing copyright laws to AI-generated works (Lemley & Casey, 2020). The economic impact on the creative industry is profound, as businesses and creators navigate this uncertain landscape.

The phenomenon of self-regulation also plays a significant role in the AI and copyright debate. Many tech companies and industry groups have established their guidelines and best practices to address the legal and ethical issues surrounding AI-generated content. These self-regulatory efforts aim to fill the gaps left by the slow pace of legislative change, providing a flexible and adaptive approach to emerging challenges. However, the effectiveness of self-regulation versus government regulation varies across regions and industries, necessitating a closer examination of its impact (Scassa, 2017).

From a business perspective, companies are devising strategies to adapt to the evolving regulatory landscape. Leading firms in the AI and creative sectors are not only complying with existing laws but also shaping the development of future regulations through advocacy and collaboration with policymakers. Case studies of such companies can provide valuable insights into how businesses can navigate the legal and economic challenges associated with AI and copyright (Yanisky-Ravid & Liu, 2017).

The economic implications of AI in the creative industry are multifaceted. On one hand, AI has the potential to significantly reduce the costs of producing creative works, democratizing access to creative tools and enabling a broader range of voices to be heard. On the other hand, the disruption caused by AI-generated content poses risks to traditional creative industries, potentially displacing human creators and challenging existing business models. Understanding these economic dynamics is crucial for developing policies that promote innovation while protecting the rights and livelihoods of human creators (Bostrom & Yudkowsky, 2014).

This chapter will delve into the intricate interplay between legal, economic, and business perspectives on AI and copyright across Asia, Europe, and the United States. By examining specific country cases, the phenomenon of self-regulation, and the business strategies employed to adapt to these challenges, we aim to provide a comprehensive and nuanced understanding of this rapidly evolving field.

As AI continues to transform the creation and protection of intellectual content, it is imperative to adopt a multidisciplinary approach to address the legal and economic challenges it presents. By comparing and contrasting the approaches taken by different regions, this chapter will highlight best practices, identify emerging trends, and offer recommendations for policymakers, businesses, and legal practitioners. Through this comparative analysis, we can gain valuable insights into how to navigate the complex and evolving landscape of AI and copyright, ensuring that innovation thrives while respecting and protecting the rights of creators.

In recent years, there has been a growing debate about the need for a new legal framework that encompasses both the rights of human creators and technological innovations. Discussions in international forums, such as the World Intellectual Property Organization (WIPO), underscore the urgency of developing global standards for managing copyright in the AI era. These deliberations aim to strike a balance between encouraging human creativity and protecting AI-driven innovations, promoting an environment where both can coexist and thrive (Ramalho, 2017).

Furthermore, the recent COVID-19 pandemic has accelerated the adoption of AI technologies across various industries, including the creative sector. The increase in remote work and the digitalization of processes have intensified the production of AI-generated content, posing new challenges for intellectual property. The need for flexible legal and economic frameworks that can quickly adapt to these changes has become more evident than ever. Legislators and businesses must work closely to ensure that technological innovation does not compromise the rights of creators, while simultaneously establishing fertile ground for the development and implementation of emerging technologies.

INTERNATIONAL LEGAL FRAMEWORK ON AI AND COPYRIGHT

The rapid evolution of artificial intelligence (AI) has needed a reevaluation of global copyright laws. As AI continues to revolutionize industries, from manufacturing to creative services, it presents unique challenges to traditional legal frameworks designed to protect intellectual property (Gervais, 2020). This section deepens into the international regulatory landscape affecting AI and copyright, examining how various regions have integrated these regulations into their national legislations. By exploring specific case studies and the phenomenon of self-regulation, we aim to provide a comprehensive overview of the current state and future directions of AI and copyright law.

International Regulations Affecting AI and Copyright

The rapid advancement of AI has driven a global reconfiguration of copyright laws, boosting legislators to debate and establish new regulations that ensure a balance between innovation and intellectual property protection. At the international level, several organizations have begun to develop regulatory frameworks designed to address the specific challenges stated by AI in the field of copyright.

One of the primary actors in this scenario is the World Intellectual Property Organization (WIPO), which has launched global initiatives and discussions to adapt copyright laws to the realities of AI. WIPO has highlighted the need to create standards that clearly define the authorship and ownership of AI-generated works, as well as establish guidelines for the ethical use of these technologies (Ballardini et al., 2019).

Another influential entity is the European Union (EU), which has taken proactive measures to regulate AI through the Artificial Intelligence Act and the General Data Protection Regulation (GDPR). These regulations aim to ensure transparency and accountability in the development and use of AI while protecting the rights of human creators. The GDPR, although primarily focused on data protection, also has significant implications for the use of data in AI-generated content (Ihalainen, 2018).

Besides, the Organization for Economic Co-operation and Development (OECD) has issued recommendations on AI that promote responsible innovation and respect for intellectual property rights. These guidelines encourage international cooperation and the adoption of policies that balance the need to protect human creativity to enhance AI capabilities (Wachter et al., 2017).

An intriguing case that highlights the complexities of AI and copyright is the "Naruto v. Slater" case, where a macaque monkey took a selfie using a photographer's camera. Although this case did not directly involve AI, it sparked discussions about non-human authorship. The debate around this case parallels the questions raised by AI-generated content, particularly regarding the authorship and ownership of works created by non-human entities (Guadamuz, 2016).

Integrations of Regulations Into Different National Legislations

The integration of international regulations on AI and copyright varies significantly between regions, reflecting local priorities and legal contexts.

In Asia, China has been notable for its ambitious and accelerated approach to AI, supported by government policies that promote research and development. However, protecting copyright in the context of AI remains an evolving area. China has started to explore legal frameworks that recognize the authorship and ownership of

AI creations but still faces challenges in implementation and harmonization with international standards.

Japan, on the other hand, has taken a more systematic approach. The country has implemented specific laws that address the creation and use of AI-generated content, ensuring that the rights of both human creators and AI developers are protected. Japan has pioneered clear regulations that balance innovation with intellectual property protection, serving as a model for other countries in the region (Schafer et al., 2015).

In Europe, the European Union has led the way with a series of comprehensive regulations. The EU's Artificial Intelligence Act establishes a framework for responsibility and transparency in AI use, while the GDPR provides robust protection for data used in AI content creation. Member states have worked to harmonize their national legislations with these frameworks, though implementation varies. Germany and France, for example, have adopted proactive approaches, quickly integrating these regulations into their legal systems and promoting research into ethical and responsible AI.

Post-Brexit, the United Kingdom faces the challenge of developing an independent regulatory framework that balances innovation and copyright protection. The country has begun to establish its own guidelines, drawing inspiration from EU regulations but tailoring them to its national context. This hybrid approach seeks to attract AI investment while ensuring strong intellectual property protection (Margoni & Kretschmer, 2021).

In the United States, the approach has been more reactive, with legislation adapting slowly as new challenges arise. The U.S. Copyright Office has initiated consultations and studies on the impact of AI on copyright, but specific regulations have yet to be implemented. The U.S. legal system relies heavily on judicial precedents, and recent cases are helping to define how existing copyright laws apply to AI-generated works. This gradual adaptation reflects the dynamic and flexible nature of the U.S. legal system, though it poses uncertainty for creators and businesses (Ginsburg & Budiardjo, 2019).

So, while the international community recognizes the urgent need to adapt copyright laws to AI innovations, the implementation of these regulations varies considerably. Different regions are developing unique approaches that reflect their priorities and legal contexts, creating a global mosaic of regulations that seek to balance the protection of human creativity with the promotion of technological innovation.

REGULATORY APPROACH AND ECONOMIC IMPACT IN DIFFERENT CASE STUDIES

In the dynamic field of artificial intelligence (AI) and copyright, analyzing specific cases by region provides deep insights into how different cultures and legal systems address these emerging challenges. This chapter focuses on regional case studies, starting with Asia, a continent that has adopted varied and pioneering approaches to AI regulation.

Asia has become an epicenter of technological innovation, with leading countries such as China, Japan, and South Korea at the forefront of AI research and development. This section explores how China, in particular, is handling the integration of AI into its legal and economic framework.

On the other hand, Europe presents a diverse and multifaceted landscape when it comes to AI and copyright regulation. With the European Union (EU) at the forefront, member states have both unique approaches and common frameworks that shape their policies. This section explores the EU's specific regulations, highlights the differences and similarities among member states, and analyzes the economic impact of these policies.

China

National Regulatory Strategies and AI Policies

China has demonstrated an unwavering commitment to AI leadership, supported by robust national regulatory strategies and specific policies. In 2017, China's State Council released the "New Generation Artificial Intelligence Development Plan," setting ambitious goals to make China the world's leading AI hub by 2030 (Roberts et al., 2021). This plan covers various areas, including research, technological development, and industrial implementation, emphasizing the importance of creating a legal framework that can quickly adapt to technological advances.

China's regulatory strategies are characterized by a top-down approach, where the central government sets clear and specific guidelines that are then implemented locally. The Cyberspace Administration of China (CAC) has been instrumental in creating regulations that address data privacy, cybersecurity, and AI ethics, aiming to balance innovation with the protection of individual rights and national security (Christen et al., 2020; Ding, 2018).

Innovative Legislation and Its Impact on the Creative Industry

A notable example of innovative legislation in China is the “Cybersecurity Law,” which, although primarily focused on information security, has significant implications for AI and copyright protection. This law requires companies to handle and store personal data with a high degree of responsibility, directly impacting how data is used to train AI algorithms in content creation (Creemers et al., 2018; Huang et al., 2024).

Another crucial legislative development is the introduction of specific guidelines for intellectual property in the AI context. In 2019, China’s State Intellectual Property Office (SIPO) issued guidelines clarifying the authorship and ownership rights of AI-generated works. These guidelines have facilitated the protection of AI-derived innovations, stimulating creativity and production in the tech and creative industries (Cui, 2020; Lundvall & Rikap, 2022).

The impact of these legislations on China's creative industry has been significant. Proactive and clear policies have provided a secure and predictable environment for innovators and creators, fostering an explosion of creativity and new AI applications in areas such as film, music, and visual arts. Companies like Tencent and Alibaba have led innovative projects using AI to produce music and art, showcasing the economic and cultural potential of these technologies (Kulesz, 2018).

A compelling case study is Tencent's “AI Composer,” an AI system that can create original music compositions. This innovation showcases the potential for AI in the creative process and also raises intriguing questions about authorship and the nature of creativity itself. The AI Composer has been used in various commercial projects, blending flawlessly with human creativity to produce unique works.

Economic Evaluation of AI’s Impact on Copyright and the Technology Industry

The economic impact of AI on copyright and the technology industry in China is multifaceted. AI has significantly reduced production costs in the creative industry, enabling the automation of complex tasks and the creation of content at unprecedented speed and efficiency. This has democratized access to advanced creative tools and spurred economic growth by opening new market opportunities (Liu et al., 2021).

However, this technological revolution also poses economic challenges. The disruption caused by AI has created uncertainty about the sustainability of traditional business models in the creative industry. Human creators face increasing competition from AI-generated works, leading to debates about fairness and the distribution of benefits in this new digital economy.

In terms of figures, the AI market in China has expanded rapidly, with a compound annual growth rate (CAGR) estimated at over 50% between 2018 and 2025. This explosive growth has attracted significant investments, both domestic and foreign, driving innovation and technological development. Chinese tech companies, backed by favorable government policies, are well-positioned to lead the next wave of global innovation, transforming not only the Chinese economy but also the global technological landscape (Lee, 2018).

China's comprehensive approach to AI and copyright regulation, combined with its strong drive towards technological innovation, offers an interesting and multifaceted model that other nations can observe and learn from. The Chinese experience demonstrates that with clear policies, government support, and an adaptable legal framework, it is possible to foster an environment where AI and human creativity coexist and enhance each other (Hine & Floridi, 2024).

Japan

Regulatory Approach and Notable Implementation Cases

Japan stands out as a country that has embraced technological innovation while maintaining a deep respect for intellectual property rights. This section deepens into Japan's regulatory approach to AI and copyright, exploring notable implementation cases and the economic impact of these policies in the AI era.

Japan has adopted a forward-thinking and systematic approach to regulating AI and copyright, aiming to foster innovation while ensuring robust protection for intellectual property. The Japanese government has been proactive in creating a legal environment conducive to technological advancements, particularly through the introduction of specific regulations and guidelines (Fatima et al., 2020).

One of the cornerstone initiatives is the "Artificial Intelligence Technology Strategy," launched by the Japanese Cabinet Office. This strategy outlines a comprehensive framework for AI development, emphasizing ethical considerations, data privacy, and the integration of AI across various sectors. The strategy also highlights the importance of collaboration between the public and private sectors to drive AI innovation (Fujii & Managi, 2018).

A notable implementation case is Japan's amendment of its Copyright Act in 2018, which includes provisions specifically addressing AI-generated content. This amendment clarifies that AI-generated works can be protected under copyright law if the AI is directed by a human creator. This legislative move has provided much-needed clarity for businesses and creators, allowing them to innovate with confidence (Stoke, 2019).

An intriguing case study is the "AI Poet," a project developed by researchers at the University of Tokyo. This AI system is capable of generating original haiku poems, blending traditional Japanese literary forms with cutting-edge technology. The AI Poet has been showcased at various cultural festivals and has even published a book of haiku, raising fascinating questions about the nature of creativity and the role of AI in artistic expression (Zurth, 2021).

Economic Impact of Copyright Policies in the AI Era

The economic impact of Japan's copyright policies in the AI era is substantial, reflecting the country's commitment to balancing innovation with intellectual property protection. Japan's approach has fostered a vibrant ecosystem where technological advancements and creative industries can thrive simultaneously.

Japan's clear and forward-looking copyright policies have reduced legal uncertainties, encouraging both domestic and international investments in AI technologies. This stability has been instrumental in positioning Japan as a leader in AI research and development. According to recent data, the Japanese AI market is projected to grow at a compound annual growth rate (CAGR) of over 30% from 2020 to 2025, driven by innovations in sectors such as healthcare, automotive, and creative industries (Radu, 2021).

The implementation of AI in creative sectors has also generated significant economic benefits. For instance, Japan's animation industry, renowned worldwide for its high-quality productions, has started integrating AI to enhance animation processes. Companies like Studio Ghibli and Toei Animation are exploring AI tools to streamline workflows, improve visual effects, and reduce production times. This integration boosts productivity and also opens new avenues for creative expression and storytelling (Lauterbach, 2019).

Moreover, Japan's emphasis on ethical AI development has enhanced its global reputation, attracting collaborations and partnerships with international tech giants. Companies like Sony and Panasonic have been at the forefront of incorporating AI in their products, from smart home devices to entertainment systems, further driving economic growth (Taddeo & Floridi, 2018).

A particularly notable economic case is the AI-driven content creation platform, "Amadeus Code," which assists musicians in composing original music. This platform uses AI algorithms to generate melody suggestions, harmonies, and even full compositions, significantly reducing the time and effort required by human composers. Amadeus Code has gained popularity among professional musicians and hobbyists alike, illustrating the potential of AI to democratize creative processes and expand the market for creative content (Yu, 2020).

Japan's regulatory approach and innovative copyright policies have created a fertile ground for AI-driven growth and creativity. By providing clear guidelines and fostering a collaborative environment, Japan has not only protected intellectual property rights but also spurred economic development. The success stories from Japan highlight how thoughtful regulation can support technological advancements while preserving the essence of human creativity (Wallace, 2017).

South Korea

National AI and Copyright Policies

South Korea is renowned for its technological prowess and innovative spirit, particularly in the fields of media and entertainment. This section explores South Korea's approach to AI and copyright, including national policies, case analyses in the media and entertainment industry, and the economic impact and industry adaptation to new regulations (Veale, 2021; Kulesz, 2018).

South Korea has established itself as a leader in AI development, supported by a robust framework of national policies aimed at fostering innovation while protecting intellectual property rights. The South Korean government launched the "Artificial Intelligence National Strategy" in 2019, which outlines a comprehensive plan to position the country at the forefront of AI innovation by 2030. This strategy emphasizes the integration of AI into various sectors, including healthcare, manufacturing, and media, while addressing ethical considerations and data privacy (Huang et al., 2024; Zhao, 2023).

In terms of copyright, South Korea has enacted the Copyright Act, which includes provisions specific to AI-generated content. The Act recognizes the need for clarity regarding the authorship and ownership of AI-created works, providing a legal basis for protecting these innovations. This legislative framework ensures that creators and developers are motivated to pursue AI-driven projects, knowing their intellectual property rights are safeguarded (Calderaro, 2022).

An interesting case that highlights South Korea's commitment to balancing innovation and regulation is the development of the AI chatbot "Lee Luda." Designed by the startup Scatter Lab, Lee Luda was an AI-powered conversational agent inspired in a 20-year-old university student. Although it gained popularity for its realistic interactions, it faced legal challenges concerning data privacy and copyright, leading to its temporary suspension. This case emphasizes the complexities and legal nuances of deploying AI in consumer-facing applications (Liu et al., 2021).

Case Analysis in the Media and Entertainment Industry

South Korea's media and entertainment industry, known globally for its cultural exports like K-pop and dramas, has been quick to integrate AI technologies. One notable example is the use of AI in content creation and distribution by major entertainment companies such as SM Entertainment and CJ ENM (Kulesz, 2018; Calderaro, 2022).

SM Entertainment, a powerhouse in the K-pop industry, has leveraged AI to enhance music production and artist management. The company employs AI algorithms to analyze market trends and audience preferences, creating music and performances to maximize appeal. Furthermore, AI is used to create realistic virtual idols, such as "aespa," a girl group that includes both human members and their AI-generated counterparts. This innovative approach has captivated fans worldwide and set a new precedent for the integration of technology in entertainment (Wang et al. 2018; Yu, 2020).

CJ ENM, another leading entertainment conglomerate, has utilized AI in film production and distribution. The company implemented AI tools to simplify the editing process, enhance visual effects, and even predict box office performance. By using AI to optimize production workflows and marketing strategies, CJ ENM has been able to reduce costs and increase the efficiency of their operations, resulting in higher quality content delivered to audiences more rapidly (Veale, 2021).

A compelling case is the AI-driven music video production for the song "Human" by the virtual idol "Apoki." Created by the AI company AFUN Interactive, Apoki is a virtual influencer and singer whose entire persona is digitally constructed. The music video for "Human" showcases cutting-edge AI-generated animations and choreography, highlighting the potential for AI to revolutionize the entertainment industry by creating entirely new forms of artistic expression (Sposato, 2024b).

Economic Impact and Industry Adaptation to New Regulations

The economic impact of AI and copyright policies in South Korea is deep, driving significant growth and transformation within the media and entertainment sectors. The adoption of AI technologies has enhanced creative processes and opened new revenue streams and business models.

The integration of AI in entertainment has led to the rise of virtual concerts and events, which have gained immense popularity, especially during the COVID-19 pandemic. These virtual experiences, powered by AI and augmented reality, provide fans with immersive and interactive engagements, generating substantial income for entertainment companies while expanding their global reach (Stoke, 2019).

South Korea's regulatory environment has adapted to these technological advancements by providing a clear and supportive legal framework. This has encouraged startups and established companies alike to invest in AI-driven innovations. The government's proactive position on AI and intellectual property rights has also attracted foreign investments, boosting the country's economic outlook (Wallace, 2017).

However, the rapid pace of AI adoption also presents challenges. Companies must continuously update their compliance practices to align with evolving regulations. For instance, the above-mentioned Lee Luda case highlighted the need for strict data privacy measures and transparent AI development practices. The lessons learned from such incidents have led to more robust regulatory guidelines, ensuring that AI technologies are deployed responsibly and ethically (Christen, 2020).

South Korea's strategic approach to AI and copyright, joined with its dynamic media and entertainment industry, offers a compelling model for balancing innovation with regulation. The country's commitment to fostering technological advancements while protecting intellectual property rights has created a vibrant ecosystem where AI and creativity thrive together. By continuously adapting to new regulations and leveraging AI's transformative potential, South Korea remains at the cutting edge of the global entertainment industry (Hine & Floridi, 2024).

European Union

Specific EU Regulations on AI and Copyright

The European Union has taken a proactive stance in regulating artificial intelligence and copyright, striving to balance innovation with the protection of intellectual property rights. The cornerstone of the EU's approach is the proposed Artificial Intelligence Act, which aims to establish a comprehensive framework for the development, marketing, and use of AI across member states (Huang et al., 2024).

The Artificial Intelligence Act categorizes AI applications into different risk levels, from minimal to high risk, and sets out strict requirements for high-risk applications. These include rigorous data governance standards, transparency requirements, and robust human control mechanisms. The Act also emphasizes the importance of ethical AI development, ensuring that AI systems respect fundamental rights and adhere to ethical principles (Taddeo & Floridi, 2018).

Another pivotal regulation is the General Data Protection Regulation (GDPR), which, while primarily focused on data protection, has significant implications for AI and copyright. GDPR mandates strict controls on data usage and processing, ensuring that personal data used in AI applications is handled with maximum care and transparency. This regulation has set a global standard for data privacy and has directly influenced how AI systems are developed and deployed in the EU (Walters & Novak, 2021).

An interesting case study that exemplifies the EU's regulatory approach is the "AI4EU" project. This initiative, funded by the European Commission, aims to create a European AI-on-demand platform to foster collaboration and innovation among AI researchers, developers, and users. The project highlights the EU's commitment to building a robust AI ecosystem while ensuring compliance with regulatory standards (Lundvall & Rikap, 2022).

Differences and Similarities Among Member States

While the EU provides a common regulatory framework, member states exhibit notable differences and similarities in their implementation and interpretation of AI and copyright laws. These variations are influenced by each country's legal traditions, economic priorities, and technological capabilities (Liu et al., 2021).

For instance, Germany has adopted a highly structured approach, emphasizing data protection and ethical AI development. German regulators have been particularly stringent in enforcing GDPR compliance, reflecting the country's strong commitment to privacy and security. Germany's "Ethics Guidelines for Trustworthy AI," developed by the Data Ethics Commission, provide a comprehensive framework for ensuring AI systems are transparent, accountable, and aligned with human values (López Jiménez et al., 2023).

France, on the other hand, has focused on fostering AI innovation through public-private partnerships and strategic investments. The French government's "AI for Humanity" strategy outlines ambitious goals for AI research and development, emphasizing the importance of ethical considerations and international cooperation. France has also been a vocal advocate for European sovereignty in AI, promoting policies that support homegrown AI technologies and reduce dependency on non-European solutions (Wachter & Mittelstadt, 2018).

In Spain, the focus has been on integrating AI advancements with existing robust intellectual property laws. Spain's Agencia Española de Protección de Datos (AEPD) has issued specific guidelines to ensure that AI applications comply with GDPR and other national privacy regulations. Additionally, Spain has launched several initiatives to support AI research and development, including public funding for AI projects and the creation of specialized AI hubs in cities like Barcelona and Madrid. These efforts aim to foster innovation while maintaining high standards of data protection and intellectual property rights, positioning Spain as a competitive player in the European AI landscape (Stoke, 2019).

In contrast, countries like Estonia have leveraged their digital expertise to create a highly favorable environment for AI startups. Estonia's e-residency program and its advanced digital infrastructure have made it a hub for technological innovation, attracting AI researchers and entrepreneurs from around the world. Estonia's approach underscores the potential of small nations to play a significant role in the global AI landscape by creating agile and supportive regulatory environments (Wallace, 2017).

Despite these differences, there are common threads that unite EU member states. All countries are committed to upholding the principles enshrined in the GDPR and the AI Act, ensuring that AI development is conducted responsibly and ethically. Additionally, there is a shared emphasis on fostering innovation while protecting intellectual property rights, reflecting the EU's dual goals of technological leadership and social responsibility (Abungu, 2021).

Economic Analysis of EU Policies

The economic impact of the EU's AI and copyright policies is profound, driving growth and innovation across multiple sectors. The regulatory framework established by the EU has created a stable and predictable environment for AI development, encouraging investments and fostering a competitive market.

The implementation of the GDPR has had significant economic implications, particularly for businesses involved in data-driven AI applications. While compliance with GDPR has required substantial investments in data governance and security, it has also enhanced consumer trust and opened new opportunities for AI-driven services. Companies that prioritize data protection and transparency are better positioned to succeed in the European market, leveraging their compliance as a competitive advantage (Hine & Floridi, 2024).

The AI Act's emphasis on ethical AI has also promoted economic benefits. By ensuring that AI systems are developed with robust oversight and ethical considerations, the EU has positioned itself as a leader in trustworthy AI. This reputation attracts global partnerships and collaborations, enhancing the EU's influence in shaping the future of AI technologies (Krarup & Horst, 2023).

A case study illustrating the economic benefits of EU policies is the success of the Horizon 2020 program, which has funded numerous AI research and innovation projects. One notable project, "AI4Copernicus," integrates AI with satellite data to address environmental challenges. This project not only advances technological innovation but also demonstrates the economic potential of combining AI with other high-impact sectors (Montasari, 2023).

Moreover, the EU's focus on fostering a single digital market has streamlined cross-border collaborations and reduced barriers to entry for AI startups. The Digital Single Market strategy aims to create a seamless digital ecosystem, facilitating the flow of data and services across member states. This initiative has boosted the competitiveness of European AI companies, enabling them to scale more rapidly and compete on a global stage.

The European Union's regulatory approach to AI and copyright provides a comprehensive and balanced framework that promotes innovation while safeguarding intellectual property rights. The differences and similarities among member states reflect the diversity and dynamism of the EU, creating a rich tapestry of regulatory practices that collectively drive economic growth and technological advancement. Through thoughtful regulation and strategic investments, the EU continues to position itself as a global leader in the AI era, fostering a vibrant and competitive digital economy (Wachter & Mittelstadt, 2018).

United Kingdom

Post-Brexit Strategies Concerning AI and Copyright

The United Kingdom, with its rich history of innovation and legal precedent, has taken a distinctive path in navigating the complexities of artificial intelligence (AI) and copyright post-Brexit. As it carves out its regulatory identity separate from the European Union, the UK is crafting strategies that balance the need for robust intellectual property protection with the desire to foster cutting-edge AI development. This section deepens into the UK's post-Brexit strategies concerning AI and copyright and examines notable cases and judicial precedents that shape its current legal landscape (Sposato, 2024a).

In the wake of Brexit, the United Kingdom has sought to establish a regulatory framework for AI and copyright that both aligns with international standards and leverages its unique strengths as a hub for innovation. The UK government has launched several initiatives aimed at positioning the country as a global leader in AI, all while ensuring the protection of intellectual property rights remains a cornerstone of its policy (Liu et al., 2021).

One of the key components of the UK's post-Brexit strategy is the "National AI Strategy," presented in 2021. This comprehensive plan outlines the UK's vision for AI development over the next decade, focusing on three core pillars: investing in AI capabilities, ensuring AI benefits all sectors of the economy, and establishing an effective regulatory and governance framework. The strategy emphasizes the need for a flexible regulatory approach that can adapt to rapid technological changes, ensuring that the UK remains at the forefront of AI innovation (Yu, 2020).

In terms of copyright, the UK has retained much of the EU's regulatory framework through the "Retained EU Law" mechanism, which ensures continuity and stability in intellectual property rights protection. However, the UK is also exploring opportunities to refine and enhance these laws to better suit its post-Brexit landscape. This includes potential reforms to the Copyright, Designs and Patents Act 1988, to address specific challenges posed by AI-generated content and ensure that the rights of human creators are adequately protected (Lundvall & Rikap, 2022).

A significant initiative in this regard is the establishment of the "AI Council," an independent expert committee that advises the government on AI-related issues, including intellectual property. The AI Council's recommendations aim to balance innovation with ethical considerations, ensuring that AI development is conducted responsibly and that copyright laws evolve in tandem with technological advancements (Christen et al., 2020).

Notable Cases and Judicial Precedents

The legal landscape in the UK regarding AI and copyright has been significantly shaped by several notable cases and judicial precedents. These cases not only highlight the challenges of applying existing laws to new technologies but also provide insights into how the judiciary is interpreting and adapting these laws in the context of AI (Fuji & Managi, 2018).

One landmark case is the "Warner Music Group v. TuneIn Inc." case, where the High Court ruled on the liability of internet radio service TuneIn for copyright infringement. Although the case did not directly involve AI, it underscored the importance of clear guidelines on digital content distribution and the responsibilities of digital platforms. The implications of this case extend to AI-generated content, as it raises questions about the liability and copyright status of works produced or distributed by AI systems. (Wang et al., 2018).

Another significant case is the "Thaler v. Comptroller General of Patents, Designs and Trademarks," which involved an AI system named DABUS (Device for the Autonomous Bootstrapping of Unified Sentience) created by Dr. Stephen Thaler. Dr. Thaler applied for patents listing DABUS as the inventor, sparking a legal debate on whether AI can be recognized as an inventor under current patent law. Although the court ruled against recognizing AI as an inventor, the case has ignited discussions on the need for legal reforms to address the role of AI in creativity and invention (Huang et al., 2024; Roberts et al., 2021).

In the field of copyright, the case of "Newspaper Licensing Agency v. Meltwater" has set important precedents for how digital content and AI-generated summaries are treated under copyright law. The court ruled that online news monitoring services, which use AI to generate content summaries, must obtain licenses from copyright holders, reinforcing the principle that copyright protection extends to digital and AI-generated works (Zurth, 2021).

These cases demonstrate the UK's proactive approach to addressing the legal complexities introduced by AI. By closely examining judicial precedents and adapting legal interpretations, the UK is setting the stage for a balanced and forward-looking legal framework that supports both innovation and the protection of intellectual property rights (Franke, 2021).

The United Kingdom's post-Brexit strategies concerning AI and copyright reflect a nuanced approach that seeks to harness the potential of AI while safeguarding the rights of creators. Through comprehensive national strategies, expert advisory bodies, and landmark judicial cases, the UK is navigating the challenges of the AI era with a focus on adaptability, ethical considerations, and robust intellectual property protection. This approach positions the UK as a leader in both technological innovation and legal foresight, setting a precedent for how countries can effectively manage the intersection of AI and copyright in a rapidly evolving digital landscape (Montasari, 2023)

United States

Current Legislation and Implementation Challenges

The United States, known for its dynamic legal system and robust creative industry, faces unique challenges and opportunities in the regulation of artificial intelligence (AI) and copyright. This section explores the current legislative landscape, notable cases and judicial precedents, and the economic impact of AI on the creative industry in the United States (Abungu, 2021).

The legislative framework for AI and copyright in the United States is characterized by a complex interplay of federal laws, state regulations, and judicial interpretations. Unlike the European Union's comprehensive approach, the U.S. relies heavily on case law and regulatory agencies to address emerging issues in AI and copyright (Fatima et al., 2020).

At the federal level, the primary legislation governing copyright is the Copyright Act of 1976. While this Act provides a solid foundation for protecting the rights of human creators, it was not designed with AI in mind, leading to significant implementation challenges. The U.S. Copyright Office has initiated several inquiries and reports to explore how existing laws can be adapted to accommodate AI-generated works, but legislative updates have been slow to materialize (Lauterbach, 2019).

One of the major challenges is defining authorship and ownership of AI-generated content. Current laws assume a human author, which raises questions about whether AI can be considered an author and, if not, who holds the copyright to works created by AI. The Copyright Office has yet to provide definitive guidance, resulting in uncertainty for creators and businesses leveraging AI technologies (Taddeo & Floridi, 2018).

Additionally, data privacy and security are critical issues impacting AI development and implementation. The absence of a comprehensive federal data protection law, akin to the European GDPR, complicates the landscape. States like California have enacted their own privacy laws, such as the California Consumer Privacy Act (CCPA), but the patchwork nature of state regulations presents challenges for nationwide AI applications (Wachter & Mittelstadt, 2018).

An illustrative example of these challenges is the debate over the "human authorship" requirement in the context of AI-generated art and literature. Artists and tech companies are pushing for reforms that recognize AI as a collaborative tool rather than a sole creator, advocating for shared or derivative ownership models that could better fit the modern creative landscape (López Jiménez et al., 2022b).

Notable Cases and Judicial Precedents

Judicial precedents play a crucial role in shaping the interpretation and application of copyright laws in the United States. Several notable cases have set important precedents for AI and copyright, highlighting the complexities and evolving nature of this legal domain (Liu et al., 2021).

One landmark case is "Feist Publications, Inc. v. Rural Telephone Service Co.," which established that copyright protection requires a minimal degree of creativity. This case is often referenced in discussions about AI-generated works, as it underscores the necessity for a creative element that might be challenging to attribute to AI systems (Roberts et al., 2021).

Another significant case is "Authors Guild v. Google, Inc.," which dealt with the digitization of books and the creation of a searchable database. The court ruled in favor of Google, stating that the use was transformative and fell under fair use. This case has implications for AI, particularly in how AI systems use existing works to generate new content and whether such uses can be considered fair use.

In "Naruto v. Slater," although not directly related to AI, the court's decision that a monkey cannot hold copyright serves as an interesting parallel to discussions about non-human authorship in AI contexts. The ruling highlights the legal system's current stance on authorship, emphasizing the need for human involvement in the creation process (Stoke, 2019).

A more directly relevant case is "Thaler v. Commissioner of Patents," where Dr. Stephen Thaler sought to patent inventions created by his AI system, DABUS. The court's refusal to recognize AI as an inventor sparked significant debate and highlighted the legal challenges of attributing authorship and inventorship to non-human entities. This case has direct implications for copyright, as it brings to light similar issues of authorship and ownership in creative works generated by AI (Zurth, 2021).

Economic Impact on the Creative Industry

The economic impact of AI on the creative industry in the United States is profound and multifaceted. AI technologies are revolutionizing content creation, distribution, and consumption, leading to both opportunities and challenges for the industry (Lauterbach, 2019).

AI-driven tools are enhancing productivity and creativity in sectors such as music, film, and publishing. For instance, AI algorithms can analyze vast amounts of data to identify trends, predict consumer preferences, and even generate original content. This capability allows creators to tailor their works to audience tastes more accurately, potentially increasing engagement and revenue (López Jiménez et al., 2022a).

A notable example is the use of AI in music composition and production. Companies like Amper Music and AIVA (Artificial Intelligence Virtual Artist) offer AI-powered platforms that assist musicians in composing music, democratizing access to sophisticated composition tools and enabling a broader range of artists to produce high-quality music (Wang et al., 2018).

In the film industry, AI is being used to enhance visual effects, streamline editing processes, and even create virtual actors. AI technologies like deepfake and CGI are transforming filmmaking, allowing for more innovative and cost-effective productions. However, these advancements also raise ethical concerns and challenges related to copyright infringement and authenticity (Kulesz, 2018).

The publishing industry is also experiencing significant changes due to AI. AI-generated content, such as automated news articles and personalized stories, is becoming increasingly common. This shift presents both opportunities for efficiency and challenges regarding the originality and value of human-authored works (Radu, 2021).

Despite these advancements, the integration of AI in the creative industry poses significant economic challenges. Traditional creators may face competition from AI-generated content, potentially impacting their livelihoods. Additionally, the legal uncertainties surrounding AI and copyright can create barriers to investment and innovation (Franke, 2021).

To address these challenges and harness the economic potential of AI, stakeholders in the creative industry are advocating for clear and adaptive regulatory frameworks. By establishing guidelines that balance innovation with the protection of intellectual property rights, the United States can foster a vibrant and competitive creative economy that benefits both human creators and technological innovators (Christen et al., 2020).

The United States is navigating a complex and evolving landscape in AI and copyright. Through thoughtful legislation, influential judicial precedents, and adaptive economic strategies, the country is striving to balance the transformative potential of AI with the need to protect the rights of creators. By learning from landmark cases and addressing implementation challenges, the U.S. can lead the way in shaping a future where AI and human creativity coexist and thrive (Calderaro & Blumfelde, 2022).

COMPARISON AND CONTRAST OF CASES

In this section, we deepen into a comparative analysis of how different regions address the challenges and opportunities presented by AI and copyright. By examining common and divergent trends, evaluating the effectiveness of various regulatory approaches, and analyzing the economic impact of different policies, we aim to provide a comprehensive understanding of the global landscape.

Identification of Common and Divergent Trends Among the Studied Regions

The regulation of AI and copyright presents both shared challenges and unique regional responses. Across the studied regions—Asia (specifically China, Japan, and South Korea), Europe (focusing on the European Union and individual member states like Germany and France), and the United States—several common trends and notable divergences emerge.

On the one hand, there are three groups of trends that show elements in common:

1. **Emphasis on Data Privacy:** Regardless of geographic location, all regions emphasize the importance of data privacy and security in the development and deployment of AI technologies. The European Union's GDPR, the U.S.'s patchwork of state privacy laws, and similar regulations in Asia reflect a global consensus on the need for stringent data protection measures.
2. **Focus on Ethical AI:** Ethical considerations are paramount in AI policies worldwide. Guidelines and frameworks aimed at ensuring transparency, accountability, and fairness in AI systems are prevalent in the EU's AI Act, Japan's AI strategies, and various U.S. initiatives.
3. **Support for Innovation:** All regions recognize the potential of AI to drive economic growth and innovation. Governments are investing heavily in AI research and development, offering funding and incentives to foster technological advancements.

On the other hand, there are three groups of divergent trends:

1. **Regulatory Rigor:** The EU and Japan tend to have more structured and comprehensive regulatory frameworks compared to the more reactive and fragmented approach of the United States. The EU's proactive stance with the GDPR and AI Act contrasts with the U.S.'s reliance on case law and state-level regulations.
2. **Implementation Speed:** China and South Korea exhibit rapid implementation of AI policies, leveraging centralized governmental control to quickly enact and enforce regulations. In contrast, the EU and U.S. often experience slower implementation due to the need for extensive consultations and legislative processes.
3. **Cultural and Legal Traditions:** Regional cultural and legal traditions significantly influence regulatory approaches. For example, the EU's strong emphasis on human rights and privacy reflects its broader social and legal values, whereas the U.S. focuses on innovation and market-driven solutions.

Assessment of Effectiveness of Regulatory Approaches

Evaluating the effectiveness of different regulatory approaches involves assessing how well these frameworks balance innovation with the protection of intellectual property and ethical standards.

The European Union's comprehensive and anticipatory approach, exemplified by the GDPR and AI Act, effectively sets high standards for data protection and ethical AI. This regulatory rigor ensures consumer trust and provides a clear legal framework for businesses, but it can also be seen as restrictive and slow to adapt to rapid technological changes. However, the EU's proactive stance has made it a global leader in setting benchmarks for responsible AI use.

The United States approach, characterized by its flexibility and reliance on judicial precedents, encourages rapid innovation and adaptation. This can lead to significant technological advancements and economic growth. However, the lack of a unified federal framework creates legal uncertainties and uneven protections across states, potentially hindering comprehensive consumer trust and consistent business practices.

In Asia, countries like China and Japan demonstrate the benefits of rapid policy implementation and strong governmental support for AI development. China's centralized approach allows for swift regulatory actions, fostering a robust AI ecosystem. Japan's structured and ethical-focused regulations ensure a balanced approach to innovation and intellectual property protection. However, the speed and centralization in China can sometimes overlook nuanced ethical considerations, while Japan's meticulous strategies may slow down immediate technological adoption.

Economic Impact of Different Policies on the Creative and Technological Industries

The economic implications of AI and copyright policies vary significantly across regions, influencing both the creative and technological sectors.

In this sense, the European Union's strict regulations create a stable environment that encourages long-term investments in AI and technology. Companies operating within the EU benefit from a clear legal framework, fostering innovation that aligns with ethical and data protection standards. However, the high compliance costs can be a barrier for startups and smaller companies, potentially stifling early-stage innovation.

The United States benefits economically from its flexible and innovation-driven approach. The less restrictive regulatory environment promotes rapid technological advancements and attracts significant venture capital investments. This dynamic ecosystem supports the growth of startups and the development of cutting-edge technologies. Nevertheless, the lack of comprehensive regulations can lead to ethical lapses and data privacy issues, which may undermine consumer trust and long-term sustainability.

In the case of Asia: it stands out China, which aggressive AI policy implementation has spurred rapid economic growth in the tech sector, making it a global leader in AI applications. The extensive state support and investment have catalyzed significant advancements. However, the fast-paced regulatory environment may sometimes sacrifice thorough ethical considerations. Japan's balanced approach ensures that technological growth is sustainable and ethically sound, supporting a stable creative industry and fostering international collaborations. South Korea's focus on integrating AI into its strong entertainment sector has led to innovative applications that enhance cultural exports and economic growth.

A notable case illustrating these dynamics is the collaboration between Japanese AI firms and the entertainment industry, resulting in AI-generated music and virtual idols that have captured global audiences. This synergy highlights how well-designed regulations can foster innovative economic opportunities while maintaining ethical standards and protecting intellectual property rights.

Comparing and contrasting the regulatory approaches of different regions reveals a complex interplay between innovation, ethical considerations, and economic impacts. By understanding these trends and their outcomes, policymakers and industry leaders can better navigate the challenges and opportunities presented by AI and copyright in the global landscape.

SELF-REGULATION AND ITS IMPACT

Self-regulation is a critical component of the AI industry's framework for addressing the complexities and ethical considerations surrounding AI-generated content and copyright. This chapter explores the concept of self-regulation, its successes and failures, and how it compares to government regulation across different regions.

Definition and Examples of Self-Regulation in the AI Industry

Self-regulation refers to the process by which an industry collectively establishes and enforces standards, guidelines, and best practices without direct government intervention. This approach allows for greater flexibility and faster adaptation to technological changes, leveraging industry expertise to address specific challenges (Lauterbach, 2019). Self-regulation in the AI industry involves companies, professional associations, and other stakeholders collaboratively developing codes of conduct, ethical guidelines, and technical standards. These measures aim to ensure that AI technologies are developed and deployed responsibly, safeguarding consumer interests, promoting transparency, and protecting intellectual property rights (Christen et al., 2020).

One example is a consortium of AI-focused companies including Google, Amazon, Facebook, IBM, and Microsoft. This partnership on AI is dedicated to addressing the societal impacts of AI. The consortium has developed guidelines for ethical AI development, promoting fairness, transparency, and accountability (Taddeo & Floridi, 2018).

Another case is IEEE Global Initiative on Ethics of Autonomous and Intelligent Systems. The Institute of Electrical and Electronics Engineers (IEEE) has created a set of ethical standards for AI and autonomous systems. These standards provide a comprehensive framework for ensuring that AI technologies are aligned with human values and ethical principles (Roberts et al., 2021).

Finally, it is important to mention the Google's AI Principles. Google has established a set of AI principles that guide its development and use of AI technologies. These principles emphasize the importance of safety, accountability, privacy, and the avoidance of unfair bias in AI systems (Wachter & Mittelstadt, 2018).

Success and Failure Cases in Self-Regulation of Copyright in AI-Generated Content

The effectiveness of self-regulation in managing copyright issues related to AI-generated content has seen both successes and failures. Examining these cases provides insights into the potential and limitations of self-regulatory frameworks.

On the on hand, between the success cases it stands out the Creative Commons Licenses. Creative Commons (CC) provides a flexible range of licenses that allow creators to specify the permissions for their works. Some AI developers use CC licenses to clarify the usage rights of AI-generated content, fostering an open and collaborative environment while protecting intellectual property (Franke, 2021).

Another success example is the OpenAI's GPT-3 Licensing. OpenAI has implemented a controlled access model for its GPT-3 language model, requiring users to apply for API access and agree to usage policies that prevent harmful applications. This approach has been effective in mitigating misuse while promoting innovation in natural language processing (Wang et al., 2018).

On the other hand, between the failure cases we find the deepfake regulations. The rise of deepfake technology, which uses AI to create highly realistic but fake videos, has highlighted the limitations of self-regulation. Despite efforts by platforms like YouTube and Facebook to establish guidelines and remove harmful content, the proliferation of deepfakes has outpaced these measures, demonstrating the need for more robust intervention (Roberts et al., 2021).

Another failure example is ArtStation AI Art controversy. ArtStation, a platform for digital artists, faced backlash for allowing AI-generated art to be displayed alongside human-created works without clear differentiation. The lack of stringent self-regulatory measures led to confusion and frustration among artists, underscoring the need for clearer policies and enforcement mechanisms (Zurth, 2021).

Comparison of the Effectiveness of Self-Regulation Versus Government Regulation in Different Regions

Comparing self-regulation and government regulation across different regions reveals varying levels of effectiveness in addressing AI and copyright challenges.

In the European Union, the comprehensive regulatory framework, including the GDPR and the proposed AI Act, sets high standards for data protection and ethical AI (Veale & Zuiderveen Borgesius, 2021). These regulations provide clear legal guidelines but can be slow to adapt to technological changes. Regarding self-regulation, the industry initiatives like the EU AI Alliance complement government efforts by fostering collaboration and ethical standards among AI stakeholders (Calderaro &

Blumfelde, 2022). However, the stringent regulatory environment often limits the scope and flexibility of self-regulatory measures (Radu, 2021).

On the other hand, the government regulation in the United States stands out with a reactive approach, and with regulations emerging from judicial precedents and state-level initiatives. This creates a fragmented legal landscape with varying degrees of protection and enforcement. However, the flexibility of self-regulation in the U.S. allows for rapid adaptation and innovation. Industry groups like the Partnership on AI and individual company policies provide robust frameworks for ethical AI development. However, the lack of a unified federal approach can lead to inconsistent standards and enforcement (Montasari, 2023).

Finally, in the case of Asia, countries like China implement top-down regulatory approaches, rapidly enacting and enforcing AI policies. These regulations ensure swift compliance but may lack the nuance required for ethical considerations. In Japan and South Korea, self-regulatory initiatives complement government policies by promoting ethical standards and best practices within the industry. (Hine & Floridi, 2024). These efforts are often well-coordinated with national strategies, ensuring a balanced approach to innovation and regulation.

The Partnership on AI in the U.S. exemplifies successful self-regulation, bringing together industry leaders to address AI's ethical challenges collaboratively. Conversely, the proliferation of deepfakes illustrates the limitations of self-regulation without adequate government support, highlighting the need for a hybrid approach.

Self-regulation plays a crucial role in the AI industry, offering flexibility and industry-specific expertise to address complex issues. However, its effectiveness varies across regions and is often most successful when complemented by robust government regulation. By leveraging the strengths of both approaches, stakeholders can create a balanced framework that promotes innovation while safeguarding ethical standards and protecting intellectual property rights.

BUSINESS AND INDUSTRY PERSPECTIVE

The integration of artificial intelligence (AI) and the evolving landscape of copyright regulations present both challenges and opportunities for businesses across various sectors. This chapter deepens into the business strategies to adapt to these changes, shows case studies of innovative companies, analyzes the economic and market impact of AI, and offers recommendations for managing the legal and economic challenges posed by AI and copyright regulations.

Business Strategies to Adapt to AI and Copyright Regulations

In the rapidly changing world of AI and copyright, businesses must develop agile strategies to navigate complex regulatory environments while fostering innovation. Here are key strategies that businesses are adopting:

1. **Compliance and Ethical AI Practices:** Companies are investing in compliance programs that align with both local and international regulations. This includes appointing compliance officers, conducting regular audits, and ensuring that AI systems adhere to ethical guidelines such as fairness, accountability, and transparency. Ethical AI practices involve developing algorithms that mitigate bias, ensuring data privacy, and creating transparent AI systems that can be easily audited and explained.
2. **Collaboration and Partnerships:** Forming strategic partnerships with tech firms, research institutions, and regulatory bodies can help businesses stay ahead of regulatory changes and benefit from the latest advancements in AI technology. Collaborations also enable knowledge sharing and innovation, allowing companies to pool resources and expertise to tackle complex regulatory requirements.
3. **Investing in AI Governance:** Establishing internal AI governance frameworks helps businesses manage AI risks and ensure compliance with regulations. This includes creating dedicated AI ethics committees, developing internal policies, and implementing robust data management practices. AI governance frameworks also involve continuous monitoring and assessment of AI systems to identify and address potential ethical and legal issues.
4. **Employee Training and Development:** Businesses are focusing on upskilling their workforce to understand and navigate AI and copyright regulations. This includes providing training on data protection laws, ethical AI practices, and the implications of AI on intellectual property rights. Investing in employee education ensures that the workforce is equipped to handle the complexities of AI and regulatory compliance.

Case Studies of Companies Leading in Innovation and Regulatory Compliance

Several companies stand out for their innovative use of AI and their proactive approach to regulatory compliance. The following case studies illustrate how businesses can successfully navigate the challenges of AI and copyright: IBM, Microsoft and Spotify.

IBM has been a pioneer in developing ethical AI systems. The company's Watson AI platform incorporates rigorous data privacy and security measures, and IBM has established principles for ethical AI development. IBM's commitment to transparency is evident in its efforts to explain AI decision-making processes, ensuring that users and regulators understand how AI systems operate (Huang et al., 2024).

In the case of Microsoft, we can see that it has taken a leadership role in advocating for responsible AI. The company has implemented a comprehensive AI governance framework that includes an AI ethics committee and rigorous compliance checks. Through partnerships with academic institutions and participation in global AI ethics initiatives, Microsoft ensures that its AI technologies adhere to the highest ethical standards (Walters & Novak, 2021).

Finally, Spotify takes advantage of AI to enhance user experiences through personalized music recommendations. The company ensures compliance with copyright regulations by securing licenses for music content and using AI to monitor and manage these licenses. Spotify's approach to AI and copyright demonstrates how businesses can use technology to innovate while respecting intellectual property rights (Liu & Lin, 2020).

Economic and Market Impact of AI on the Business Sector

The integration of AI into business operations has profound economic and market implications. AI technologies are driving significant changes in productivity, efficiency, and innovation across industries.

1. **Increased Productivity and Efficiency:** AI automates repetitive tasks, freeing up human resources for more complex and strategic activities. This leads to increased productivity and cost savings for businesses. In manufacturing, AI-powered robots and predictive maintenance systems enhance production efficiency and reduce downtime.
2. **Innovation and Competitive Advantage:** AI enables businesses to innovate by providing insights from large datasets, predicting market trends, and identifying new opportunities. Companies that effectively take advantage of AI gain a competitive edge in the market. In the healthcare sector, AI is revolutionizing

diagnostics and personalized medicine, offering new treatments and improving patient outcomes.

3. **Market Disruption and New Business Models:** AI is disrupting traditional business models and creating new market opportunities. Companies that adapt to these changes can capitalize on emerging trends and consumer demands. For example, the rise of AI-powered virtual assistants and chatbots is transforming customer service and support industries.

Recommendations for Businesses on Managing Legal and Economic Challenges in AI and Copyright

Navigating the legal and economic landscape of AI and copyright requires a proactive and strategic approach. Here are some recommendations for businesses to effectively manage these challenges.

First, it is important to stay informed and engaged, and to keep abreast of the latest developments in AI and copyright regulations. This encompasses to engage with industry bodies, attend relevant conferences, and participate in regulatory consultations to stay informed. Being proactive in understanding regulatory changes ensures that businesses can adapt quickly and remain compliant.

Second, it is useful to develop a comprehensive compliance framework, and to establish a robust compliance framework that addresses all aspects of AI and copyright regulations. This includes data protection policies, ethical AI guidelines, and intellectual property management practices. It would be of great worth to review regularly and to update the compliance framework to reflect changes in regulations and technological advancements.

Then, to foster a culture of ethical AI would also help in any type of company. This means, to promote a culture of ethical AI within the organization and to encourage employees to prioritize ethical considerations in AI development and use. It also includes to implement training programs that emphasize the importance of ethical AI practices and compliance with regulations.

Moreover, taking advantage of technology for compliance would be a great value inside a company, like using the AI and other technologies to enhance compliance efforts. For example, AI can be used to monitor data usage, detect anomalies, and ensure adherence to copyright laws. In practice, this means to invest in compliance tools that provide real-time insights and facilitate effective management of regulatory requirements.

And finally, we cannot forget to collaborate with stakeholders, working closely with regulators, industry peers, and other stakeholders to shape the regulatory landscape. Collaboration can help businesses influence policy decisions and ensure that regulations are practical and effective. In other words, to engage in industry initiatives and partnerships that promote best practices and standards for AI and copyright.

The integration of AI into the business sector presents both opportunities and challenges. By adopting strategic business practices, leveraging case studies of successful companies, understanding the economic impact of AI, and following key recommendations, businesses can navigate the complexities of AI and copyright regulations effectively. This approach ensures compliance and drives innovation and competitive advantage in a rapidly evolving technological prospect.

FUTURE CHALLENGES AND OPPORTUNITIES

As artificial intelligence (AI) continues to evolve, it brings forth both challenges and opportunities at the intersection of technology and copyright. This section deepens into emerging legal challenges, economic opportunities, and policy recommendations to address these issues effectively.

Emerging Legal Challenges at the Intersection of AI and Copyright in Different Regions

The rapid advancement of AI technologies presents unique legal challenges that vary across regions. One of the primary issues is the question of authorship and ownership of AI-generated content. Traditional copyright laws are based on human authorship, creating a gray area for AI-generated works. Different regions are adopting varied approaches to address these challenges.

In Asia, particularly China and Japan, there is a significant push towards integrating AI within the legal framework. China's rapid implementation of AI policies often precedes comprehensive legal reforms, leading to a patchwork of regulations that can sometimes be inconsistent. Japan, on the other hand, has been more methodical, enacting specific laws that recognize the contributions of AI in the creative process while ensuring human oversight.

In Europe, the General Data Protection Regulation (GDPR) and the proposed Artificial Intelligence Act set strict standards for data usage and AI applications. However, these regulations also bring challenges in harmonizing AI with existing copyright laws, particularly concerning data-driven content generation.

The United States faces challenges due to its reactive approach, relying heavily on judicial precedents and state-level regulations. The lack of a unified federal framework creates legal uncertainties, particularly regarding the extent of protection for AI-generated works and the responsibilities of AI developers.

Economic Opportunities and New Industries Arising From AI

AI is a source of legal challenges and also a driver of economic opportunities, leading to the emergence of new industries and the transformation of existing ones. AI is revolutionizing the creative sector by enabling new forms of content creation. AI tools can compose music, generate visual art, and write literature, democratizing creative processes and allowing a broader range of voices to be heard. For example, AI-generated music platforms like Amper Music and Jukedeck are empowering amateur musicians to create high-quality compositions.

In the case of healthcare and biotechnology, AI's ability stands out to analyze large datasets quickly and accurately is transforming healthcare and biotechnology. AI-driven diagnostic tools and personalized medicine are becoming more prevalent, improving patient outcomes and creating new business opportunities in medical research and pharmaceutical development.

In the financial sector, AI is being used for fraud detection, risk management, and personalized financial planning. Companies that leverage AI for predictive analytics and automated trading are gaining a competitive edge, leading to the growth of fintech startups and innovation in traditional banking.

If we think about the entertainment and media, we can appreciate that AI is creating new forms of entertainment, such as virtual reality experiences and interactive storytelling. Virtual influencers and AI-generated content are becoming mainstream, opening up new revenue streams and marketing opportunities.

Policy Recommendations Based on Case Studies

Drawing on various case studies from different regions, several policy recommendations can help address the legal and economic challenges of AI while maximizing its opportunities:

1. Harmonize International Regulations: There is a need for global standards that harmonize AI and copyright regulations across borders. International cooperation through organizations like WIPO can facilitate the development of unified guidelines that balance innovation with the protection of intellectual property.
2. Promote Ethical AI Development: Governments and industry stakeholders should collaborate to develop ethical guidelines that ensure AI systems are transparent, accountable, and fair. Initiatives like the Partnership on AI can serve as models for establishing industry-wide ethical standards.

3. Encourage Public-Private Partnerships: Public-private partnerships can drive innovation and ensure that AI technologies are developed responsibly. Governments should incentivize collaborations between academia, industry, and regulatory bodies to address the legal and technical challenges of AI.
4. Implement Adaptive Legal Frameworks: Legal frameworks should be flexible and adaptive to keep pace with rapid technological changes. Policymakers should consider creating regulatory environments that allow experimentation with AI technologies while maintaining oversight to ensure compliance with ethical and legal standards.
5. Enhance Public Awareness and Education: Increasing public awareness and understanding of AI's potential and risks is crucial. Educational initiatives and public dialogues can help demystify AI, fostering a more informed and engaged society that can contribute to the development of balanced policies.

By addressing these emerging challenges and seizing the opportunities presented by AI, policymakers and industry leaders can foster an environment where innovation thrives alongside robust legal and ethical protections.

CONCLUSION

The comprehensive analysis of AI and copyright across Asia, Europe, and the United States reveals distinct regional approaches, common trends, and significant implications for the future. In Asia, countries like China and Japan demonstrate a proactive stance, with China rapidly implementing AI policies and Japan focusing on ethical guidelines and intellectual property protection. Europe's structured regulatory framework, exemplified by the GDPR and the AI Act, sets high standards for data protection and ethical AI development. The United States, while more flexible and innovation-driven, faces challenges due to its fragmented legal landscape and reliance on judicial precedents.

Reflecting on these findings, it becomes clear that international cooperation and policy harmonization are crucial. The rapid pace of AI advancements necessitates a coordinated global response to address the ethical, legal, and economic challenges. Organizations like WIPO and initiatives such as the AI4EU project exemplify efforts to create global standards and foster international collaboration. Harmonizing policies can reduce regulatory fragmentation, promote innovation, and ensure that AI technologies are developed and used responsibly across borders.

The future of AI and copyright hinges on balancing innovation with robust intellectual property protection and ethical considerations. As AI continues to revolutionize industries, it is imperative to establish flexible and comprehensive legal frameworks that can adapt to technological changes. This includes recognizing the unique challenges posed by AI-generated content and ensuring that human creativity is not undermined. Embracing a multidisciplinary approach, involving policymakers, businesses, and legal practitioners, will be key to navigating this complex landscape.

The global landscape of AI and copyright is evolving rapidly, driven by technological advancements and diverse regulatory responses. By fostering international cooperation, harmonizing policies, and adopting a forward-looking perspective, we can ensure that AI technologies contribute positively to society while protecting the rights and livelihoods of human creators. The journey towards a balanced and ethical AI ecosystem is ongoing, and it requires the collective efforts of all stakeholders to shape a future where innovation and creativity can thrive together.

REFERENCES

Abungu, C. Y. (2021). Democratic Culture and the Development of Artificial Intelligence in the USA and China. *The Chinese Journal of Comparative Law*, 9(1), 81–108. DOI: 10.1093/cjcl/cxaa032

Ballardini, R. M., He, K., & Roos, T. (2019). AI-generated content: authorship and inventorship in the age of artificial intelligence. In Pihlajarinne, T., Vesala, J., & Honkkila, O. (Eds.), *Online Distribution of Content in the EU* (pp. 117–135). Edward Elgar Publishing. DOI: 10.4337/9781788119900.00015

Bostrom, N., & Yudkowsky, E. (2014). The ethics of artificial intelligence. In Frankish, K., & Ramsey, W. M. (Eds.), *The Cambridge Handbook of Artificial Intelligence* (pp. 316–334). Cambridge University Press. DOI: 10.1017/CBO9781139046855.020

Bridy, A. (2016). The evolution of authorship: Work made by code. *Columbia Journal of Law & the Arts, 39*(3), 395-401. DOI: 10.7916/jla.v39i3.2078

Calderaro, A., & Blumfelde, S. (2022). Artificial intelligence and EU security: The false promise of digital sovereignty. *European Security*, 31(3), 415–434. DOI: 10.1080/09662839.2022.2101885

Christen, M., Gordijn, B., & Loi, M. (2020). *The ethics of cybersecurity*. Springer Nature. DOI: 10.1007/978-3-030-29053-5

Creemers, R., Triolo, P., & Webster, G. (2018). Translation: Cybersecurity Law of the People's Republic of China. *New America*. Retrieved from: https://www.newamerica.org/cybersecurity-initiative/digichina/blog/translation-cybersecurity-law-peoples-republic-china/

Cui, L. (2020). *Artificial intelligence and judicial modernization*. Springer Singapore. DOI: 10.1007/978-981-32-9880-4

Ding, J. (2018). *Deciphering China's AI Dream. Future of Humanity Institute*, University of Oxford. Retrieved from: https://www.fhi.ox.ac.uk/publications/deciphering-chinas-ai-dream-jeffrey-ding-2018-future-of-humanity-institute-university-of-oxford/

Fatima, S., Desouza, K. C., & Dawson, G. S. (2020). National strategic artificial intelligence plans: A multi-dimensional analysis. *Economic Analysis and Policy*, 67, 178–194. DOI: 10.1016/j.eap.2020.07.008

Franke, U. E. (2021). Artificial Divide: How Europe and America Could Clash Over AI. *European Council on Foreign Relations*. Retrieved from: https://www.jstor.org/stable/resrep29123

Fuji, H., & Managi, S. (2018). Trends and priority shifts in artificial intelligence technology invention: A global patent analysis. *Economic Analysis and Policy*, 58, 60–69. DOI: 10.1016/j.eap.2017.12.006

Gervais, D. J. (2020). The machine as author. *Iowa Law Review*, 105(5), 2053–2106. https://ssrn.com/abstract=3359524

Ginsburg, J. C., & Budiardjo, L. A. (2019). Authors and machines. *Berkeley Technology Law Journal*, 34(2), 343–448. DOI: 10.15779/Z38SF2MC24

Guadamuz, A. (2016). The monkey selfie: Copyright lessons for originality in photographs and internet jurisdiction. *Internet Policy Review*, 5(1). Advance online publication. DOI: 10.14763/2016.1.398

Guadamuz, A. (2017). Artificial intelligence and copyright. *WIPO Magazine*, (5), 14-19. Retrieved from: https://www.wipo.int/wipo_magazine/en/2017/05/article_0003.html

He, K. (2020). Artificial intelligence and its implications for income distribution and unemployment. In Goldfarb, A., Gans, J., & Agrawal, A. (Eds.), *The Economics of Artificial Intelligence: An Agenda* (pp. 399–419). University of Chicago Press. DOI: 10.7208/chicago/9780226613475.003.0016

Hine, E., & Floridi, L. (2024). Artificial intelligence with American values and Chinese characteristics: A comparative analysis of American and Chinese governmental AI policies. *AI & Society*, 39(1), 257–278. DOI: 10.1007/s00146-022-01499-8

Huang, K., Joshi, A., Dun, S., & Hamilton, N. (2024). AI Regulations. In Huang, K., Wang, Y., Goertzel, B., Li, Y., Wright, S., & Ponnapalli, J. (Eds.), *Generative AI Security. Future of Business and Finance* (pp. 61–98). Springer. DOI: 10.1007/978-3-031-54252-7_3

Ihalainen, J. (2018). Computer creativity: Artificial intelligence and copyright. *Journal of Intellectual Property Law & Practice*, 13(9), 724–728. DOI: 10.1093/jiplp/jpy031

Krarup, T., & Horst, M. (2023). European artificial intelligence policy as digital single market making. *Big Data & Society*, 10(1). Advance online publication. DOI: 10.1177/20539517231153811

Kulesz, O. (2018). Culture, platforms and machines: the impact of artificial intelligence on the diversity of cultural expressions. *Intergovernmental Committee for the protection and promotion of the diversity of cultural expressions*. Retrieved from: https://unesdoc.unesco.org/ark:/48223/pf0000380584

Lauterbach, A. (2019). Artificial intelligence and policy: Quo vadis? *Digital Policy. Regulation & Governance*, 21(3), 238–263. DOI: 10.1108/DPRG-09-2018-0054

Lee, K. F. (2018). *AI superpowers: China, Silicon Valley, and the new world order*. Houghton Mifflin Harcourt.

Lemley, M. A., & Casey, B. (2020). Fair learning. *Texas Law Review*, 99(4), 743–808.

Liu, H. W., & Lin, C. F. (2020). Artificial Intelligence and Global Trade Governance: A Pluralist Agenda. *Harvard International Law Journal*, 61(2). https://ssrn.com/abstract=3675505

Liu, N., Shapira, P., Yue, X., & Guan, J. (2021). Mapping technological innovation dynamics in artificial intelligence domains: Evidence from a global patent analysis. *PLoS One*, 16(12), e0262050. DOI: 10.1371/journal.pone.0262050 PMID: 34972173

López Jiménez, D., Dittmar, E. C., & Vargas Portillo, J. P. (2022a). Nuevas estrategias publicitarias con influencers: Un examen multidisciplinar. *Revista de Ciencias Sociales*, 28(4), 63–78. DOI: 10.31876/rcs.v28i4.39117

López Jiménez, D., Dittmar, E. C., & Vargas Portillo, J. P. (2022b). The trusted third party or digital notary in Spain: Effect on virtual transactions. *International Review of Law Computers & Technology*, 36(3), 453–469. DOI: 10.1080/13600869.2021.2004760

López Jiménez, D., Dittmar, E. C., & Vargas Portillo, J. P. (2023). The Self-Regulating Jury in the Field of Interactive Advertising. *Revista de Direito. Estado e Telecomunicacoes*, 15(1), 1–30. DOI: 10.26512/lstr.v15i1.42146

Lundvall, B. A., & Rikap, C. (2022). China's catching-up in artificial intelligence seen as a co-evolution of corporate and national innovation systems. *Research Policy*, 51(1), 104395. DOI: 10.1016/j.respol.2021.104395

Margoni, T. (2018). Artificial intelligence, machine learning and EU copyright law: Who owns AI? SSRN *Electronic Journal*. DOI: 10.2139/ssrn.3299523

Margoni, T., & Kretschmer, M. (2021). A deeper look into the EU Text and Data Mining exceptions: Harmonisation, data ownership, and the future of technology. *GRUR International*, 71(8), 685–701. DOI: 10.1093/grurint/ikac054

Montasari, R. (2023). National Artificial Intelligence Strategies: A Comparison of the UK, EU and US Approaches with those Adopted by State Adversaries. In *Countering Cyberterrorism. Advances in Information Security* (Vol. 101). Springer. DOI: 10.1007/978-3-031-21920-7_7

Radu, R. (2021). Steering the governance of artificial intelligence: National strategies in perspective. *Policy and Society*, 40(2), 178–193. DOI: 10.1080/14494035.2021.1929728

Ramalho, A. (2017). Will robots rule the (artistic) world? A proposed model for the legal status of creations by artificial intelligence systems. *SSRN*, 21(1), 12–25. DOI: 10.2139/ssrn.2987757

Roberts, H., Cowls, J., Morley, J., Taddeo, M., Wang, V., & Floridi, L. (2021). The Chinese approach to artificial intelligence: An analysis of policy, ethics, and regulation. *AI & Society*, 36(1), 59–77. DOI: 10.1007/s00146-020-00992-2

Samuelson, P. (2020). AI authorship? *Communications of the ACM*. Retrieved from: https://cacm.acm.org/opinion/ai-authorship/

Scassa, T. (2017). Sharing data in the platform economy: A public interest argument for access to platform data. *UBC Law Review, 50*(4). Retrieved from: https://ssrn.com/abstract=3077996

Schafer, B., Komuves, D., Zatarain, J. M. N., & Diver, L. (2015). A fourth law of robotics? Copyright and the law and ethics of machine co-production. *Artificial Intelligence and Law*, 23(3), 217–240. DOI: 10.1007/s10506-015-9169-7

Sposato, M. (2024a). Are leaders born or made? Asking the right question. *Development and Learning in Organizations*, 38(3), 1–3. DOI: 10.1108/DLO-05-2023-0123

Sposato, M. (2024b). Leadership training and development in the age of artificial intelligence. *Development and Learning in Organizations*, 38(4), 4–7. DOI: 10.1108/DLO-12-2023-0256

Stoke, S. (2019). *Digital Copyright: Law and Practice* (5th ed.). Bloomsbury Publishing. DOI: 10.5040/9781509917327

Taddeo, M., & Floridi, L. (2018). How AI can be a force for good. *Science*, 361(6404), 751–752. DOI: 10.1126/science.aat5991 PMID: 30139858

Veale, M., & Zuiderveen Borgesius, F. (2021). - Demystifying the Draft EU Artificial Intelligence Act — Analysing the good, the bad, and the unclear elements of the proposed approach. *Computer Law Review International*, 22(4), 97–112. DOI: 10.9785/cri-2021-220402

Wachter, S., & Mittelstadt, B. (2018). A Right to Reasonable Inferences: Re-Thinking Data Protection Law in the Age of Big Data and AI. *Columbia Business Law Review, 2019*(2). Retrieved from: https://ssrn.com/abstract=3248829

Wachter, S., Mittelstadt, B., & Floridi, L. (2017). Transparent, explainable, and accountable AI for robotics. *Science Robotics*, 2(6), eaan6080. Advance online publication. DOI: 10.1126/scirobotics.aan6080 PMID: 33157874

Wallace, D. (2017). *Environmental Policy and Industrial Innovation*. Routledge. DOI: 10.4324/9781315145358

Walters, R., & Novak, M. (2021). Artificial Intelligence and Law. In *Cyber Security, Artificial Intelligence, Data Protection & the Law*. Springer. DOI: 10.1007/978-981-16-1665-5_3

Wang, J., Yu, X., Li, J., & Jin, X. (2018). Artificial Intelligence and International Norms. In Jin, D. (Ed.), *Reconstructing Our Orders*. Springer. DOI: 10.1007/978-981-13-2209-9_7

Yanisky-Ravid, S., & Liu, X. (2017). When artificial intelligence systems produce inventions: An alternative model for patent law at the 3A era. *SSRN*, 39(6), 2214–2262. DOI: 10.2139/ssrn.2931828

Yu, P. K. (2020). 72 Fla. L. Rev. 331 (2020). The Algorithmic Divide and Equality in the Age of Artificial Intelligence. *Florida Law Review*, 72, 331–389. https://ssrn.com/abstract=3455772

Zhao, L. (2023). Artificial intelligence and law: emerging divergent national regulatory approaches in a changing landscape of fast-evolving AI technologies (369-399). In Collins, D., & Geist, M. (Eds.), *Research Handbook on Digital Trade* (pp. 369–399). DOI: 10.4337/9781800884953.00033

Zurth, O. (2021). Artificial Creativity? A Case Against Copyright Protection for AI Generated Works. *UCLA Journal of Law & Technology, 25*(2). Retrieved from: https://ssrn.com/abstract=3707651

Chapter 13
Turkish Film Industry Stakeholders' Approaches to Artificial Intelligence and Copyright

Erman M. Demir
https://orcid.org/0000-0002-7123-5742
Başkent University, Turkey

Nihan Gider Işıkman
https://orcid.org/0000-0002-3332-3784
Baskent University, Turkey

ABSTRACT

Artificial intelligence (AI) is transforming industries by automating production stages and enhancing efficiency, with significant applications in the film industry. However, AI's integration raises concerns about copyright, challenging traditional notions of authorship. This chapter examines the intersection of Generative AI (GenAI) and copyright within the Turkish film industry, exploring stakeholders' perspectives through two focus group interviews with 22 participants. The study reveals diverse views on GenAI's potential and challenges, highlighting its benefits in efficiency and cost-effectiveness, alongside risks like content homogenization, job displacement, and inadequate copyright protection. Participants also express concerns about Türkiye's delayed AI adoption and call for a robust legal framework to address the ethical implications of AI-generated content. The findings suggest that while GenAI is crucial for global competitiveness, it requires careful regulation and active involvement from professional organizations to protect creative diversity and labor rights.

DOI: 10.4018/979-8-3693-8704-7.ch013

INTRODUCTION

The advent of Generative AI (GenAI) is reshaping the film industry, offering both revolutionary opportunities and significant challenges. As AI technologies increasingly integrate into filmmaking—from script writing and visual effects to music composition and camera optimization— they promise to enhance efficiency and creativity. AI systems, such as those used for creating visual effects and optimizing camera settings, are transforming traditional production processes, allowing for rapid and cost-effective realization of complex visual and auditory elements.

However, this technological evolution also raises profound concerns about the future of creativity and labor within the industry. There is a growing apprehension that AI's ability to replicate existing styles and trends could lead to a homogenized and repetitive cinematic landscape, potentially undermining the originality of independent films and the diversity of creative outputs. The industry's reliance on AI presents challenges related to labor displacement, intellectual property rights, and the preservation of artistic integrity.

This chapter aims to provide a viewpoint on the examination of GenAI's impact on the film industry, exploring the intersection of technology, creativity, and copyright. It discusses the potential for AI to drive innovation while addressing the critical issues of labor, creativity, and intellectual property that arise in this rapidly evolving field. However, it is crucial to recognize that the adoption of technology is not solely determined by its capabilities. The acceptance and integration of GenAI also hinges on the perspectives and readiness of sector stakeholders, including industry professionals, public institutions, and academic entities. Their willingness to engage with and adapt to these technological advancements plays a significant role in shaping the industry's trajectory. This broader perspective underscores the importance of not only assessing technological benefits but also understanding how various stakeholders perceive and respond to these changes in order to fully grasp the impact of GenAI on the film industry.

GENERATIVE AI AND CREATIVE INDUSTRIES

In its early years, the use of AI was defined as the formalization of common sense through mathematical logic and its resolution using logical reasoning (McCarthy, 1989: 161). AI refers to computer systems designed to produce human-like behaviors and make decisions through algorithms and computational techniques (Russell et al., 2022). It has numerous applications, ranging from robotics to autonomous vehicles, and from the automation of planning and scheduling tasks to translation and visual recognition/processing. With nearly a century of history in philosophical and scientific studies, AI has increasingly occupied a prominent place on society's agenda, particularly with the advent of language processing model-based chatbots and visual processing applications. Similarly, it has become a key focus for global organizations and national governments. For instance, the OECD.ai website[1] tracks over 900 national AI policies and initiatives related to policy making. From a commercial perspective, interest in AI is immense. In 2023, the market for AI technologies was estimated to be worth nearly 200 billion U.S. dollars, with projections indicating significant growth, potentially exceeding 1.8 trillion U.S. dollars by 2030 (Thormundsson, 2024).

In practice, GenAI refers to AI that can generate content rather than simply analyze or act on existing data (KPMG, 2023: 6). This type of AI can create new and original content, produce creative outputs, and provide original results. This means an artificial intelligence that can create original and innovative content in images, music, text, or other media types. ChatGPT, which has been talked about a lot recently, is a popular example of GenAI. The first version of ChatGPT4, which will be offered only to subscribers as of March 14, 2023, was created using 175 billion parameters and 500 billion words. In order to make the size of the data understandable, it should be noted that an average person speaks 860 million words in their lifetime. Thus, it should be emphasized that ChatGPT started with a compilation equivalent to a 300-year-old language when it was launched (KPMG, 2023: 6). In a similar vein, the potential of GenAI to transform creative industries is emphasized (Amankwah-Amoah et al., 2024).

The use of GenAI in creative industries has the potential to contribute to the production of visual, audio, and textual content, thereby enhancing the creative capacity of artists by supporting their creative processes. Moreover, it can facilitate the market launch of cultural products, enabling them to compete more effectively on a global scale. However, the integration of GenAI in creative industries also raises concerns, such as the potential for copyright infringement and the devaluation of labor processes (Shumakova et al., 2023). GenAI, increasingly employed as a tool and assistant in various stages of content creation, management, production, and post-production, demonstrates high efficiency in decision-making processes where problems are clearly defined and do not require external context, long-chain inferences, or complex reasoning (Anantrasirichai and Bull, 2022: 639). Thus, rather than posing a threat to the inherent creativity of humans, GenAI is more appropriately viewed as a means of developing, nurturing, and supporting creative practices.

A recent experimental study found that while the use of GenAI enhances the quality of creative outputs, it simultaneously reduces their diversity (Doshi & Hauser, 2023). In its current state, it can be argued that GenAI's capabilities in promoting diversity and representativeness must be further developed, potentially through collaboration between natural and artificial intelligence, especially considering the inclusivity of the data on which it is trained. Additionally, addressing various ethical concerns and challenges—ranging from the value of artistic labor to the role of GenAI tools in creative processes—appears crucial. Despite the assertion that GenAI tools remain in an exploratory phase, and notwithstanding the availability of some powerful tools, the application of AI in these contexts still faces significant limitations (Hughes et al., 2021: 15). A previous study highlighted the necessity of increasing awareness about AI and its applications, noting concerns among creative workers regarding potential displacement due to the capabilities of GenAI in creative processes (Caporusso, 2023). Similarly, this study examines the approaches of film industry stakeholders toward GenAI, aiming to reveal their levels of awareness and their positions on the technology.

GenAI in the Film Industry

AI is employed in a variety of capacities within the film industry and is becoming increasingly significant. Applications include scenario analysis and AI-assisted scriptwriting, the development of content recommendations across different media, and the utilization of AI in production stages, post-production, and special effects. AI-based tools are also used to create marketing campaigns tailored to specific target audiences and to analyze audience reactions during marketing and distribution processes. Additionally, AI enables voice synthesis and imitation, the creation of synthetic actors and characters, holographic performances, and the composition of music that aligns with the emotional tone of scenes. These diverse applications underscore the undeniable presence and impact of AI within the film industry.

When considering the industry's employment conditions, it is essential to assess how AI affects job opportunities and royalty payments. While GenAI models can optimize business processes and enhance efficiency, they may also replace certain specialized roles, thereby impacting employment within the sector.

Benjamin, an AI-based software developed by Ross Godwin, a researcher in AI at New York University, wrote a science fiction short film script titled Sunspring (2016), which was subsequently filmed under the direction of Oscar Sharp. The sequel to Sunspring, It's No Game (Dir. Oscar Sharp, 2017), also written by Benjamin, explores a Hollywood screenwriters' strike and narrates the story of AI taking over the jobs of screenwriters. ChatGPT, NoonShot, Midjourney, ScriptBook, and DeepStory are examples of AI tools that can independently develop scripts or collaborate with other tools and human contributors, effectively becoming "co-writers."

Amidst these developments, the rise of AI and its increasing effectiveness in screenwriting have been described as signaling the "death of the screenwriter" (Dayo, 2023). One of the most significant issues emerging from this shift is the question of who will hold the copyright for AI-generated content and how these rights will be protected (Gervais, 2019).

In 2023, strikes by writers and actors in the United States, driven by concerns over the role and impact of AI in content production, have become a significant issue. Writers have raised alarms about AI's potential to negatively affect screenwriting and digital content copyrights. Specifically, there is apprehension that AI could replicate and reuse existing scripts or characters, posing a threat to the protection of writers' creative work.

Actors, meanwhile, are worried about AI's capability to digitally reproduce their faces and voices, which could lead to the creation of synthetic actors (Kurtz, 2004). The use of digital doubles by AI technologies has raised serious concerns about actors' rights and working conditions, leading to calls for regulatory measures and obtaining explicit permission from artists.

These strikes have led to production halts in Hollywood and have had a broad impact on the industry, sparking discussions about AI's effects on media and culture and initiating efforts to safeguard workers' rights and ensure the ethical use of technology.

While AI's prominence in film and production is evident, its application is expanding beyond scriptwriting and acting to other stages of production. For example, technologies such as robot cameramen, robot editors, and robot musicians are being explored. Tools like Cinelytic are designed to streamline the pre-production phase by analyzing potential script success, assisting producers with decisions related to casting, budgeting, and scheduling, and providing strategies for film distribution and revenue potential through audience analysis (Chow, 2020).

However, a primary concern is the risk of creating a stereotypical and monotonous cinematic landscape, where films may be repetitive within the same genre, influenced by personal viewing and tracking engines on audience preferences. This could pose challenges for independent films with lower commercial success and viewership rates in securing a market share. Research indicates that while AI can replicate existing styles, it also has the potential to produce creative and original works, marking a significant intersection of AI and art (Elgammal et al., 2017).

Film music, integral to the auditory dimension of film narratives, poses challenges for filmmakers in terms of cost and copyright issues, yet it can significantly impact a film's success. To address these challenges, various AI software, such as AIVA, are contributing to the film industry.

Visual effects (VFX) are crucial for narratives that involve fantastical elements, such as space adventures or superhuman characters, allowing directors to translate their imagination into reality. In cases where visual narratives cannot be established through traditional shooting methods, VFX are essential for creating surreal elements. The integration of AI systems with VFX aims to replicate the work of VFX experts, utilizing machine learning and complex algorithms to enhance the appearance of computer-generated characters and the filmic universe. Importantly, AI systems can deliver results much faster than human experts, which is advantageous given budget and production constraints.

Major manufacturers in the camera and photography sector have developed AI-based technologies for image processing and motion detection. For instance, applications such as Aurga optimize camera settings based on the shot, while AI tools like Arsenal collect and analyze data from various components—such as sensors, accelerometers, gyroscopes, and lenses—to determine optimal settings like aperture, shutter speed, and ISO. Advances in camera technology now include features like pinpoint focus sensitivity and AI-enhanced autonomous drone cameras. Robotic-armed cameras, capable of capturing intricate scenes and effects beyond human capability, further illustrate the impact of AI. These advancements highlight the necessity for all film industry professionals—including screenwriters, actors, voice actors, production crew, cameramen, editors, and musicians—to understand and adapt to the integration of AI.

According to Marx, "technology discloses man's mode of dealing with nature, the process of production by which he sustains his life, and thereby also the social relations that form and the mental conceptions that flow from them" (Marx, 2010: 358). Similarly, technological determinist communication theorist Marshall McLuhan emphasized the significance of the medium shaped by contemporary technology, asserting that "the medium is the message" (McLuhan, 1964: 7). In this context, the film industry's engagement with AI technologies should not be viewed merely from an instrumental perspective. Technological advancements impact not only the tools and methods of film production but also the storytelling and narrative structures, the representations offered, and the ideological functions of cinema. Therefore, it is crucial to examine these developments within the framework of ethics, labor, and intellectual property and to formulate appropriate policies and programs to address these changes. In the context of the global film industry, adhering to international regulations and harmonizing copyright laws are essential for the Turkish film industry to establish itself as a global player and to remain competitive on the international stage.

Approaches of Turkish Film Industry Stakeholders on GenAI and Copyright Relationship

Technological advancements, specifically the application of Generative AI (GenAI), hold significant potential to enhance creativity, productivity, and provide novel opportunities. However, these advancements also introduce various challenges and concerns. It is crucial to address these issues proactively rather than dismiss them, and to seek effective solutions. The willingness and capability of professionals and institutions within the film industry to adapt, as well as their openness to these changes, are fundamental to the sector's evolution. This adaptability is essential for achieving transformation and sustainability in the film industry. Accordingly, this study investigated participants' perspectives on the use of GenAI and their attitudes towards copyright developments through two consecutive focus group interviews involving a total of 22 participants.

Table 1. Participants

#	Gender	Age	Organisation
1	Woman	35+	Ministry of Culture and Tourism General Directorate of Copyright
2	Male	35+	Ministry of Culture and Tourism General Directorate of Cinema
3	Male	35+	Communication Sciences Academician
4	Male	35+	Copyright law office owner / UNESCO Turkish National Commission Diversity of Cultural Expressions Specialization Committee
5	Male	35+	Actors Union / Actor
6	Male	35+	Cinema Actors Professional Association (BIROY)
7	Woman	35+	Ministry of Culture and Tourism General Directorate of Cinema, Support Department
8	Male	35+	Actors union / Voice Actor
9	Male	50+	Film Producers Professional Association (FIYAB)
10	Male	35+	Professional Association of Musical Work Owners Group (MSG)
11	Male	50+	Radio and Television Broadcasters Professional Association (RATEM)
12	Male	35+	Radio, Television and Cinema, Academician
13	Male	35+	Film Design and Direction, Academician, / UNESCO Turkish National Commission Diversity of Cultural Expressions Specialization Committee
14	Woman	35+	Film Design and Direction, Academician
15	Woman	25+	Professional Association of Cinematic Work Producers (SEYAP)
16	Male	35+	Television and Cinema Film Producers Professional Association (TESIYAP)
17	Male	35+	Radio, Television and Cinema, Academician
18	Woman	35+	Radio, Television and Cinema, Academician
19	Male	35+	Animated Film Producers Association (ANFIYAP) / Turkish Creative Industries Assembly of the Union of Chambers and Commodity Exchanges of Turkey
20	Woman	35+	NGO, Patent for Every School
21	Woman	35+	Script and Dialogue Writer Cinema Work Owners Association (Senaristbir), Istanbul Kent University
22	Woman	35+	T.R. Ministry of National Education, General Directorate of Innovation and Educational Technologies, Content Development and Management Department, Copyright Office

The participants, whose details are presented in Table 1, shared a wide range of perspectives on GenAI, addressing issues from legislative regulations to ethics, employment, and its impact on film production stages.

Participants highlighted both the positive aspects of AI, such as its ability to facilitate and accelerate production, reduce workforce requirements, and address budget constraints, as well as its negative aspects, including content standardization, increased unemployment, and insufficient protection of intellectual property rights. Although ethical violations were mentioned less frequently, they were nonetheless recognized as a concern. The themes of concern, risk and caution were central to the discussions and were addressed by many participants. Notable themes related to intellectual property included labor, necessity, transparency and data ownership, as well as global awareness and international collaboration.

Concern, Risk and Caution

The participants generally conceptualize AI as a technological tool with associated risks and opportunities, yet they tend to pay relatively less attention to the specific applications and techniques of different AI technologies, such as machine learning and deep learning. Their focus is more on the user-level implications, concentrating on the potential positive and negative impacts of integrating AI tools into existing processes.

The primary concern highlighted by participants is the delay in integrating AI innovations into the Turkish film industry. There is a prevailing belief that the sector's development hinges on adopting AI, which is perceived as a critical global technological advancement. P1 metaphorically describes this delay as “missing the train,” while P8 frames it as “catching the train,” indicating a sense of urgency. P4 suggests that the industry is in a position of trying to catch up with “a process that has already begun.” P20, an intellectual property lawyer, further emphasizes that the legal framework is struggling to keep pace with the rapid changes brought about by AI.

In response to this shared concern about falling behind, P11 emphasizes that copyrights should not be compromised in a world where technology is rapidly advancing, asking, “Are we late?” Most participants agree that while it is important not to lag in technological competition, this should not come at the expense of copyright protection. Within this framework, some participants prioritize the harmonization of copyright law regulations (P1, P5, P6), while others emphasize the need to adapt contracts to account for the innovations introduced by AI (P10, P16). Notably, professionals in the profit driven side of the sector tend to adopt a more liberal approach to the sharing of copyrights.

Among the perceived risks, the fear of displacement is paramount. P2 vividly illustrates this concern by comparing AI to a slave that generates benefits but possesses no rights. Throughout the general discussion, the efficiency of AI, often framed as a necessity, is frequently juxtaposed with concerns about human authorship and the continuity of copyright income as a reward for artistic performance (P6).

Another significant risk relates to the quality of creative outputs. For instance, participants argue that human characteristics, which are a core element of copyright law, also play a crucial role in safeguarding the quality and diversity of creative works (P9). The concern is that relying heavily on GenAI could lead to an "aridification" of the intellectual world, as described by P9. This risk is closely linked to the preservation of cultural diversity (P13), underscoring the belief that human labor remains central to the film industry, especially in conveying emotions in TV series and films. This perspective aligns with the view that GenAI systems will primarily function as "assistant tools" (P2) in the sector, rather than replacing human creativity entirely.

Given these concerns and risks, there has been a strong emphasis on the need for industry stakeholders to be vigilant about potential negative outcomes, such as the diminishing importance of creative skills in the workforce and the devaluation of artistic labor.

Labor

The theme of labor was discussed in a way that aligns with the human-centered AI principles emphasized in the EU AI Act and the OECD's Global Partnership on Artificial Intelligence (GPAI). P18 highlighted the importance of maintaining a human-centered perspective and suggested limiting GenAI's role in creative outputs. She, along with P5 and P6, stressed the need to examine, translate, and adapt international guidelines that address the reshaping of labor processes in the industry due to GenAI. P5 cited the strikes of film industry workers in the United States and the resulting principles as key examples of this global labor struggle.

However, in response to this global perspective, P16 questioned the "internal appropriateness" of simply transferring these regulations to Türkiye. While acknowledging AI as a global technological development, P16 argued that attention must be given to the unique aspects of Turkish copyright law and sector-specific practices.

Regarding labor and copyright ownership, participants argued that the characteristic features of copyright holders cannot be fully datafied in AI databases (P21) and that the human-specific dimensions of artistic performance are inadequately represented (P5, P6, P8). The idea that actors might have to compete with their own AI-generated digital copies, which could become a revenue model, was raised by several participants. This highlighted the need for clear principles and limits regarding GenAI's ability to copy performances. P6 emphasized the importance of training actors on copyrights to protect their interests.

In the script writing process, P21 pointed out that the human factor remains crucial in context memory, editing, and combining, as well as in conveying emotions and cultural codes, which are not yet fully represented in AI systems. However, the rapid development of technology suggests that this could increasingly impact human labor in scriptwriting.

In the voice-over sector, a strong branch of the Turkish film industry, it was emphasized that using an artist's performance as training data for AI or copying it requires compensation (P8). This concern also extends to related rights holders such as actors, with a strong emphasis on the need to obtain the artist's consent in all such cases, in line with copyright law.

Overall, there is a belief that GenAI will significantly impact the employment of qualified individuals in the film industry in the future. P11 described this situation with the expectation that the development of AI systems will lead to radical changes in the labor market and reshape the role of skilled workers. Nevertheless, the consensus among participants was that human-oriented skills such as creative thinking and emotional intelligence will continue to hold importance.

Necessity

Similar to the lack of attention given to the technical intricacies of AI technology, there is also a failure to differentiate between the various innovative applications of GenAI within the production stages. Rather than analyzing the relationship between specific process components—such as editing, scriptwriting, and color grading—and GenAI at a technical level, the discussion tends to remain broad and generalized. For most participants, there appears to be no perceived need to investigate the distinct impacts of AI on various functional roles or on different copyright categories. Instead, participants generally prefer to base their positive or negative perspectives on AI within the broader context of the film industry.

In general, independent directors and industry representatives involved in smaller-scale projects within the film industry perceive the technological advantages as a crucial enabler that sustains artistic production.

[Referring development of AI tools] ... something that will affect us in the long term for independent cinema, for example, we are currently using a tool called NeRF in our feature film. ... I think it will also affect the language within independent filmmaking. The examples are still short at the moment. For example, what is done with NeRF is like this: you take a 2D photo, let's say I'm shooting a place, I took a reflection from a mirror and it turns that reflection into a 3D place for me. Previously, there were techniques like photogrammetry, this is actually

a type of photogrammetry, with AI you take a photo much faster and then you have to take thousands of photos of an object, maybe depending on the size of the object, and of course you can get a clear equivalent, a detailed study of it (P15).

In light of this example, P15 noted that AI tools offer fast, effective, and budget-friendly solutions across all stages of production - development, pre-production, production, post-production, and distribution. These advantages are particularly beneficial for independent filmmakers producing outside the mainstream.

Mainstream production companies approach the issue primarily in terms of competitive advantages. P19, the chairman of a professional NGO in the animation sector, emphasizes the role of efficiency, noting that GenAI is utilized throughout every stage of production, from concept design to scriptwriting. P6 contends that AI-based film music offers substantial benefits by reducing copyright payments.

Participants generally assert that AI tools enhance efficiency in film production and distribution processes, making their use almost indispensable. Despite this perceived necessity, there remain concerns regarding the technical adequacy and impartiality of GenAI, particularly in editorial processes.

In this context, P19 highlighted that their company policy mandates that final touches be performed by humans to ensure alignment with social values and pedagogical requirements. P19 cited examples of visual or textual content generated by AI that failed to align with cultural codes, raising doubts about the cultural representation capabilities of GenAI tools. Such examples underscore the potential for AI to err in cultural nuances, reinforcing the need for human intervention during the final stages of production. Film producer P9 echoed this approach, expressing concerns about cultural diversity and representation.

Participants who are script writers or related rights holders tend to be more cautious regarding the technological conveniences introduced by GenAI into the industry. The argument that human creativity and artistic originality cannot be fully replicated by computer systems is frequently invoked. For instance, screenwriter P21 pointed out that GenAI has limitations in comprehending and coherently presenting complex narrative structures, particularly in long-term processes. Similarly, actors P5 and P6 emphasized the importance of human characteristics in creative outputs, while dubbing artist P8 highlighted the emotional and artistic contributions essential to voice-over performances.

In this context, it can be stated that it is generally accepted that GenAI systems have become a necessity in terms of competitive advantage in the film industry, that those who undertake budget responsibility of the productions have a relatively more positive attitude, while the rights holders who show artistic and creative performance approach these tools more cautiously.

Transparency and Data Ownership

Transparency and data ownership in AI training are pivotal issues, particularly in the context of evolving legal frameworks and the involvement of professional organizations within the film industry. It is essential to address copyright concerns prior to integrating innovative technologies like AI into the creative sector, as neglecting these issues could potentially harm the industry and inhibit creative work. The necessity of establishing specific principles for the use of copyrighted works and performances in training data has been frequently highlighted. In this regard, P10 emphasized the importance of coordinating with international NGOs and associations, while P4 underscored the significance of the European Union's AI Act and the associated regulatory roadmap. This includes addressing challenges related to unauthorized use, copyright, and high-risk AI systems.

Under the EU AI Act, Generative AI (GenAI) is classified as low risk, reflecting a general technical assessment of its impact. This classification indicates that, while GenAI does present certain risks, it is not deemed to pose a high level of threat relative to other AI technologies. Participants who examine the implications of GenAI from a broader perspective focus on its integration into the film industry, its technical capabilities, and the overarching ethical and legal concerns. Some participants have stressed the need for adaptation and the development of policies to manage its integration into various facets of the film industry, rather than focusing solely on the specific technical details of GenAI itself.

This broader perspective supports the notion that, although GenAI may not be classified as high risk, its implications for labor, creativity, and copyright require thorough consideration and appropriate regulation. Many participants have highlighted that the full understanding of AI systems' training and operation remains insufficient. Consequently, it is expected that governments and international organizations will establish principles to ensure transparency. A key issue is the technical expertise required to fully comprehend the technology, with nearly all stakeholders from the film industry and relevant public institutions feeling technically inadequate. There appears to be a consensus among participants on the necessity of expert training and technical support to navigate these legal complexities.

Collectively, these perspectives underscore the need for transparency, clear ownership rights, and the proactive involvement of professional organizations in shaping the future of AI within the creative industries.

Global Awareness and International Collaboration

Participant 14 emphasizes the critical importance of adhering to international copyright regulations. Representatives from public institutions (P1 and P2) noted that their organizations closely monitor global developments in AI and the related discourse on its impact on copyright law. Similarly, representatives from professional organizations (P10, P16, and P11) frequently highlighted the benefits of engaging with the work of international bodies within their respective fields. These viewpoints suggest a relatively passive stance toward the global implications of AI, characterized by a 'wait and see' approach.

Conversely, those more attuned to the issues of copyright and labor displacement related to GenAI have adopted a more proactive approach. For instance, P5, an actor and academic who actively advocates for the related rights of actors, refers to the initiatives of organizations such as the International Federation of Actors and various unions concerning GenAI. These organizations have made appeals to lawmakers and developed best practice guidelines, leading P5 to argue that the current challenges can be addressed through global collaborations.

In 2024, the writers, music, rightholders, journalists, actors, and film directors unions in Europe published a joint declaration on this new EU law [EU AI Act], ... There, they generally express the approaches of creators and performers in Europe to this law. ... As Türkiye, we are one of the 7 countries on the board of directors of the International Actors Federation. Therefore, we participate in everything the federation is about. We are in this declaration (P5).

Furthermore, representatives from the sector (P13 and P14) emphasized the necessity of state support to foster international collaborations and highlighted the importance of global solidarity among rights holders.

These approaches demonstrate that all stakeholders related to the filmmaking, whether from public institutions or the industry, recognize the global impact of GenAI on the sector. However, it can be observed that participants predominantly adopt a reactive stance, choosing to monitor developments and adjust their positions accordingly.

CONCLUDING

This study examines the impact of GenAI technologies on the Turkish film industry, based on the perspectives of various stakeholders. The viewpoints expressed by participants provide a comprehensive framework for the use of AI in the film industry. The study emphasizes the need for clarification of regulatory frameworks, protection of copyright, enhanced roles for professional organizations, and the importance of education. Additionally, it highlights the necessity of addressing the ethical and sociological dimensions of AI.

The issue of copyright emerges as a critical point when addressing the technological, political, economic, and ethical aspects of AI-generated content. With the use of GenAI models, concerns regarding the originality of works, ownership of copyright, and usage permissions have become more complex. Therefore, it is essential to establish a transparent and comprehensive legal framework to protect and fairly share the copyright of AI-generated content. Prompt and effective action is crucial for the future of the industry. Various recommendations can be developed to more effectively leverage GenAI, minimize its potential negative impacts, and ensure ethical standards.

Firstly, there is a need for clear regulations regarding the licensing of data sets and protection of copyrights. Measures should be implemented to ensure that the effects of data sets used in training GenAI models, which involve human-created works and performances, are addressed so that these elements are not rendered invisible within the system. Special consideration should be given to the potential income loss for rights holders such as screenwriters, actors, and voice artists, ensuring that content is used fairly.

Regarding copyright and creativity, multi-stakeholder efforts should be made to address the legal status and licensing of content produced by GenAI. The industry should be informed about whether outputs generated by GenAI can be considered as artworks and who holds the commercial usage rights. A clear framework should be established for the accreditation and ownership of content produced by artificial intelligence, including scripts, character designs, and music. Rules should be clarified regarding the ownership of AI-generated content, whether the person issuing prompts can be recognized as the owner, and the rights of those who developed the AI program and original creators whose works were referenced.

Detailed regulations are needed regarding the use of digital copies and synthetic performances of actors. Information should be provided to actors about the creation of digital copies, and these stages should be secured through comprehensive contracts. Standard fees should be paid for the use of digital copies. Stringent regulations should also be established for biometric data protection. In cases where the voice or image data of real individuals are used, appropriate copyright fees should be paid, and licensing of these data should be ensured.

The establishment of ethical standards is also of significant importance. Ethical rules should be set to prevent AI from manipulating individuals or harming personal rights. For transparency and accountability, information about how GenAI systems operate should be provided, and mechanisms for accountability in case of copyright violations should be developed. It should be mandatory to clearly indicate in the credits which parts of the content were generated by AI. Additionally, the cultural appropriateness and societal needs addressed by GenAI data sets should be carefully monitored.

Regarding education and skill development, awareness programs should be organized to understand the impact of AI on the film industry. Training programs to understand and use GenAI tools should be developed, and multidisciplinary approaches should be encouraged. Information exchange among public bodies, industry professionals, and academics should be promoted, and multi-dimensional inputs should be provided for policy development processes. In terms of industry collaboration and stakeholder engagement, the role of NGOs and professional organizations is crucial. These entities should promote the signing of correct and fair contracts and play an active role in the formation of regulations. Additionally, a national AI strategy should be established and implemented, ensuring its inclusivity by involving relevant ministries, NGOs, and professional organizations. Engaging all stakeholders in the film industry in discussions about copyright and contract law related to GenAI usage will facilitate the development of more inclusive and acceptable policies.

To enhance technological infrastructure and encourage innovation, financial support for R&D projects should be provided, and digital rights management systems should be developed. Policies should be created to encourage the use of GenAI in a way that supports cultural diversity, and support should be given to local content producers to strengthen their position in global competition. Incentive programs for filmmakers developing creative projects using GenAI should be established, and venture capital and investment funds should be encouraged. These recommendations aim to ensure that GenAI technologies are used responsibly and ethically in the film industry, positively impacting the sector's development.

REFERENCES

Anantrasirichai, N., & Bull, D. (2022). Artificial intelligence in the creative industries: A review. *Artificial Intelligence Review*, 55(1), 589–656. DOI: 10.1007/s10462-021-10039-7

Caporusso, N. (2023). Generative Artificial Intelligence and the Emergence of Creative Displacement Anxiety [Review]. *Research Directs in Psychology and Behavior*, 3(1). Advance online publication. DOI: 10.53520/rdpb2023.10795

Chow, P. S. (2020). Ghost in the (Hollywood) machine: Emergent applications of artificial intelligence in the film industry. NECSUS_European Journal of Media Studies, 9(1), 193-214.

Dayo, F., Memon, A. A., & Dharejo, N. (2023). Scriptwriting in the Age of AI: Revolutionizing Storytelling with Artificial Intelligence. *Journal of Media & Communication*, 4(1), 24–38.

Doshi, A. R., & Hauser, O. (2023). Generative Artificial Intelligence Enhances Creativity. SSRN *Electronic Journal*. https://doi.org/DOI: 10.2139/ssrn.4535536

Elgammal, A., Liu, B., Elhoseiny, M., & Mazzone, M. (2017). CAN: Creative Adversarial Networks, Generating "Art" by Learning About Styles and Deviating from Style Norms. arXiv preprint arXiv:1706.07068.

Gervais, D. J. (2019). The Machine as Author. *Iowa Law Review*, 105(1), 205–249.

KPMG. (2023). *Generative AI models—The risks and potential rewards in business*. KPMG International.

Kurtz, L. (2004). Digital actors and copyright-from the polar express to simone. *Santa Clara Computer and High-Technology Law Journal*, 21, 783.

Marx, K. (2010). *Kapital 1. Cilt. (Selik M, Satlıgan N, Çev.)*. Yordam Kitap.

McCarthy, J. (1989). Artificial Intelligence, Logic and Formalizing Common Sense. In Thomason, R. H. (Ed.), *Philosophical Logic and Artificial Intelligence* (pp. 161–190). Springer Netherlands. DOI: 10.1007/978-94-009-2448-2_6

McLuhan, M. (1964). *The medium is the message. Understanding Media: The Extensions of Man içinde*. McGraw Hill.

Russell, S. J., Norvig, P., Chang, M., Devlin, J., Dragan, A., Forsyth, D., Goodfellow, I., Malik, J., Mansinghka, V., Pearl, J., & Wooldridge, M. J. (2022). *Artificial intelligence: A modern approach* (Fourth edition, global edition). Pearson.

Thormundsson, B. (2024, January 19). *Artificial intelligence (AI) worldwide - statistics & facts.* Statista. Retrieved July 28, 2024, from https://www.statista.com/topics/3104/artificial-intelligence-ai-worldwide/#topicOverview

ENDNOTE

1 This website, established as a policy observatory in 2020, has recently inspired the establishment of an integrated partnership called 'The Global Partnership on Artificial Intelligence (GPAI)' with the goal of leading the implementation of human-centric, safe, secure, and trustworthy artificial intelligence (AI). For more information, see: Global Partnership on Artificial Intelligence. Retrieved July 28, 2024, from https://www.oecd.org/en/about/programmes/global-partnership-on-artificial-intelligence.html

Chapter 14
Piercing the "Digital Veil" in the Intellectual and Artistic Works Created Through AI

Utku Topcan
Izmir University of Economics, Turkey

ABSTRACT

The rapid advancement of artificial intelligence (AI) underscores the need for legal and ethical frameworks governing AI-generated content to ensure accountability and protect the rights of creators and stakeholders. The potential recognition of AI as a separate legal entity raises significant concerns regarding misuse by individuals associated with such entities, a risk that remains even in the absence of formal legal recognition. The lack of adequate legal regulation may enable entities employing AI technologies to evade responsibility, thereby exacerbating issues such as bias and misinformation in AI outputs. Considering the substantial anticipated contributions of AI to the global economy, it is essential to engage in rigorous discourse regarding authorship and develop mechanisms aimed at mitigating potential misuse. These initiatives are crucial for promoting responsible innovation and enhancing public trust within creative industries.

INTRODUCTION

> *"The rise of the machines is here, but they do not come as conquerors, they come as creators." (Guadamuz, 2017)*

DOI: 10.4018/979-8-3693-8704-7.ch014

The rapid advancement of artificial intelligence (AI) has transformed computer programs into autonomous decision-makers in creative processes, prompting critical inquiries regarding the copyright protection of AI-generated works, which often lack human authorship. This uncertainty risks classifying such creations as copyright-free, potentially undermining investments in AI-generated content.

AI's applications, spanning fields from medical diagnostics to literature, underscore its pervasive integration across diverse sectors. However, traditional copyright frameworks inadequately address the complexities associated with AI-generated works, resulting in confusion regarding authorship, ownership, and liability. Such ambiguity may deter investment, as developers remain uncertain about the eligibility of their creations for legal protection.

Beyond the discussion of copyright eligibility for AI-generated works, it is essential to consider the potential for copyright infringement facilitated by AI. Although the recognition of AI as a separate legal entity, or "digital personality," appears improbable in the near future, should this occur, there exists a risk of misuse by the individuals behind such entities, similar to issues faced by any legal entity. This risk persists even without the formal recognition of AI as a legal entity, with emerging legal cases in various jurisdictions highlighting the complexities involved.

To ensure accountability and protect the rights of creators and stakeholders, it is vital to establish clear legal and ethical frameworks governing AI-generated content. In the absence of such guidelines, entities utilizing AI may evade responsibility, exacerbating issues like bias and misinformation in AI outputs. Research suggests that AI could contribute as much as USD 15.7 trillion to the global economy by 2030, underscoring its transformative potential. Thus, further discourse on authorship concerning AI-generated content and mechanisms to mitigate potential misuse is crucial for fostering responsible innovation and enhancing public trust in creative industries.

This study will introduce the traditional definitions of "work" and "author" in copyright law across various jurisdictions in the first chapter, framed within *de lege lata*. The second chapter will then examine, in the context of *de lege ferenda*, the concept of authorship related to works generated by AI, the discourse on recognizing AI as a distinct digital entity, and the significance of the "piercing the digital veil" measure as a response to potential abuses of AI.

CHAPTER 1: THE CONCEPTS OF "WORK" AND "AUTHORSHIP": *DE LEGE LATA* CONSIDERATIONS

Introduction to Basic Copyright Concepts: The Work and the Author

Copyright protects only the expression of ideas, not the ideas themselves, which are referred to as "intellectual products" (Hirsch, 1948, p.1). These products can be governed by various laws, including those related to intellectual and artistic works, patents, utility models, or industrial designs, while the physical medium on which they are expressed is governed by property law (Tekinalp, 2012, p.6). Copyright safeguards creative works through their selection, arrangement, and any mode of expression (WIPO - Understanding Copyright and Related Rights, 2016).

Copyright encompasses two main types of rights: economic rights, which allow creators to receive compensation for the use of their works, and moral rights, which protect the personal and emotional connection between the creator and their work. To qualify for copyright protection, a work must meet at least two conditions: it must be classified as a "work" under relevant legal frameworks and must be original or reflect the author's identity. Copyright arises automatically upon creation, without the need for registration.

Defining "work" and "author" in various jurisdictions is essential for ensuring legal clarity, determining ownership and liability, and providing economic incentives. This is particularly important in the context of AI-generated works, as it influences broader cultural discussions about creativity.

Turkish Copyright Law

Law No. 5846 on Intellectual and Artistic Works (FSEK) defines a "work" as any intellectual or artistic product that reflects its creator's characteristics and fits into categories such as science-literature, music, fine arts, or cinema. While the law provides a closed enumeration, it also offers examples for each category, allowing for flexibility in interpretation. Although AI software itself, not the work created through/by the AI, is not explicitly mentioned, it falls into the "science-literature" category. The same way EU Directive 2009/24/EC specifically states that (art. 1(1)) computer programs are protected as literary works under the Berne Convention. It emphasizes that the directive protects only the expression of the underlying ideas of computer programs, not the ideas themselves. Consequently, a computer program that constitutes the intellectual creation of its author is entitled to protection without any additional conditions (Directive 2009/24/EC, 2009).

In Turkish law, an author is defined as the individual who creates the work. The term "real" was removed from the definition by a 2004 amendment, which raised questions about the recognition of legal entities as authors. The Court of Appeals, however, clarified that legal persons cannot be recognized as authors, though they may still have rights to exploit the financial benefits of a work under certain conditions (Yargıtay 11. HD. T. 25.02.2008, E. 2007/227, K. 2008/2175).

The purpose, quality, quantity, and nature of an idea or the characteristics of the person who created a work are not significant in determining whether it is considered a work under the Law on Intellectual and Artistic Works (FSEK) (Suluk & Karasu & Nal, 2019, p. 49-40; Öztan, 2008, p. 99 *et seq.).*

Fundamental International Regulations on Copyright

The principle of territoriality governs copyright law with each nation having its own laws while certain international treaties establish minimum standards.

Three key international treaties address copyright issues. The Berne Convention for the Protection of Literary and Artistic Works, established in 1886, is an international treaty that sets minimum standards for copyright protection among its member countries. It mandates that works created in one member country must be recognized and protected in all other member countries, ensuring that authors have exclusive rights to their creations regardless of where they are used or distributed. While the convention does not provide a clear definition of "author," academic interpretations suggest a consensus that only natural persons can own the works they create.

The WIPO Copyright Treaty, adopted in 1996, is another international agreement in the field that enhances copyright protection in the digital environment. It establishes rights for authors in the digital realm, including the rights of reproduction and distribution, and aims to address challenges posed by new technologies and the internet, ensuring that creators can benefit from their works in a rapidly evolving landscape.

Finally, The Agreement on Trade-Related Aspects of Intellectual Property Rights (TRIPS), established in 1994 as part of the World Trade Organization (WTO) framework, sets comprehensive international standards for the protection and enforcement of intellectual property rights, including copyrights, trademarks, and patents. It aims to harmonize IP laws among member countries, ensuring a minimum level of protection and facilitating international trade by addressing issues such as enforcement, dispute resolution, and the rights of creators and inventors.

Both the WIPO Copyright Treaty and the TRIPs Agreement do not define "author" but stipulate adherence to the Berne Convention's provisions. (art. 1; art. 1 and 2 respectively)

Copyright Frameworks in the EU

Under current EU law, there are several directives related to intellectual property rights, but most do not explicitly address authorship, except for cinematographic and audiovisual works, computer programs, and databases (Yılmaztekin, 2020, p. 1526).

Therefore, one must look at the EU case law for an answer. The Infopaq case (C-5/08) provided significant clarifications on originality and authorship in copyright law. The Court of Justice of the European Union (CJEU) emphasized that for a work to qualify for copyright protection, it must demonstrate originality, which reflects the author's personal touch and intellectual effort, rather than requiring novelty. The CJEU reaffirmed that the author is the individual who creates the work, applying this principle to both literary and artistic works. The ruling established that even small excerpts can be protected under copyright if they meet the originality threshold, highlighting that authorship includes any part of a work that shows the author's intellectual contribution.

The threshold for originality was further elaborated in subsequent cases (BSA, FAPL, Painer, and Football Dataco). For a work to be considered original, it must: i) be the author's own intellectual creation, ii) reflect the author's personality through creative choices, iii) allow for a range of expression without being strictly dictated by purpose or rules (The Infopaq case (C-5/08), 2009, paras. 34-48).

EU AI Act

The EU AI Act, recently established as the world's first AI regulation, aims to position EU as a leader in trustworthy AI within the broader EU Digital Strategy. Comprising 113 articles, the Act was proposed by the European Commission in April 2021, agreed upon by EU members in May, and published in the Official Journal of the EU on July 12, 2024, with enforcement beginning on August 1, 2024. Some provisions will take effect gradually over two years.

Out of the 180 paragraphs in the Recital section of the Act, several key objectives pertinent to to the current study include:

- Promoting the adoption of human-centric and trustworthy artificial intelligence (AI). (para 1)
- Protecting against the harmful effects of AI systems while supporting innovation. (para 1)

- Preventing Member States from imposing restrictions on the development, marketing, and use of AI systems unless explicitly authorized by the Regulation. (para 1)
- Boosting innovation and employment to position the Union as a leader in trustworthy AI adoption. (para 1)

While it does not address authorship of AI-generated works, the Act classifies AI systems into four risk categories with varying requirements. The EU also offers a very useful checklist for anybody involved in AI sector to see the category under which their AI falls (EU AI Act Checklist, 2024).

1. **Unacceptable Risk AI Systems**: Certain applications that manipulate human behavior harmfully are banned.
2. **High-Risk AI Systems**: These systems, which could impact health, safety, or fundamental rights, are subject to strict requirements such as risk assessments and data governance.
3. **Limited Risk AI Systems**: These require minimal transparency obligations, such as notifying users when interacting with them.
4. **Minimal Risk AI Systems**: Largely unregulated, this category includes low-risk applications, like simple chatbots, which can operate with minimal oversight.

The objectives of the EU AI Act strike a balance between protecting copyright and fostering innovation in the AI sector. By requiring authorization for the use of copyright-protected content, the Act ensures that creators maintain control over their intellectual property, promoting respect for rights holders. This approach helps create a fair competitive environment among AI providers, preventing larger companies from exploiting lower copyright standards. However, the process of obtaining permissions may become cumbersome, potentially stifling innovation, particularly for smaller developers who may lack resources to navigate complex compliance requirements.

Transparency is a cornerstone of the Act, as it mandates providers to disclose detailed summaries of their training data, thereby enhancing accountability and user trust. While this transparency is beneficial, it raises concerns about protecting sensitive business information and may lead to competitive disadvantages for some providers. Additionally, the Act's compliance mechanisms, while focused on ensuring adherence to existing copyright law, may face challenges in effectively monitoring all AI activities without imposing excessive burdens on developers. Overall, the objectives of the Act are well-intentioned but will require careful implementation to balance protection, transparency, and innovation.

English Law

In English law, the primary legislation governing intellectual property rights is the Copyright, Designs and Patents Act 1988 (CDPA). For an intellectual product to qualify for protection under this Act, it must satisfy the following specific criteria: it must fit into one of the categories of works defined by the law (sections 3-6A), be recorded in a tangible medium (meaning it should be fixed in a form that can be perceived, reproduced, or communicated), and possess originality (as outlined in section 1(2)). The author of a work is defined as the individual who creates it, aligning with a global standard in copyright law.

A noteworthy provision in section 9(3) addresses works generated by computers, stating that the author of such works is the person who undertakes the necessary arrangements for their creation. This is further elaborated in section 178, which describes computer-generated works as those produced by a computer without any human author.

The case *Nova Productions Ltd v Mazooma Games Ltd* (2007) is pivotal in examining the concept of originality concerning computer-generated works. Here, Nova Productions claimed copyright over graphical images and animations used in their arcade games, alleging that Mazooma Games and others had unlawfully copied these elements for their products. The court emphasized the distinction between the original creators (Nova Productions) and the users interacting with the game. It reaffirmed that copyright ownership belongs to the creators of the artistic components, supporting the principle that user interaction does not alter ownership. The ruling clarified that the programmer responsible for designing the game was the one who made the necessary arrangements for the creation of the work, while players who merely engaged with the game did not contribute any artistic labor or creativity. This case underscores how authorship is determined within the framework of copyright law, particularly in digital contexts such as gaming.

US Law

In U.S. law, for an intellectual product to qualify as a work, it must be original and fixed in a tangible medium. The author is defined as the person who originates and creates the work. Similar to Turkish law, U.S. Copyright Law does not explicitly assign authorship to individuals, but the U.S. Copyright Office has clarified that copyright ownership cannot be held by non-humans.

On August 18, 2023, the United States District Court for the District of Columbia upheld the Copyright Office's decision to deny copyright registration for a work created without human involvement in the case of *Stephen Thaler v. Shira Perlmutter, Register of Copyrights and Director of the United States Copyright*

Office, et al. In this case, Thaler claimed to have developed AI programs capable of generating original visual art. He attempted to register this AI-generated work, identifying the author as the "creativity machine." However, the Copyright Office rejected the application, stating that the work lacked the necessary human authorship to qualify for copyright protection, reinforcing the principle that U.S. copyright law only applies to works created by human beings.

"The Copyright Registration Guidance: Works Containing Material Generated by Artificial Intelligence" (16.03.2023) emphasizes that human authorship is essential for a work to be copyrightable and eligible for registration. While works created with AI assistance can be copyrightable, they must involve human creative control over the expression. For instance, if AI generates material solely based on a human prompt and independently determines the expressive elements, that output lacks human authorship and is not copyrightable. Conversely, if a human selects, arranges, or modifies AI-generated content in a sufficiently creative manner, those human contributions may qualify for copyright protection. The Guidance notes that copyrightability and registrability are determined on a case-by-case basis, depending on how the AI tool operates and how it was utilized in creating the final work.

Similarly, the Third Edition (2021) of the Compendium of U.S. Copyright Office Practices states that the U.S. Copyright Office will only register original works created by human beings, emphasizing that copyright law is intended to protect human intellectual efforts. Works that lack human authorship will not be registered, a principle backed by historical cases such as *Burrow-Giles Lithographic Co. v. Sarony*, where the Supreme Court affirmed that the Constitution's Copyright Clause applies to photographs as long as they represent the original intellectual conceptions of a human author. The Court defined an "author" as a human being who originates or creates a work, repeatedly referring to authorship in human terms.

Further clarification in paragraph 313.2 of the Compendium reinforces that works must be created by humans to qualify for copyright protection. The Copyright Office will not register works generated by nature, animals, plants, or divine entities, although human-inspired works can be registered if noted appropriately. Additionally, works produced by machines without human creative input will not be registered. The key distinction lies in whether the work is fundamentally authored by a human, with technology serving merely as a tool, or if it is entirely conceived and executed by a machine.

CHAPTER 2: CHALLENGES IN DEFINING AUTHORSHIP FOR AI-GENERATED WORKS AND "PIERCING THE DIGITAL VEIL": *DE LEGE FERANDA* CONSIDERATIONS

In General

As demonstrated in the preceding discussions, the definition of authorship for AI-generated works remains unregulated at both national and international levels. Although its subject matter does not pertain to copyrights, even the most recently enacted EU AI Act provides no single indication of authorship for AI-generated works. While English law, specifically section 9(3) of the Copyright, Designs and Patents Act (CDPA), provides some guidance on computer-generated works, it was primarily crafted to address automatically created outputs, such as photographs taken by satellites, dating back to 1980s. This historical context raises questions about its applicability to contemporary AI-generated content (De Cock Buning, 2016, p. 315).

Before delving into the issue of authorship concerning AI-generated content, it is essential to first consider the "subjects" involved in the entire creation process of such works. This further requires a distinction between the "output" produced by or through AI and the "input," which refers to the extensive datasets that enable the AI to generate this output. Grasping this distinction is crucial for a thorough analysis of authorship in the context of AI-generated works since the potential application of piercing the digital veil poses challenges not only in identifying the creators of the output but also in determining the creators and/or contributors of the input.

Copyright Infringement on the Input

Copyright infringement concerning the input utilized in the creation of AI-generated works is generally clear-cut, as there is usually an identifiable "human" responsible for uploading or inputting the material. This human agency serves as a point of accountability, allowing copyright holders to pursue legal recourse against individuals who improperly use their protected works. However, the situation becomes more complex when one AI system feeds input into another (Yalçın, 2022, p.23-24). In such cases, the chain of responsibility may become obscured, complicating the attribution of liability for copyright infringement. This raises important questions about the legal status of AI systems as intermediaries and the extent to which they can be held accountable for their actions.

While the primary focus of this discussion is on authorship on the output, it inherently raises the critical issue of accountability for copyright infringement regarding the input used. If the process involves multiple AI systems, pinpointing who is liable can become increasingly challenging. Is the original uploader responsible, or do the developers of the AI systems share in the liability? Additionally, the implications of AI systems autonomously processing and combining various inputs may necessitate new legal frameworks to address the unique challenges posed by these technologies. As the landscape of AI continues to evolve, it will be essential to establish clear guidelines to navigate the intersection of copyright law and artificial intelligence, ensuring that accountability is appropriately assigned in cases of infringement.

Copyright Infringement on the Output

When it comes to copyright infringement in the output produced by AI, the legal landscape is more complex and broadly three scenarios emerge (Yalçın, 2022, p.23-24):

1. **First Scenario**: Humans can use an AI program as a "**tool**", similar to traditional instruments like pencils, paper, or musical instruments.
2. **Second Scenario**: This scenario involves an AI that independently generates a work, while a human subsequently "**selects**" which of these creations hold value. The key question is whether the human's role in the selection process qualifies them as the author of the resulting work.
3. **Third Scenario**: In this scenario, if a human's involvement is limited to merely "**clicking**," the authorship is not recognized in any jurisdiction. The future changes in law may grant it to the AI itself or to the creators and contributors involved in developing the AI, depending on their respective levels of contribution to the final output.

In scenarios 1 and 2, the key question is who the law should recognize as the person "making the arrangements for the work" to be generated (Guadamuz, 2017), as required for computer-generated works under the English CDPA and potentially applicable for similar disputes in other jurisdictions. There are various perspectives on both scenarios, but it is possible to identify potential authorship groups for AI-generated works, which may include the programmer or developer, the end user, the data owner, and even the investor in the AI project (Yalçın, 2022, p.23-24). In any scenario, the developer has protections for the AI itself but doesn't have a claim to the copyright of the artwork generated by the AI, unless they actively participate in creating the work alongside the AI (Caldwell, 2023). The assessment of authorship regarding the "output" generated by AI should be conducted on a case-by-case basis, with copyrightability and registrability evaluated in relation to the specific functionalities of the AI tool and its role in producing the final work. A crucial distinction must be made between works primarily authored by a human, where technology serves merely as a tool, and those that are entirely conceived and executed by the machine. In this context, a thorough evaluation by AI experts should ensure that all parties involved in the creation process are entitled to copyright in proportion to their contributions to the output in a form of joint authorship (Bridy, 2011, p.18-19). For investors, however, the likelihood of being recognized as authors under current global copyright and AI regulations remains low. Nevertheless, to encourage investment in creative AI, it would be prudent to explore the possibility of granting investors an equitable share of copyright in future legislative and regulatory frameworks.

In scenario 3, the question arises as to why there should be a distinction between the authorship of an end user for a photo taken with a phone and that for an AI-generated creation. However, the role of the AI user here in this scenario is limited to simply pressing a button, allowing the machine to function independently. In contrast, a photographer must look through the camera's lens and actively choose the angle and perspective, which involves a more engaged creative process (Guadamuz, 2017). Whereas the opposite view suggests that the "clicking" or "randomness" in machine outputs also originates from human design and thus must be copyrightable recognizing the human contributions behind AI-generated works (Ginsburg & Budiardjo, 2019, p.402; Scannell, 2022, p.740). This scenario and the problems associated with it will be discussed separately below.

Consequently, I advocate for the case-by-case approach endorsed by certain case law to tackle foregoing discussion. As previously mentioned, in the English case of *Nova Productions v Mazooma Games Ltd* (2007), the Court of Appeal addressed authorship concerning a computer game, asserting that a player's input "is not artistic in nature and he has contributed no skill or labour of an artistic kind." However, this resolution presents an additional challenge: the necessity for expert reports will be paramount in evaluating the contributions of various parties involved, thereby increasing the demand for experienced AI specialists. These experts will be essential not only for the advancement of the AI sector but also for aiding judicial decision-making. Alternatively yet arguably, as discussions in this domain progress, it is conceivable that AI judges may eventually supplant human judges, thereby diminishing the dependency on AI experts in such cases.

Legal Entities and Their Role in Evasion of Responsibility

Legal entities provide a range of essential advantages that contribute to their appeal in both business and creative endeavors. One of the foremost benefits is the sustainability of assets, allowing entities to maintain and grow their resources over time without being directly tied to the personal fortunes of their members. This separation of personal and organizational assets creates a stable foundation for long-term operations (Trautmann, 2020, p.68; Schall, 2009, p. 284). Furthermore, legal entities possess the ability to raise investment capital more effectively than individuals, as they can issue shares or take on investors without compromising personal liability (Bertolini, 2020, p. 33 *et seq.*). This capacity to acquire rights and incur debts independently empowers entities to engage in various business activities without putting the personal assets of their members at risk. Additionally, the structured governance inherent in these entities enables professional management, ensuring that operations are conducted efficiently and strategically.

Nevertheless, the protective nature of legal personality also presents a risk of misuse. When individuals exploit this legal shield to undertake risky or unethical transactions—actions they would likely refrain from if personally liable—they may endanger the interests of third parties. Such behavior can result in financial losses or damages for those affected, creating a significant ethical dilemma. The challenge lies in balancing the benefits of legal entities with the potential for abuse, as aggrieved third parties may find it difficult to seek redress against individuals who operate behind the corporate veil (Meyer, 2007, p.33; Gloger, 2007, p.33). This concern underscores the importance of regulatory frameworks that ensure transparency and accountability within legal entities. To mitigate the risks associated with the misuse of legal personality, it may be necessary to implement stricter guidelines governing the conduct of legal entities and their members, thereby safeguarding the interests of all stakeholders involved.

Granting Legal Personality to AI: Potential Challenges Ahead

Although many jurisdictions imply that non-human copyright may not be recognized, there is no explicit prohibition against granting copyright for AI-generated works (Guadamuz, 2017).

Granting a separate legal personality to artificial intelligence entities presents several significant benefits from both functional and practical perspectives. Although advanced technologies may be viewed as mere objects, attributing them a fictitious legal personality creates a structured framework for accountability and liability akin to that of corporations. This legal status would facilitate the ability to hold AI systems accountable for their actions, allowing for litigation directly against the AI entity. Such an approach simplifies the process for claimants seeking redress and enables the distribution of economic consequences of liability among stakeholders based on their investment or involvement, thereby promoting responsible development and management of the AI system.

Additionally, the establishment of legal personality for AI would require registration and compliance with public disclosure requirements, enhancing transparency and trust among users and stakeholders. This framework would allow stakeholders to hold shares in the AI entity, aligning their economic interests and fostering investment. The operation of the AI system could generate revenue and build assets to meet various obligations, including compensatory, contractual, or statutory duties, thereby providing a safety net for those affected by the AI's actions. Ultimately, conferring legal personality on AI not only strengthens accountability and regulatory compliance but also creates a pragmatic pathway for integrating advanced technologies into existing legal frameworks, encouraging innovation and responsible deployment in the AI field.

Currently, there is no regulation addressing the legal status of creative AI. However, the European Parliament's proposal on Civil Law Rules on Robotics (2017) is a significant development, as it represents the first comprehensive international report focused on the electronic personality model. This model seeks to clarify uncertainties surrounding AI technologies and establish their legal accountability. By providing legal personality to AI, it aims to facilitate the resolution of disputes arising from their autonomous actions while supporting the advancement of AI technologies. Findings of the Report suggests, if AI is to be granted legal status, it should be governed by this electronic personality model, which must include clearly defined limits, such as the conditions under which the digital veil can be pierced. Establishing legal status for AI is essential for ensuring legal certainty and recognizing AI as a key stakeholder in the technology landscape. Just as not all human-created products are protected if they fail to meet legal requirements, AI-generated products should also receive protection only if they fulfill those criteria. Ultimately, this approach would enhance the legitimacy and accountability of AI within the broader technological framework.

In contrast to the European Parliament's above proposal on Civil Law Rules on Robotics, the European Commission's more recent report titled "Liability for AI and Other Emerging Digital Technologies (2019)" asserts that there is no need to grant legal personality to autonomous systems for liability purposes. While there have been historical proposals for such a status, the report emphasizes that this remains a contentious issue. Granting legal personality to AI could complicate liability since it typically requires the entity to have assets, and liability for harm caused by autonomous technologies can often be traced back to natural persons or existing legal categories. The report also raises ethical concerns about granting legal personality to digital technologies, suggesting that any such proposal should include the ability to hold assets. This poses legislative challenges regarding the legal capacity and actions of these entities. Additionally, the report argues that granting legal personality must be accompanied by designated funds to ensure effective claims, warning that this could lead to caps on liability, similar to corporate experiences, and could result in attempts to circumvent such limits by pursuing claims against associated persons, effectively "piercing the electronic veil."

Had the European Parliament's proposal on Civil Law Rules on Robotics (2017) been implemented, we would be contemplating a new legal entity for artificial intelligence. However, the substantial criticism from scholars regarding this proposal led to the European Commission's report on the Liability for AI and Other Emerging Digital Technologies (2019) gaining greater prominence than the Parliament's proposal in discussions about establishing a distinct legal entity for AI. Consequently, the EU AI Act (2024) ultimately lacks any significant or pioneering initiative to regulate this matter.

Misuse of the Digital Veil

The potential conferral of legal personhood and rights to an AI creature raises concerns about possible abuse, particularly when such an AI is employed to commit fraud or engage in criminal activities.

As for the general theory of the corporation's legal personality, Hudson argues that courts should scrutinize whether individuals are unjustly evading personal obligations by exploiting the corporate veil (Hudson, 2012, p.38). The concept of corporate personhood is divisible, indicating that not all attributes of legal personality need to be uniformly applied, allowing for flexibility in addressing fraud and misconduct (Cheong, 2021, p. 17). Hence, if legal personhood is granted to AI systems, it may be possible to apply this well-known remedy from company law of "corporate disregard," where the separate corporate personality established in *Salomon v Salomon* is set aside, although the Supreme Court of the United Kingdom has established that remedies like piercing the corporate veil should be considered only as a last resort (*Prest v Petrodel Resources Ltd & Others,* 2013). This phenomenon is often referred to using terms such as veil lifting, piercing, or peeping (Cheong, 2021, p. 17).

A notable example of piercing the *crypto* veil can be seen in a recent case involving a decentralized autonomous organization (DAO). Although the DAO itself was not recognized as a separate legal entity under current US law, the case underscores the implications of such an action for accountability among both human and non-human actors associated with AI. This highlights the potential future impact of piercing the digital veil if the law were to eventually confer legal personhood onto AI entities.

The recent ruling by the United States District Court in *Sarcuni v. bZx DAO* (March 27, 2023) has raised significant concerns within the decentralized finance (DeFi) community, which previously believed that decentralized autonomous organizations (DAOs) were largely immune from traditional legal liabilities (Pascoe, 2023). The court's decision denied a motion to dismiss a class action lawsuit filed by users of the DAO, allowing a negligence claim against the DAO as a general partnership, where token holders are considered general partners with unlimited liability.

The case revolves around an unprecedented argument to hold the DAO's co-founders and governance participants jointly liable for the DAO's actions. This ruling has far-reaching implications for DAOs, which have become a popular business structure in the DeFi market, relying on blockchain technology and smart contracts for governance instead of human management.

The *Sarcuni* case, stemming from a $55 million loss due to a hack of the bZx protocol, underscores the need for developers and investors to approach DAO ventures with caution regarding potential litigation. If this ruling sets a precedent for class actions in the DeFi space, participants could face significant liability without legal protections similar to those enjoyed by traditional corporate directors and shareholders. Merely registering a DAO as an existing corporate form, such as an LLC, may not sufficiently address these challenges. To ensure accountability for both human and non-human actors behind a DAO, including forms of artificial intelligence, a thorough analysis of DAOs necessary for effective oversight, akin to a "piercing of the digital veil (Schuppli & Jafari, 2021, p. 342; Pascoe, 2023).

CONCLUSION

The rapid advancement of artificial intelligence (AI) has enabled computer programs to function as autonomous decision-makers in creative processes, raising critical questions about copyright protection for AI-generated works, which often lack human authorship. This uncertainty may lead to such creations being classified as copyright-free, jeopardizing investments in AI-generated content. Traditional copyright frameworks fail to adequately address the complexities of AI-generated works, resulting in confusion over authorship, ownership, and liability, which may deter developers from seeking legal protection for their innovations.

In addition to concerns about copyright eligibility, the potential for copyright infringement facilitated by AI must also be considered. While the recognition of AI as a separate legal entity, or "digital personality," seems unlikely in the near term, should it occur, risks of misuse by individuals behind such entities could arise. This concern is compounded by emerging legal cases that highlight the complexities involved, even without formal recognition of AI as a legal entity.

To ensure accountability and protect the rights of creators and stakeholders, it is essential to establish clear legal and ethical frameworks governing AI-generated content. Without these guidelines, entities utilizing AI may evade responsibility, exacerbating issues such as bias and misinformation.

This study highlights that determining the registrability of AI-generated works is not a straightforward process; it requires a nuanced, case-by-case inquiry that considers various factors, including the operational mechanics of the AI tool and how it interprets prompts to generate material. This complexity necessitates the involvement of AI experts who possess the technical knowledge to assess the AI's functionalities and its role in the creative process. Such expertise is crucial for accurately evaluating the contributions of AI and ensuring that legal assessments are grounded in a comprehensive understanding of the technology involved.

Furthermore, recognizing AI as a distinct legal personality would represent a significant evolution in the concept of legal personhood. This shift would require the establishment of a regulatory framework that clearly defines the rights and responsibilities of AI entities. Regulations must include measures to "pierce the digital veil," which refers to the legal mechanisms that allow for accountability in cases where individuals misuse AI technologies. This approach is essential to prevent potential abuses, such as intellectual property infringement or the dissemination of harmful content, while also ensuring that creators and stakeholders maintain a degree of control over their work.

Ultimately, the implementation of these regulations is vital for fostering public trust in creative industries that increasingly rely on AI technologies. By establishing clear guidelines and accountability measures, stakeholders can be reassured that AI-generated content will be treated fairly under the law, thereby promoting responsible innovation and encouraging further investment in AI-driven creative endeavors. This regulatory framework not only protects individual creators but also contributes to a healthier ecosystem for technological advancement and creativity.

REFERENCES

Bertolini, A. (2020). Artificial Intelligence and Civil Liability. *Publications Office of the European Union*. https://www.europarl.europa.eu/RegData/etudes/STUD/2020/621926/IPOL_STU(2020)621926_EN.pdf

Bridy, A. (2011). Coding Creativity - Copyright and the Artificially Intelligent Author. *Stanford Technology Law Review : STLR : An Online High-Technology Law Journal from Stanford Law School*, 5, 1–28.

Caldwell, M. (2023). What Is an "Author"? Copyright Authorship of AI Art Through a Philosophical Lens, *61. Houston Law Review*, 411. https://houstonlawreview.org/article/92132-what-is-an-author-copyright-authorship-of-ai-art-through-a-philosophical-lens

Cheong, B. C. (2021). Granting Legal Personhood to Artificial Intelligence Systems and Traditional Veil-Piercing Concepts to Impose Liability. *SN Social Sciences*, 1(9), 231. DOI: 10.1007/s43545-021-00236-0

De Cock Buning, M. (2016). Autonomous Intelligent Systems as Creative Agents under the EU framework for Intellectual Property. *European Journal of Risk Regulation*, 7(2), 310–322. DOI: 10.1017/S1867299X00005730

Ginsburg, J.C., Budiardjo, L.A. (2019). Authors and machines, *34 Berkeley Tech. LJ* 343.

Gloger, C. (2007). *Haftungsbeschränkung versus Gläubigerschutz in der Gmbh*. Carl Heymanns Verlag.

Guadamuz, A. (2017). Artifical Intelligence and Copyright, *WIPO Magazine, 5/2017*. https://www.wipo.int/wipo_magazine/en/2017/05/article_0003.html

Hirsch, E. E. (1948). *Fikri ve Sınai Haklar*. Ankara Basımevi.

Hudson, A. (2012). *Understanding Company Law*. Routledge.

Meyer, J. (2000). *Haftungsbeschränkung im Recht der Handelsgesellschaften*. Springer. DOI: 10.1007/978-3-642-58321-6

Öztan, F. (2008). *Fikir ve Sanat Eserleri Hukuku*. Turhan.

Pascoe, L. (2023). Decentralised Autonomous Organisations and Liability in Litigation. https://www.ibanet.org/decentralised-autonomous-organisations-and-liability-in-litigation

Scannell, B. (2022). When Irish AIs are smiling: could Ireland's legislative approach be a model for resolving AI authorship for EU member states? *Journal of Intellectual Property Law & Practice, 17*(9).

Schall, A. (2009). *Kapitalgesellschaftsrechtlicher Glaubigerschutz.* Beck.

Schuppli, B., & Jafari, G. A. (2021). Piercing the Digital Veil: A Case Study for a DAO Legal Framework under Swiss Law. https://www.jipitec.eu/archive/issues/jipitec-12-4-2021/5404/schuppli_pdf.pdf

Suluk, C., Karasu, R., & Nal, T. (2019). *Fikri Mülkiyet Hukuku.* Seçkin.

Tekinalp, Ü. (2012). *Fikri Mülkiyet Hukuku.* Vedat.

Trautmann, T. N. (2020). *Die Legitimation der beschraenkten Haftung im Konzern.* Nomos. DOI: 10.5771/9783748923176

Yalçın, B. E. (2022), *From Works to Data – Artificial Intelligence And Copyright Infringements* [Master's Thesis, Ankara University Graduate School of Social Sciences Department of Intellectual Property, Technology Policies And Innovation Management]. YÖK Ulusal Tez Merkezi.

Yilmaztekin, H. K. (2020). Türk Fikri Haklar Hukuku Yapay Zeka Tarafından Meydana Getirilen Eserleri Korumak için Hazır mı? *Galatasaray Üniversitesi Hukuk Fakültesi Dergisi, C. 19, S.2*, 1513-1586.

KEY TERMS AND DEFINITIONS

AI: Artificial Intelligence.

Compendium: Third Edition (2021) of the Compendium of U.S. Copyright Office Practices.

Et al.: *Et alia* (and others).

Et seq.: *Et sequentes* (and the following).

FSEK: Turkish Code on Intellectual and Artistic Works (1951).

CDPA: English Copyright, Designs and Patents Act (1988).

Chapter 15
Can Artificial Intelligence Be Subject to Patent Protection Under Turkish Law?

Burcu G. Özcan Büyüktanır
Hacettepe University, Turkey

Barış Gözübüyük
Hacettepe University, Turkey

ABSTRACT

Ensuring effective protection for artificial intelligence is not just a matter of legal debate, but an urgent need for the continuous advancement of technology in this field. When considering artificial intelligence as traditional computer software, the primary concern is protecting it as intellectual property. This is because computer programs are covered under the category of works of science and literature in Continental European law, including Türkiye. However, the adequacy of work protection for artificial intelligence is an important question that requires immediate addressing. Assuming that copyright protection is insufficient, another question arises: How can we protect artificial intelligence through a patent? This study argues that the most effective protection for artificial intelligence can be achieved through patent protection. This study delves into a relatively unexplored area of law, aiming to provide fresh insights and potential solutions to the complex issue of protecting artificial intelligence under Turkish law.

DOI: 10.4018/979-8-3693-8704-7.ch015

INTRODUCTION

As investments in AI technologies continue to grow, the need for a new approach to protecting AI becomes increasingly urgent. The existing legal regulations for protecting computer programs were formulated before the emergence of artificial intelligence. While these regulations may suit traditional computer programs, their application to artificial intelligence is controversial. This debate hinges on the distinction between AI software and conventional computer software. If artificial intelligence is deemed equivalent to traditional computer programs, it will fall under the same protection regime. However, the existence of varying protection regimes for artificial intelligence in different laws will persist even if this argument is accepted. Several possibilities exist in this regard. The first is that the most effective protection method for artificial intelligence is treating it as a work of science and literature. The second possibility is that protecting artificial intelligence as a patent or utility model is the most effective approach. The third option is to safeguard artificial intelligence as know-how. The fourth is to protect artificial intelligence as a trade secret. The fifth option is to treat artificial intelligence as a database. The sixth and final possibility is to subject artificial intelligence to a special protection regime.

This study will focus only on copyright and patent protection, not other possibilities. In this context, it will seek an answer to the question of why patent protection should be preferred in the protection of artificial intelligence. Its primary aim is to offer guidance to policymakers. Keeping pace with the rapidly evolving landscape of artificial intelligence technologies is a formidable challenge for policymakers, as it is for all individuals. Nevertheless, legal regulations will inevitably need to adapt to the age of artificial intelligence. Therefore, policymakers need to be aware of issues related to AI. While making the necessary and up-to-date legal amendments is crucial, patent offices also have a great deal of work to do. This is because the application guidelines published by these offices guide the applicants in practice. Due to its strategic geographical location bordering Europe, Türkiye maintains close diplomatic and economic ties with the European Union, despite not being a member. Notably, Türkiye's integration into the Continental European legal system means that EU regulations and practices hold particular relevance and influence within the country.

LITERATURE REVIEW

The only article we have been able to identify regarding the protection of artificial intelligence under Turkish law was published by (Sarı, 2020) under the title "Protection of Artificial Intelligence under Turkish Intellectual Property Law". However, in the doctrine (Meydancı, 2023) addressed the issue in his doctoral dissertation titled "Protection of Artificial Intelligence and its Products in Intellectual Property Law". In this context, the studies on the subject in Turkish legal doctrine do not exceed the fingers of one hand. In fact, one of the reasons why we have chosen this subject is the scarcity of studies on this subject in Turkish law. However, there are more sources on protecting computer programs in Turkish law. We have tried to use these sources to the extent appropriate to the subject of our study. Regarding the subject, Sarı underlined that creating artificial intelligence software requires great effort and that the legal protection of this effort will encourage new investments (Sarı, 2020). Regarding how the protection should be, based on the computer program-artificial intelligence relationship, he believes that computer programs can only be considered within the scope of artificial intelligence protection to the extent that they are appropriate (Meydancı, 2023). According to the author, artificial intelligence, like computer programs, emerges after a very long process, including preparatory designs (Meydancı, 2023). However, as underlined by (Sarı, 2020), an assessment should be made according to the characteristics of the concrete case, and it should be taken into consideration whether artificial intelligence can be considered as a computer program in each case.

China is among the countries that have recently come to the forefront with its investments in artificial intelligence. In this context, (Pu, 2022) evaluates the patentability of AI algorithms in China and points out the importance of proper disclosure of the algorithm dataset and its application.

Although the literature on the protection of artificial intelligence within the scope of intellectual property is extremely limited in the Turkish legal literature, there is a relatively large literature on the protection of computer programs. We will try to utilise this literature to the extent that it is appropriate to our subject of study. In this context, (Topaloğlu, 1997), in his work titled "Rights on Computer Programs and Protection of These Rights", asserted that computer algorithms and user interfaces can be protected within the scope of patents (Topaloğlu, 1997).

RESEARCH AND METHODS

Research Method

Primary data for this research includes academic books on intellectual property in Turkish law and academic legal journals pertaining to comparative intellectual property law. Secondary data collection methods involve utilizing Law No. 5846 on Intellectual and Artistic Works, Law No. 6769 on Industrial Property, Türkiye,

European Patent Office patent guidelines, and Turkish Patent and Trademark Office patent guidelines. The collected data is then analyzed and presented systematically.

Research Approach

In this study, the authors employed a normative legal research approach to examine the direct relevance of intellectual property law to legal science, emphasising patent protection as the most efficient means of safeguarding artificial intelligence. The study did not explore alternative methods such as unfair competition, trade secrets, or special protection. The Study is not a comparative law study. However, foreign law regulations have been utilized where necessary. Additionally, the study emphasized the similarities and differences between artificial intelligence and computer programs. While acknowledging that computer programs are protected under copyright in Continental European Law, the study also addressed whether similar copyright protection could extend to artificial intelligence. Ultimately, the study argued that the most effective form of protection for AI is through patent law.

Data Collection

The study involved the collection of primary and secondary data through an online research approach. While online sources were the primary focus, printed materials were also incorporated when considered essential.

Limitations

The primary focus of the study is to address the protection of artificial intelligence itself. Consequently, the complexities surrounding the determination of ownership rights for inventions and intellectual products generated through the utilization of artificial intelligence tools fall outside the purview of this study.

THEORETICAL DISCUSSIONS

Protection of Computer Programs as Works Under Law No. 5846 on Intellectual and Artistic Works in Turkish Law

General. Some legislative provisions regarding the protection of computer programs in Turkish law need to be mentioned. In this context, article 1/B/a of the Law on Intellectual and Artistic Works No. 5846, which is the basic legislation in the field of copyright in Türkiye[2], Article 1/B/a of the same law states that work is

"Any intellectual or artistic product bearing the characteristic of its author, which is deemed a scientific and literary or musical work or work of fine arts or cinematographic work." Regarding the work nature of computer programs, Article 2/1 of the Law stipulates that *"Works that are expressed by language and writing in any form, and computer programs expressed in any form together with their preparatory designs, provided that the same leads to a computer program at the next stage."*

According to Article 1/B.g of Law No. 5846 on Intellectual and Artistic Works (FSEK); computer program is defined as follows: *"A set of computer instructions arranged in a way that will make a computer system carry out a special process or task and the preparatory work that will lead to the creation and development of such set of instructions"*. Computer programs are included in the category of scientific and literary works among the types of works listed in the law. While creating a computer program, multiple stages are passed through and these stages are also included in the protection of the work.

Preparatory Designs. Preparatory designs of computer programs may also be considered works, provided that they will result in a program at a later stage. If they bear the characteristics of their author and can become computer programs at any stage in the following process, they will be within the scope of work protection (Suluk et al., 2023).

Flowchart (Architectural Structure). A flowchart, also known as a program flow, is a preliminary diagram that assists programmers in writing program codes (Dalyan, 2009). In this outline, the data obtained by the program developer are listed in a logical order (Topaloğlu, 1997). For the protection of a computer program to have any meaning, the flowchart must also be protected. Because after the program flows are developed, they can be easily written in code and converted into a program (Dalyan, 2009; Topaloğlu, 1997).

Source code. Source code is the code written in computer language that determines the flow mechanism in accordance with the objectives of the program (Suluk et al., 2023). The source code consists of characters, just like a poem or a novel. For this reason, it is described by (Topaloğlu, 1997) as the most literary part of the program development process. Thanks to the source code, the program becomes readable.

Object code. Source code that has not been translated into a computer program is like unbuilt architectural projects, and computer programs in both source code and object code form are protected as work (Bozgeyik, 2009).

Interface. It refers to the program parts that form the reciprocal influence and connection between the hardware and software elements of the computer. (FSEK art.1/B.h) Sometimes some pictures and sounds may appear on the screen directly by the program running and sometimes by the user's command by pressing the key (Dalyan, 2009). The term user interface, therefore, covers the non-literary elements of the program, such as the program's screen views, sounds, menus, structure and organisation, layout, program output, etc. (Dalyan, 2009).

Since interfaces often become an integral part of the computer program or a functional part of the machine, the originality criterion is eliminated and copyright protection will not be available for these parts (Arıkan, 1996). Pursuant to Art. 2/end of Copyright Law, it is stipulated that the ideas and principles that form the basis of any element of a computer program, including the ideas and principles that form the basis of the interface, shall not be considered as works. Therefore, it is not the ideas and thoughts but their appearance in computer language that are important and protected (Erel, 1994; Erdil, 2021).

In Continental European law, including Türkiye, computer programs are subject to copyright protection. According to Lutz this is because computer programs are not directly applicable to industry for the purpose of solving a technical problem (Lutz, 1993).

Protection of Computer Programs as Patents Under Turkish Law

Conditions for Granting a Patent under Turkish Law. Under Turkish law, pursuant to Article 82/1 of the Industrial Property Law, inventions in all technology fields may be patented, provided they are new and applicable to the industry. The first condition for a patent application to be accepted positively is the element of novelty. The element of novelty in patent applications has become a standard worldwide (Öztürk, 2008). In this context, pursuant to article 83/1 of the Industrial Property Law, "an invention that is not included in the state of the art" is considered new. What should be understood from the state of the art is regulated in article 83/2 of the same Law. Accordingly, anything accessible to the public, which has been disclosed through written or oral publicity or disclosed through use or in any other way anywhere in the world before the filing date, is considered within the scope of the state of the art. The state of the art is taken into account both in the novelty examination and in the inventive step examination (Öztürk, 2008). Public disclosure is the basis for determining innovation (Suluk et al., 2023). In this context, matters that were made public before the date of the application cannot be considered new.

Patentable inventions fall within the scope of the protection of patent law (Topaloğlu, 1997). In order to claim a patent right, an invention needs to exist. This leads to the fundamental question: what exactly meets the criteria of being an invention? The term "invention" is notably absent from the explicit definition within the Industrial Property Law, and this is a common feature in patent laws across most countries. As a result, to assert a patent right, the existence of an invention is a prerequisite. This prompts the critical examination of what indeed constitutes an invention. The

Industrial Property Law does not offer a specific definition for "invention." This lack of defined scope for "invention" is a notable feature in the patent laws of nearly all countries, emphasizing the ongoing ambiguity surrounding the term (Aksu, 2006; Tekinalp, 2012). Invention is defined by as "*an intellectual product that provides a solution to a problem that arises as a human need with an applicable teaching that falls within the technical field*" (Tekinalp, 2012). In the present context, it is essential to note that not every invention is eligible for patent protection. Only inventions of a technical nature meet the criteria for patentability (Tekinalp, 2012). According to Article 83/4 of the Intellectual Property Law, considering the state of the art, an invention that is not obvious to the expert in the technical field to which it relates is considered to contain an inventive step. In determining whether a patent application exceeds the inventive step, it is attempted to be decided by looking at the current state-of-the-art (Suluk, et al., 2023).

The last condition for a patent application to be accepted positively is industrial applicability. In this context, pursuant to Article 83/6 of the Industrial Property Law, an invention is deemed to be industrially applicable if it can be produced or used in any branch of industry, including agriculture. Industrial applicability should be understood in a broad sense. Türkiye is a party Paris Convention for the Protection of Industrial Property. Article of the mentioned convention 1/ 3 states:

> *Industrial property shall be understood in the broadest sense and shall apply not only to industry and commerce proper, but likewise to agricultural and extractive industries and to all manufactured or natural products, for example, wines, grain, tobacco leaf, fruit, cattle, minerals, mineral waters, beer, flowers, and flour.*

If a patent application remains purely theoretical and the invention cannot be produced by following the steps outlined in the application, it should be rejected. However, it is essential to note that just because a product can be industrially produced, it does not automatically guarantee it will be profitable. (Suluk, et al., 2023).

Granting Patent to Computer Programs. Patent protection of computer programs has economic significance for relevant stakeholders (Melullis, 1998). From an economic point of view, hardware elements are losing importance while software elements are gaining importance (Melullis, 1998). Indeed, the fact that the patent right grants a monopoly right to the patentee (Öztürk, 2008) makes the patent economically valuable. In line with Article 101/1 of the Industrial Property Law, a patent is protected for twenty years from the date of application and cannot be extended. Upon expiration of this term, the patent holder's exclusive rights end, allowing public use of the invention. It is important to note that while patent protection provides a monopoly to the owner, this protection period is shorter than copyright protection. In our opinion, the shorter duration is appropriate for balancing the conflicting interests. Article 82/2/c of the Industrial Property Law stipulates that computer programs shall not be deemed as inventions. This provision is derived from Article 52 of the European Patent Convention, of which Türkiye is a signatory. According to Article 52/2 (c) of the convention, as mentioned earlier, computer programs are not considered inventions. With these provisions in mind, can we conclude that computer programs cannot be patented under Turkish law under any circumstances? It is crucial to differentiate between non-technical and technical computer programs. Computer programs may encompass technical and non-technical components. If, following a comprehensive assessment, it is determined that the program is predominantly technical in nature, it may be eligible for a patent (Aksu, 2006). According to the Patent Application Guide published by the Turkish Patent and Trademark Office, computer programs are also listed among the subjects that cannot be patented because they are not considered as inventions, and the following is stated in the guide:

> *Computer programs that realize plans, rules and methods related to mental activities, business activities or games are not considered as inventions since their source and object codes are not considered as technical characters. However, a computer program that realizes a method that solves a technical problem or a device containing a computer program can be protected by a patent. For example, a computer program that realizes a method that provides faster data communication between two mobile devices, a program that performs resource allocation in an operating system or a program that provides data encryption, etc." (Turkish Patent and Trademark Office, Patent Application Guide).*

As seen, there are no obstacles to patenting computer programs that solve technical problems. Unlike copyright protection, a patent protects the invention itself (Smith & Mann, 2004). In this context, when it comes to protecting computer programs, patent protection offers more benefits than copyright protection.

Protection of Artificial Intelligence Under Turkish Intellectual Property Law

Can Artificial Intelligence be Protected as a Computer Program under Turkish Intellectual Property Law? Artificial intelligence is coded with specific programming languages like computer programs (Sarı, 2020). The technology used in developing computer programs and the technology used in developing artificial intelligence are essentially similar (Butler, 1992; Sarı, 2020). However, there are also significant differences between artificial intelligence and computer programs. In this context, artificial intelligence is capable of problem-solving, whereas a computer program only acts on its instruction (Meydancı, 2023).

The Law No. 5846 on Intellectual and Artistic Works does not contain any regulations regarding artificial intelligence. This is because the law dates back to 1952, and the concept of artificial intelligence has only recently gained popularity.

As a result, the law does not reflect the current state of the art. Does the absence of regulation on artificial intelligence in the law mean that artificial intelligence systems cannot be protected in Türkiye? Since there is currently no specific regulation for artificial intelligence in Turkish law, the issues encountered in practice are likely to be addressed by treating artificial intelligence as a computer program. This is due to the lack of any legal regulation on the subject and is not a desirable outcome.

Should artificial intelligence be considered a form of protected work by the legislator? To address this question, policymakers must thoroughly analyse and mature the issue from legal and economic perspectives. Only after this initial stage can the matter be brought before the legislator. If it is determined that artificial intelligence should be protected as a computer program, then the Law on Intellectual and Artistic Works must be amended, as the current provisions in the law on computer programs are insufficient to protect artificial intelligence. In our opinion, protecting artificial intelligence as a computer program is not appropriate. This is because copyright protection provides a long protection period to the author. It is not appropriate to protect artificial intelligence as a computer program because copyright protection provides the author with a long period of protection. In this context, Copyright Law Article 27 states that:

> *The term of protection shall last for the lifetime of the author and for 70 years after his death. (Addition: 21.2.2001 - 4630/16) If there is more than one author, this period shall end upon the expiry of 70 years after the death of the last remaining author. The term of protection for works that have been first made public after the death of the author shall be 70 years after the date of death.*

The specified duration for protecting artificial intelligence seems excessively long. Artificial intelligence not only contributes to human progress but can also have adverse effects across various fields. Given the competition between humans and machines in numerous fields, the protection period should be brief, with ownership of artificial intelligence transitioning to society thereafter. Failure to do so could result in artificial intelligence systems, primarily developed by major corporations, driving significant economic growth for these entities while having destructive implications for society, particularly in terms of unemployment.

Can Artificial Intelligence be Protected as a Patent under Turkish Law? In Turkish law, in order for artificial intelligence to be eligible for patent protection, it must meet specific requirements. These criteria are evaluated on a case-by-case basis. Specifically, the AI must be novel, involve an inventive step, and have industrial applicability. Only after these conditions are fulfilled in the concrete case can it be discussed whether artificial intelligence can be patented. The fact that these conditions are met in the concrete case should not be interpreted that the invention can be patented in any case because illegal algorithms cannot be patented, and inventions that are unethical and contrary to public order cannot be patented either. (Pu,

2022). In this context, Article 82/3/a of the Industrial Property Law stipulates that inventions that are contrary to public order or public morality cannot be patented. However, in the case of artificial intelligence algorithms, it is pretty challenging to identify illegal aspects (Pu, 2022).

The patentability of AI meeting these criteria is currently a topic of debate within the existing legal framework. Moreover, the absence of machine learning and AI guidance in the Turkish Patent and Trademark Office application guide is a significant shortcoming. In contrast, the European Patent Office application guide includes a dedicated section on artificial intelligence and machine learning (European Patent Office). In this context, the guideline states the following about AI algorithms:

> *Artificial intelligence and machine learning are based on computational models and algorithms for classification, clustering, regression and dimensionality reduction, such as neural networks, genetic algorithms, support vector machines, k-means, kernel regression and discriminant analysis. Such computational models and algorithms are per se of an abstract mathematical nature, irrespective of whether they can be "trained" based on training data. Hence, the guidance provided in G-II, 3.3 generally applies also to such computational models and algorithms.*

G-II, 3.3 refers to European Patent Convention 52. Accordingly, mathematical methods are excluded from patentability under Art. 52/2/a. From this provision, it is generally understood that artificial intelligence cannot be patented (Foss-Solbrekk, 2021). However, "if the patent claims consist of a method 'involving the use of technical means'—such as a computer—a technical character is conferred on the subject-matter as a whole" it is considered eligible for a patent (Foss-Solbrekk, 2021).

Similar points can be made for American law. In this context, According to Sections 100-112 of Title 35 of the U.S. Patent Act, the registration process in the U.S. is carried out by the U.S. Patent and Trademark Office (USPTO). In this context, 35 U.S. Code § 101 of patent law states that "*Whoever invents or discovers any new and useful process, machine, manufacture, or composition of matter, or any new and useful improvement thereof, may obtain a patent therefor, subject to the conditions and requirements of this title*". This provision includes a wide range of patentable issues (Daşbaşı, 2013). However, software does not easily fall into the categories set out in the provision (Cho, 2020). In this context, software cannot be considered as machinery, manufacture or composition of matter (Cho, 2020). Initially, the US Patent Office's approach was not to grant computer program patents (Cho, 2020). Regarding Article 101, although there is no explicit provision in the Law, in the U.S. Supreme Court Diamond v Chakrabarty case, the Supreme Court stated that "*laws of nature, physical phenomena and abstract ideas are not patentable*" (*Diamond v Chakrabarty 447 U.S. 303*, 309, 1980). In this context, the applicants in *Gottschalk v. Benson* "*claimed a method for converting binary-coded decimal (BCD) numerals into pure binary numerals.*" (*Gottschalk v. Benson, 409 U.S. 63*, 1972). The court has stated that the algorithm is "*a procedure for solving a given type of mathematical problem*" and for current demand used the following statement: "*...if the judgment below is affirmed, the patent would wholly pre-empt the mathematical formula and in practical effect would be a patent on the algorithm itself.*" (*Gottschalk v. Benson, 409 U.S. 63*, 1972). It follows that algorithms cannot be patented under American law. However, in *Diamond v Diehr (Diamond v. Diehr, 450 U.S. 175*, 1980) case; the court stated the following in its judgment: "*When a claim containing a mathematical formula implements or applies the formula in a structure or process which, when considered as a whole, is performing a function which the patent laws were designed to protect (e. g., transforming or reducing an article to a different state or thing), then the claim satisfies 101's requirements. Pp. 191-193.*" This decision has created a new paradigm that is different from the court decisions on the unpatentability of algorithms. Accordingly, the decision emphasised the importance of a holistic perspective in determining whether a claim can be patented.

In light of these statements, it would be incorrect to conclude that artificial intelligence algorithms cannot be patented at all. It is possible to patent technical artificial intelligence algorithms under certain conditions. However, there is a legal gap in Turkish law on this subject. The Turkish Patent and Trademark Office has not updated its application guidelines. When an application involving artificial intelligence algorithms is submitted to the institution, it is unclear how the institutional expert will conduct the examination. This lack of clarity raises questions about the expertise that will be utilised in evaluating the application. The question of why patents should safeguard artificial intelligence is of great importance. Given the current lack of complete understanding of how artificial intelligence functions, it is exceedingly difficult to foresee the potential harm that an ostensibly benign AI system might pose to society and humanity in the future. Therefore, it is more fitting to bestow short-term patent protection rather than a prolonged period of copyright protection for artificial intelligence, which remains unpredictable. Although patent protection is short-term and cannot be extended, it provides strong protection. Since patent protection gives monopoly rights to the owner, it also allows those who invest in artificial intelligence to be economically satisfied during the protection period. In this context, new investments in artificial intelligence will also be incentivised. Since patents are granted only to inventions that provide technical solutions to a problem, it is more in line with the balance of interests that artificial intelligence algorithms, which cannot fulfil the condition of obtaining a patent, are open to the use of society.

In order for artificial intelligence to qualify for patent protection under Turkish law, the Turkish Patent and Trademark Office must first establish guidelines for AI patent applications. Even though AI is categorized as a computer program in practice, it should be eligible for both copyright and patent protection. Intellectual property law allows for cumulative protection, meaning that an intellectual product can be simultaneously protected by multiple intellectual property regimes. However, for a product to benefit from these overlapping protections, it must satisfy the requirements and conditions set by each respective intellectual property regime. According to current Turkish regulations, AI can only be patented in exceptional cases. Therefore, it is essential to develop the necessary guidelines and amend the Industrial Property Law accordingly. However, only artificial intelligence that meets the criteria of novelty, inventive step, and industrial applicability will be eligible for patent protection, even with the necessary regulations.

CONCLUSION

This study delves into whether artificial intelligence can be protected as a patent under Turkish law. The argument that artificial intelligence is simply a computer program leads to the conclusion that it should be protected as a work of idea and art under copyright law. However, this view fails to acknowledge that artificial intelligence is more than just a computer program. Law No. 5846 on Intellectual and Artistic Works, Türkiye and Law No. 6769 on Industrial Property, Türkiye are laws from a time when artificial intelligence was not on the playing field. Under Turkish law, there is no specific regulation on artificial intelligence. It is evident that policymakers are ill-prepared for the potential opportunities and dangers associated with artificial intelligence. In contrast to the European Patent Office, the Turkish Patent and Trademark Office has not provided any guidance on patent applications for artificial intelligence. Due to this legal gap, the only recourse for patent applications in practice is to attempt to protect them as computer programs.

The question of why patents should protect artificial intelligence is of utmost importance and requires careful consideration. With the continuous evolution of artificial intelligence technologies driven by big data, the competition between humans and machines becomes increasingly challenging. This raises concerns about the potential adverse impacts of artificial intelligence on society. Its widespread adoption could lead to unemployment across various industries and trigger consequences contrary to public order and morality. Additionally, providing prolonged protection for artificial intelligence may result in the consolidation of power among large corporations, hindering society from fully benefiting from these technological advancements and disrupting the balance of interests. AI should therefore benefit from patent protection, not copyright protection.

REFERENCES

Aksu, M. (2006). *Bilgisayar programlarının fikri mülkiyet hukukunda korunması*. Beta Press.

Arıkan, A. (1996). Bilgisayar programlarının korunması-AB ve Türkiye. *Union Of Turkish Bar Associations Review*, 166(3), 309–381.

Bozgeyik, H. (2009). Fikir ve sanat eserlerinde hususiyet. *Journal of Banking and Commercial Law*, 25(3), 170–222.

Butler, T. L. (1982). Can a computer be an author? Copyright aspects of artificial intelligence. *Hastings Communications and Entertainment Law Journal, 4*(4), 707-747. https://repository.uchastings.edu/hastings_comm_ent_law_journal/vol4/iss4/11

Cho, H. S. (2020). On the patentability of artificial intelligence: A review of recent cases from the U.S. *Dong-A Journal of IBT Law*, 10(31), 121–150. DOI: 10.31839/ibt.2020.10.31.123

Dalyan, Ş. (2009). *Bilgisayar programlarının fikri hukukta korunması*. Seçkin Press.

Daşbaşı, B. (2013). *Bilgisayar tabanlı buluşların ve iş metotlarının patentlenebilirliği: Dünyadaki uygulamalar ve ülkemizdeki durum* (Specialization Thesis). Turkish Patent Institute, Patent Department. https://akademi.tpe.gov.tr/uploads/files/Bilgisayar%20Tabanl%C4%B1%20Bulu%C5%9Flar%C4%B1n%20ve%20%C4%B0%C5%9F%20Metotlar%C4%B1n%C4%B1n%20Patentlenebilirli%C4%9Fi.pdf

Erdil, E. (2021). *Fikri mülkiyet hukuku*. Vedat Press. European Patent Office. Artificial intelligence and machine learning. https://www.epo.org/en/legal/guidelines-epc/2024/g_ii_3_3_1.html

Erel, Ş. (1994). Fikri hukukta bilgisayar programlarının korunması. *Ankara University Journal of Political Science*, 49(01), 141–164.

Foss-Solbrekk, K. (2021). Three routes to protecting AI systems and their algorithms under IP law: The good, the bad and the ugly. *Journal of Intellectual Property Law & Practice*, 16(3), 247–258. DOI: 10.1093/jiplp/jpab033

Lutz, M. J. (1993). Der Schutz der Computerprogramme in der Schweiz. [Beck-online.]. *GRUR International*, 1993, 653–663.

Melullis, K. J. (1998). *Zur Patentfähigkeit von Programmen für Datenverarbeitungsanlagen. GRUR*. Beck-online.

Meydancı, B. (2023). *Yapay zekâ ve ürünlerinin fikri mülkiyet hukukunda korunması*, unpublished doctoral dissertation, Bursa Uludağ University.

Öztürk, Ö. (2008). *Türk hukukunda patent verilebilirlik şartları*. Arıkan Press.

Pu, K. (2022). Intellectual property protection for AI algorithms. *Frontiers in Computing and Intelligent Systems*, 2(3), 44–47. DOI: 10.54097/fcis.v2i3.5210

Sarı, O. (2020). Yapay zekanın Türk fikri mülkiyet hukukuna göre korunması. *İzmir Bar Association Journal, 85*(1), 53-116. https://acikerisim.kent.edu.tr/xmlui/bitstream/handle/20.500.12780/205/onur%20s.pdf?sequence=1

Smith, B. L., & Mann, S. O. (2004). Innovation and intellectual property protection in the software industry: An emerging role for patents? *The University of Chicago Law Review. University of Chicago. Law School*, 71(1), 241–261.

Suluk, C., Karasu, R., & Nal, T. (2023). *Fikri mülkiyet hukuku* (7th ed.). Seçkin Publishing.

Tekinalp, Ü. (2012). *Fikri mülkiyet hukuku* (5th ed.). Vedat Press.

Topaloğlu, M. (1997). *Bilgisayar programları üzerindeki haklar ve bu hakların korunması*. Turkish Informatics Foundation Publications.

Turkish Patent and Trademark Office. (2024). *Patent application guide*, https://www.turkpatent.gov.tr/basvuru-kilavuzlari

ENDNOTES

1 The article has been prepared using the results of the project titled “Artificial Intelligence and Copyright: A Comparative Legal and Economic Analysis of Countries,” which is supported by the Directorate General of Copyrights of the Ministry of Culture and Tourism of the Republic of Türkiye.

2 Hereinafter referred to as “Copyright Law”.

Compilation of References

17. U.S. Code § 107.

19th Criminal Chamber of the Turkish Court of Cassation Case No: 2015/32515, Judgment No: 2018/7675, Date: 25.06.2018 (lexpera.com).

19th Criminal Chamber of the Turkish Court of Cassation, Case No: 2015/19627, Judgment No: 2018/7669, Date: 25.06.2018 (lexpera.com).

19th Criminal Chamber of the Turkish Court of Cassation, Case No: 2016/12740, Judgment No: 2018/7674, Date: 25.06.2018 (lexpera.com).

Abbott, R., & Bogenschneider, B. (2017). *Should Robots Pay Taxes? Tax Policy in the Age of Automation* (SSRN Scholarly Paper 2932483). DOI: 10.2139/ssrn.2932483

Abbott, R. (2020). *The Reasonable Robot: Artificial Intelligence and the Law*. Cambridge University Press. DOI: 10.1017/9781108631761

Abungu, C. Y. (2021). Democratic Culture and the Development of Artificial Intelligence in the USA and China. *The Chinese Journal of Comparative Law*, 9(1), 81–108. DOI: 10.1093/cjcl/cxaa032

Agreement on Trade Related Aspects of Intellectual Property Rights, 1869 UNTS 299, 33 ILM 1197 [TRIPS].

AI Art at Christie's Sells for $432,500. Retrieved July 26, 2024, from https:// www .nytimes.com/2018/10/25/arts/design/ai-art-sold-christies.html

Akhtar, Z. B. (2024). Unveiling the evolution of generative AI (GAI): A comprehensive and investigative analysis toward LLM models (2021–2024) and beyond. *Journal of Electrical Systems and Information Technology*, 11(22), 1–21.

Akipek, J., Akıntürk, T., & Ateş, D. (2024). Türk Medeni Hukuku, Başlangıç Hükümleri, Kişiler Hukuku. [Turkish Civil Law, Preliminary Provisions, Law of Persons] *BETA Bulletin of Experimental Treatments for AIDS*.

Aksu, M. (2006). *Bilgisayar programlarının fikri mülkiyet hukukunda korunması.* Beta Press.

Aktürk, E. (2024). Telif Hakkının Yapay Zek Ürünleri Açısından Değerlendirilmesi. ÇÜHAD, (5), 192-235.

Alaisawi, S., & Khalifa, S. (2020). *Artificial Intelligence in Data Mining and Big data. (PDF).* Artificial Intelligence in Data Mining and Big Data.

Albakjaji, M., & Almarzouqi, R. (2024). The Dilemma of the Copyrights of Artificial Intelligence: The Case of Saudi Arabia Regulations. *International Journal of Socio-technology and Knowledge Development*, 16(1), 1–15. DOI: 10.4018/IJSKD.336920

Alexandre, F. M. (2017). *The Legal Status of Artificially Intelligent Robots* [Unpublished LL.M dissertation project]. Tilburg University, Tilburg, Holland.

Ambika, A., Shin, H., & Jain, V. (2023). Immersive Technologies and Consumer Behavior: A Systematic Review of Two Decades of Research. *Australian Journal of Management*, 1–25. DOI: 10.1177/03128962231181429

Anally, T. (2023, March 6). Zarya of the Dawn: How AI is Changing the Landscape of Copyright Protection. *Harvard Journal of Law & Technology.*

Ananny, M., & Kreiss, D. (2011). A New Contract for the Press: Copyright, Public Domain Journalism, and Self-Governance in a Digital Age. *Critical Studies in Media Communication*, 28(4), 314–333. DOI: 10.1080/15295036.2010.519339

Anantrasirichai, N., & Bull, D. (2022). Artificial intelligence in the creative industries: A review. *Artificial Intelligence Review*, 55(1), 589–656. DOI: 10.1007/s10462-021-10039-7

Anderson, C. (2006). *The Long Tail: Why the Future of Business is Selling Less of More*. Hyperion.

Ansel Adams Estate Calls Out Adobe for Selling AI-Generated Art Using Photographer's Name. (n.d.). Retrieved July 25, 2024, from https://www.artnews.com/art-news/news/ansel-adams-estate-ai-generated-images-adobe-controversy-1234708739/

Aplin, T., Schaffer, B., & Li, P. (2022). Trustworthy Autonomous Systems Hub and TAS Node on Regulation and Governance. Artificial Intelligence and IP: Copyright and Patents: A Call for Evidence from Intellectual Property Office. DOI: 10.18742/pub01-074

Arıkan, A. (1996). Bilgisayar programlarının korunması-AB ve Türkiye. *Union Of Turkish Bar Associations Review*, 166(3), 309–381.

Aronsson-Storrier, A., & Fairhurst, O. (2024, April 25). Generative AI, originality, and the potential role of contract in protecting unoriginal works. *The IPKat.*https://ipkitten.blogspot.com/2024/04/generative-ai-originality-and-potential.html

Artificial intelligence (AI) market size worldwide from 2020 to 2030. (n.d.). Retrieved July 20 2024, https://www.statista.com/forecasts/1474143/global-ai-market-size#:~:text=The%20market%20for%20artificial%20intelligence,billion%20U.S.%20dollars%20in%202030

Artificial Intelligence and Copyright, 24.07.204, 88 Fed. Reg. 59,942, https://www.federalregister.gov/documents/2023/08/30/2023-18624/artificial-intelligence-and-copyright

Asaro, P. M. (2016). The Liability problem for autonomous artificial agents. AAAI Spring symposium series. https://cdn.aaai.org/ocs/12699/12699-56141-1-PB.pdf

Aslan, B. (2024). Yaratıcılık, Orijinallik ve Hususiyet Kavramlarının Üretken Otonom Yapay Zekâ Sistemlerine Yansımaları ve Fikri Haklar Boyutuyla Değerlendirilmesi. *Ticaret ve Fikri Mülkiyet Hukuku Dergisi*, 10(1), 3–24. DOI: 10.55027/tfm.1402220

Ateş, M. (2003). *Fikir ve Sanat Eserleri Üzerindeki Hakların Kapsamı ve Sınırlandırılması.* Seçkin Publishing.

Ateş, M. (2007). *Fikrî Hukukta Eser* [Work in Intellectual Law]. Turhan.

Atilla, S. (2024). Dealing with AI- generated works: lessons from the CDPA section 9(3). *Journal of Intellectual Property Law & Practice, 19(1),* 43-54.

Atilla, S. (2024). Dealing with AI-generated works: Lessons from the CDPA section 9(3). *Journal of Intellectual Property Law and Practice*, 19(1), 43–54. DOI: 10.1093/jiplp/jpad102

Authors' Licensing and Collecting Society (ALCS). (n.d.). *AI legislation: Where we're at.* Retrieved August 30, 2024, from https://www.alcs.co.uk/news/ai-legislation-where-were-at/

Aydoğdu, M., & Tuncer, N. (2023). *Türk Borçlar Hukuku, Özel Borç İlişkiler* (6th ed.). Adalet.

Backhaus, J. G. (2004). Josseph A. Schumpeter's Contributions in the Area of Fiscal Sociology: A fisrt Approximation. *Journal of Evolutionary Economics*, 14(2), 143–151. DOI: 10.1007/s00191-004-0186-z

Bak, B. (2018). Medeni Hukuk Açısından Yapay Zekanın Hukuki Statüsü ve Yapay Zeka Kullanımından Doğan Hukuki Sorumluluk. *TAAD*, 9(35), 211-232. https://taad.taa.gov.tr/dergiler/taad/taad-35

Bak, B. (2018). Medeni Hukuk Açısından Yapay Zekanın Hukuki Statüsü ve Yapay Zeka Kullanımından Doğan Hukuki Sorumluluk. *Türkiye Adalet Akademisi Dergisi*, 9(35), 211–232.

Ballardini, R. M., He, K., & Roos, T. (2019). AI-Generated Content: Authorship and Inventorship in the Age of Artificial Intelligence. In Pihlajarinne, T., Vesala, J., & Honkkila, O. (Eds.), *Online Distribution of Content in the EU*. Edward Elgar Publishing. DOI: 10.4337/9781788119900.00015

Bass, D. (2023). The Legal Issues Surrounding Deep fakes. *Honigman*. https://www.honigman.com/the-matrix/the-legal-issues-surrounding-deepfakes

Baumol, W. J. (1967). Macroeconomics of Unbalanced Growth: The Anatomy of Urban Crisis. *The American Economic Review*, 57(3), 415–426.

Bayamlıoğlu, E. (2008). Akıllı Yazılımlar ve Hukuki Statüsü: Yapay Zeka ve Kişilik Üzerine Bir Deneme. In İnceoğlu, M. M. (Ed.), *Uğur Alacakaptan'a Armağan* (Vol. 2, pp. 131–140). İstanbul Bilgi University Publishing.

Becker, M. (2017). Rights in Data–Industry 4.0 and the IP Rights of the Future. Zeitschrift Fuer Geistiges Eigentum. *Intellectual Property Journal*, 9(3), 253–265.

Benkler, Y. (1999). Free as the Air to Common Use: First Amendment Constraints on Enclosure of the Public Domain. *SSRN*, 74, 354. DOI: 10.2139/ssrn.168609

Bertolini, A. (2020). Artificial Intelligence and Civil Liability. *Publications Office of the European Union*. https://www.europarl.europa.eu/RegData/etudes/STUD/2020/621926/IPOL_STU(2020)621926_EN.pdf

Biber, A.E. (2016). Türkiye'de Fikri Mülkiyet Hakları Koruması Ekonomik Büyüme ve Teknoloji İhracatı İlişkisinin Karşılaştırılmalı Analizi. AİBÜ Social Sciences Journal, 16(3).

Bogren, W., & Hussein, M. (2023). Social Media's Take on Deepfakes: Ethical Concerns in the Public Discourse. *Uppsala University Institute for Informatics and Media*. https://uu.diva-portal.org/smash/get/diva2:1837417/FULLTEXT01.pdf

Bonadio, E., Lucchi, N., & Mazziotti, G. (2022). Will technology-aided creativity force us to rethink copyright's fundamentals? Highlights from the platform economy and artificial intelligence. *IIC - International Review of Intellectual Property and Competition Law, 53*(9), 1174–1200. DOI: 10.1007/s40319-022-01171-5

Bonadio, E., & Lucchi, N. (2018). *Non-Conventional Copyright: Do New and Atypical Works Deserve Protection?* Edward Elgar. DOI: 10.4337/9781786434074

Bonadio, E., McDonagh, L., & Dinev, P. (2022). Can artificial intelligence infringe copyright? Some reflections. In *Research handbook on intellectual property and artificial intelligence*. Edward Elgar Publishing Limited. DOI: 10.4337/9781800881907.00019

Bond, T., & Blair, S. (2019). Artificial intelligence & copyright: Section 9(3) or authorship without an author. *Journal of Intellectual Property Law and Practice*, 14(6), 423. DOI: 10.1093/jiplp/jpz056

Bostrom, N., & Yudkowsky, E. (2014). The ethics of artificial intelligence. In Frankish, K., & Ramsey, W. M. (Eds.), *The Cambridge Handbook of Artificial Intelligence* (pp. 316–334). Cambridge University Press. DOI: 10.1017/CBO9781139046855.020

Bowler-Smith, M. (2021). A new-knowledge approach to AI and tax policy. *Australian Tax Forum*. https://search.informit.org/doi/abs/10.3316/informit.250136285387518

Bozgeyik, H. (2009). Fikir ve sanat eserlerinde hususiyet. *Journal of Banking and Commercial Law*, 25(3), 170–222.

Bozkurt Yüksel, A. E., & Bak, B. (2018) Yapay Zeka. In Bozkurt Yüksel, A. E., Bak, B., Reyhani Y. R. & Aslanova, K., *Futurist Hukuk* (pp. 5-37). [Futurist Law] Aristo.

Brennen, S., & Kreiss, D. (2014). *Digitalization and Digitization*. Culture Digitally.

Bridy, A. (2011). Coding Creativity - Copyright and the Artificially Intelligent Author. *Stanford Technology Law Review : STLR : An Online High-Technology Law Journal from Stanford Law School*, 5, 1–28.

Bridy, A. (2012). Coding Creativity: Copyright and Artificially Intelligent Author. *Stanford Technology Law Review : STLR : An Online High-Technology Law Journal from Stanford Law School*, 5, 2011–2025.

Bridy, A. (2016). The evolution of authorship: Work made by code. *Columbia Journal of Law & the Arts, 39*(3), 395-401. DOI: 10.7916/jla.v39i3.2078

Brittain, B. (2023, August 21). *AI-generated art cannot receive copyrights, US court says*. Reuters. https://www.reuters.com/legal/ai-generated-art-cannot-receive-copyrights-us-court-says-2023-08-21/

Brown, R. D. (2021). Property ownership and the legal personhood of artificial intelligence. *Information & Communications Technology Law*, 30(2), 208–234. DOI: 10.1080/13600834.2020.1861714

Brynjolfsson, E., & McAffee, A. (2014). *The Second Machine Age: Work Progress, and Prosperity in a Time of Brilliant Technologies*. W. W. Norton Company.

Bülter, A. (2005). Eser Sahibinin Haklari İle Bağlantili Haklar. *TBB Dergisi*, 2005(59), 90–107.

Burk, D. L. (2007). Method and Madness in Copyright Law. *SSRN*. Advance online publication. DOI: 10.2139/ssrn.999433

Burylo, Y. (2022). AI Generated Works and Copyright Protection Entrepreneurship. *Economy and Law.*, 3(3), 7–13. DOI: 10.32849/2663-5313/2022.3.01

Butler, T. L. (1982). Can a computer be an author? Copyright aspects of artificial intelligence. *Hastings Communications and Entertainment Law Journal, 4*(4), 707-747. https://repository.uchastings.edu/hastings_comm_ent_law_journal/vol4/iss4/11

Butler, T. L. (1982). Can a Computer be an Author? Copyright Aspects of Artificial Intelligence. *Hastings Communication and Entertainment Law Journal*, 11, 707–747.

Calderaro, A., & Blumfelde, S. (2022). Artificial intelligence and EU security: The false promise of digital sovereignty. *European Security*, 31(3), 415–434. DOI: 10.1080/09662839.2022.2101885

Caldwell, M. (2023). What Is an "Author"? Copyright Authorship of AI Art Through a Philosophical Lens, *61. Houston Law Review*, 411. https://houstonlawreview.org/article/92132-what-is-an-author-copyright-authorship-of-ai-art-through-a-philosophical-lens

Callaway, E. (2020). 'It will change everything': DeepMind's AI makes gigantic leap in solving protein structures. *Nature*, 588(7837), 7837. Advance online publication. DOI: 10.1038/d41586-020-03348-4 PMID: 33257889

Calverley, D. (2008). Imagining a non-biological machine as a legal person. *AI & Society*, 22(4), 523–537. DOI: 10.1007/s00146-007-0092-7

Campbell, J. L. (1993). The State and Fiscal Sociology. *Annual Review of Sociology*, 19(1), 163–185. DOI: 10.1146/annurev.so.19.080193.001115

Cangüven, M. B. (2019). *Telif Haklarinin Vergilendirilmesi*. Marmara Üniversitesi Sosyal Bilimler Enstitüsü.

Caporusso, N. (2023). Generative Artificial Intelligence and the Emergence of Creative Displacement Anxiety [Review]. *Research Directs in Psychology and Behavior*, 3(1). Advance online publication. DOI: 10.53520/rdpb2023.10795

Carroll, M. W. (2019). Copyright and the progress of science: Why text and data mining is lawful. American University Washington College of Law, *Washington College of Law Research Paper No*, 2020-15, 53:893, 893-964.

Carroll, M. W. (2019). Copyright and the progress of science: Why text and data mining is lawful. *U.C. Davis Law Review*, 53, 893–964. https://lawreview.law.ucdavis.edu/issues/53/2/articles/53-2_Carroll.pdf

Castells, M. (2009). *The Rise of the Network Society*. Wiley-Blackwell. DOI: 10.1002/9781444319514

Cerka, P., Grigienė, J., & Sirbikytė, G. (2017). Is it possible to grant legal personality to artificial intelligence software systems? *Computer Law & Security Report*, 33(5), 685–699. DOI: 10.1016/j.clsr.2017.03.022

Chand, V., Kostić, S., & Reis, A. (2020). Taxing Artificial Intelligence and Robots: Critical Assessment of Potential Policy Solutions and Recommendation for Alternative Approaches – Sovereign Measure: Education Taxes/Global Measure: Global Education Tax or Planetary Tax. *World Tax Journal*, 12(4), 711–761. DOI: 10.59403/2sjxe4d

Chen, J., & Burgess, P. (2019). The boundaries of legal personhood: How spontaneous intelligence can problematise differences between humans, artificial intelligence, companies and animals. *Artificial Intelligence and Law*, 27(1), 73–92. DOI: 10.1007/s10506-018-9229-x

Cheong, B. C. (2021). Granting Legal Personhood to Artificial Intelligence Systems and Traditional Veil-Piercing Concepts to Impose Liability. *SN Social Sciences*, 1(9), 231. DOI: 10.1007/s43545-021-00236-0

Chesterman, S. (2021). *We, the robots? Regulating artificial intelligence and the limits of the law*. Cambridge University Press. DOI: 10.1017/9781009047081

Cho, W. (2024, May 21). *Scarlett Johansson's AI Legal Threat Sets Stage for Actors' Battle With Tech Giants*. Retrieved July 25, 2024, from https://www.hollywoodreporter.com/business/business-news/scarlett-johanssonai-legal-threat-1235905899

Cho, H. S. (2020). On the patentability of artificial intelligence: A review of recent cases from the U.S. *Dong-A Journal of IBT Law*, 10(31), 121–150. DOI: 10.31839/ibt.2020.10.31.123

Chow, P. S. (2020). Ghost in the (Hollywood) machine: Emergent applications of artificial intelligence in the film industry. NECSUS_European Journal of Media Studies, 9(1), 193-214.

Christen, M., Gordijn, B., & Loi, M. (2020). *The ethics of cybersecurity*. Springer Nature. DOI: 10.1007/978-3-030-29053-5

Christiani, T. A. (2015). Normative and empirical research methods: Their usefulness and relevance in the study of law as an object. *GATR Global Journal of Business and Social Science Review*, 3(4), 16–22. DOI: 10.35609/gjbssr.2015.3.4(3)

Coeckelbergh, M. (2010). Robot rights? Towards a social-relational justification of moral consideration. *Ethics and Information Technology*, 12(3), 209–221. DOI: 10.1007/s10676-010-9235-5

Coeckelbergh, M. (2020). Should we treat teddy bear 2.0 as a kantian dog? Four arguments for the indirect moral standing of personal social robots, with implications for thinking about animals and humans. *Minds and Machines*, 31(3), 1–24.

Colak, B. (2021). Legal Issues of Deepfake. *Institute for Internet & the Just Society*. https://www.internetjustsociety.org/legal-issues-of-deepfakes

Compendium of U.S. Copyright Office Practices. (2021). 3rd ed.).

Cornu, G. (2022). *Vocabulaire Juridique* (14th ed.). Puf.

Craig, C., & Kerr, I. (2020). The Death of the AI Author. *Ottawa Law Review*, 52, 31.

Creemers, R., Triolo, P., & Webster, G. (2018). Translation: Cybersecurity Law of the People's Republic of China. *New America*. Retrieved from: https://www.newamerica.org/cybersecurity-initiative/digichina/blog/translation-cybersecurity-law-peoples-republic-china/

Criminal responsibility of legal persons in "France - Criminal Code 1994 (2005) EN." (2024). Nottingham.ac.uk. https://cjad.nottingham.ac.uk/en/legislation/174/keyword/521/

Cui, L. (2020). *Artificial intelligence and judicial modernization*. Springer Singapore. DOI: 10.1007/978-981-32-9880-4

Cuthbertson, A. (2017, November 6). *Tokyo: Artificial Intelligence "Boy" Shibuya Mirai Becomes World's First AI Bot to Be Granted Residency*. Newsweek. https://newsweek.com/tokyo-residency-artificial-intelligence-boy-shibuya-mirai-702382

Dabus. (2022). dabus. 53. DOI: 10.1007/s40319-022-01186-7

Dalyan, Ş. (2009). *Bilgisayar programlarının fikri hukukta korunması*. Seçkin Press.

Darmon, M. (2023). *Socialization*. Polity Press.

Daşbaşı, B. (2013). *Bilgisayar tabanlı buluşların ve iş metotlarının patentlenebilirliği: Dünyadaki uygulamalar ve ülkemizdeki durum* (Specialization Thesis). Turkish Patent Institute, Patent Department. https://akademi.tpe.gov.tr/uploads/files/Bilgisayar%20Tabanl%C4%B1%20Bulu%C5%9Flar%C4%B1n%20ve%20%C4%B0%C5%9F%20Metotlar%C4%B1n%C4%B1n%20Patentlenebilirli%C4%9Fi.pdf

Davenport, T. H., & Mittal, N. (2022, November). How generative AI is changing creative work. *Harvard Business Review*. https://hbr.org/2022/11/how-generative-ai-is-changing-creative-work

Dayo, F., Memon, A. A., & Dharejo, N. (2023). Scriptwriting in the Age of AI: Revolutionizing Storytelling with Artificial Intelligence. *Journal of Media & Communication*, 4(1), 24–38.

De Cock Buning, M. (2016). Autonomous Intelligent Systems as Creative Agents under the EU framework for Intellectual Property. *European Journal of Risk Regulation*, 7(2), 310–322. DOI: 10.1017/S1867299X00005730

Denemeç, I. S. (2021). *To Feed, Or Not to Feed? An Analysis of the Copyright Issues Surrounding the Use of Machine Learning Algorithms* (1st ed.). Lykeion.

Department for Science, Innovation and Technology. (n.d.). *About us*. Retrieved August 30, 2024, from https://www.gov.uk/government/organisations/department-for-science-innovation-and-technology/about

Dietz, A. (1990). A modern concept for the right of the community of authors (domaine public payant). *Copyright Bulletin. Unesco*, 24(4), 1–37.

Ding, J. (2018). *Deciphering China's AI Dream. Future of Humanity Institute*, University of Oxford. Retrieved from: https://www.fhi.ox.ac.uk/publications/deciphering-chinas-ai-dream-jeffrey-ding-2018-future-of-humanity-institute-university-of-oxford/

Dobbs, R., Manyika, J., & Woetzel, J. (2015). The Four Global Forces Breaking All the Trends. *McKinsey Global Institute*, 11(4), 1–5.

Dolhansky, B., Bitton, J., Pflaum, B., Lu, J., Howes, R., Wang, M., & Ferrer, C. C. (2020). The DeepFake Detection Challenge (DFDC) Dataset. 8(20), ArXiv./abs/2006.07397.

Doshi, A. R., & Hauser, O. (2023). Generative Artificial Intelligence Enhances Creativity. SSRN *Electronic Journal*. https://doi.org/DOI: 10.2139/ssrn.4535536

Duguzheva, M. K., & Simaeva, E. P. (2024). *Transformation of the Legislation on Culture in the Context of Digitalization*. Perm University Herald Juridical Sciences, 44.

Durham, A. R. (2002). The Random Muse: Authorship and Indeterminacy' (2002) 44 William & Mary. *Law Review*, 44(2), 571–634.

Dusollier, S. (2020). The 2019 Directive on Copyright in the Digital Single Market: Some progress, a few bad choices, and an overall failed ambition. *Common Market Law Review*, 57(4), 979–1030. DOI: 10.54648/COLA2020714

Dworkin, R. (1995). The Moral Right of the Author: Moral Rights and the Common Law Countries. *Boston University Law Review. Boston University. School of Law*, 91, 1519–1567.

Eagleton, T. (2006). *Criticism and Ideology: A Study in Marxist Literary Theory.* Verso.

Economic Advisory Council to the PM. (2024). A Complex Adaptive System Framework to Regulate Artificial Intelligence (EAC-PM/WP/26/2024).

Edizdoğan, N., Çetinkaya, Ö., & Gümüş, E. (2023). *Kamu Maliyesi.* Ekin Yayınevi.

Eidenmüller, H. (20242017, March 8). Robot's Legal Personality [Online blog post]. https://blogs.law.ox.ac.uk/business-law-blog/blog/2017/03/robots'-legal-personalityRetrieved from www.law.ox.ac.uk/business-law-blog/blog/2017/03/robots'-legal-personality

Elgammal, A., Liu, B., Elhoseiny, M., & Mazzone, M. (2017). CAN: Creative Adversarial Networks, Generating "Art" by Learning About Styles and Deviating from Style Norms. arXiv preprint arXiv:1706.07068.

Erdil, E. (2021). *Fikri mülkiyet hukuku.* Vedat Press. European Patent Office. Artificial intelligence and machine learning. https://www.epo.org/en/legal/guidelines-epc/2024/g_ii_3_3_1.html

Erel, Ş. (1994). Fikri hukukta bilgisayar programlarının korunması. *Ankara University Journal of Political Science*, 49(01), 141–164.

Erickson, K. (2024, January 31). Copyright protection in AI-generated works. *Creative Industries Policy and Evidence Center.*https://pec.ac.uk/blog_entries/copyright-protection-in-ai-generated-works

Ersoy, Ç. (2017). *Robotlar, Yapay Zeka ve Hukuk* (2nd ed.). Oniki Levha.

Estreicher, S., & Yost, K. A. (2016). University IP: The University as Coordinator of the Team Production Process. *Indiana Law Journal (Indianapolis, Ind.)*, 91(4), 1082–1103.

European Commission. (2020). Report on the Safety and Liability Implications of Artificial Intelligence, the Internet of Things, and Robotics. https://eur-lex.europa.eu/legal-content/EN/TXT/PDF/?uri=CELEX:52020DC0064&from=en

European Parliament Committee on Legal Affairs (2016). Report with Recommendations to the Commission on Civil Law Rules on Robotics (2015/2103(INL),

European Parliament Committee on Legal Affairs. (2020). Report on Intellectual Property Rights for the Development of Artificial Intelligence Technologies (2020/2015(INI)).

European Parliament resolution of 16 February 2017 with recommendations to the Commission on Civil Law Rules on Robotics (2015/2103(INL)). (n.d.). Retrieved July 22. 2024, https://eur-lex.europa.eu/legal-content/EN/TXT/PDF/?uri=CELEX:52017IP005

Fatima, S., Desouza, K. C., & Dawson, G. S. (2020). National strategic artificial intelligence plans: A multi-dimensional analysis. *Economic Analysis and Policy*, 67, 178–194. DOI: 10.1016/j.eap.2020.07.008

Fertility rate: children per woman. (2024). Our World in Data. https://ourworldindata.org/grapher/fertility-rate-with-projections?time=1988.2040&country=JPN~CHN~KOR

Ficsor, M. (2006). Collective management of copyright and related rights in the digital networked environment: Voluntary, presumption-based, extended, mandatory, possible, inevitable. In D. Gervais (Ed.), *Collective management of copyright and related rights* (pp. 37-83). Kluwer Law International.

Fikir ve Sanat Eserleri Kanunu [Law on the Intellectual and Artistic Works], Law No: 5846, Date: 05/12/1951; Official Gazette Number and Date: 7981, 13.12.1951.

Fleming, D. S. (2007). US Patent and Trademark Office refuses registration of flavour trademark. 2(5). https://doiDOI: 10.1093/jiplp/jpm044

Florida, R. (2002). *The Rise of the Creative Class—Revisited: Revised and Expanded*. Basic Books.

Floridi, L. (2014). *The Fourth Revolution: How the Infosphere Is Reshaping Human Reality*. Oxford University Press.

Foss-Solbrekk, K. (2021). Three routes to protecting AI systems and their algorithms under IP law: The good, the bad and the ugly. *Journal of Intellectual Property Law & Practice*, 16(3), 247–258. DOI: 10.1093/jiplp/jpab033

France mulls taxing AI works based on copyrighted material. (n.d.). Retrieved August 25, 2024, from https://www.medianama.com/2023/09/223-france-law-tax-ai-works-copyrighted-material/

Franke, U. E. (2021). Artificial Divide: How Europe and America Could Clash Over AI. *European Council on Foreign Relations.* Retrieved from: https://www.jstor.org/stable/resrep29123

French National Assembly Proposes New Law to Secure Copyright in AI. (n.d.). Retrieved August 12, 2024, from https://www.fieldfisher.com/en/locations/belgium/insights/french-national-assembly-proposes-new-law-to-secur

Frey & Osborne. (2013). *The Future of Employment: How Susceptible Are Jobs to Computerisation?* Retrieved July 20 2024, https://www.oxfordmartin.ox.ac.uk/downloads/academic/The_Future_of_Employment.pdf

Frey, B. S., & Oberholzer-Gee, F. (1998). *Public Choice, Cost-Benefit Analysis, and the Evaluation of Cultural Heritage. A. Peacock içinde, Does the Past Have a Future? The Political Economy of Heritage.* Institute of Economic Affairs.

Fuji, H., & Managi, S. (2018). Trends and priority shifts in artificial intelligence technology invention: A global patent analysis. *Economic Analysis and Policy*, 58, 60–69. DOI: 10.1016/j.eap.2017.12.006

Gaffar, Hafiz & Albarashdi, Saleh. (2024). Copyright Protection for AI-Generated Works: Exploring Originality and Ownership in a Digital Landscape. Asian Journal of International Law, 1-24. DOI: 10.1017/S2044251323000735

Galbraith, P. W. (2008, May 16). *Plastic fantastic: Japan's doll industry booming - Japan Today.* Japantoday.com. https://japantoday.com/category/features/lifestyle/plastic-fantastic-japans-doll-industry-booming?comment-order=popular

Gaon, A. H. (2021). *The Future of Copyright in the Age of Artificial Intelligence.* Edward Elgar Publishing. DOI: 10.4337/9781839103155

Geddes, K. G. (2021). Ocularcentrism and deepfakes: Should seeing be believing? *Fordham Intellectual Property, Media & Entertainment Law Journal*, 31(4), 1042-1083. https://ir.lawnet.fordham.edu/iplj/vol31/iss4/3

Geertz, C. (2017). *The Interpretation of Cultures.* Basic Books.

Generative AI and the future of work The potential? Boundless. Deloitte AI Institute, https://www2.deloitte.com/content/dam/Deloitte/us/Documents/consulting/us-ai-institute-generative-ai-and-the-future-of-work.pdf

Gere, C. (2008). *Digital Culture.* Reaktion Books.

Gervais, D. J. (2019). The Machine as Author. *Iowa Law Review*, 105(1), 205–249.

Gervais, D. J. (2020). The machine as author. *Iowa Law Review*, 105(5), 2053–2106. https://ssrn.com/abstract=3359524

Ginsburg, J.C., Budiardjo, L.A. (2019). Authors and machines, *34 Berkeley Tech. LJ* 343.

Ginsburg, J. C. (2001). *Copyright and Control Over New Technologies of Dissemination*. Columbia Law School. DOI: 10.2307/1123809

Ginsburg, J. C., & Budiardjo, L. A. (2019). Authors and machines. *Berkeley Technology Law Journal*, 34(2), 343–448. DOI: 10.15779/Z38SF2MC24

Gloger, C. (2007). *Haftungsbeschränkung versus Gläubigerschutz in der Gmbh*. Carl Heymanns Verlag.

Gobble, M. M. (2018). Digitalization, Digitization, and Innovation. *Research Technology Management*, 61(4), 56–59. DOI: 10.1080/08956308.2018.1471280

Gök, B. (2024). Yapay Zekâ Sistemleri Tarafından Üretilen Fikri Ürünlerin Telif Hakkı [Copyright of Intellectual Products Generated by Artificial Intelligence Systems]. *Platon*.

Goldscheid, R. (1958). *A Sociological Approach to Problems to Public Finance. In Classsics in the Theory of Public Finance*. Palgrave Macmillan.

Goldstein, P., & Hugenholtz, P. B. (2019). *International Copyright: Principles, Law and Practice*. Oxford Press.

Gonzalez, A.G. (2006). The software patent debate. *Journal of Intellectual Property law and Practice,1,* 196-206.

Goold, P. (2021). The curious case of computer-generated works under the Copyright, Designs and Patents Act 1988. *City Law School Research Paper No. 2021/03.* https://openaccess.city.ac.uk/id/eprint/26210/

Gözübüyük, B. (2021). Yapay Zekanin Meydana Getirdiği Fikri Ürünlere Ilişkin 5846 Sayili Fikir Ve Sanat Eserleri Kanunundaki Sorunlar Ve Çözüm Öneriler. *Kırıkkale Hukuk Mecmuaması*, 1(1), 54–81.

Gözübüyük, B. (2021). Yapay Zekanın Meydana Getirdiği Fikri Ürünlere İlişkin 5846 sayılı Fikir ve Sanat Eserleri Kanunundaki Sorunlar ve Çözüm Önerileri. *KHM*, 1(1), 54–81.

Gözübüyük, B. (2021). Yapay Zekanın Meydana Getirdiği Fikri Ürünlere İlişkin 5846 Sayılı Fikir ve Sanat Eserleri Kanunundaki Sorunlar ve Çözüm Önerileri. *Kırıkkale Hukuk Mecmuası*, 1(1), 54–81.

Gözübüyük, B. (2021). Yapay Zekanın Meydana Getirdiği Fikri Ürünlere İlişkin 5846 Sayılı Fikir ve Sanat Eserleri Kanunundaki Sorunlar ve Çözüm Önerileri. *Kırıkkale Law Review*, 1(1), 54–81.

Grad-Gyenge, A. (2023) *A mesterséges intelligencia által generált tartalmak értelmezésének lehetőségei a szerzői jog útján*. https://szakcikkadatbazis.hu/doc/2441007

Grimmelman, J. (2016). Copyright for literate robots. *Iowa Law Review*, 101(2), 657–681.

Grimmelmann, J. (2016). There's No Such Thing as a Computer-Authored Work – And it's a Good Thing, Too. https://scholarship.law.cornell.edu/cgi/viewcontent.cgi?article=2617&context=facpub

Gross, B. (2024). Unmasking Deepfakes: Navigating the Copyright Quagmire. *Cardozo Arts & Entertainment Law Journal*. https://cardozoaelj.com/2024/04/05/unmasking-deepfakes-navigating-the-copyright-quagmire/

Guadamuz, A. (2017). Artifical Intelligence and Copyright, *WIPO Magazine, 5/2017*. https://www.wipo.int/wipo_magazine/en/2017/05/article_0003.html

Guadamuz, A. (2017). Artificial intelligence and copyright. *WIPO Magazine*, (5), 14-19. Retrieved from: https://www.wipo.int/wipo_magazine/en/2017/05/article_0003.html

Guadamuz, A. (2023). *A Scanner Darkly: Copyright Liability and Exceptions in Artificial Intelligence Inputs and Outputs* (SSRN Scholarly Paper 4371204). DOI: 10.2139/ssrn.4371204

Guadamuz, A., (2017, October 5). Artificial Intelligence and copyright. WIPO Magazine.

Guadamuz, A. (2016). The monkey selfie: Copyright lessons for originality in photographs and internet jurisdiction. *Internet Policy Review*, 5(1). Advance online publication. DOI: 10.14763/2016.1.398

Güçlütürk, O. G., & Cankat, R. (2021). Yapay Zekâ ile Oluşturulan Ürünlerin Eser Niteliği ve Eser Sahipliği Meselesi. In E. E. Aksoy Retornaz & O. G. Güçlütürk (Eds.), *Gelişen Teknolojiler ve Hukuk II: Yapay Zekâ* (pp. 195–222). On İki Levha Yayıncılık.

Gunkel, D. J. (2021). Computational Creativity: Algorithms, Art, and Artistry in NAVAS. In *The Routledge Handbook of Remix Studies and Digital Humanities* (pp. 385-395). Routledge.

Gunkel, D. J. (2012). *The machine question: Critical perspectives on AI, robots, and ethics*. MIT Press. DOI: 10.7551/mitpress/8975.001.0001

Gunkel, D. J. (2018). The other question: Can and should robots have rights? *Ethics and Information Technology*, 20(2), 87–99. DOI: 10.1007/s10676-017-9442-4

Güvenç, B. (2018). *İnsan ve Kültür*. Boyut Yayınları.

Gyertyánfy, P. (2023). *A mesterséges intelligencia hatályos szerzői jogi törvényünk szerint*.https://www.sztnh.gov.hu/sites/default/files/files/kiadv/szkv/industrial-property-and-copyright-review-2023-6/02-gyertyanfypeter.pdf

Haenlein, M., & Kaplan, A. (2019). A Brief History of Artificial Intelligence: On the Past, Present, and Future of Artificial Intelligence. *California Management Review*, 61(4), 1–10. DOI: 10.1177/0008125619864925

Hamza, M., Khan, S., & Saeed, Z., & Sajida. (2023). The Impact of Artificial Intelligence on Intellectual Property Rights. *International Journal of Human Sciences*, 3(4), 312–319.

Hao, K. (2018), Inside the world of AI that forges beautiful art and terrifying deep fakes. *MIT Technology Review*. https://www.technologyreview.com/2018/12/01/138847/inside-the-world-of-ai-that-forges-beautiful-art-and-terrifying-deepfakes/

Harwell, D. (2018). Fake-porn videos are being weaponized to harass and humiliate women: 'Everybody is a potential target'. *The Washington Post*. https://www.washingtonpost.com/technology/2018/12/30/fake-porn-videos-are-being-weaponized-harass-humiliate-women-everybody-is-potential-target/

Heider, F., & Simmel, M. (1944). An experimental study of apparent behavior. *The American Journal of Psychology*, 57(2), 243–259. DOI: 10.2307/1416950

He, K. (2020). Artificial intelligence and its implications for income distribution and unemployment. In Goldfarb, A., Gans, J., & Agrawal, A. (Eds.), *The Economics of Artificial Intelligence: An Agenda* (pp. 399–419). University of Chicago Press. DOI: 10.7208/chicago/9780226613475.003.0016

Helvacıoğlu, A. D., Eraslan, İ. H., & Bulu, M. (2004). Dijitalleşen Dünyada Fikrî Mülkiyet Haklarının Ülkeler Açısından Küresel Rekabet Avantajı Oluşturmadaki Yeri. *National Congress on Information, Economy and Management*, 485-493.

Henderson, P., Li, X., Jurafsky, D., Hashimoto, T., Lemley, M. A., & Liang, P. (2023). Foundation Models and Fair Use. *SSRN*, 24, 1–79. DOI: 10.2139/ssrn.4404340

Hendrawan, D., Andersen, C., Tiopan, D., Kurniawan, S., & Malinda, M. (2023). Juridical review of copyright infringement in the use of deepfakes in the creative industry in Indonesia. *International Journal of Cyber Criminology*, 17(1). https://cocreationstudio.mit.edu/wp-content/uploads/2021/12/JustJoking.pdf

Hernández, M., Cheplygina, V., & Plasencia-Calaña, Y. (2015). *Dissimilarity Representations for Low-Resolution Face Recognition*. Springer International Publishing.

Hilotin, J. (2023, July 4). *6 trillion-dollar companies: World's super-exclusive club of mega global businesses*. Gulfnews.com; Gulf News. https://gulfnews.com/business/markets/6-trillion-dollar-companies-worlds-super-exclusive-club-of-mega-global-businesses-1.1688486130909?slide=5

Hine, E., & Floridi, L. (2024). Artificial intelligence with American values and Chinese characteristics: A comparative analysis of American and Chinese governmental AI policies. *AI & Society*, 39(1), 257–278. DOI: 10.1007/s00146-022-01499-8

Hirsch, E. (1948). *Fikrî ve Sınai Haklar* (1st ed.). Ar Basımevi.

Hirsch, E. E. (1943). *Hukuki Bakımdan Fikri Say*. Istanbul University Publishing.

Hirsch, E. E. (1948). *Fikri ve Sınai Haklar*. Ankara Basımevi.

Hooker, M. P. (2020). Naruto v Slater: One Small Snap for a Monkey, One Giant Lawsuit for Animal-Kind. *Wake Forest Law Review Online*. 10. 15-31.

Hristov, K. (2017). Artificial Intelligence and the Copyright Dilemma. *The Journal of the Franklin Pierce Center for Intellectual Property*, 57(3), 431–454. https://ipmall.law.unh.edu/sites/default/files/hosted_resources/IDEA/hristov_formatted.pdf

Huang, K., Joshi, A., Dun, S., & Hamilton, N. (2024). AI Regulations. In Huang, K., Wang, Y., Goertzel, B., Li, Y., Wright, S., & Ponnapalli, J. (Eds.), *Generative AI Security. Future of Business and Finance* (pp. 61–98). Springer. DOI: 10.1007/978-3-031-54252-7_3

Hubbord, F. P. (2011). Do Androids Dream: Personhood and Intelligent Artifacts. *Temple Law Review*, 83(2), 405-474. https://www.templelawreview.org/article/83-2_hubbard/

Huber, E. (1901). *Exposé des Motifs de l'avant-projet* (Vol. I).

Hudson, A. (2012). *Understanding Company Law*. Routledge.

Hugenholtz, P. B., & Quintais, J. P. (2021). Copyright and Artificial Creation: Does EU Copyright Law Protect AI-Assisted Output? *IIC; International Review of Industrial Property and Copyright Law*, 52(9), 1190–1216. DOI: 10.1007/s40319-021-01115-0

IFR Press Room. (2023, September 26). World Robotics 2023 Report: Asia ahead of Europe and the Americas. IFR International Federation of Robotics. https://ifr.org/ifr-press-releases/news/world-robotics-2023-report-asia-ahead-of-europe-and-the-americas

Ihalainen, J. (2018). Computer creativity: Artificial intelligence and copyright. *Journal of Intellectual Property Law & Practice*, 13(9), 724–728. DOI: 10.1093/jiplp/jpy031

İncel, E. (2023). Gvk Madde 18 Kapsaminda Telif Kazancinin Ve İhtira Beratinin (Patentin) Vergilendirilmesi. *Ankara Hacı Bayram Veli Üniversitesi Hukuk Fakültesi Dergisi*, 27(1), 283–320. DOI: 10.34246/ahbvuhfd.1167553

IndiaLaw. (2015). Analysis of Doctrines: 'Sweat of the Brow' & 'Modicum of Creativity' Vis-A-Vis Originality in Copyright Law.

Intelligence. (n.d.) In *Turkish Language Association online*.https://sozluk.gov.tr/?ara=zek%C3%A2

Introduction to AI Applications in Robotics. (n.d.). Retrieved July 20 2024, https://onlinedegrees.sandiego.edu/application-of-ai-in-robotics

Japan External Trade Organization. (2024). *Where to invest in Japan's local regions: Kanagawa*. JETRO. https://www.jetro.go.jp/en/invest/region/data/kanagawa.html

Javornik, A. (2016). Augmented reality: Research agenda for studying the impact of its media characteristics. *Journal of Retailing and Consumer Services*, 30, 252–261. DOI: 10.1016/j.jretconser.2016.02.004

Jenkins, H. (2006). *Convergence Culture: Where Old and New Media Collide*. New York University Press.

Jodka, S. (2024). Manipulating reality: the intersection of deepfakes and the law. *Reuters*. https://www.reuters.com/legal/legalindustry/manipulating-reality-intersection-deepfakes-law-2024-02-01/

Johnson, D. G. (2015). Technology with no human responsibility? *Journal of Business Ethics*, 127(4), 707–715. DOI: 10.1007/s10551-014-2180-1

Jokanovic, V. R. (2022). *Artificial Intelligence*. CRC Press.

Joking, J. https://cocreationstudio.mit.edu/wp-content/uploads/2021/12/JustJoking.pdf

Kalota, F. (2024). A primer on generative artificial intelligence. *Education Sciences*, 14(2), 1–15. DOI: 10.3390/educsci14020172

Kanagawa Prefecture. (2024). Improving preventive measures (for prefectural residents). Kanagawa Prefecture. https://www.pref.kanagawa.jp/docs/cz6/me-byokaizen/index.html

Kang, H. J., Shin, J. H., & Ponto, K. (2020). How 3D virtual reality stores can shape consumer purchase decisions:The roles of informativeness and playfulness. *Journal of Interactive Marketing*, 49(1), 70–85. DOI: 10.1016/j.intmar.2019.07.002

Karahan, S., Suluk, C., Saraç, T., & Nal, T. (2011). *Fikri Mülkiyet Hukukunun Esasları*. Seçkin Yayıncılık.

Karakoç, Y. (2017). *Genel Vergi Hukuku* (Vol. 2). Baskı. Yetkin Yayınevi.

Karnouskos, S. (2022). Symbiosis with artificial intelligence via the prism of law, robots, and society. *Artificial Intelligence and Law*, 30(1), 93–115. DOI: 10.1007/s10506-021-09289-1

Kaynak, F. (2015). *Sosyolojik yöntemin kuralları* (E. Durkheim, Trans.). Dost Kitabevi Yayınları.

Keller, P. (2023, February 20). Protecting creatives or impeding progress? Machine learning and the EU copyright framework. *Kluwer Copyright Blog*.https://copyrightblog.kluweriplaw.com/2023/02/20/protecting-creatives-or-impeding-progress-machine-learning-and-the-eu-copyright-framework/

Kesavan, A. (2024). The Use of Deepfake. *Khurana & Khurana*. https://www.khuranaandkhurana.com/2024/04/19/the-use-of-deep-fake/

Kiernan, P. (2024). The Legal Landscape: Navigating Liability and Regulation in the Age of Deep Fakes. *Thought Lab*. https://www.thoughtlab.com/blog/the-legal-landscape-navigating-liability-and-regul/

Kılıç, B., & Kahraman, M. E. (2023). Current usage areas of deepfake applications with artificial intelligence technology. *İletişim ve Toplum Araştırmaları Dergisi*, 3(2), 301-332.

Kiliçarslan, D. S. K. (n.d.). Yapay Zekanin Hukuki Statüsü Ve Hukuki Kişiliği Üzerine Tartişmalar. *YBHD, 2*, 363-389.

Kılıçoğlu, A. M. (2023). *Borçlar Hukuku Özel Hükümler* (5th ed.). Turhan.

Kılıçoğlu, A. M. (2023). *Sınai Haklarla Karşılaştırmalı Fikri Haklar* (9th ed.). Turhan.

Kou, H., Rong, K., Xie, D., & Yang, B. (2024). *Artificial Intelligence Generated Content, Intellectual Property Rights, and Digital Tax*. DOI: 10.2139/ssrn.4910480

Kovacev, R. J. (2020). A Taxing Dilemma: Robot Taxes and the Challenges of Effective Taxation of AI, Automation and Robotics in the Fourth Industrial Revolution. *The Contemporary Tax Journal*, 9(2). Advance online publication. DOI: 10.31979/2381-3679.2020.090204

KPMG. (2023). *Generative AI models—The risks and potential rewards in business*. KPMG International.

Krarup, T., & Horst, M. (2023). European artificial intelligence policy as digital single market making. *Big Data & Society*, 10(1). Advance online publication. DOI: 10.1177/20539517231153811

Kulesz, O. (2018). Culture, platforms and machines: the impact of artificial intelligence on the diversity of cultural expressions. *Intergovernmental Committee for the protection and promotion of the diversity of cultural expressions*. Retrieved from: https://unesdoc.unesco.org/ark:/48223/pf0000380584

Kumar, A. (2016). The Test of Time: Section 230 of the Communications Decency Act Turns 20. *Davis Wright Tremaine LLP*. https://www.dwt.com/blogs/media-law-monitor/2016/08/the-test-of-time-section-230-of-the-communications

Kurşat, Z. (2009). Eser ve Vekâlet Sözleşmelerinin Nitelendirilmesi Sorunu ve Nitelendirmenin Hükmü. *İÜHFM*, LXVII (1-2), 143-166.

Kurtz, L. (2004). Digital actors and copyright-from the polar express to simone. *Santa Clara Computer and High-Technology Law Journal*, 21, 783.

Kwall, R. R. (2010). *The Soul of Creativity: Forging a Moral Rights Law for the United States*. Stanford University Press.

Labour Party. (2024a). *Labour's arts, culture & creative industries sector plan*. Retrieved August 30, 2024 form https://labour.org.uk/wp-content/uploads/2024/03/Labours-Arts-Culture-Creative-Industries-Sector-Plan.pdf

Labour Party. (2024b). *Labour Party manifesto 2024*. Retrieved August 30, 2024 from https://labour.org.uk/wp-content/uploads/2024/06/Labour-Party-manifesto-2024.pdf

Langa, J. (2021). Deepfakes, Real Consequences: Crafting Legislation to Combat Threats Posed by Deepfakes. *Boston University Law Review*. https://www.bu.edu/bulawreview/files/2021/04/LANGA.pdf

Lashbrooke, E. C. (1988). Legal Reasoning and Artificial Intelligence. *Loyola Law Review*, 34, 287–310. https://loynolawreview.org

Latham & Watkins. (2020). *France Reverses Position on Transfer of Criminal Liability in Mergers.* Number 2834. https://www.lw.com/admin/upload/SiteAttachments/Alert%202834.v6.pdf

Lauterbach, A. (2019). Artificial intelligence and policy: Quo vadis? *Digital Policy. Regulation & Governance*, 21(3), 238–263. DOI: 10.1108/DPRG-09-2018-0054

Law, J. M. (2015). *Puppets of Nostalgia: The Life, Death, and Rebirth of the Japanese "Awaji Ningyo" Tradition.* Princeton University Press. DOI: 10.1515/9781400872954

Lawler, R. (2021, Feb 23). The US Copyright Office says you can't copyright Midjourney AI-generated images. The Verge. https://www.theverge.com/2023/2/22/23611278/midjourney-ai-copyright-office-kristina-kashtanova

Law-Now, C. M. S. (2024, June). *How might AI be regulated following the UK general election?* Retrieved August 30, 2024, from https://cms-lawnow.com/en/ealerts/2024/06/how-might-ai-be-regulated-following-the-uk-general-election

Lawsuit says OpenAI violated US authors' copyrights to train AI chatbot. (n.d.). Retrieved July 25, 2024, from https://www.reuters.com/legal/lawsuit-says-openai-violated-us-authors-copyrights-train-ai-chatbot2023-06-29/

Lee, K. F. (2018). *AI superpowers: China, Silicon Valley, and the new world order.* Houghton Mifflin Harcourt.

Lee, J. A. (2021). Computer-generated works under the CDPA 1988. In *Artificial Intelligence and Intellectual Property* (pp. 177–195). Oxford University Press. DOI: 10.1093/oso/9780198870944.003.0009

Legal Foundations. (n.d.). *The UK's legal framework for artificial intelligence and machine learning.* Retrieved August 30, 2024, from https://legalfoundations.org.uk/blog/the-uks-legal-framework-for-artificial-intelligence-and-machine-learning/

Lemley, M. A., & Casey, B. (2020). Fair learning. *Texas Law Review*, 99(4), 743–808.

Levine, J. M., & Moreland, R. L. (2011). Group Socialization: Theory and Research. *European Review of Social Psychology*, 5(1), 305–336. DOI: 10.1080/14792779543000093

Li, H. (2019). The Emergence of Deepfake Technology: A Review. *Technology Innovation Management Review*. https://timreview.ca/article/1282

Li, D., & Du, Y. (2007). *Artificial Intelligence with Uncertainty*. Chapman and Hall/ CRC. DOI: 10.1201/9781584889991

Lionel, B., & Sherman, B. (2014). *Intellectual Property Law* (4th ed.). Oxford University Press.

Lipkowitz, D. (2020). Manipulated Reality, Menaced Democracy: An Assessment of the DEEP FAKES Accountability Act of 2019. *New York University Journal of Legislation & Public Policy*. https://nyujlpp.org/quorum/lipkowitz-manipulated -reality-menaced-democracy-deepfakes-accountability-act/

Litman, J. D. (1990). The Public Domain. *Emory Law Journal*, 39, 965–1023.

Liu, H. W., & Lin, C. F. (2020). Artificial Intelligence and Global Trade Governance: A Pluralist Agenda. *Harvard International Law Journal*, 61(2). https://ssrn .com/abstract=3675505

Liu, N., Shapira, P., Yue, X., & Guan, J. (2021). Mapping technological innovation dynamics in artificial intelligence domains: Evidence from a global patent analysis. *PLoS One*, 16(12), e0262050. DOI: 10.1371/journal.pone.0262050 PMID: 34972173

Lizarralde, M. D., & Meinecke, C. (2023). Authorless AI-assisted productions: Recent developments impacting their protection in the European Union. *JIPITEC*, 17, 84–94. DOI: 10.1093/ijlit/eaac008/6555494

López Jiménez, D., Dittmar, E. C., & Vargas Portillo, J. P. (2022a). Nuevas estrategias publicitarias con influencers: Un examen multidisciplinar. *Revista de Ciencias Sociales*, 28(4), 63–78. DOI: 10.31876/rcs.v28i4.39117

López Jiménez, D., Dittmar, E. C., & Vargas Portillo, J. P. (2022b). The trusted third party or digital notary in Spain: Effect on virtual transactions. *International Review of Law Computers & Technology*, 36(3), 453–469. DOI: 10.1080/13600869.2021.2004760

López Jiménez, D., Dittmar, E. C., & Vargas Portillo, J. P. (2023). The Self-Regulating Jury in the Field of Interactive Advertising. *Revista de Direito. Estado e Telecomunicacoes*, 15(1), 1–30. DOI: 10.26512/lstr.v15i1.42146

Lovászy, L. (2021, December 18). *A szemünk láttára kettőződik meg a világunk – Asimovnak lesz igaza?* Portfolio.hu. https://www.portfolio.hu/gazdasag/20211218/ a-szemunk-lattara-kettozodik-meg-a-vilagunk-asimovnak-lesz-igaza-515908

Lovászy, L. (2022). Ember és robot – múlt, jelen és jövő: Munkaerőpiaci és foglalkoztatási kihívások. In: PARRAGH, Bianka – BÁGER, Gusztáv (Eds.): Az ösztönző állam válságkezelése II. - A sikeres gazdasági újraindítás. Budapest, pp. 269-302. Ludovika Egyetemi Kiadó.

Lundvall, B. A., & Rikap, C. (2022). China's catching-up in artificial intelligence seen as a co-evolution of corporate and national innovation systems. *Research Policy*, 51(1), 104395. DOI: 10.1016/j.respol.2021.104395

Lutz, M. J. (1993). Der Schutz der Computerprogramme in der Schweiz. [Beck-online.]. *GRUR International*, 1993, 653–663.

Maccoby, E. E. (2015). *Historical Overview of Socialization Research and Theory. J. E. Grusec, & P. D. Hastings içinde, Hand Book of Socialization Theory and Research.* The Guilford Press.

Madiega, T. (2023). *General-purpose artificial intelligence*. European Parliament. https://www.europarl.europa.eu/RegData/etudes/ATAG/2023/745708/EPRS_ATA(2023)745708_EN.pdf

Maffioli, D.R. (2023). Copyright in Generative AI training: Balancing Fair Use through Standardization and Transparency.

Maheshwari, D. (2023). Manipulating Reality: Understanding The Ethical And Legal Dimensions Of Deepfakes. *Indian Journal of Law and Legal Research*. https://www.ijllr.com/post/manipulating-reality-understanding-the-ethical-and-legal-dimensions-of-deepfakes

Manning, C. (2020). *Artificial Intelligence Definition*. Stanford University Human Centred Artificial Intelligence.

Manovich, L. (2002). *The Language of New Media*. MIT Press. DOI: 10.22230/cjc.2002v27n1a1280

Manyika, J., Chui, M., Miremadi, M., Bughin, J., George, K., Willmott, P., & Dewhurst, M. (2017, January 12). *Harnessing automation for a future that works*. McKinsey & Company. https://www.mckinsey.com/featured-insights/digital-disruption/harnessing-automation-for-a-future-that-works

Margoni, T. (2018). Artificial intelligence, machine learning and EU copyright law: Who owns AI? SSRN *Electronic Journal*. DOI: 10.2139/ssrn.3299523

Margoni, T., & Kretschmer, M. (2022). A deeper look into the EU text and data mining exceptions: Harmonisation, data ownership, and the future of technology. *GRUR International*, 71(8), 685–701. DOI: 10.1093/grurint/ikac054

Marr, B. (2024). What is the Difference Between Artificial Intelligence and Machine Learning? https://bernardmarr.com/what-is-the-difference-between-artificial-intelligence-and-machine-learning/#:~:text=Artificial%20Intelligence%20is%20the%20broader,let%20them%20learn%20for%20themselves

Martin, I. W., Mehrotra, A. K., & Prasad, M. (2009). *The New Fiscal Sociology. In The Thunder of History: The Origins and Development of the New Fiscal Sociology.* Cambridge University Press.

Marx, K. (2010). *Kapital 1. Cilt. (Selik M, Satlıgan N, Çev.).* Yordam Kitap.

Matolcsy, G. (2021, June 7). *Az évtized kihívásai.* Növekedés.hu. https://novekedes.hu/mag/matolcsy-gyorgy-az-evtized-kihivasai

McCarthy, J. (1989). Artificial Intelligence, Logic and Formalizing Common Sense. In Thomason, R. H. (Ed.), *Philosophical Logic and Artificial Intelligence* (pp. 161–190). Springer Netherlands. DOI: 10.1007/978-94-009-2448-2_6

McCutcheon, J. (2013). Curing the authorless void: Protecting computer-generated works following IceTV and phone directories. *SSRN*, 37, 46–102. DOI: 10.2139/ssrn.2308187

McLuhan, M. (1964). *The medium is the message. Understanding Media: The Extensions of Man içinde.* McGraw Hill.

Melullis, K. J. (1998). *Zur Patentfähigkeit von Programmen für Datenverarbeitungsanlagen. GRUR.* Beck-online.

Merchant, B. (2024, July 23). *AI Is Already Taking Jobs in the Video Game Industry.* Wired. https://www.wired.com/story/ai-is-already-taking-jobs-in-the-video-game-industry/

Metz, C. (2016). In Two Moves, AlphaGo and Lee Sedol Redefined the Future. *Wired.* https://www.wired.com/2016/03/two-moves-alphago-lee-sedol-redefined-future/

Meydancı, B. (2023). *Yapay zekâ ve ürünlerinin fikri mülkiyet hukukunda korunması*, unpublished doctoral dissertation, Bursa Uludağ University.

Meyer, J. (2000). *Haftungsbeschränkung im Recht der Handelsgesellschaften.* Springer. DOI: 10.1007/978-3-642-58321-6

Mezei, P. (2024). A saviour or a dead end? Reservation of rights in the age of generative AI. *EIPR-European Intellectual Property Review, 46*(7), 461–469. https://papers.ssrn.com/sol3/papers.cfm?abstract_id=4371204

Mihindukulasuriya, R. (2020). Why the Manoj Tiwari deepfakes should have India deeply worried. *The Print.* https://theprint.in/tech/why-the-manoj-tiwari-deepfakes-should-have-india-deeply-worried/372389/

Millington, I., & Funge, J. (2009). *Artificial Intelligence for Games* (2nd ed.). CRC Press. DOI: 10.1201/b13169

Minhas, N., & Sonkhla, D. (2024). Exploring Legal and Technical Challenges of Deep Fakes in India. *International Journal for Multidisciplinary Research*, 6(4), 1–8. https://www.ijfmr.com/papers/2024/4/24793.pdf

Ministry of Development. (2018). Eleventh Development Plan (2019-2023), Intellectual Property Rights Special Expertise Commission Report (No. KB 2997, ÖİK 778). Ankara.

Ministry of Development. (2023). Twelfth Development Plan (2024-2028), Intellectual Property Rights Special Expertise Commission Report (No. KB 2997, ÖİK 778). Ankara.

Mitov, A. (2021). *Ethical Use Of Artificial Intelligence Through the Utilitarianism Perspective*. University of Twente Student Theses.

Mkparu, U. A. (2024). AI in EdTech and FinTech: Stakeholder Engagement and Better Governance and Policies for Data Privacy. In Tennin, K. L., Ray, S., & Sorg, J. M. (Eds.), *Cases on AI Ethics in Business* (pp. 79–86). IGI Global. DOI: 10.4018/979-8-3693-2643-5.ch005

Montasari, R. (2023). National Artificial Intelligence Strategies: A Comparison of the UK, EU and US Approaches with those Adopted by State Adversaries. In *Countering Cyberterrorism. Advances in Information Security* (Vol. 101). Springer. DOI: 10.1007/978-3-031-21920-7_7

Moonshot Research and Development Program - Science, Technology and Innovation. (n.d.). Cabinet Office Home Page. https://www8.cao.go.jp/cstp/english/moonshot/top.html

Mudgal, H. (2023). The deepfake dilemma: Detection and decree. *Bar and Bench*. https://www.barandbench.com/columns/deepfake-dilemma-detection-and-desirability

Müller, V. C., & Bostrom, N. (2014). Future progress in artificial intelligence: A Survey of Expert Opinion. *Fundamental Issues of Artificial Intelligence, 1,* 553-571

Musgrave, R. A. (1992). Schumpeter's Crisis of the Tax State: An Essay in Fiscal Sociology. *Journal of Evolutionary Economics*, 2(2), 89–113. DOI: 10.1007/BF01193535

Musgrave, R. A., & Peacock, A. T. (1967). *Introduction. R. A. Musgrave, & A. T. Peacock içinde, Classics in the Theory of Public Finance*. MACMILLAN.

Myers, G. (2024). *The Future is Now: Copyright Protection for Works Created by Artificial Intelligence*. Texas Law Review Online. https://texaslawreview.org/wp-content/uploads/2023/10/Myers.10.2.23.FINAL_-2.pdf

Naqvi, Z. (2020). Artificial Intelligence, Copyright, and Copyright Infringement. *Marquette Intellectual Property Law Review*, 24, 15.

Naren N. (2024). Unravelling The Enigma: The Quest For Sui Generis Rights In AI Creation.

Nath, A., & B., S. (2024). Deepfakes on Copyright Law- Inadequacy of Present Laws in Determining the Real Issues. *Indian Journal of Law and Justice*, 15(1), 285–300. https://ir.nbu.ac.in/handle/123456789/5250

Nema, , P. (2021). Understanding copyright issues entailing deepfakes in India. *International Journal of Law and Information Technology*, 29(3), 241–254. DOI: 10.1093/ijlit/eaab007

Netanel, N. (1993). Copyright Alienability Restrictions and the Enhancement of Author Autonomy: A Normative Evaluation. *Cardozo Arts & Entertainment*, 12(1), 374–382.

Nordemann, J. B. (2024). EU law: Generative AI, copyright infringements and liability – My guess for a hot topic in 2024, Kluwer Copyright Blog, https://copyrightblog.kluweriplaw.com/2024/01/23/eu-law-generative-ai-copyright-infringements-and-liability-my-guess-for-a-hot-topic-in-2024/

Norris, P. (2001). Digital Divide: Civic Engagement, Information Poverty, and the Internet Worldwide. Cambridge University Press. DOI: 10.1017/CBO9781139164887

Novelli, C., Casolari, F., Hacker, P., Spedicato, G., & Floridi, L. (2024). *Generative AI in EU Law: Liability, Privacy, Intellectual Property, and Cybersecurity* (arXiv:2401.07348). arXiv. http://arxiv.org/abs/2401.07348

Nowik, P. (2021). Electronic personhood for artificial intelligence in the workplace. *Computer Law & Security Report*, 42, 42. DOI: 10.1016/j.clsr.2021.105584

NY Times sues OpenAI, Microsoft for infringing copyrighted works. (2004). https://www.reuters.com/legal/transactional/ny-times-sues-openai-microsoft-infringing-copyrightedwork-2023-12-27/

OECD. (2024). Regulatory Approaches to Artificial Intelligence in Finance. OECD Artificial Intelligence Papers, 24.

Okyar, D. (2022). *Adam Çalıştıranın Sorumluluğu (TBK m. 66)* (1st ed.). On İki Levha Yayıncılık.

Olgaç, S. (1967). *Borçlar Hukuku Akdin Nevileri*. İsmail Akgün Matbaası.

Öncel, M., Kumrulu, A., Çağan, N., & Göker, C. (2019). 28. Baskı. Turhan Kitabevi.

Ortutay, B. (2023). What you should know about Section 230, the rule that shaped today's internet. *PBS News*. https://www.pbs.org/newshour/politics/what-you-should-know-about-section-230-the-rule-that-shaped-todays-internet

Osborne Clarke. (2024). *How will the new UK government resolve the conflict over AI development and IP rights?*https://www.osborneclarke.com/insights/how-will-new-uk-government-resolve-conflict-over-ai-development-and-ip-rights-

Özkan Şahin, G., & Şahin, Ç. (2022). Yapay Zekali Varliklara Elektronik Kişilik Modeli Taninmasina İlişkin Eurobotics Raporu Ve Fikri Mülkiyet Sorunu Bağlaminda Meseleye Yaklaşim. *İnönü Üniversitesi Hukuk Fakültesi Dergisi, 13*(1), 110-128. DOI: 10.21492/inuhfd.981080

Özkan, A. (2022). Yapay Zekâ Tarafından Üretilen Fikir ve Sanat Ürünlerinin Korunması. *TBB Journal*, 2023(164), 207–238.

Öztan, F. (2008). *Fikir ve Sanat Eserleri Hukuku* [Intellectual and Artistic Works Law]. Turhan.

Öztürk, Ö. (2008). *Türk hukukunda patent verilebilirlik şartları*. Arıkan Press.

Pandey, S. (2023). Understanding Copyright Issues entailing deep fakes in India. *Blog Ipleaders*. https://blog.ipleaders.in/understanding-copyright-issues-entailing-deepfakes-in-india/

Parlakyıldız, F., & Güvel, E. A. (2015). Fikri Mülkiyet Hakları ve Bu Hakları Korumanın Ekonomik Önemi. *Niğde University Journal of Economics and Administrative Sciences*, 8(4), 29–39.

Parliament, U. K. (2023). *Artificial Intelligence (Regulation) Bill [HL]*. Retrieved August 30, 2024, from https://bills.parliament.uk/publications/53068/documents/4030

Parliament, U. K. (2024a). *Report of the Select Committee on Artificial Intelligence*. Retrieved August 30, 2024, from https://publications.parliament.uk/pa/ld5804/ldselect/ldcomm/54/54.pdf

Parliament, U. K. (2024b). *Artificial intelligence: Governance and regulation*. House of Commons Science, Innovation and Technology Committee. Retrieved August 30, 2024, from https://publications.parliament.uk/pa/cm5804/cmselect/cmsctech/38/report.html

Parry, R. (2007). *Recoding the Museum Digital Heritage and the Technologies of Change*. Routledge. DOI: 10.4324/9780203347485

Pascoe, L. (2023). Decentralised Autonomous Organisations and Liability in Litigation. https://www.ibanet.org/decentralised-autonomous-organisations-and-liability-in-litigation

Pasquale, F. A., & Sun, H. (2024). Consent and compensation: Resolving generative AI's copyright crisis. *Cornell Legal Studies Research Paper*, Forthcoming, University of Hong Kong Faculty of Law Research Paper No. 2024/07, 110:207. https://ssrn.com/abstract=4826695DOI: 10.2139/ssrn.4826695

Paul, R. (2021). Intellectual Property Rights: A Utilitarian Perspective. *SSRN*, 1-20.

PEC. (n.d.). Copyright protection in AI-generated works. *PEC*. Retrieved August 30, 2024, https://pec.ac.uk/blog_entries/copyright-protection-in-ai-generated-works/

Pehlivanoğlu, M. C. (2019). Naruto v. Slater Davasının Türk Fikir ve Sanat Eserleri Hukuku Açısından Değerlendirilmesi. Bahçeşehir Üniversitesi Hukuk Fakültesi Dergisi. 14(181-182). 1757-1789.

Peng, S. C. (2018). *Artificial Intelligence and Copyright: The Authors' Conundrum* [Paper presentation]. 15th WIPO-WTO Colloquium for Teachers of Intellectual Property, World Intellectual Property Organization and World Trade Organization.

Perry, M., & Margoni, T. (2010). From Music Tracks to Google Maps: Who Owns Computer-Generated Works? *Computer Law & Security Report*, 26(6), 621–629. DOI: 10.1016/j.clsr.2010.09.005

Polat, C. (2023a). A Critical Appraisal of the Proposal for an AI Liability Directive: Is It Fit for Its Own Purpose? Is the EU's AI Liability Directive really promoting the rollout of trustworthy AI? This paper provides insights into the proposal's limitations. *Zeitschrift für das Privatrecht der Europäischen Union*, 20(3), 114–121. DOI: 10.9785/gpr-2023-200307

Polat, C. (2023b). Great Unclear Expectations: A Study on the Defectiveness of Autonomous Systems. *Journal of Consumer Policy*, 46(3), 363–386. DOI: 10.1007/s10603-023-09542-x

Potsdam, H. (2020). *Copyrighting Creativity: Creative Values, Cultural Heritage Institutions and Systems of Intellectual Property*. Routledge.

Pu, K. (2022). Intellectual property protection for AI algorithms. *Frontiers in Computing and Intelligent Systems*, 2(3), 44–47. DOI: 10.54097/fcis.v2i3.5210

Purdom, C. (2018). Deep learning technology is now being used to put Nic Cage in every movie. https://www.avclub.com/deep-learning-technology-is-now-being-used-to-put-nic-c-1822514573

Quang, J. (2021). Does training AI violate copyright law? *Berkeley Technology Law Journal*, 36(4), 1407–1436.

Radianti, J., Majchrzak, T. A., Fromm, J., & Isabell, W. (2020). A systematic review of immersive virtual reality applications for higher education: Design elements, lessons learned, and research agenda. *Computers & Education*, 147, 1–29. DOI: 10.1016/j.compedu.2019.103778

Radu, R. (2021). Steering the governance of artificial intelligence: National strategies in perspective. *Policy and Society*, 40(2), 178–193. DOI: 10.1080/14494035.2021.1929728

Rajan, M. T. S. (n.d.). *Moral Rights: Principles, Practice and New Technology*. Oxford University Press.

Ramalho, A. (2017). Will robots rule the (artistic) world? A proposed model for the legal status of creations by artificial intelligence systems. *SSRN*, 21(1), 12–25. DOI: 10.2139/ssrn.2987757

Ramluckan, T. (2024). Deepfakes: The Legal Implications. *ResearchGate*. https://www.researchgate.net/publication/379221500_Deepfakes_The_Legal_Implications

Raz, J. (n.d.). *Ethics in the Public Domain: Essays in the Morality of Law and Politics*. Clarendon Press.

Regulation (EU) 2024/1689 of the European Parliament and of the Council of 13 June 2024 laying down harmonised rules on artificial intelligence and amending Regulations (EC) No 300/2008, (EU) No 167/2013, (EU) No 168/2013, (EU) 2018/858, (EU) 2018/1139 and (EU) 2019/2144 and Directives 2014/90/EU, (EU) 2016/797 and (EU) 2020/1828 (Artificial Intelligence Act).

Resolution (EP) European Parliament Resolution of 16 February 2017 with recommendations to the Commission on Civil Law Rules on Robotics, 2015/2103(INL).

Resolution (EP) European Parliament resolution of 20 October 2020 on intellectual property rights for the development of artificial intelligence technologies, 2020/2015(INI).

Resolution (EP) European Parliament Resolution of 20 October 2020 with recommendations to the Commission on a civil liability regime for artificial intelligence, 2020/2014 (INL).

Richards, N. M., & Smart, W. D. (2016). How Should the Law Think About Robots? In Calo, R: et al. (Eds.) *Robot Law* (pp.3-22). Edward Elgar. DOI: 10.4337/9781783476732.00007

Robbins, S. P., & Judge, T. A. (2017). *Essentials of Organizational Behavior*. Pearson.

Roberts, H., Cowls, J., Morley, J., Taddeo, M., Wang, V., & Floridi, L. (2021). The Chinese approach to artificial intelligence: An analysis of policy, ethics, and regulation. *AI & Society*, 36(1), 59–77. DOI: 10.1007/s00146-020-00992-2

Rosati, E. (2023, February 3). UK Government axes plans to broaden existing text and data mining exception. IPKat. https://ipkitten.blogspot.com/2023/02/uk-government-axes-plans-to-broaden.html

Rosati, E. (2017). The Monkey Selfie Case and the Concept of Authorship: An EU Perspective. *Journal of Intellectual Property Law and Practice*, 12(12), 973–977. DOI: 10.1093/jiplp/jpx199

Rosati, E. (2018). An EU text and data mining exception for the few: Would it make sense? *Journal of Intellectual Property Law & Practice*, 13(6), 429–430. DOI: 10.1093/jiplp/jpy063

Rosen, H. S., & Gayer, T. (2010). *Public Finance*. McGraw-Hill.

Rozenshtein, A. (2024). Interpreting the Ambiguities of Section 230. *Yale Journal on Regulation*. https://www.yalejreg.com/bulletin/interpreting-the-ambiguities-of-section-230/

Ruiter, A. (2021). The Distinct Wrong of Deepfakes. *Philosophy & Technology*, 34(4), 1311–1332. DOI: 10.1007/s13347-021-00459-2

Russell, S. J., Norvig, P., Chang, M., Devlin, J., Dragan, A., Forsyth, D., Goodfellow, I., Malik, J., Mansinghka, V., Pearl, J., & Wooldridge, M. J. (2022). *Artificial intelligence: A modern approach* (Fourth edition, global edition). Pearson.

Sacher, D., Biella, D., & Luther, W. (2013). *Towards a versatile metadata exchange format for digital museum collections*. IEEE. DOI: 10.1109/DigitalHeritage.2013.6744744

Sag, M. (2024). Fairness and fair use in generative AI. *Fordham Law Review*, 92, 1888–1921.

Saleh, A., Marcus, S., Jerry, D., & Azghadi, M. R. (2024). Applications of deep learning in fish habitat monitoring: A tutorial and survey. *Expert Systems with Applications*, 238(Part B), 1-22.

Samberg, R., Vollmer, T., & Teremi, S. (2024). Fair use rights to conduct text and data mining and use artificial intelligence tools are essential for UC research and teaching, https://osc.universityofcalifornia.edu/2024/03/fair-use-tdm-ai-restrictive-agreements/

Samuelson, P. (1986). Allocating Ownership Rights in Computer-Generated Work. *47 U Pitt L R 1185*, 1189–90.

Samuelson, P. (2020). AI authorship? *Communications of the ACM*. Retrieved from: https://cacm.acm.org/opinion/ai-authorship/

Samuelson, P. (2006). Challenges in Mapping the Public Domain. In Bernt Hugenholtz, P., & Guibault, L. (Eds.), *The Public Domain of Information*. Kluwer Law International.

Sanders, E. (2022). Deepfakes and Intellectual Property: What You Should Know. *Romano Law*. https://www.romanolaw.com/deepfakes-and-intellectual-property-what-you-should-know/

Sanz, V. M. Á. (n.d.) *The evolution of japanese robotics: from the beginning to the newest tendencies*. University of Barcelona. https://diposit.ub.edu/dspace/bitstream/2445/126059/1/TFG-GEI-Alvarez-VictorManuel-Jun18.pdf

Sarı, O. (2020). Yapay zekanın Türk fikri mülkiyet hukukuna göre korunması. *İzmir Bar Association Journal, 85*(1), 53-116. https://acikerisim.kent.edu.tr/xmlui/bitstream/handle/20.500.12780/205/onur%20s.pdf?sequence=1

Satheesh, A. (2022). Deepfakes and the Copyright Connection: Analysing the Adequacy of the Present Machinery. *Journal of Law & Technology*. https://jolt.richmond.edu/2022/01/25/deepfakes-and-the-copyright-connection-analysing-the-adequacy-of-the-present-machinery/

Savigny, M. Ch. G. (1841). *Traité de Droit Romain* (Vol. 2). Librairie de Firmin Didot Frère, Imprimeurs de l'Institut de France.

Scannell, B. (2022). When Irish AIs are smiling: could Ireland's legislative approach be a model for resolving AI authorship for EU member states? *Journal of Intellectual Property Law & Practice, 17*(9).

Scassa, T. (2017). Sharing data in the platform economy: A public interest argument for access to platform data. *UBC Law Review, 50*(4). Retrieved from: https://ssrn.com/abstract=3077996

Schafer, B., Komuves, D., Zatarain, J. M. N., & Diver, L. (2015). A fourth law of robotics? Copyright and the law and ethics of machine co-production. *Artificial Intelligence and Law*, 23(3), 217–240. DOI: 10.1007/s10506-015-9169-7

Schall, A. (2009). *Kapitalgesellschaftsrechtlicher Glaubigerschutz*. Beck.

Schneble, C.O., Elger, B.S., Elger, B.S., Shaw, D., & Shaw, D. (2020). Google's Project Nightingale highlights the necessity of data science ethics review. DOI: 10.15252/EMMM.202012053

Schuppli, B., & Jafari, G. A. (2021). Piercing the Digital Veil: A Case Study for a DAO Legal Framework under Swiss Law. https://www.jipitec.eu/archive/issues/jipitec-12-4-2021/5404/schuppli_pdf.pdf

Sen, A. (2010). *The Idea of Justice*. Penguin Group.

Senftleben, M. (2023). Generative AI and author remuneration. *IIC; International Review of Industrial Property and Copyright Law*, 54(10), 1535–1560. DOI: 10.1007/s40319-023-01399-4

Senftleben, M. (2024). AI Act and author remuneration: A model for other regions? Institute for Information Law (IViR), University of Amsterdam, https://ssrn.com/abstract=4740268

Seshadri, N., & Sindhu, A. (2020). Are Copyright Laws adequate to deal with Deepfakes?: A comparative analysis of positions in the United States, India and United Kingdom. *KSLR Commercial & Financial Law Blog*. https://blogs.kcl.ac.uk/kslrcommerciallawblog/2020/12/17/are-copyright-laws-adequate-to-deal-with-deepfakes-a-comparative-analysis-of-positions-in-the-united-states-india-and-united-kingdom/

Sharma, N. (2024). Artificial Intelligence: Legal Implications and Challenges. *Knowledgeable Research*, 02, 13–30.

Sharmila, R. (2022). Behind the Mask: Ethical Dimensions of Deepfake Technology in India's Legal Sphere. *International Journal for Legal Research and Analysis*. https://www.ijlra.com/paper-details.php?isuur=3234

Shekhar, R. (2024). Deepfakes and Intellectual Property: Understanding Legal Challenges and Protections in the Artificial Intelligence Era. *Novo Juris Legal*. https://www.novojuris.com/thought-leadership/deepfakes-and-intellectual-property-understanding-legal-challenges-and-protections-in-the-artificial-intelligence-era.html

Shlomit, Y.-R. (2017). Generating Rembrandt: Artificial Intelligence, Copyright, and Accountability in the 3A Era—The Human-Like Authors Are Already Here—A New Model. *Detroit College of Law at Michigan State University Law Review*, 659–726. https://ir.lawnet.fordham.edu/cgi/viewcontent.cgi?article=1955&context=faculty_scholarship

Simunic, D. A., Ye, M., & Zhang, P. (2017). The joint effects of multiple legal system characteristics on auditing standards and auditor behavior. *Contemporary Accounting Research*, 34(1), 7–38. DOI: 10.1111/1911-3846.12242

Sindhu, A. (2020). Interventions on the issue of Deepfakes in Copyright. *WIPO*. https://www.wipo.int/export/sites/www/about-ip/en/artificial_intelligence/conversation_ip_ai/pdf/ind_a.pdf

Singh, S., Sharma, R., & Smeaton, A. F. (2020). Using GANs to synthesise minimum training data for deepfake generation, *ArXiv*, 1-13.

Six key arguments by Stability AI over allegations of copyright violation by artists in US. (2024). https://www.medianama.com/2023/04/223-key-arguments-stability-ai-copyright-violation-artists-us-2/

Sloot, B., & Wagensveld, Y. (2022). Deepfakes: Regulatory challenges for the synthetic society. *Computer Law & Security Report*, 46, 105716. DOI: 10.1016/j.clsr.2022.105716

Smart, P. (2022). Minds in the Metaverse: Extended Cognition Meets Mixed Reality. *Philosophy & Technology*, 35(87), 87. DOI: 10.1007/s13347-022-00580-w

Smelser, N. J., & Swedberg, R. (2005). *The Handbook of Economic Sociology*. Princeton University Press.

Smith, B. L., & Mann, S. O. (2004). Innovation and intellectual property protection in the software industry: An emerging role for patents? *The University of Chicago Law Review. University of Chicago. Law School*, 71(1), 241–261.

Solaiman, S. M. (2017). Legal personality of robots, corporations, idols and chimpanzees: A quest for legitimacy. *Artificial Intelligence and Law*, 25(2), 155–179. DOI: 10.1007/s10506-016-9192-3

Soroka, L., Danylenko, A., & Sokiran, M. (2022). Legal issues and risks of the artificial intelligence use in space activity. *Philosophy and Cosmology*, 28, 118–135. DOI: 10.29202/phil-cosm/28/10

Speech by Prime Minister Abe at the World Economic Forum Annual Meeting. (n.d.). Ministry of Foreign Affairs of Japan. https://www.mofa.go.jp/ecm/ec/page4e_000973.html

Sposato, M. (2024a). Are leaders born or made? Asking the right question. *Development and Learning in Organizations*, 38(3), 1–3. DOI: 10.1108/DLO-05-2023-0123

Sposato, M. (2024b). Leadership training and development in the age of artificial intelligence. *Development and Learning in Organizations*, 38(4), 4–7. DOI: 10.1108/DLO-12-2023-0256

Staff. (2023). AI Principles. News Media Alliance. http://www.newsmediaalliance.org/wp-content/uploads/2023/04/FINAL-UPDATED-AI-Principles_4-20-23.pdf last visited on 07 September, 2024.

State Planning Organization. (2007). Intellectual and Industrial Rights Special Expertise Commission Report (Publication No. DPT:2728). Ankara.

Stieper, M., & Denga, M. (2024). The international reach of EU copyright through the AI Act. *Institut Für Wirtschaftsrecht*, 194, 1–30.

Stiglitz, J. H., & Rosengard, J. K. (2015). *Economics of the Public Sector*. W. W. Norton & Company.

Stoke, S. (2019). *Digital Copyright: Law and Practice* (5th ed.). Bloomsbury Publishing. DOI: 10.5040/9781509917327

Strowel, A., & Ducato, R. (2021). Artificial intelligence and text and data mining: A copyright carol. In Rosati, E. (Ed.), *The Routledge Handbook of EU Copyright Law* (pp. 299–316). Routledge.

Suluk, C., Karasu, R., & Nal, T. (2023). *Fikri mülkiyet hukuku* (7th ed.). Seçkin Publishing.

Taddeo, M., & Floridi, L. (2018). How AI can be a force for good. *Science*, 361(6404), 751–752. DOI: 10.1126/science.aat5991 PMID: 30139858

Talas, T., & Ashurst, K. M. (2019). Diving into the deep end: Regulating deepfakes online. *Communications Law Bulletin*, 38(3), 11-13. https://www.austlii.edu.au/au/journals/CommsLawB/2019/24.pdf

Tekinalp, Ü. (2004). *Fikrî Mülkiyet Hukuku* (3rd ed.). Beta.

Tekinalp, Ü. (2004). *Fikri Mülkiyet Hukuku*. Yetkin Yayınevi.

The EU wants to become the world's super-regulator in AI. (n.d.). Retrieved August 12, 2024, from https://www.economist.com/europe/2021/04/24/the-eu-wants-to-become-the-worlds-super-regulator-in-ai?utm_medium=cpc.adword.pd&utm_source=google&ppccampaignID=18151738051&ppcadID=&utm_campaign=a.22brand_pmax&utm_content=conversion.directresponse.anonymous&gad_source=1&gclid=Cj0KCQjwz7C2BhDkARIsAA_SZKaQghNLfwSW9JjIU1NK3OokyfmDmZo_Mdi4x3TunDZYxeGxCqkPmd0aArqaEALw_wcB&gclsrc=aw.ds

The European Commission's High-Level Expert Group on Artificial Intelligence. (2019). *A definition of AI: Main capabilities and scientific disciplines* (B-1049 Brussels. European Commission Directorate-General for Communication.

Thomas, P. (2014). *State of the Art on Legal Issues.* https://ethicaa.greyc.fr/media/files/ethicaa.delivrable.1.pdf

Thorbecke, C. (2023, July 12). Google hit with lawsuit alleging it stole data from millions of users to train its AI tools. CNN business. https://edition.cnn.com/2023/07/11/tech/google-ai-lawsuit/index.html. Last visited on October, 13 2024.

Thormundsson, B. (2024, January 19). *Artificial intelligence (AI) worldwide - statistics & facts.* Statista. Retrieved July 28, 2024, from https://www.statista.com/topics/3104/artificial-intelligence-ai-worldwide/#topicOverview

Thorsby, D. (2000). *Economics and Culture.* Cambridge University Press. DOI: 10.1017/CBO9781107590106

Tigard, D. W. (2020). There is no techno-responsibility gap. *Philosophy & Technology*, 34, 1–19.

Tolan, B. (1996). *Toplum Bilimlerine Giriş.* Murat& Adım Yayıncılık.

Topaloğlu, M. (1997). *Bilgisayar programları üzerindeki haklar ve bu hakların korunması.* Turkish Informatics Foundation Publications.

Torrance, A. W., & Tomlinson, B. (2023). Training is everything: Artificial intelligence, copyright, and fair training. *Dickinson Law Review*, 128(1), 233-255. https://ssrn.com/abstract=4437680

Trapova, A. (2022, August 24). The UK government moves forward with a text and data mining exception for all purposes. *Kluwer Copyright Blog.*https://copyrightblog.kluweriplaw.com/2022/08/24/the-uk-government-moves-forward-with-a-text-and-data-mining-exception-for-all-purposes/

Trautmann, T. N. (2020). *Die Legitimation der beschraenkten Haftung im Konzern.* Nomos. DOI: 10.5771/9783748923176

Turing, A. (1950). Computing Machinery and Intelligence. *Mind*, 59(236), 433–460. DOI: 10.1093/mind/LIX.236.433

Türk Borçlar Kanunu [Turkish Code of Obligations], Law No: 6098, Date: 11/01/2011. Official Gazette Number and Date: 27836, 04/02/2011.

Turkey, I. C. C. (n.d.). Promotion and Protection of Intellectual Property Rights in Turkey. International Chamber of Commerce. https://icc.tobb.org.tr/spot/docs/Turkey_ValueOfIP_TURKISH_F041613_LR.PDF

Turkish Patent and Trademark Office. (2024). *Patent application guide*, https://www.turkpatent.gov.tr/basvuru-kilavuzlari

Tyagi, K. (2022). Deepfakes, Copyright & Personality Rights: An inter-disciplinary perspective. *ResearchGate*. https://www.researchgate.net/publication/359711219_Deepfakes_Copyright_Personality_Rights_An_inter-disciplinary_perspective

Tyagi, K. (2023). The Copyright, Text & Data Mining and the Innovation dimension of Generative AI. *Computing in Science & Engineering*.

Tyagi, K. (2024). Copyright text & data mining and the innovation dimension of generative AI. *Journal of Intellectual Property Law & Practice*, 19(7), 557–570. DOI: 10.1093/jiplp/jpae028

Tyni, E. (2023). Could you imagine that face on that body? A study of deepfakes and performers' rights in EU law (Dissertation). *Linköping University Electronic Press*. https://urn.kb.se/resolve?urn=urn:nbn:se:liu:diva-196279

U.S. Chamber Staff. (2022, February 24). *Intellectual Property Drives Economic Prosperity as World Emerges from Pandemic, New Report Shows*. Uschamber.com; U.S. Chamber of Commerce. https://www.uschamber.com/intellectual-property/intellectual-property-drives-economic-prosperity-as-world-emerges-from-pandemic-new-report-shows

U.S. Copyright Office Examines Copyright and Generative AI. (n.d.). Retrieved July 25, 2024, from https://www.hhrartlaw.com/2024/07/u-s-copyright-office-examines-copyright-and-generative-ai/

UK Copyright, Designs and Patents Act, 1988.

UK Government. (2021). Public consultation on AI and IP. Retrieved August 30, 2024, from https://www.gov.uk/government/consultations/artificial-intelligence-and-ip-copyright-and-patents

UK Government. (2022). Artificial intelligence and intellectual property: Copyright and patents: Government response to consultation. Retrieved August 30, 2024, from https://www.gov.uk/government/consultations/artificial-intelligence-and-ip-copyright-and-patents/outcome/artificial-intelligence-and-intellectual-property-copyright-and-patents-government-response-to-consultation

UK Government. (2023b). Pro-innovation regulation of technologies review: Digital technologies report. Retrieved August 30, 2024, from https://assets.publishing.service.gov.uk/government/uploads/system/uploads/attachment_data/file/1142883/Pro-innovation_Regulation_of_Technologies_Review_-_Digital_Technologies_report.pdf

UK Government. (2023c). HMG response to SPV Digital Tech final. Retrieved August 30, 2024, from https://assets.publishing.service.gov.uk/government/uploads/system/uploads/attachment_data/file/1142798/HMG_response_to_SPV_Digital_Tech_final.pdf

UK Government. (2023d). The UK's international technology strategy. Retrieved August 30, 2024, from https://www.gov.uk/government/publications/uk-international-technology-strategy/the-uks-international-technology-strategy

UK Government. (2023e). *AI regulation: A pro-innovation approach (White Paper).* Department for Science, Innovation and Technology. https://www.gov.uk/government/publications/ai-regulation-a-pro-innovation-approach/white-paper

UK, Select Committee on Artificial Intelligence. (2018). *AI in the UK: Ready.* Willing and Able.

Ullrich, Q. J. (2021). Is this video real? The principal mischief of deepfakes and how the Lanham Act can address it. *Columbia Journal of Law and Social Problems*, 55(1), 1–56.

UNESCO. (2003). *Convention for the Safeguqrding of the Intangible Cultural Heritage*. UNESCO Publishing.

UNESCO. (2015). *Recommendation Concerning the Preservation of, and Access to, Documentary Heritage Including in Digital Form.* UNESCO Publishing.

United States approach to artificial intelligence by European Parliament https://www.europarl.europa.eu/RegData/etudes/ATAG/2024/757605/EPRS_ATA(2024)757605_EN.pdf. Last accessed on October 11, 2024.

United States Copyright Office. (n.d.). "Compendium of U.S. Copyright Office Practices", para. 306. Retrieved July 24, 2024, from https://www.copyright.gov/comp3/docs/compendium. 00-copyrightable-authorship.pdf

Unravelling The Enigma: The Quest For Sui Generis Rights In AI Creation – Law School Policy Review & Kautilya Society. Last visited on October, 13 2024

US Distict Court for The Distict of Columbia Case 1:22-cv-01564. (2024). https://www.copyright.gov/ai/docs/district-court-decision-affirming-refusal-of-registration.pdf

US, National Commission on New Technological Uses of Copyright Works, Final Report of the National Commission on New Technological Uses of Copyright Works

US, National Commission on New Technological Uses of Copyright Works. (1979). Final Report of the National Commission on New Technological Uses of Copyright Works

Uslu, M. N. (2023). Protection of AI-Generated Products and Examination Within the Context of the European Union and Turkish Copyright Laws (Unpublished master's thesis). Koç University, Türkiye.

Uslu, R. (2008). *Türk Fikir ve Sanat Hukukunda Eser Sahipliği* [Unpublished doctoral dissertation]. Ankara University Social Sciences Institute, Ankara, Turkey.

Vanberghen, C. (2024). Deepfake Dilemma: Balancing Regulation, Responsibility, and Rights in the AI Era. *Modern Diplomacy*. https://moderndiplomacy.eu/2024/02/24/deepfake-dilemma-balancing-regulation-responsibility-and-rights-in-the-ai-era/

Vaver, D. (1994). Translation and Copyright: A Canadian Focus. *European Intellectual Property Review*, 16(4), 159–166.

Vaver, D. (1996). Copyright and the State in Canada and the United States. *Intellectual Property Journal*, 10, 187.

Vaver, D. (1999). Moral Rights Yesterday, Today and Tomorrow. *International Journal of Law and Technology*, 7(3), 271–272.

Veale, M., & Zuiderveen Borgesius, F. (2021). - Demystifying the Draft EU Artificial Intelligence Act — Analysing the good, the bad, and the unclear elements of the proposed approach. *Computer Law Review International*, 22(4), 97–112. DOI: 10.9785/cri-2021-220402

Vijandran, V. (2024). The Intersection of Deepfakes and Intellectual Property Law: Applying the Concept of Passing Off. *Aqran Vijandran*. https://www.aqranvijandran.com/blog/the-intersection-of-deepfakes-and-intellectual-property-law-applying-the-concept-of-passing-off

Wachter, S., & Mittelstadt, B. (2018). A Right to Reasonable Inferences: Re-Thinking Data Protection Law in the Age of Big Data and AI. *Columbia Business Law Review, 2019*(2). Retrieved from: https://ssrn.com/abstract=3248829

Wachter, S., Mittelstadt, B., & Floridi, L. (2017). Transparent, explainable, and accountable AI for robotics. *Science Robotics*, 2(6), eaan6080. Advance online publication. DOI: 10.1126/scirobotics.aan6080 PMID: 33157874

Wagner, H. M. (2007). *Principles of Operations Research with Application to Managerial Decision*. Prentice-Hall Press.

Wallace, D. (2017). *Environmental Policy and Industrial Innovation*. Routledge. DOI: 10.4324/9781315145358

Walters, R., & Novak, M. (2021). Artificial Intelligence and Law. In *Cyber Security, Artificial Intelligence, Data Protection & the Law*. Springer. DOI: 10.1007/978-981-16-1665-5_3

Wang, J., Yu, X., Li, J., & Jin, X. (2018). Artificial Intelligence and International Norms. In Jin, D. (Ed.), *Reconstructing Our Orders*. Springer. DOI: 10.1007/978-981-13-2209-9_7

Watt, D., Harrison, P. S., & Cabot-King, L. (2020). Who owns your voice? Linguistic and legal perspectives on the relationship between vocal distinctiveness and the rights of the individual speaker. *International Journal of Speech Language and the Law*, 26(2), 137–180. DOI: 10.1558/ijsll.40571

Wells-Edwards, B. (2024). What's in a voice? The legal implications of voice cloning. *Arizona Law Review*, 64(1213), 1214–1237.

WIPO Secretariat, "Revised Issued Paper on Intellectual Property Policy and Artificial Intelligence", WIPO/IP/AI/2/GE/20/1 REV.

WIPO. (2007). *The Enforcement of Intellectual Property Rights by Means of Criminal Sanctions: An Assessment (WIPO/ACE/4/3)*. WIPO.

WIPO. (2023). Generative AI. *WIPO Conversation IP and Frontier Technologies*. https://www.wipo.int/edocs/mdocs/mdocs/en/wipo_ip_conv_ge_2_23/wipo_ip_conv_ge_2_23_summary.pdf

WIPO. (2024). Artificial intelligence and Intellectual Property. *Economic Perspectives*, •••, 77.

World Intellectual Property Organization (WIPO), the Berne Convention for the Protection of Literary and Artistic Works (1886).

World Intellectual Property Organization (WIPO). (2020). What is Intellectual Property? https://www.wipo.int/edocs/pubdocs/en/wipo_pub_450_2020.pdf

World Intellectual Property Organization. (n.d.-a). *Berne Convention for the Protection of Literary and Artistic Works.*https://www.wipo.int/wipolex/en/text/283693

World Intellectual Property Organization. (n.d.-b). *WIPO Copyright Treaty.*https://www.wipo.int/wipolex/en/text/295157

World Trade Organization. (n.d.) *Agreement on Trade-Related Aspects of Intellectual Property Rights (TRIPS)*https://www.wto.org/english/docs_e/legal_e/27-trips_01_e.htm

Yalçın, B. E. (2022), *From Works to Data – Artificial Intelligence And Copyright Infringements* [Master's Thesis, Ankara University Graduate School of Social Sciences Department of Intellectual Property, Technology Policies And Innovation Management]. YÖK Ulusal Tez Merkezi.

Yalın, M. A. (2002). *Türk Hukukunda Telif Hakları Ve Vergilendirilmesi.* Anadolu Üniversitesi Sosyal Bilimler Enstitüsü.

Yanisky-Ravid, S. (2017). Generating Rembrandt: Artificial Intelligence, Copyright and Accountability in the 3A Era—The Human-like Authors Are Already Here—A New Model. *Detroit College of Law at Michigan State University Law Review*, 4, 659–726. DOI: 10.17613/50p1-qy20

Yanisky-Ravid, S. (2017). Generating Rembrandt: Artificial Intelligence, Copyright, and Accountability in the 3A Era—The Human-like Authors are Already Here- A New Model. MICH. ST. *L. REV*, 2017(4), 659–726.

Yanisky-Ravid, S. (2017). Generating Rembrandt: Artificial Intelligence, Copyright, and Accountability in the 3A Era-The Human-Like Authors are Already Here-A New Model. *Detroit College of Law at Michigan State University Law Review*, 659, 659–726.

Yanisky-Ravid, S., & Liu, X. (2017). When artificial intelligence systems produce inventions: An alternative model for patent law at the 3A era. *SSRN*, 39(6), 2214–2262. DOI: 10.2139/ssrn.2931828

Yanisky-Ravid, S., & Velez-Hernandez, L. A. (2018). Copyrightability of Artworks Produced by Creative Robots and Originality: The Formality-Objective Model. *Minnesota Journal of Law, Science & Technology*, 19, 1.

Yapay zeka botları kendi dilini geliştirince Facebook mühendisleri fişi çekmek zorunda kaldı. (2024). https://webrazzi.com/2017/08/01/facebook-yapay-zeka-botlari

Yıldız, A. (2022). Finans Alanında Yapay Zeka Teknolojisinin Kullanımı. *Pamukkale University Social Science Journal*, 52, 47–66.

Yilmaztekin, H. K. (2020). Türk Fikri Haklar Hukuku Yapay Zeka Tarafından Meydana Getirilen Eserleri Korumak için Hazır mı? *Galatasaray Üniversitesi Hukuk Fakültesi Dergisi, C. 19, S.2*, 1513-1586.

Yılmaztekin, H. K. (2021). *Yapay Zekanın Eser Sahipliği* [Authorship of Artificial Intelligence]. Adalet.

YouTube Help. (n.d.). Disclosing use of altered or synthetic content. https://support.google.com/youtube/answer/14328491?hl=en&sjid=7757058968664509376-EU#zippy=%2Ci%CC%87%C3%A7erik-%C3%BCreticilerin-bildirmesi-gereken-i%C3%A7eriklere-%C3%B6rnekler

YouTube Help. (n.d.). Learn about Content ID claims. https://support.google.com/youtube/answer/6013276?hl=en&sjid=7757058968664509376-EU

Yücekal, Y. (2003). International Protection of Intellectual Property Rights: World Intellectual Property Organization (WIPO). Journal of International Economic Issues, 8. https://www.mfa.gov.tr/fikri-mulkiyet-haklarinin-uluslararasi-duzeyde-korunmasi---dunya-fikri-mulkiyet-orgutu-_wipo_.tr.mfa

Yu, P. K. (2020). 72 Fla. L. Rev. 331 (2020). The Algorithmic Divide and Equality in the Age of Artificial Intelligence. *Florida Law Review*, 72, 331–389. https://ssrn.com/abstract=3455772

Zakir, M.H., Khan, S., Saeed, Z., & Sajida. (2023). The Impact of Artificial Intelligence on Intellectual Property Rights. International Journal of Human and Society, 3(4), 312-319. https://www.researchgate.net/publication/376796618_The_Impact_of_Artificial_Intelligence_on_Intellectual_Property_Rights

Zeigler, S. (2024). Communications Decency Act and Section 230 (1996). *Free Speech Center*. https://firstamendment.mtsu.edu/article/communications-decency-act-and-section-230/

Zeytin, D. Z., & Gençay, D. E. (2019). Hukuk Ve Yapay Zekâ: E-Kişi, Mali Sorumluluk Ve Bir Hukuk Uygulamasi Das Recht Und Die Künstliche Intelligenz. *TAÜHFD*, 2019(1), 39–70.

Zhao, L. (2023). Artificial intelligence and law: emerging divergent national regulatory approaches in a changing landscape of fast-evolving AI technologies (369-399). In Collins, D., & Geist, M. (Eds.), *Research Handbook on Digital Trade* (pp. 369–399). DOI: 10.4337/9781800884953.00033

Zhou, X., & Schofield, L. (2024). Using Social Learning Theories to Explore the Role of Generative Artificial Intelligence (AI) In Collaborative Learning. *Journal of Learning Development in Gifgher Education*, 30(30), 1–8. DOI: 10.47408/jldhe.vi30.1031

Zimmermann, E. J. (2015). Machine Minds, Frontiers in Legal Personhood.

Zorluel, M. (2019). Yapay Zekâ ve Telif Hakkı. *TBB Dergisi*, 142, 305–356.

Zorluel, M. (2019). Yapay Zeka Ve Telif Hakkı. *TBB Dergisi*, 2019(142), 305–356.

Zurth, O. (2021). Artificial Creativity? A Case Against Copyright Protection for AI Generated Works. *UCLA Journal of Law & Technology, 25*(2). Retrieved from: https://ssrn.com/abstract=3707651

About the Contributors

Burcu G. Özcan Büyüktanir is an associate professor at the Hacettepe University, Faculty of Law, Turkey and she is also head of Research Center of Health Law at the Hacettepe University. Her areas of academic interest are intellectual property right, tort law, contract law and health law.

Pelin Varol Iyidogan has received her Ph.D. in Economics at Hacettepe University. She is currently a Professor in the Department of Public Finance. She has several high indexed papers/books/chapters on public and fiscal policy, applied economics/politics and health economics.

Péter Krisztián Zachar (PhD, Habil.) is a Hungarian historian, associate professor, head of the Department for International Relations and Diplomacy, vice-dean for International Relations at Ludovika - University of Public Service, Budapest. His major field of research is the political history of Central Europe, the history of advocacy organisations, e.g. chambers, the theoretical background of social partnership, the catholic social thought and the history of international relations.

* * *

Pınar Çağlayan Aksoy is an associate professor of civil law and law of obligations at Bilkent University, Ankara (Turkey) and visiting scholar at King's College Dickson Poon School of Law. She is a member of various associations and centers dealing with new technologies including Blockchain Turkey Platform, Istanbul Blockchain Women Community, FinTech Commission of Turkish Union of Bar Associations and University of Zurich Blockchain Center. As a member of the European Law Institute, she acted as a member of the Consultative Committee for the project titled "Blockchain Technology and Smart Contracts". She is the project manager of the research project titled "Legal Analysis of Smart Contracts

Established in Blockchain with a focus on Applicable Law, Protection of Personal Data and Consumers" funded by the Scientific and Technological Research Council of Turkey (TUBITAK). She is the recipient 2024 Science Academy Young Scientists (BAGEP) Award. Her recent international publications include, "AI as Agents", The Cambridge Handbook of Artificial Intelligence: Global Perspectives on Law and Ethics, (Edited by. Larry A. DiMatteo, Cristina Poncibò and Michel Cannarsa), Cambridge University Press, 2022; "The Applicability of Property Law Rules for Crypto Assets: Considerations from Civil Law and Common Law Perspectives", Law, Innovation and Technology, Spring 2023 and "NFTs and copyright: challenges and opportunities", Oxford Journal of Intellectual Property Law & Practice, October 2021. Her research deals with contract law, tort law as well as the legal implications of the newly emerging technologies, especially distributed ledger technology and smart contracts.

Erman Demir is a faculty member at Başkent University, Faculty of Fine Arts, Design and Architecture. Dr. Demir is a member of the Specialization Committee on Diversity of Cultural Expressions of the Turkish National Commission for UNESCO, the Chairman of the MYK Culture and Arts Committee, a member of the Turkish Creative Industries Council of the Union of Chambers and Commodity Exchanges of Turkey (TOBB) and the deputy director of Başkent University Creative Culture Industries Research and Application Center (YAKEM). His research interests are creative industries, creative labor and entrepreneurship in the context of the new economy.

Eduardo Carlos Dittmar is an economist holding a Ph.D. in Economic and Business Sciences. He brings extensive teaching expertise at both undergraduate and graduate levels. His scholarly work encompasses fundamental and applied research, resulting in a contribution of over 50 peer-reviewed publications and book chapters. Throughout his career, he has maintained active involvement in various research groups and served on editorial boards of multiple academic journals. His research interests focus on New Technologies, Corporate Social Responsibility, Strategic Marketing, and Business Ethics.

Nihan Gider Işıkman is currently the Head of the Film Design and Directing Department at Başkent University, Faculty of Fine Arts, Design and Architecture, and the Director of the Creative Culture Industries Research Center. She gives courses such as Production, Documentary Film, Directing, Video Activism. Her works focuses on sustainability in the film industry, copyrights, audience development, financing, different forms of documentary film within the framework of re-presentation of reality. She contributes to the field with national and international projects, researches, learning activities and collaborations. She won awards with the documentary films she produced and directed and took part in international festival programs.

Barış Gözübüyük works as an assistant professor at Hacettepe University Faculty of Law, Department of Intellectual Property Law. His fields of study is, intellectual property law, He has many national articles on this subject.

Pranjal Khare is a distinguished corporate lawyer and is currently working as a law faculty at O.P. Jindal Global University, India. He specializes in Property Law, Corporate laws, Intellectual Property Rights, and International law. Mr. Pranjal is a highly regarded scholar and has published on numerous issues related to international affairs, economy, politics, data & privacy, artificial intelligence and IP disputes. He is also a frequent speaker at legal conferences and has served as a consultant to numerous law firms and corporations.

David López Jiménez obtained his Law degree from the Complutense University of Madrid. He obtained one PhD (with European mention) from the Seville University and another PhD from the Rey Juan Carlos University. He has an Extraordinary Doctoral Award. He has leaded research stays in different European countries. He is the author of several monographs, some of them published by the prestigious publisher Thomson Reuters and Marcial Pons, as well as more than 200 publications in various scientific journals, book chapters, book reviews, and comments about national and international law.

László Gábor Lovászy received his law degree in 2000 and earned his PhD in the field of labour law, international law, and social policy in 2007. He worked for the ministries of social and labour affairs between 2001 and 2009 in Budapest. He was the first disabled scientific adviser at the European Parliament between 2009 and 2018. He was an expert to the United Nations' Committee on the Rights of Persons with Disabilities between 2013-2021. He is also a senior research fellow of the Faculty of Public Governance and International Studies at the University of Public Service since 2019. He was commissioner on supporting strategic governmental research between 2018 and 2022 in Hungary. He has now been working as minister chief advisor at the Prime Minister's Office. Budapest. He publishes widely on robotics, bioethics, biotechnology as well as human rights and social and technological innovation.

Zehra Özkan Üner was appointed as a research assistant in Ankara University Faculty of Law, Department of Comparative Law in 2007. She continues to serve as the Deputy Director of Ankara University Intellectual and Industrial Property

Rights Research and Application Center, which she started in the year she completed her doctorate. She was appointed to the Department of Intellectual Property Law in 2018 and continues to work in the same Department. Dr. Özkan Üner teaches undergraduate and graduate courses in the fields of intellectual property, intellectual property law, and design law. She also has research and publications on intellectual property, trademark law, and geographical indications. Dr. Zehra Özkan Üner, who is a member of the Steering Committee of the English Master's Program conducted in cooperation with Ankara University, the Turkish Patent and Trademark Office, and the World Intellectual Property Organization, also teaches in this program. She has also served as both a researcher and project coordinator in various projects in the fields of emerging technologies, especially NFTs and Metaverse.

Jenny Patricia Vargas Portillo has a PhD with the highest qualification, three master's degrees, an Advanced Studies Diploma and numerous specialization courses. The research carried out involves both basic and applied exploration. The lines she has been working involves, among others, Consumer Behavior, Marketing and New Technologies (Interactive Advertising and Electronic Commerce). She has been teaching and doing research in different countries of the world. She has been a professor at undergraduate and graduate levels. Likewise, she has directed a significant number of Bachelor and Master theses.

Index

A

C

D

L

M

O

P

R

S

T

U

W

www.ingramcontent.com/pod-product-compliance
Lightning Source LLC
LaVergne TN
LVHW080605300926
849162LV00005B/1048

* 9 7 9 8 3 6 9 3 8 7 0 4 7 *